A Delicate Arrangement

Books By Arnold C. Brackman

The Luck of Nineveh

The Search for the Gold of Tutankhamen

The Gold of Tutankhamen

The Dream of Troy

The Last Emperor

and other works

A DELICATE ARRANGEMENT

The Strange Case of
Charles Darwin
and Alfred Russel Wallace

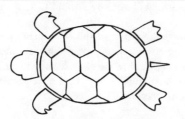

ARNOLD C. BRACKMAN

𝕿imes
BOOKS

Published by TIMES BOOKS, a division
of Quadrangle/The New York Times Book Co., Inc.
Three Park Avenue, New York, N.Y. 10016

Published simultaneously in Canada by
Fitzhenry & Whiteside, Ltd., Toronto.

Library of Congress Cataloging in Publication Data

Brackman, Arnold C.
    A delicate arrangement.

    Includes index.
    1. Darwin, Charles Robert, 1809–1882.
2. Wallace, Alfred Russel, 1823–1913.
3. Evolution—History. 4. Naturalists—England—
Biography. I. Title.
QH31.D2B745   1980   575.01′62′0924   79-19384
ISBN 0-8129-0883-X

Manufactured in the United States of America.

for Cat,
a companion on
many journeys into history

Contents

Illustrations follow page 86.

Foreword

DARWIN is a household name. Homer would have described Charles Robert (who rarely used his middle name) Darwin as an earth-shaker, and the publication of *The Origin of Species* in 1859 certainly shook the earth—and still does. Indeed, there is hardly a literate person who does not recognize the name Darwin and does not associate it with the theory of evolution.

Cities have been named for Darwin, postage stamps issued in his honor, and medals struck to commemorate his hypothesis (the theory of man's descent by natural selection from closely allied, preexisting species has never been proven, and probably never will). Bookshelves creak under the weight of Darwinian biographies, monographs, and Ph.D. theses.

The story of the origin of the *Origin* has been told again and again, and, like Topsy, grows with the retelling.

It is therefore hardly surprising that, as Garrett Hardin, microbiologist and author of a popular college paperback on biology and man's fate, wrote, "Of Darwin's life and thought we have perhaps the most complete record in the history of science." This is the long-standing, widespread conclusion within and without the scientific community.

More than half a century ago the same theme was sounded. Yale University published a biography of Darwin in which the author observed that "though a considerable amount—the withheld parts of Darwin's biography, personal letters, manuscripts and notebooks—

must be in existence somewhere . . . I do not think the omission matters much for I cannot believe that any secrets remain to be revealed."

Thus, it may come as a shock to discover that many—if not most—
of the books about Darwin engage in outrageous errors of both omission and commission.

In Darwin's own time, particularly as he grew older, he frequently
referred to "our theory" when discussing evolution by descent with
modification through variation and natural selection. Mid-Victorian
scientists identified Darwin as a "co-discoverer" or "co-adjutor" of
the theory. August Weismann, the celebrated German biologist and
a founder of genetics who died in 1914, wrote, "Everyone knows that
Darwin was not alone in discovering the principle of selection, and
that the same idea occurred . . . independently to Alfred Russel
Wallace. . . . These names will always shine side by side as two of
the brightest stars in the scientific sky."

Everyone?

In his own correspondence, Darwin referred to "Wallace and my
views" and employed similar expressions to describe their relationship.
On one occasion he wrote Wallace, "I do not think your share of the
theory will be overlooked by the real judges."

Overlooked?

For all practical purposes and with the exception of a handful of
specialists, who may almost be counted on the fingers of one hand,
Wallace is completely forgotten.

T. H. Huxley, the brilliant essayist and friend of Darwin (Huxley
called himself "Darwin's bulldog"), wrote in defense of the theory that
"science is the sworn interpreter in the high court of reason." For that
matter, the same should be said of historians and biographers. But what
if innocence, ignorance, or—worse—duplicity is the judge, and prejudice the foreman of the jury?

When I visited Wallace's gravesite in Broadstone, Dorset, a young
caretaker at the cemetery pointed to the spot. He had never heard of
Wallace before, nor, he added, had anyone else on the heath upon
which we stood. At the school attended by the great-granddaughter of
Wallace, Susan Wallace—who in college became a student of audi-
ology—an instructor asked if any member of the class could claim
descent from an historical figure. Reserved, like her great-grandfather,
the youthful Ms. Wallace waited until after the class had ended and
privately cited, with pride, Alfred Russel Wallace as an ancestor.

"Who?" the instructor asked with a quizzical look. "I never heard of him."

If, as the record makes plain, Wallace was a copilot on the epic flight toward a revolutionary understanding of the development of the human species, why is he unknown today? The question is compounded by evidence that Wallace, not Darwin, first wrote out the *complete* theory of the origin and divergence of species by natural selection—the theory which is today universally ascribed to Darwin.

The explanation for Wallace's disappearance from history is basically threefold. In part, he was the victim of a conspiracy by the scientific aristocracy of the day and was robbed in 1858 of his priority in the proclaiming of the theory. "This delicate arrangement," Huxley's son Leonard termed the incident. "This delicate situation," Darwin characterized it in a letter to Sir Joseph Dalton Hooker, the great botanist and intimate friend of Darwin.

In part, the explanation for Wallace's disappearance from history is also found in his relatively lowly social status at a time—the Victorian period—of which rampant snobbery was a hallmark.

And in part, Wallace's subsidence stems from the nature of his own character. He turned the other cheek.

What follows is the largely untold story of the conspiracy against Wallace and its cover-up, and the story of Alfred Russel Wallace himself. It is also the tale of the strange relationship between Wallace and Darwin. For without Wallace there would have been no Darwin. And without Darwin, Wallace's story may have had a different ending.

ARNOLD C. BRACKMAN

Broadstone, Dorset, England, 1978
Brookfield Center, Connecticut, 1980

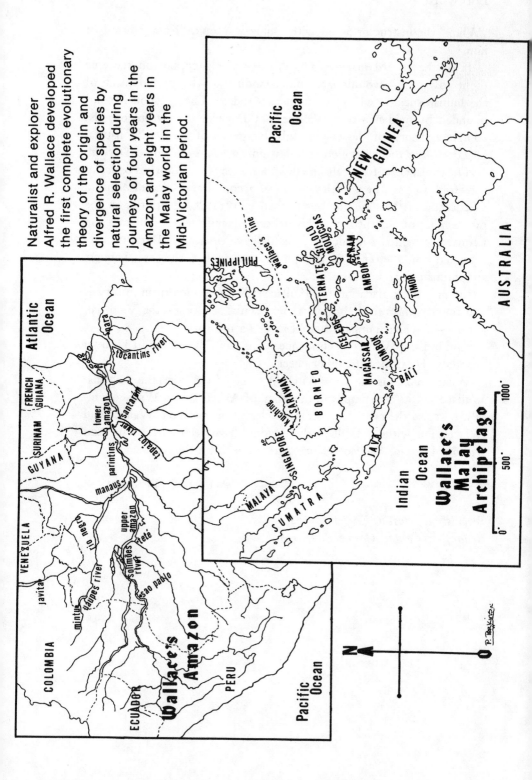

Naturalist and explorer Alfred R. Wallace developed the first complete evolutionary theory of the origin and divergence of species by natural selection during journeys of four years in the Amazon and eight years in the Malay world in the Mid-Victorian period.

Wallace's Amazon

Pacific Ocean

Atlantic Ocean

COLOMBIA
VENEZUELA
GUYANA
SURINAM
FRENCH GUIANA
ECUADOR
PERU

javita
mintu
vaupes river
rio negro
manaus
parintins
upper amazon
Solimoes river
sao pablo
tefe
lower amazon
tapajoz river
Santarem
tocantins river
para

Wallace's Malay Archipelago

Indian Ocean

Pacific Ocean

MALAYA
SUMATRA
SINGAPORE
Kuching
SARAWAK
BORNEO
JAVA
BALI
LOMBOK
MACASSAR
CELEBES
TERNATE
GILOLO
MOLUCCAS
CERAM
AMBON
TIMOR
PHILIPPINES
NEW GUINEA
AUSTRALIA
Wallace's line

0°   500°   1000°

N

P. Perkins

PART I

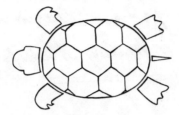

A Delicate Arrangement

Wallace's paper had come like a bolt from the blue. . . . Yet . . . when this delicate situation had been arranged [Darwin wrote Hooker], "You must let me once again tell you how deeply I feel your generous kindness and Lyell's on this occasion; but in truth it shames me."

Leonard Huxley, *The Life and Letters*
of Joseph Dalton Hooker, 1918

The manner in which you have given Darwin the whole credit of the theory of natural selection is very handsome, but if anyone else had done it [*The Origin of Species*] without allusion to your papers, it would have been wrong.

Sir Charles Lyell, in a letter
to Wallace, 1864

I never did pick anyone's pocket.

Charles Darwin, in a letter to
Hooker, 1859

The first 8 letters I received from Darwin — while in the Malay Archipelago)

N.B. The Mss. of my Paper sent to Darwin and printed in the Journal of the Linnean Society, was not returned to me, and seems to be lost. The proofs with the Mss. were perhaps sent to Sir Charles Lyell, or to the Secretary of the Linn. Soc. & may some day be found. It was written on thin foreign note paper.

Alfred R. Wallace

The inscription on the envelope in which Wallace kept the first eight letters he received from Darwin. Mysteriously, *all* of Wallace's early correspondence to Darwin, with the exception of one fragment, is missing. (Courtesy of the New York Public Library. Reprinted by permission.)

Chapter 1

THE POSTRIDER AT DOWN, a secluded hamlet tucked among narrow lanes, cherry trees, high hedgerows, and hop fields in the shire of Kent, rarely deposited Charles Darwin's mail through the black, wrought-iron letter slot built into the door of Down House, as the Darwins called their elegant, white Georgian mansion. There was simply too much mail. The Darwin family tree was thickly branched. Darwin's wife, Emma, a first cousin (his mother's niece), was the daughter of Josiah Wedgwood, the legendary eighteenth-century potter whose name lent itself to a style of pottery in vogue to this day. The Darwins and Wedgwoods were perpetual letter writers. Had the telephone been invented, they would have, much to Darwin's despair, been on the phone daily.

Down House was also the recipient of a heavy flow of letters from Darwin's scientific colleagues in Britain and abroad, the daily edition of the London *Times*, and a plethora of journals of every description, from the *Gardeners' Chronicle* to the *Entomological Weekly Intelligence*, *Annals and Magazine of Natural History*, and the *Geological Society Journal*. Indeed, Darwin was a contributor to several of these and other periodicals.

Clearly, the postrider must have sighed with relief when he trotted his horse up Luxted Road, a lane built before the Norman Conquest, emptied his bag at Down House, and galloped on to Biggin Hill, the next stop.

There was another reason that the postrider rarely deposited his mail through the regular letter slot at Down House: Joseph Parslow, Darwin's butler, almost invariably answered the postrider's knock and personally collected the day's mail. He placed it on a table in the spacious, economically appointed drawing room, the floor-to-ceiling French windows of which looked out on Darwin's fifteen-acre estate of formal and wild gardens, open fields, and woodland. Parslow had entered the service of Charles and Emma Darwin when they were married in 1839, and he moved with them into Down House when Darwin's father, a prominent physician, purchased the home as a gift for the couple three years later. In 1891, at age seventy-nine and six years after Darwin had died at eighty-two years of age on the second floor of that same house, Parslow continued to plead with Emma for a full day's work. From respect and fondness for him, she refused this, but contributed to his upkeep.

During the more than forty years that Darwin concealed himself in the isolation of the Dickens' countryside—as Kent is sometimes called —he tried to hew to the same schedule. Each day, he ate breakfast alone at about 7:45 A.M. and then went immediately to work in his "capital study," as he was fond of describing the eighteen-by-eighteen-foot room.

The study was attractive and comfortable. It was also cluttered. Piles of books and periodicals littered it. The walls were covered with pictures. Specimen boxes and jars crowded two wooden tables. A brass-plated microscope—as simply constructed as a teenager's Christmas present today—and a set of dissecting instruments were strategically placed near a window which extended almost the height of the wall. The window faced north by east and on sunlit mornings was flooded with cold light. The most curious feature in the room was a unique chair built on casters and equipped with a writing board. This was truly a worker's room, not a showplace study, and Darwin considered the period between 8:00 and 9:30 A.M. his most productive.

At 9:30, Darwin joined Emma in the drawing room, and read the day's mail. "He rejoiced if the post was a light one," son Francis wrote, "and . . . worried if it was not." After an hour of culling through correspondence (Emma read the family letters aloud), Darwin returned to the study, taking important mail with him, and worked until 12:00 noon or a quarter past. At that point, wrote daughter Henrietta in a memoir, he would be "at the end of his tether."

Emerging for a second time from his workroom, Darwin would often mumble aloud in a satisfied tone, "I've done a good day's work."

Sometimes he probably cursed softly to himself, "Another day wasted."

While Emma supervised the kitchen staff, as lunch was prepared, Darwin and Polly, his white terrier and constant companion, strolled around the "Sandwalk," a footpath which in winter encircled a dark and somber wood situated about three hundred yards from the house. The stand included cherry, hazel, birch, ash, lime, beech, Scotch pine, and dogwood, and was bordered on one side by holly. But in spring and summer the Sandwalk was a palette of color, with bluebells, anemones, cowslips, primroses, and wild ivy. One of Darwin's daughters—the couple had ten children; eight survived to adulthood—later remarked that her parents "loved this wood and took pains in later years to make it a sort of wild garden."

This was Darwin's private world. Here, his granddaughter Gwen Raverat observed, he was "quite cut off from human society." But in this remembrance, the operative word is *human*, for in the Sandwalk, Darwin was hardly cut off from society. Indeed, he was amidst the real world, Genesis, abounding in life: plants, insects, birds, and small mammals. Darwin knew, and felt, that he shared a common heritage, a common bond with them all.

In a letter he wrote to Emma in the spring of 1858, there is a poignant sentence which strikingly illuminates Darwin's love for this real world. "At last I fell fast asleep on the grass, and awoke with a chorus of birds singing around me and squirrels running up the trees, and some woodpeckers, laughing, and it was as pleasant and rural a scene as ever I saw . . . and I did not care one penny how any of the beasts or birds had been formed."

As William, his first son, later said, he did not think his father could have written that passage "without a deep sense of the beauty and the poetry of the world and of life." The judgment cannot be faulted.

One day, while walking through the Sandwalk, Darwin came across a fox asleep in his path. On another occasion, while the mother looked on anxiously, several youthful squirrels mistook him for a tree and ran up his back and legs, clinging to his cloak.* The Sandwalk's beasts and birds possessed no fear of man. Man was accepted as part of nature.

When he and Emma made their first visit to Down in 1842, Darwin found the village astonishingly quiet. "It is really surprising," he wrote, "to think London is only sixteen miles off." This observation holds fast to the present, although in Darwin's time it took two hours by coach

* The Sandwalk, along which I strode for the first time in 1978, still abounds with wildlife.

to Tower Bridge, while the same distance can be covered in a quarter of that time today. Yet in spirit and scenery, Down might as well be sixteen light-years from London. On his initial visit, the observant Darwin noted that "there is one . . . post-office." There still is only one today, crammed into the corner of a grocery store and situated literally a stone's peg from the George and Dragon Inn, where the Darwins spent their first night at Down while making up their minds whether or not to buy the estate they had inspected earlier that day. Across the road from the Inn, a few steps from the greengrocer, the Down Chapel, built in 1290, still stands. Parslow is buried there.

On June 18, 1858, according to Darwin—and perhaps as early as June 4, as suggested by circumstantial evidence—the postrider must have handed Parslow that memorable post.

It was certainly too bulky to slip through the mail slot of the door. And when Darwin entered the drawing room later that morning and ran his eyes over the day's delivery, he must have turned violently ill.

Scholars still debate the nature of Darwin's chronically poor health. After returning in 1836 from his vigorous, five-year voyage around the world as naturalist aboard H.M.S. *Beagle*, a refitted ten-gun brig of 242 ton burthen—"the most important event in my life," Darwin termed the journey—he considered himself an invalid. It was in the course of this cruise—having reached the Galápagos archipelago, a cluster of fourteen main islands and numerous atolls scattered roughly six hundred miles off the west coast of South America and which Herman Melville called "the enchanted islands"—Darwin later alleged, that he asked himself why the animals and plants of the archipelago were so alike and yet so different from island to island and from those of the South American mainland. It was the question of the origin of species.

But as a result of that voyage, Darwin assumed the life of the shawl. Rarely thereafter did he pass a comfortable day or night. To this day some believe he was a hypochondriac, others that he used his assorted ailments as a pretext for avoiding the claims of society, still others that during the cruise he had acquired a tropical malady known as Chagas' disease. Recent and more convincing evidence indicates that Darwin's symptoms were largely psychogenic. Unfortunately, the psychogenic theory has also carried with it such claims as those of one psychiatrist who apparently considered it significant that Darwin settled in Down at the age of thirty-three, the same age at which Christ was crucified— the point presumably being that the "Darwinian" theory of the origin of species crucified God.* This has opened the door to what Sir Hedley Atkins, president of the Royal College of Surgeons—which now owns and maintains Down House—has called "a lot of psychological 'claptrap.'"

Lady Nora Barlow, like Gwen Raverat a granddaughter of Charles Darwin, has also held such claims up to ridicule. "Psychiatrists too often select their evidence so as to suit their special school of thought," she complained in 1954 in the *Lancet*, Britain's prestigious medical journal. Bitingly, she went on to recall a joke in *The New Yorker* magazine in which one person at a bar is overheard telling another, "Of course, success in any field is a neurosis." So, Lady Barlow observed, is failure, and she asked, "What then is left in between?"

And ten years later, writing in the *New Statesman*, a journal of London's intellectual left, zoologist and Nobel Prize winner P. B. Medawar, concluded, "I believe that Darwin was organically ill (the case for his having Chagas' disease is clearly a strong one) but was also the victim of neurosis; and that the neurotic element in his illness may have been caused by the very obscurity of its origins, by his being 'genuinely' ill . . . and having nothing to show for it—surely a great embarrassment to a man whose whole intellectual life was a marshalling and assay of hard evidence."

Clearly, as one academic refreshingly admitted recently, "No really satisfactory explanation for Darwin's illness has yet been given." Darwin himself had no illusions. "Many of my friends," he conceded, "think me a hypochondriac."

Darwin's illnesses varied, ranging from attacks of nausea, indigestion, and heart palpitations, through bouts of uncontrollable drowsiness and fatigue, to eczema and boils. He was a pharmacist's delight and took a variety of medicinal preparations, including small doses of arsenic— a common prescription in the mid-Victorian era. Conceivably, he may have suffered from a touch of arsenic poisoning.

Yet his illnesses—real or perceived—notwithstanding, Darwin ac-

---

* Running wild, Edward J. Kempf, clinical psychiatrist at the former Government Hospital for the Insane at Washington, D.C., added this observation in the journal *Psychopathology* in 1920: "Probably the same biological cravings that dominate us all and have insisted upon cherishing the fantasies and renunciations of envy by Christ in the Garden of Gethsemane, the Crucifixion and Burial of all selfish, worldly (sporting) interests, and the conversion and ascension in life through seeking truth and generously tolerating censure, urged Darwin irresistibly onward."

complished a prodigious amount of work: more than seven thousand pages of scientific research. He not only wrote books, articles, and monographs, but maintained notebooks, diaries, and his heavy correspondence. "Work makes me for the time forget," he said, "or drives quite away my daily discomfort." Nevertheless, during moments of great stress, his medical log showed that he often suffered bouts of grave discomfort, especially intense shivering and attacks of vomiting. It is against this documented medical history that one can fairly conclude that when Darwin ran his fingers over the day's mail that sunlit June morning, he took violently ill.

Chapter 2

AMONG DARWIN'S letters and journals that June morning of 1858 was a relatively thick envelope containing some twenty sheets of a thin "foreign" stationery, probably rice paper, and probably pale violet in color. The manuscript was accompanied by a note from Alfred Russel Wallace, who had initiated a correspondence with Darwin only some twenty months earlier from Sarawak, Borneo. Wallace, a "fly-catcher" who sold specimens to English naturalists and institutions for a living, had dispatched his manuscript from the Malay archipelago, the largest archipelago in the world. A thousand Galápagos rolled into one, an emerald necklace of 13,000 islands strung along the equator on the periphery of Southeast Asia, the bulk of the archipelago then made up the Netherlands East Indian empire; today it forms the Republic of Indonesia. The insular chain still boasts New Guinea and Borneo, the second and third largest islands in the world, respectively, after Greenland, and is a region where almost every landscape is or seems also to be a seascape. Many of the islands are dotted with volcanoes, some active, others extinct. The archipelago is truly east of Eden.

Wallace's envelope bore no stamps. Postage stamps had not yet come into usage in that part of the world, although in England they had been introduced as early as 1840. Indeed, they would not make their appearance among the Dutch islands until 1864, and, among the British, Spanish, and Portuguese colonial possessions in the archipelago, not for another three years and more after that.

Since post offices and postage stamps had not yet come into fashion in the Malay archipelago, Wallace had employed the popular method of the day for dispatching private mail. He paid the captain of a Dutch vessel two or three Dutch Indies cents to carry the manuscript to Singapore. At Singapore the envelope was transferred to a Southampton-bound packet. Upon its delivery at Down House, via London and Down's solitary post office, Parslow dipped into the Darwin household's petty cash and paid the postrider 1 shilling 9 pence, or possibly 2 shillings (about 20 cents), the routine postage-due charge in England at that time for unfranked overseas mail. The Victorian postal service, given the primitive means of transportation at the time, was extremely efficient, remarkably so as compared with present-day standards.

It is reasonable to surmise, given the known postal history of the period, that a series of cancellation marks or "chops," as they are called in the Far East, recorded the journey of Wallace's communication halfway around the world. One cancellation mark may have given the point of origin, Ternate, a palm-thronged island belonging to the group known as the Moluccas—the Spice Islands of antiquity, which Columbus had set out in search of when he stumbled across a New World. Another chop probably indicated that the envelope passed through Singapore, the seat of British power in East Asia and today an independent city-state. Still another cancellation mark was probably affixed at London before the parcel reached Down.

A letter from the Dutch East Indies normally took about three months to reach Europe. This particular letter was apparently dispatched early in March and, according to notations in Wallace's diary, most likely March 9, when a Dutch cargo vessel, a forerunner of the Koninklijke Pakketvaart Maatschappij intracoastal service, with its familiar house flag—a Dutch crown in a white diamond on a red field—put into Ternate on her regular run. Dutch ships monopolized intrainsular traffic among the islands.

Wallace, of course, ran a risk sending his manuscript to Darwin in this manner. But he had no alternative. And until the recipient replied, half a year or more would pass before he knew whether or not the mail got through. There was, of course, always the possibility that a ship would founder at sea, and its contents with it. On one occasion, for example, Darwin wrote a correspondent, "It has been a great disappointment to me that I have never received your long letter written to me from the Canary Islands." A ship from the Canaries, a Spanish possession off the northwest coast of Africa, had gone down en route to England.

For parochial Down, Darwin was the local oddity, and these letters from unheard of places added to his reputation. Darwin's immediate neighbor, Sir John Lubbock, a zoologist and paleontologist whose estate covered three thousand acres, once recalled that Darwin was "something of a puzzle to the villagers—looked on as a necromancer." And, Lubbock reminisced, on one occasion a friend asked Darwin's head gardener about his employer's chronically poor health. "Oh," the gardener said, "my poor master has been very sadly. I often wish he had something to do. He moons about in the garden, and I have seen him stand for nothing before a flower for ten minutes at a time. If he had something to do I really believe he would be better."

Wallace's letter got through.

Darwin immediately recognized the obscure name scrawled on the return address. And Darwin must have been terror-stricken.

Why should a letter from Wallace upset Darwin?

He had known since December of 1855, and possibly by September of that year, that Wallace, working independently in Sarawak, in the wilds of Borneo, on the other side of the globe, had developed and published the Sarawak Law and was seeking a solution to the riddle as old as mankind itself—the origin of man.

As for the background of the Sarawak Law, the scientific community of the period largely believed in the permanence or fixity of species. A housefly was ordained a housefly, and would forever remain so. It had not descended from some closely allied species; it had been "created" by an act of Divine Providence. Evolution itself, however, was *not* at issue. The process of evolution was widely acknowledged in the West, and had been since the Greeks; the housefly, for example, was known to evolve through four stages: egg, larva, pupa, and adult. But the scientists of the day agreed that this evolutionary process was, like the housefly itself, immutable—it always produced the same result.

Yet a small and increasingly sophisticated band of observers, among them Darwin and Wallace, had doubts about the origin of the housefly and every other species. Naturalists of that era, like taxonomists today, sought to fit all living things into a system of classification or chain of relationship. In the eighteenth century, the Swedish botanist Carl von Linné had developed the first workable system. In shorthand, as it affects man, for example, the Linnaean system runs as follows: kingdom (animal); subkingdom (vertebrate, i.e., having a backbone); class (mammal); order (primate); family (anthropoid, i.e., resembling man); genus (homo [man]); species (sapiens, i.e., resembling contemporary as distinguished from fossil man); and variety (dwarf, albino, etc.).

Darwin (and Wallace) recognized that all species are constantly producing varieties, few of which have survived, most of which have perished. The disturbing question was: When did a variety become a species?—a problem that confronts taxonomists to this day. More profoundly, when did the chain of relationships lead to a completely new creature? The suggestion that varieties developed into species put into jeopardy the concepts of immutability and special creation. Beneath the seemingly technical search for the origin and diversity of species lurked that greatest of all mysteries—the very origin of man. The line of inquiry pursued by both Darwin and Wallace courted heresy.

When Darwin embarked on the voyage of the *Beagle* he believed, like his colleagues, in the permanence of species. "Occasionally," he admitted later, "doubts flitted across my mind." Chiefly as the result of experiments at Down with domesticated species, such as the pigeon, Darwin concluded that species were not immutable. This was an especially frightening conclusion for a man who, as a student at Cambridge, had been trained initially for the clergy and who, in his youth, had never entertained "in the least doubt the strict and literal truth of every word in the Bible."

By the 1840s Darwin had developed a theory of artificial selection in the breeding of domesticated animals and had worked out a theory of selection, based in part on the availability of food, for the survival of a species in nature. But Darwin was troubled about "the possible and probable application" of his theory of natural selection in the wild. He knew that there was a serious drawback in the crossbreeding of domesticated animals, that the new variety was either sterile or in time reverted to type, to its original "wild" state in nature. What check prevented animals in the wild from reverting to type in the evolution of new species? Darwin was also troubled by his failure to understand the principle of divergence in the order of classification.

Like Darwin, Wallace had also, in the 1840s, independently cast aside the story of Biblical creation, the rigidity of species (which Wallace apparently had never entertained very strongly anyway). He had concluded that species undergo "a natural process of gradual extinction and creation" and that "no group of species has come into existence twice." Unlike Darwin and all other naturalists who toyed with theories of evolution, however, Wallace recognized evolution as "change," not necessarily "progress." However, as far as Darwin knew, Wallace had not yet worked out either the mechanism of natural selection or the principle of divergence.

Even so, Wallace posed a direct and open threat to Darwin in establishing priority on the species question, having published his first species paper in September 1855. And his conclusions startled his readers, including Darwin. Darwin knew from the forthright tone and originality of Wallace's published paper that Wallace was not only hot on the species trail, but gave every indication of outpacing him.

For Darwin, it probably was a bitter, large pill to swallow. The difficulty for Darwin was partly social in character, and partly psychological.

Wallace was a relative upstart, fourteen years Darwin's junior, the offspring of an impoverished, albeit genteel, middle-class family—a family of no distinction in an era when individuals were born and locked into a social status as fixed and permanent as, presumably, were the species around them.

By comparison, Darwin was an old species hand. He had been working on the question since his days aboard the *Beagle*, and had opened the first page of his species notebook in 1837 when Wallace, a lad of fourteen, his family in deepening financial straits, was compelled to go out and look for work. Moreover, while Wallace was a newcomer to the field, Darwin already ranked among England's preeminent naturalists. He dazzled the world with his technical ability and range, and was the imposing author of such diverse monographs as *Notes Upon Rhea Americana, Origin of Saliferous Deposits, The Structure and Distribution of Coral Reefs, A Monograph on Fossil Lepadidae*, and so on. Darwin was also an original member of the Entomological Society, an elected member of the Royal Geographical Society, the Royal Society of London, the Geological Society, and the Linnean Society, and a correspondent member, as early as 1831—when Wallace was eight years old—of the Zoological Society. Among Darwin's close associates were Sir Charles Lyell, the renowned author of *The Principles of Geology*, to whom Darwin dedicated his now classic *Voyage of the Beagle*; Sir Joseph Dalton Hooker, the great botanist and director of Kew Gardens, the preeminent botanical institution of Britain; his neighbor Lubbock, the zoologist whom Victoria later elevated to the peerage as Lord Avebury; Thomas H. Huxley, the anatomist and irascible essayist; and other scientific luminaries.

Lyell, twelve years Darwin's senior, and Hooker, eight years Darwin's junior, were Darwin's most intimate friends; Hooker had become his confessor and it was to him that Darwin, in a letter, admitted to "murder" in 1844. In the letter, dated June 8 of that year, Darwin wrote that "at last gleams of light have come, and I am almost convinced (quite to the contrary of the opinion I started with) that species are not (it is like confessing to a murder) immutable." The murder, of course, was the murder of God, for the theory that species are not special creations killed the Mosaic cosmogony. Did not the First Book of Moses—commonly called Genesis—read that, "In the beginning God created the heavens and the earth"? And did it not continue that God said "let the water bring forth abundantly the moving creatures that hath life"? Yet it is as well worth noting as it is overlooked that Genesis depicts God's creation of life in evolutionary stages—birds, beasts, and, finally, man. There is a sense of timing, of evolution, in the Old Testament.

Scientific interests aside, Lyell, Hooker, and Darwin shared attributes beyond their religiosity. The trio were men of wealth and social and academic station. Moreover, they were so in the increasingly stratified society which came to characterize the Victorian age. In bleak contrast, Wallace was not only impoverished, but uneducated. He was lucky to own a tie, much less a proper school tie. He never finished the equivalent of American junior high school. And he was perched on a low rung of the social ladder, a rung lower than his father's as the family's fortunes ebbed in his youth. Moreover, Wallace was not much of a climber. He felt awkward, uneasy, and uncomfortable in society. In sum, Darwin, Lyell, and Hooker lived upstairs; Wallace, downstairs.

But Darwin's annoyance with Wallace, if not outright fear of him, coursed deeper. Wallace, whom he never even recalled having met, not only disturbed Darwin's peace of mind and the tranquility he had found at Down, but, worse, appeared to be scaling Darwin's redoubt—the field of the origin of species. In his own mind, Darwin had come to regard the species question as a private preserve. He had erected a "no trespassing" sign. He held territorial rights. Moreover, on the basis of a successful, active career, Darwin justifiably wielded great influence and power within the scientific establishment, and exercised it. Wallace was an intruder and, to boot, an "outsider."

Darwin also did not care for surprises. Surprises interrupted his lifestyle, a mode of living designed to afford him the structured quiet he needed to work out his ambitious project on the origin of species. Surprises robbed him of time and energy and above all interrupted his concentration on the species question to the exclusion of everything else except his immediate family. The species question had "haunted" him—Darwin's own word—since the voyage of the *Beagle* had opened his eyes to the immense, incredible diversity of life and raised strong doubts in his mind about beliefs in Noah's Ark and the Reverend Ussher's chronology of the Earth.

As for the latter, the Reverend Ussher, Bishop of Armagh, born in 1581, had calculated that God had created the earth at 9 A.M., October 23, 4004 B.C., and—like the story of the Ark—this date was widely accepted as gospel in Darwin's day.

Although in the 1840s Darwin had partly solved the mechanism or "how" of evolution—"natural selection"—he was baffled by its operation in nature, and so repeatedly put off writing up his evolutionary theory.

Darwin could easily demonstrate the theory of selection in the breeding of domesticated animals. Cross a donkey with a horse and get a mule—any ass could see that. But how, in nature, did the lizard and leopard diverge from the same tree of life? What was the underlying principle of divergence in natural selection? In his species notebook, Darwin confessed that "how selection could be applied to organisms living in a state of nature [is] a mystery to me." It was still a mystery when he finally began writing, a dangerous way of proceeding, for a scientist.

By the spring of 1858 Darwin was at a crossroads with his "big book," a manuscript which nobody had yet seen, not even Hooker or Lyell, his closest friends.

Chapter 3

SINCE THE MANUSCRIPT Wallace mailed from Ternate contained—in complete form—what is today known as the Darwinian theory of evolution, the date of its arrival at Down House acquires profound historical significance.

A quartet of dates is in the running as *the* date on which the postrider handed Wallace's envelope to Parslow. The first of the four—Friday, June 4—is speculative; the second—Tuesday, June 8—is the day Darwin wrote Hooker that he had suddenly found the missing "keystone" of his theory; the third—Monday, June 14—is suggested by Darwin's "little diary"; and the fourth—Friday, June 18—is the date publicly advanced by Darwin himself. Wherever the chronological reality may rest, June 1858 clearly marked for Darwin the moment of truth.

The problem is compounded by the disappearance of the Wallace envelope. That envelope, with its postmarks, which has been searched for in vain at the Linnean Society, the Royal Geographical Society, the British Museum (Natural History), the University of London, and elsewhere, contained irrefutable evidence of the precise date on which Darwin broke it open and read its contents. In all probability, it no longer exists. It has either been misplaced or, more likely, destroyed.

The postal history of the period, the survival of a number of other Wallace letters from Ternate, and a consensus among philatelists is that it would take a letter from Ternate some twelve weeks to reach Down. According to the evidence found in Wallace's papers, he wrote out his complete theory of evolution toward the end of February and posted it March 9, when the first available Dutch vessel dropped anchor at Ternate. This is corroborated by a letter Wallace sent that same day by the same ship to Frederick Bates, the brother of Henry Walter Bates with whom Wallace had scoured the Amazon for species some years earlier. H. Lewis McKinney, a member of the University of Kansas faculty, was the first to draw attention to the Bates letter, which is in the possession of Wallace's grandson, Alfred John Russel Wallace. The letter, mailed from Ternate, bears the usual series of cancellations, showing its arrival at Singapore and transit to London via Southampton and then on to Leicester, where Bates lived. It arrived at Leicester June 3 and bears a cancellation of the Leicester post office for that date.*

Wallace's letter to Darwin should have arrived the same day as Bates', June 3, or perhaps a day or two later. "It is only reasonable to assume that Wallace's communication to Darwin arrived at the same time and was delivered to Darwin at Down House on 3 June 1858, the same day as Bates' letter arrived in Leicester," said McKinney. "If this sequence is correct, as it appears to be, we must ask ourselves what Darwin was doing with Wallace's paper during the two weeks between 4 June and 18 June (when Darwin claimed he received it)."

Clearly, the evidence favoring June 3 is strong. It is further strengthened by another piece of evidence dating from June 8.

On that day, five days after probably receiving Wallace's Ternate manuscript, Darwin wrote the faithful Hooker that he, Darwin, was now suffering from an outbreak of boils but, discomfort aside, was elated to report that he had at last resolved the frustrating problem of how species diverged in nature. "I have a very great confidence it is sound," Darwin said about the new principle. In his letter he confided that the new theory "is the keystone of my book." In other words, he arrived at the complete solution of his theory on the origin of divergent species two years after he had begun writing his "big book." In the letter to Hooker, Darwin—characteristically—did not spell out his latest discovery. He kept it a secret from his best friend.

Late in life, after ascending Olympus and entering the pantheon of

---

* In the course of a visit with John Wallace and his wife Daphne at their home in Bournemouth, I had the opportunity to examine the envelope. As a former member of the China Unit of the American Philatelic Society, I can attest to the authenticity of the cancellations. The letter consists of four pages, French-fold, on light violet stationery and is dated March 2, 1858. The envelope bears an April 1858 Singapore post office chop, and June 3 London and Leicester cancellations.

the world's greatest scientists, among them Aristotle, Copernicus, and Newton, Darwin admitted in an autobiographical sketch that the principle of divergence had escaped him until almost the last moment.

"In June 1842 I first allowed myself the satisfaction of writing a very brief abstract of my theory in 35 pages," Darwin said, "and this was enlarged during the summer of 1844 into one of 230 pages." Then he added, "But at the time I overlooked one problem of great importance: and it is astonishing to me . . . how I could have overlooked it and its solution. This problem is the tendency in organic beings descended from the same stock to diverge in character as they become modified. That they diverged greatly is obvious from the manner in which species of all kinds can be classed as genera, genera under families, families under suborders, and so forth.

"I can remember," continued Darwin, "the very spot in the road, whilst in my carriage, when to my joy the solution occurred to me, and this was *long after* I had come to Down." (Italics added.)

Infuriatingly, as in other instances of crucial importance, Darwin did not pinpoint the date of his major discovery, although he was a meticulous notetaker and kept copious notes when he wanted to, right down to the number of candles he burned at Down annually. Yet the June 8 letter to his lifelong confidant indicates that he may have made the discovery shortly before that date. Did he make it after reading Wallace's Ternate Paper—assuming that the latter had arrived some five days earlier? Or did Darwin make his discovery independently? With the exception of a relative handful of scholars, the academic community at large has never seriously resolved these questions. Dr. John L. Brooks, who is presently Deputy Division Director, Division of Environmental Biology, National Science Foundation, is convinced that Darwin drew his concept of divergence from Wallace's Sarawak Law and the Ternate Essay (which Darwinphiles, incidentally, often refer to misleadingly as simply "Wallace's Ternate letter" when, in point of fact, Wallace himself termed it a "paper." [See p. 327.])

"Wallace was the first and the *only* person to conceive of the dynamics of the formation of the observed patterns of organic diversity through the action of inevitable natural process," Brooks said in a summary of his forthcoming work which appeared in the American Philosophical Society's 1968 yearbook. Brooks, who formerly taught evolutionary history at Yale, also charged that in *Origin* Darwin never acknowledged his debt to Wallace in resolving his difficulties with the principle of divergence. Further, on the basis of his still unpublished research, Brooks believes that Darwin received Wallace's Ternate Essay on May 18, 1858, providing him with one month to rework the theory in his own mind before writing Lyell on June 18 and claiming that he had "to-day" received Wallace's paper.*

Significantly, perhaps, R. C. Stauffer of the University of Wisconsin, who made a critical study of Darwin's unpublished "big book" and is a Darwin admirer who dedicated his work to Lady Barlow, concluded that Darwin completed his final revision of the chapter on divergence June 12, five days after he told Hooker that he, Darwin, had found the missing link, the "keystone" to "his" theory. If Brooks' thesis is borne out, Darwin would have had three weeks in which to rewrite his chapter on divergence.

The strength of the June 4 and 8 dates notwithstanding, there is equally strong evidence in favor of June 14 as the date that Wallace's manuscript arrived.

Darwin maintained a minilog, his "little diary," he called it, a personal annual history that was sometimes compressed into less than a page. "[The] diary or pocketbook," commented Sir Francis Darwin— his father's biographer—". . . contains little more than the dates of *the principal events* of his life." (Italics added.)

The pocket diary observes that Darwin began working on the chapter about the principle of divergence in his "big book" on May 14, 1858. According to a notation, he completed work on this most difficult chapter on June 12—that is, some nine days after having received Wallace's letter, assuming that the letter reached Down House on the same day that Wallace's other letter, dispatched simultaneously from the Malay archipelago, reached Bates, and five days after Darwin confided to Hooker that he had finally resolved the problem that had thwarted him for almost twenty years. But Darwin's June 8 date, on which he wrote to Hooker, is convenient—perhaps too convenient—if his statement that he received Wallace's manuscript on June 18 is accepted. For it was Wallace's manuscript that contained the first *complete* exposition, in writing, of descent and divergence with modification through variation and natural selection— what is now referred to as the "Darwinian" theory of evolution.

Thus, the next entry in Darwin's "little diary" acquires particular significance. It reads as follows: "June 14th pigeons (interrupted)."

*See also pp. 348-49.

Darwin was then in the midst of a major experiment with pigeons and there is no explanation for the interruption, nor for why Darwin should record the experiment as a "principal event" of that year. The subsequent entry is dated Thursday, July 20 and reads: "Began abstract of species book." This work—*The Origin of Species*—was the book that was to catapult Darwin into immortality. It was not the "big book" into which Darwin had already put more than two years' work. That book never was completed.

The jump in the "little diary" of principal dates from June 14 to July 20 excites the imagination. This is the period that included the announcement of the "Darwinian" theory of evolution to the world— July 1, 1858.

Francis Darwin, in his two-volume life and letters of his father, noted that Darwin had embarked on his "big book" on May 14, 1856, and worked steadily on it "up to June 1858, when it was *interrupted* by the arrival of Mr. Wallace's MS." (Italics added.)

For a diary which purportedly compresses into a few lines "the dates of the principal events" in Darwin's life, the entry about pigeons and the failure to note the announcement of the theory of evolution on July 1, 1858, are as astonishing as they are inexplicable. Further, if the minilog was designed to record important dates, there should at the very least have been a June 1858 entry observing the arrival of Wallace's manuscript.

Darwin's "little diary," it should be noted, only came to light about twenty years ago. It first appeared in the *Bulletin of the British Museum (Natural History)*. Sir Gavin de Beer, the distinguished geneticist and Darwinian, edited the work and, in a foreword, observed, perhaps unwittingly, that "there is always an element of indiscretion in perusing a document which was never meant by its author for publication." De Beer offered no explanation for the mysterious interruption at that critical juncture.

As for the June 18 date, this is Darwin's interpretation of events and—since he was respected for his honor and integrity—is the date almost universally accepted by biographers and historians, and cited in encyclopedias, textbooks, and other works, as the date on which Darwin received Wallace's manuscript.

In the privacy of his study a troubled Darwin opened Wallace's letter from Ternate. The contents consisted of a personal note from Wallace and an essay entitled, "On the Tendency of Varieties to Depart Indefinitely from the Original Type."

Like the envelope, the note is no longer in existence. It, too, was either lost or destroyed, accidentally or intentionally.

What does exist, however, is a letter which Darwin wrote to Lyell, and which Lyell preserved. It is dated "Down, 18th." The date is without month or year, a Darwinian idiosyncrasy, for either Darwin had neither the time nor the patience to date his correspondence or, to maintain his seclusion, he deliberately nurtured a vague sense of time as another barrier between himself and the world. Emma, his wife, was of a similar frame of mind and many of her letters are dated loosely. However, in the light of the fast-moving events in the wake of June 18, particularly between June 18 and July 1, there is not a shard of doubt that Darwin mailed his letter to Lyell on Friday, June 18, 1858.

"My dear Lyell . . . ," begins Darwin, "Wallace . . . has today sent me the enclosed, and asked me to forward it to you." And, exercising extraordinary understatement, even for an Englishman, Darwin added, "It seems to me well worth reading." The letter to Lyell interlocks with Wallace's own recollection of what he mailed to Darwin the previous March 9. In his autobiography, Wallace confirmed that he had sent his Ternate Paper to Darwin with the request that, if Darwin felt the paper had merit, he should pass it on to Lyell, the doyen of the British scientific aristocracy.

As Julian Huxley, the grandson of Thomas Huxley, later expressed it, the Wallace paper was a "bombshell."

Until the receipt of Wallace's letter, and until July 1 of that year, when the "Darwinian" theory of evolution was proclaimed publicly, Darwin—through insecurity, fear of the consequences, failure to have fully developed the theory, simply because he had studied the trees so closely and for so long that he could no longer distinguish them from the forest, or for whatever other reason that may have haunted him—had not published a single line on the species question. Not a word. Moreover, as the record shows, Darwin never took his most intimate colleagues, Hooker and Lyell, completely into his confidence about his life's work until Wallace forced his hand, and then did so only after receipt of Wallace's lucid, brilliantly conceived, and thoroughly executed presentation of the theory of evolution through natural selection, including the "keystone" of the concept, the principle of divergence.

In June 1858, Darwin understandably panicked. Indeed, he had been in a state of controlled panic since the end of 1855, when Wallace's first paper on the question appeared in print. Now the panic was uncontrollable. A logical speculation surges to the fore: Why didn't Darwin destroy Wallace's damaging manuscript? The explanation is that Darwin was in essence a true scientist, a man of honesty and integrity. His behavior following his receipt of the Ternate Essay was a tragic, human error of judgment, and the consequences were deplorable.

When panic flies in, reason flies out. Thus, in this moment of weakness which was to deeply trouble his conscience all his life, Darwin engaged in what Leonard Huxley called "a delicate arrangement," the greatest conspiracy in the annals of science.

Chapter 4

IN POINT OF FACT, the Darwinian conspiracy and cover-up were seeded two-and-a-half years before June 1858.

Early in 1855 Wallace was in Borneo, an island, then as now, larger than France but with fewer people than Denmark. Inhospitable climate and terrain account for its underpopulation. The island straddles the equator and is a panorama of jungle-clad hills, rivers with thickly overgrown banks, meandering streams choked with water plants, broad savannahs, and dense rain forests. Wallace was in that part of Borneo known as Sarawak, an area perched along the island's northern rim, overlooking the typhoon-tossed South China Sea.*

There, Wallace eked out a haphazard living with a butterfly net, collecting specimens—especially beetles, which were Wallace's (and Darwin's) favorite insects—stuffing birds, and acquiring the skins of reptiles and the orang-utan, which in the Malay language literally means the "forest man." Wallace sold the specimens to the British Museum and other interested parties through Samuel Stevens, a London agent. In the parlance of the trade, Wallace was a "fly-catcher." Stevens' job was to make the London rounds, peddling Wallace's wares.

In Wallace's day, head-hunting, piracy, and animism flourished in Sarawak, as in the rest of Borneo. The *bumi putera* or "sons of the soil"

---

* In 1946, as a correspondent en route from Hong Kong to Singapore aboard the British destroyer H. M. S. *Cossack*, I was caught in a typhoon in those waters and can confirm the violence of these tropical storms at sea.

—the "natives" of the island—were Dyaks, a cheerful and friendly people, tall, angular, and fair, who possessed a frightful reputation among Malays, Chinese, and Europeans because of their penchant for taking human heads. The Dyaks dwelt, as they still do, in longhouses, upwards of four hundred men, women, and children under one roof, a roof sometimes six hundred feet in length. The more dried heads in the rafters the better, and those of women and children were the best of all.

As for taking the heads of women and children, Dyak reasoning was sound. A warrior would have to penetrate deeply into another tribe's territory to procure such highly prized trophies. And since heads were, among other things, symbols of virility, young Dyak women encouraged their suitors to display their prowess by taking as many heads as they could. Dried heads dot the lofts of longhouses to this day; on several trips to Borneo I have sat in such homes, delightfully entertained at tea with shrunken heads above me. After a while the sight is no more startling than the view of barefooted, barebreasted Dyak maidens, attired only in a sarong wrapped around their slim waists, going about their longhouse business. I imagine Wallace also grew accustomed to these sights.

Wallace first arrived in Sarawak in 1854, five years after the United States recognized the territory, under James Brooke, as a sovereign state. Brooke was a character out of Conrad; indeed, Conrad, who plied these waters, used him as a model in several novels. Dashing, colorful, thoroughly at home among animistic Dyaks and devout Moslem Malays, Brooke had arrived on the scene several years earlier, had taken sides in one of Borneo's innumerable internecine conflicts, and was, as a reward, appointed Rajah by the Sultan of Brunei, the titular ruler of Borneo. In time, through a judicious blend of intrigue and gunpowder, the adventurous Brooke secured Sarawak's independence from the Sultan and was eventually knighted by Victoria. But the British were slow to recognize his domain, and Whitehall delayed recognizing his state until 1864.

Almost single-handedly, Brooke imposed law and order on Sarawak, and so did his descendants. By the time the clock of colonialism ran out on the White Rajahs in 1946, Brooke and his successors had put an end to head-hunting among the Dyaks and had sharply curtailed piracy. Animism, despite the conversion of many *bumi putera* to Christianity and Islam, largely held its ground. Today Sarawak is a province within the Islamic Federation of Malaysia and is governed from the Malay peninsula on the opposite rim of the South China Sea.

During Wallace's sojourn in Sarawak he was the personal guest of Brooke, who had been weakened by smallpox and malaria. The pair got along admirably. Nothing delighted the White Rajah more than to sit up at night on the *serambi* or veranda of his bungalow-palace, with its attap roof, teak beams, wicker chairs, huge library, formal gardens, and spacious grounds, sipping arak from a narrow bamboo tube and debating world affairs.

Spenser St. John, Brooke's bearded secretary and biographer, vividly recalled Wallace's first visit and wrote, "We had at this time . . . Mr. Alfred Wallace, who was then elaborating in his mind the theory . . . of the origin of species.

"If he would not convince us that our ugly neighbors, the orangutans, were our ancestors," St. John said laughingly, "he pleased, instructed, and delighted us by his clever and inexhaustible flow of talk—really good talk."

Wallace excited Brooke's mind and the pair, St. John said, debated matters of philosophy and religion almost continuously. The Rajah's palace resounded with their voices "and the energetic bangs on the table made the glasses ring," Brooke recalled in a letter to St. John. "Everybody was an atheist and pantheist by turns."

Brooke was so enamored of Wallace that he asked the "fly-catcher" to spend Christmas that year with him and his entourage at the Rajah's bungalow at the foot of the Santubong mountains, a short distance from where the muddy Sarawak River, originating in Borneo's heart of darkness, empties into the South China Sea. The hill station was, like Darwin's Sandwalk at Down, a natural retreat. Santubong was located only a few miles north of Kuching, the small *pasar* town which to this day serves as Sarawak's capital; in Malay, the word *kuching* means cat, although the reason this name was bestowed on the town is lost in history.

Like most Europeans in the Malay archipelago at that time, Wallace was repeatedly ravaged by attacks of malaria, which was then a medically unidentified malady called ague. The Rajah invited Wallace to remain a few weeks at Santubong to recuperate from his latest bout with the dread disease. On this occasion, aside from a Malay cook, whom Brooke left behind as Wallace's Man Friday, Wallace was alone in the bungalow.

Winter at Down coincides with the rainy season in Sarawak. While Charles and Emma Darwin struggled through a bitter winter—their daughter Henrietta recalled that a great snowfall enveloped Down that year and that "the snow was level with the top of the iron railings round the lawn"—Wallace waded through the monsoon season, which is known to dump as much as 150 inches of water on the island.

"During the evenings and wet days I had nothing to do but look over my books and ponder over the problem which was rarely absent from my thoughts," Wallace later recalled. That problem, the origin of species, had tormented him as it had haunted Darwin.

Wallace, however, took a novel approach to the problem. He focused on the *geographical distribution* of plants and animals, read everything on the subject he could find, and "almost knew by heart" the catalogs of insects and reptiles in the British Museum. It was, after all, his trade. These catalogs, monographs, and books provided a mass of facts, not unlike the maze of material Darwin had collected for twenty years, a labyrinth in which the master of Down House occasionally saw gleams of light, but the vast preponderance of which was still shrouded in darkness.

"It occurred to me," remembered Wallace, "that these facts had never been properly utilized as indications of the way in which species had come into existence [and] I accordingly put my facts and ideas on paper."

At the end of February 1855, he dispatched his "facts and ideas" to the prestigious *Annals and Magazine of Natural History*. The title of his essay was ambitious: "On the Law which has Regulated the Introduction of New Species."

The editorial board of the *Annals*, which was avidly read by Darwin, Lyell, and Hooker, among others, consisted of P.J. Selby, C. C. Badington, and Richard Taylor. They must have been delighted with Wallace's lucidity and originality because they published what has since become known as his Sarawak Law immediately. It appeared in their September 1855 issue. But as far as Wallace could determine from the remoteness of Borneo, he might as well have dropped the Sarawak Law down a bottomless well. There was no audible reaction to his startling thesis, not even the faintest splash.

Chapter 5

WHAT WAS "the great law," as Wallace phrased it? In less than seven thousand words, "most briefly and imperfectly," Wallace said, he drew this conclusion: *Every species has come into existence coincident both in time and space with a pre-existing closely allied species.* This is the only line in the Sarawak essay which Wallace repeatedly set forth in italics, for double emphasis. And for greater effect, he repeated the same sentence twice, word for word, at the outset and conclusion of his paper. Wallace also added a personal touch. "It is about ten years since the idea of such a law suggested itself to the writer of this essay," he said. This statement turned the clock back to 1845, a year after Darwin had written his 1844 essay, a paper which contained so many confused and incomplete lines of thought that Darwin never published it, although he considered it his most important work and left a note to his wife to publish it upon his death, suggesting Lyell, Hooker, or both, among others, as editors.

Wallace's essay displayed an astonishing grasp of scientific affairs and literary flair for a thirty-two-year-old self-educated drifter without prospect of regular employment. Wallace's technical know-how is mirrored in references in the paper which range from gloiathi, ornithopterae, heliconidae, danaidae, and other insect species, to the testaceous cephalopod. As for literary style, Wallace described the Earth as "the theatre of life."

The paper was brilliant in content and executed in a clear, direct style. In it, Wallace planted the seeds of the principle of divergence.

While a species may become extinct, as proven by the existence of strange fossils, the species may have left behind a variety or prototype, "a faint memorial" to the grandeur and luxuriance of its past. Thus, Wallace observed, every case of apparent disappearance of a species is in reality simply an expression of change.

As had the master of Down House somewhere between 1842 and 1844—although unbeknownst to his East Indian counterpart—Wallace abandoned the ladder concept of evolution first enunciated by Aristotle and later developed by the great eighteenth-century French zoologist and evolutionist, Marquis Jean Baptiste de Lamarck. Instead, Wallace envisioned life as "a forked or many branched line . . . as the twigs of gnarled oak or the vascular system of the human body." Repeatedly, he described nature in terms of a spreading chestnut tree and emphasized that while evolution may appear to some a theory of progress, "it is in reality only one of gradual change." Wallace did not confuse change with progress. Change, yes; progress, not necessarily. This solitary paper overthrew thousands of years of philosophical speculations.

These speculations go back to the earliest known literature. "There was a time in which there existed nothing but darkness and an abyss of waters," Berosus, the Chaldean priest of Babylon, wrote in a history of Assyrian and Babylonian civilization, "wherein there resided . . . creatures in which were combined the lines of every species."

In Periclean Greece, while Aristotle developed his ladder of creation and taught that "nature proceeds little by little from things lifeless to animal life," Thales—much closer to the truth—observed that "nothing comes into being out of nothing, and nothing passes away into nothing." A world away, in China, around 540 B.C., the mystic Lao Tzu suggested that survival of the fittest is a basic theme in nature. "Nature is unkind," he wrote. "It treats creation like sacrificial straw-dogs."

In the days of Rome's grandeur, Marcus Aurelius observed that "nature, which governs the whole, will soon change old things thou seest, and out of their substances will make other things, and again other things from the substance of them, in order that the world may be ever new." And Lucretius, perhaps the most advanced thinker on evolution before the Victorian Age, proclaimed that life had a definite beginning in time. Lucretius took his theory a step further, and developed a Malthusian doctrine to suggest evolution through natural selection. He concluded that "nature sought a ban on strange monsters [dinosaurs?] and they could not reach the coveted flower of age nor find food nor be united in marriage and many races of living things must then have died out and been unable to beget and continue their breed . . . while those that survived were protected and preserved by the particular qualities of their race."

Lucretius' view is so contemporary that Branislav Petronievics, in his *L'Evolution Universelle*, published in Paris in 1921, wrote with awe: "Here we feel that we are in the presence of an almost modern scientist."

Evolutionary theory emerged from the classical period only in the Age of Reason. In the eighteenth century Kant expressed a belief in a "mechanism of nature that may yet enable us to arrive at some explanation of life . . . strengthening the suspicion that species have an actual kinship due to descent from a common parent." And Erasmus Darwin, Darwin's polymath grandfather, a physician, poet, and philosopher, speculated in *Zoonomia, or the Laws of Organic Life*, that "the whole is one family of one parent." Ernest Krause, the German scientist, writing in 1879, characterized Erasmus Darwin as the forerunner of Lamarck and credited Charles Darwin's grandfather with having "first established a complete system of the theory of evolution." Indeed, it was during Darwin's grandfather's time that the word Darwinism came into vogue. Samuel Taylor Coleridge, in *Stillingfleet*, minted the word "darwinising" to describe Erasmus' wild speculations and he denounced Erasmus' concept of nature as "the Oran Outang theology of the human race," an astonishing coincidence since Wallace's Sarawak Law was drafted in the land of the orang-utan!

By 1809, with the publication of Lamarck's theory that "the simplest living things have given rise to all others" and that acquired characteristics are inherited (now disproven by modern science), the subject of evolution was "in the air" and evolution and progress were treated synonymously. Wallace's meaning of evolution, however, was not so much progress as change. This was a radical departure from the past; nevertheless, Wallace viewed evolution objectively, with dispassion, not subjectively with passion.

Wallace's essay was not footnoted. In it he drew on writers before him, as all writers do, selecting ideas notably from Lamarck, Lyell, Erasmus Darwin, and others. However, only Lyell was mentioned by name.

The revolution Lyell wrought in geology with the publication in

1832 of his *Principles* furnished Wallace, as it did Darwin, with the framework of his theory of evolution, a concept that demanded an incredibly long history of living things. Before Lyell, who broadened Hutton's views of the age of the Earth, the Mosaic cosmogony had gone largely unchallenged in the Christian and Islamic worlds.

But Wallace's theory of unity in diversity, that every species is allied to each other, postulated an Earth millions of years old, not Ussher's miserly 4,004 years (plus 1,855) as had been widely accepted. Today, of course, the Earth's age is calculated in billions of years and man's origin alone has been traced back 3.8 million years, and beyond.

In setting forth the Sarawak Law, Wallace explained that it was based on "ten well-known facts." He numbered and set them out, fact for fact. But while the ten facts may have been "well-known" to Wallace, they apparently were not well-known to anyone else, including Darwin. Nevertheless, the evidence is irrefutable that Darwin studied Wallace's law.

Darwin subscribed to the *Annals* and there are references to various articles appearing in the magazine in Darwin's correspondence with Lyell, Hooker, and others. But there is not a single reference in any of Darwin's letters to the Sarawak Law, except in one letter to Wallace after Wallace initiated a correspondence with him. In other words, Darwin gave the impression that he was either unaware of the Sarawak Law or that he had come to that conclusion so long ago that the content of the Wallace essay was common knowledge to him.

But this impression was false. Not only was Darwin aware of the publication of Wallace's paper but the law terrified him.

At Down House Darwin maintained a complete file of the *Annals*, as he did other scientific journals, and pinned to the back of the December 1855 issue, in his own scribbly hand, is a set of nineteen lines of annotations concerning the Wallace monograph which reflects Darwin's stupefaction. He called the Sarawak Law "Wallace's Paper." For example, Darwin drew two parallel lines alongside the law itself, Wallace's "fact No. 10," which Wallace had underlined and set out in italics. As for "fact No. 8," that species of one family occurring in the same geological time are more closely allied than those separated in time, Darwin jotted this notation: "Can this be true?" Obviously, this was news to Darwin.

As observed earlier, Darwin was a compulsive letter writer, as were all the Darwins and Wedgwoods. Francis Darwin's four volumes containing his father's letters fill 2,167 pages. But the tense period covering Darwin's discovery of the Sarawak Law in December 1855, and Darwin's receipt of Wallace's Ternate Paper in June 1858, gets short shrift. For the critical period of the Sarawak Law, for example, Francis' volumes leap from July 18, 1855, to August 5, 1856, with nothing in between. Henrietta, Darwin's daughter, in her two-volume edition of her mother's correspondence, also gives the period a quick brushoff. The two-volume life and letters of Hooker, Darwin's confidant, consists of 964 pages, and jumps from September 1855, when Wallace's law was published, to June 1858, when Wallace's Ternate Paper reached England, in nine pages without a solitary reference to Wallace. The two-volume life and letters of Thomas Huxley, who expanded the triumvirate of Darwin, Hooker, and Lyell into a quadrumvirate, consists of 1,080 pages and skims the critical period in less than a page.

In none of these volumes, embracing thousands of pages, is there a hint about Darwin's reaction to the Sarawak Law other than the reference to it in the Darwin correspondence edited by his son Francis and published in 1897. That reference is found in a letter Darwin sent to Wallace, which Wallace saved.

If Darwin wrote to either Hooker or Lyell about Wallace's disturbing conclusion, the letters are lost. Indeed, with the exception of a handful of letters from Darwin to Wallace, Hooker, and Lyell, *all* the pertinent Darwin correspondence of that critical thirty-one month span is missing. Yet, this period is the prologue to the raising of the curtain on the "Darwinian" theory of evolution on July 1, 1858. Credulity is strained. It is as if *Rheingold* were missing from Wagner's Ring cycle. Better still, as the evidence will demonstrate, it is as if Wagner wrote *Walküre*, *Siegfried*, and *Götterdämmerung* while an unknown composer—a complete stranger—independently had written *Rheingold before* Wagner wrote the other three parts of the Ring.

Yet, as his own notations testify, Darwin was severely shaken by Wallace's Sarawak Law. But there is additional, more convincing proof of the stunning impact of Wallace on Darwin in 1856. Leonard G. Wilson, a distinguished member of the University of Minnesota faculty, edited Lyell's scientific journals and, in the course of his work, made an astonishing discovery. Lyell's journals for 1855–1858—the crucial stretch under review—revealed that Lyell had not only read Wallace's Sarawak Law—with its reference to him and with its deep implication that man himself is the offspring of a preexisting, closely allied species—but that Lyell was so dumfounded that he began his first notebook on the species question forty-eight hours later. This was the type of species notebook that Darwin had opened twenty years earlier. Moreover, as soon as winter was spent, Lyell, Darwin's senior in age, position, and influence in the scientific aristocracy, visited Down and confronted its master with Wallace's paper. Although Darwin had never taken Lyell completely into his confidence about his speculations concerning evolution, Lyell knew that Darwin had long been studying the species question.

The electrifying tale of Lyell's pressure on Darwin as a result of the Sarawak Law is a story which is not even hinted at in Leonard Huxley's two volumes on Lyell.

The story of Wilson's discovery is fascinating. In 1961, while studying the correspondence and notebooks of Lyell at Kinnordy House, Kirriemuir, Scotland—Lyell's birthplace—Wilson stumbled across "seven notebooks in which Sir Charles Lyell had entered his notes and reflections on the question of the transmutation of species."

Wilson expressed incredulity that "apart from a very few letters, I have not been able to locate Lyell's letters to Darwin and suspect that this immense correspondence, so important for the history of science, has not survived."

Wilson offered no explanation of this shocking discovery, which is especially so since such numbers of reputable historians, biographers, and others have written so warmly that Darwin's life and work form the most completely told story in the annals of science. It was not until nine years later, with three grants of public assistance from the United States government, that Lyell's scientific journals were published.

According to Lyell's notebook entries, he read Wallace's essay in the *Annals* for the first time on November 26, 1855, and was so overwhelmed that he made a digest of it, opening two days later the first page of his own scientific journal, a running account of thought and inquiry that would extend to 1861, two years after Darwin's publication of *Origin*. Lyell's comments about and summary of Wallace's paper run almost as long as the paper itself.

Lyell apparently spent a restless winter grappling with the implications of Wallace's theory. Lyell had known for a long time that Darwin doubted the fixity of species. Finally, on Sunday, April 13, 1856, he and Lady Lyell journeyed to Down. The entry in his journal dated Wednesday, April 16, reads: "With Darwin: On the formation of Species by Natural Selection (Origin Query?)." What did Lyell and Darwin talk about? According to Lyell's journal, they discussed "Mr.

Wallace." They analyzed his theory that each species is closely related to a preexisting species. Lyell pressed Darwin for an explanation of this law and Darwin suggested, according to Lyell, that the explanation may be found in a theory he had been working on for many years, "natural selection"—what Herbert Spencer later dubbed "the survival of the fittest."

The next entry in Lyell's journal is fascinating. A religious individual who believed in acts of special creation—that species were created in one fell swoop and were permanent—Lyell struggled with the origin of origins. "How," he asked himself in his private journal, did man begin?" He left the question unanswered.

Irrefutably, Lyell's journal proves that as early as April 1856 the puzzle about the origin of species with which Darwin had struggled incessantly and inconclusively for almost a generation was in the process of being unraveled by Alfred Russel Wallace.

By reference to "natural selection" we can surmise that it was during his visit to Down that Lyell, once and for all, asked Darwin to explain his theory about the species question. Thus, for the first time, the obsessively secretive Darwin made Lyell privy to a conclusion that species were not fixed and permanent and not the result of a single act of Creation, but instead developed through "natural selection." Darwin, however, was still at a loss to explain the principle of *divergence*, how the tree of nature kept branching out in infinite, mind-boggling directions, from ladybugs and lampreys to lions and larks. The Lyell–Darwin meeting is another illustration of Darwin's character, for this was the first time that Darwin had unburdened himself of his preoccupation to Lyell in the course of a friendship that had reached back to Darwin's dedication of his *Voyage of the Beagle* to Lyell in 1835, twenty-one years earlier.

In his 1876 autobiographical sketch, Darwin disingenuously admitted that "early in 1856 Lyell advised me to write out my views pretty fully. . . ." Disingenuously, because Darwin never admitted that it was Wallace's Sarawak Law that agitated Lyell and forced Darwin to undertake his "big book" any more than he publicly acknowledged the influence of Wallace on his own thinking when he published *Origin* in 1859.

Nor is Wallace's name ever mentioned in Darwin's existing correspondence with Lyell after Lyell's visit to Down until the letter Darwin wrote to Lyell, June 18, 1858, in which Darwin, with happy simplicity, observed, "Some year or so ago you recommended me to

read a paper by Wallace in the 'Annals' which had interested you."
The reference must be to the Sarawak Law and this is buttressed by
Wilson's discovery in 1961.

But Darwin's alarm in 1856, following the publication of Wallace's
Sarawak Law and Lyell's visit to Down, is indisputable. Priority—the
irresistible passion to be first—now tormented Darwin just as the
species question had for decades. Thus, on May 3, 1856, Darwin wrote
Lyell that "I rather hate the idea of writing for priority, yet I certainly should be vexed if anyone were to publish *my* doctrine before
me." (Italics added.)

Who could that "anyone" possibly be? The reference can only be
to Wallace. And, just as obviously, how could Wallace publish
Darwin's doctrine before Darwin? How could anyone other than
Wagner write *Rheingold*? Darwin neither knew nor corresponded
with Wallace. If Wallace published such a doctrine, would it not be
Wallace's doctrine?

Darwin also displayed uneasiness about the question of priority in
a letter to Hooker six days later—again without a single reference to
Wallace. "I very much want advice and truthful consolation if you
can give it," he wrote his most intimate friend. "I had a good talk with
Lyell about my species work, and he urges me strongly to publish
something."

Darwin complained to Hooker that haste was a paramount concern,
although he never explained why. And he declared that he would at
best publish "a very thin and little volume, giving a sketch of my
views and *difficulties*; but it is really dreadfully unphilosophical to
give a resume, without exact references, of an unpublished work."
(Italics added.)

In other words, Darwin would publish without reference to his
sources, without reference to Wallace's Sarawak Law. He would
publish for reasons of priority—to lay claim to the theory of evolution by natural selection as his private possession, to secure a place in
history, and to satisfy his vaulting ego. He would soar above the
firmament like an eagle.

"In the preface," he wrote Hooker, "I would state that the work
could not be considered strictly scientific, but a mere sketch or outline
of a future work in which full reference, etc., should be given."

This was an elaborate way of circumventing Wallace and establishing priority. To his credit, however, Darwin, basically a man of
integrity, admitted that he found the stratagem distasteful, if not dis-

graceful. "I believe," he told Hooker, "I should sneer at anyone else doing this, and my only comfort is that I *truly* never dreamed of it, till Lyell suggested it." Dreamed of what? The idea of publishing a précis of the Sarawak Law?

Conveniently, Darwin quieted his conscience by shifting the blame for deviousness to Lyell. It was Lyell, he complained, who forced him to write for priority. Lyell was the *éminence gris*.

Hooker apparently approved of Lyell's suggestion and although Hooker's letter to Darwin is missing, Darwin's reply to Hooker, dated May 11 and saved by Hooker, confirms Hooker's advice and consent.

"I am extremely glad you think well [of the idea]," Darwin wrote. But Darwin admitted again that he was troubled by the affair and again put the blame on Lyell. "I begin *most heartedly* to wish that Lyell had never put the idea of an Essay into my head." Clearly, in the matter of rushing into print Lyell was the culprit, not Darwin. But who had put the Sarawak Law into Darwin's head?

"To any one but you I should apologize for such long discussion on so personal an affair," Darwin concluded.

The inseparable twins, science and truth, took a back seat to priority.

Chapter 6

NOR IS LYELL'S NOTEBOOK the only evidence of the devastating impact of the Sarawak Law on Darwin.

In the surviving correspondence of the period is a letter to Darwin from one of Darwin's regular overseas correspondents, the naturalist Edward Blyth, whose name is even more obscure in the history of science than that of Wallace.

Blyth, a year younger than Darwin, had been born into the economic ghetto of Victorian England. But like Wallace he had not let straitened circumstances stand in the way of self-education. "Never," his sister recalled, "was any youth more industrious: up at three or four in the morning, reading, making notes, sketching bones, colouring maps, stuffing birds by the hundred, collecting butterflies, and beetles— teaching himself German sufficiently to translate it readily."

Like Wallace, Blyth also spent much of his time in the reading and insect collection rooms of the British Museum "or in some kindred institution," his sister added, "trying hard to find employment." He found none in London but was ultimately offered the job of curator of the museum of the Royal Asiatic Society of Bengal, which was located in Calcutta. The pay was pitiful in the beginning, and remained so to the end of his twenty-two year sojourn in India, but he grabbed it. After he married, Blyth moonlighted to keep afloat, on one occasion purchasing a royal Bengal tiger for £2 and selling it to an English zoo for £140. But his profit was meager after deducting the costs of food and care for the animal, and the shipping of the tiger to London.

In addition to poverty and industriousness, Blyth shared two other characteristics with Wallace. As in the case of Wallace, there was not a droplet of greed or envy in Blyth, and he was entranced by the species question. Before leaving for India in 1841 he had published a series of articles in the *Magazine of Natural History* in which he explored heredity, variation, and the struggle for existence in nature. He ardently believed, however, that species were fixed and permanent, as ordained in Genesis.

Despite his religious beliefs, Blyth was a man of ideas, and Darwin furtively stole from him. Two eminent scholars provide the evidence. Loren Eiseley, the late anthropologist, in a lengthy paper for the American Philosophical Society, cited what he described as "startling" evidence for this theft: "namely, that Darwin made unacknowledged use of Blyth's work . . . that Blyth is more than a Darwinian precursor, that he is instead a direct intellectual forebear, in a phylogenetic line of descent." Eiseley was gentle. Oxford scholar C. D. Darlington was direct and brutal. Darlington noted that, in his early papers, Blyth quoted a wealth of examples from nature to make a point and that "these afterwards appear repeated, or indeed copied, by Darwin in his preliminary essays of 1842 and 1844."

Whatever the case, on December 8, 1855, Blyth wrote Darwin from India about the Sarawak Law. Unabashedly, he asked Darwin, "What do you think of Wallace's paper in the Ann. N. Hist.?" Blyth was not going to waste the better part of a year before giving Darwin his own reaction. "Good!" Blyth exclaimed, adding, "Wallace has, I think, put the matter well: and according to *his* theory, the various domestic races of animals have been fairly developed into species." (Italics added.)

Blyth described Wallace's concept as a "novelty . . . the lucid collation of facts & phenomena." Oddly enough, he asked Darwin whether it at all unsettled his ideas about "the persistence of species." The latter remark is revealing. Once again insight is acquired into Darwin's obsession with secrecy, his fear of taking anyone completely into his confidence, his ambition to monopolize the field: Darwin had been familiar with Blyth's writing since 1835, when Blyth's first monograph appeared and, as Darlington put it, Darwin "repeated, or indeed copied" Blyth's arguments in his essays of 1842 and 1844—

without attribution, of course. Yet, although Darwin was now in correspondence with Blyth, Blyth did not even know that Darwin had abandoned the Mosaic cosmogony, the grand view of Creation in six stages, as early as the 1830s.

Thomas Huxley—the Huxley who later described himself as Darwin's "general agent" and "his bulldog" in the propagation of the "Darwinian" theory of evolution—was another of Darwin's close associates who was not privy to Darwin's thoughts. But in 1887, five years after Darwin's death, when Francis Darwin completed the first volume of his father's life and letters, he asked Huxley to contribute a memoir about the reception of the *Origin* on its publication. The result may have momentarily unsettled Sir Francis, for, although the latter's volume contained not a single comment by Darwin about the Sarawak Law, Huxley—in his memoir—drew attention to Wallace.

"No enumeration of the influences at work, at the time I am speaking of, would be complete without the mention of his [Wallace's] powerful essay 'On the Law which has Regulated the Introduction of New Species' which was published in 1855," Huxley declared.

"On reading it afresh," confessed Huxley in his open, admirable way, "I have been astonished to recollect how small was the impression [the Sarawak Law] made."

But the impression made on Darwin, Lyell, and Blyth, unknown to Huxley, was not small.

History—as with Wilson's discovery of the Lyell journals almost twenty years ago—has a habit of catching up with the past. In 1959, on the occasion of the centenary of the publication of Darwin's *Origin*, the late C. F. A. Pantin, president of the prestigious Linnean Society, strode on eggshells. Positions diminishing Darwin's stature as the greatest scientific figure of the last century evoke strong emotions among his admirers, particularly in Britain where he is revered as a national hero. Yet Pantin, who taught at Oxford, was constrained to observe frankly that the Sarawak Law was "perhaps the most important 'pre-Darwinian' essay on the origin of species apart from the works of Lamarck." In the same year Pantin published, under the imprint of the Royal Society of London, a note in which he again stated his position on Wallace, whom he described as "the greatest tropical naturalist of his time."

"Although it was unrecognized at the time and has been overlooked today," said Pantin in his note, "[Wallace] had already published by far the most important 'pre-Darwinian' contribution to the theory of evolution—his Sarawak essay of 1855."

But—like Huxley before him—Pantin erred. The Sarawak Law had not been unrecognized, nor had it made a small impression. Its impression on Darwin, Lyell, and Blyth was devastating.

In far-off Sarawak, however, Wallace would have agreed with Huxley and Pantin. Wallace was keenly disppointed over the apparent failure of his Law to draw attention in London. In part, the reason for this was the seemingly outlandish character of a law that proposed the unthinkable, that therefore ran against the fashionable tenets of the Victorian period, and that had been put forward by a relatively unknown naturalist—a pedlar of insects and other forms of wildlife.

Worse, Stevens, Wallace's faithful agent, complained that "several naturalists"—that is, customers—expressed dismay that Wallace was " 'theorizing,' when what we had to do was collect more facts." By more facts, Stevens meant more specimens; for that, after all, was their business—Wallace collecting specimens and Stevens selling them. In effect, Wallace's agent told him to get on with earning a living and to stop wasting time on unprofitable theories about the laws of nature.

But Wallace, like Darwin, was obsessed, and possessed, by the species question. Living in the natural world, in the fastness of the jungle, Wallace could not abandon his speculation about man's uncertain past, inexplicable present, and unknown future.

Failing to generate interest over a law which should have shaken the world—the Sarawak Law anticipated a common ancestry for all living forms, including man; in fact, implied it—the shy, diffident Wallace made an uncharacteristic move. He wrote a letter. He probably would have preferred to write it to Lyell, doyen of the scientific aristocracy, directly on the question. But that was tantamount to writing the Queen, and he could not work up the boldness to do so. Wallace, of course, had no inkling of the extraordinary effect his theory had had on Lyell; indeed, Wallace died without knowing the truth. He was not privy to Lyell's scientific journals and there is no evidence in their later correspondence that Lyell ever told Wallace of the true impact Wallace had had upon him.

Wallace decided to draw Lyell's attention to the Sarawak Law in a circuitous fashion, by contacting the distinguished naturalist Charles Robert Darwin, a known associate of the illustrious Lyell.

Even so, it took Wallace almost a year to gather the courage to write Darwin; one may speculate that he played with the idea for months. Finally, out of desperation and frustration, he wrote to the naturalist at Down.

Wallace initiated his correspondence with Darwin on October 10, 1856. Wallace's first letter is, alas, lost. But the first eight letters Darwin wrote to Wallace were found among Wallace's papers shortly after the latter's death in 1913. Wallace preserved them in an envelope as treasures, which they were. On the outside of the envelope Wallace wrote in his legible hand: "The first 8 letters I received from Darwin— while in the Malay Archipelago."*

However, not only is Wallace's first letter to Darwin missing, so are *all* the letters which Wallace wrote Darwin in this period except for a fragment of one, which is in the Cambridge University library.

The astonishing disappearance of so many of the critical letters in the Darwinian story belies the repeated claims that the story is the most complete in scientific annals. In *The Life and Letters of Charles Darwin*, his son Francis tried to explain the mystery. "It was his custom to file all letters received, and when his slender stock of files ('spits' as he called them) was exhausted, he would burn the letters of several years, in order that he might make use of the liberated 'spits,'" Francis claimed. "This process, carried on for years, destroyed nearly all letters received before 1862." That is, until after the publication of *Origin*. After that date, according to the son, Darwin was "persuaded to keep the more interesting letters, and these are preserved in an accessible form."

Nonsense.

Take one example. In a letter from Darwin to Hooker dated July 30, 1856, Darwin wrote, "Please return Lyell's letter." Obviously, like many people, Darwin kept letters of importance. Given his agitated reaction to Wallace's Sarawak thunderbolt—"Can this be true?"—it is hardly likely that Darwin destroyed Wallace's first letter or, for that matter, those that followed, especially since Darwin recognized in Wallace a potential rival in the coveted matter of priority. Moreover, Wallace's letters were not idle social missives. They got down to the nitty-gritty of the species question, the subject that had engrossed Darwin since his youth. Most specialists who work independently in isolated places generally share one complaint, "I have nobody to talk

---

* See Frontispiece.

to." Darwin must have felt similarly, and he must have treasured his scientific correspondence.

Francis Darwin's explanation is simply too pat—or too convenient.

In 1909 Francis weakened his own case. He announced the discovery of Darwin's incomplete 1842 essay on the species question. "It only came to light after my mother's death in 1896 when the house at Down was vacated," he said. "The ms. was hidden in a cupboard under the stairs *which was not used for papers of any value, but rather as an overflow for matters which he did not wish to destroy*." (Italics added.) Obviously, there is a contradiction here. If the papers did not have "any value" why did Darwin "not wish to destroy them"? Did Francis find Wallace's letters "hidden" in the cupboard under the stairs? If so, did he suppress them—burn them—from a misguided sense of loyalty to his father? These questions cry out to be raised.

Fifty years later, Francis' position on the missing letters was further diluted, this time by another member of the Darwin family. In 1959, on the centenary of the publication of *Origin*, Lady Nora Barlow, Darwin's gracious and distinguished granddaughter, revealed that Francis had edited the autobiographical sketch which Darwin had written in 1876 at the age of sixty-seven for "his own amusement and the interest of his children and their descendants." In his editing of the short memoir, Francis killed six thousand words that might have embarrassed Darwin.

To Lady Barlow's credit, she published in 1958 the first unexpurgated edition of the *Autobiography*. "The Autobiography," she explained, "first appeared in print as part of *The Life and Letters of Charles Darwin* edited by his son Francis and published in 1887 by John Murray, five years after Charles's death, when many omissions were considered necessary."

If Francis felt it necessary to suppress parts of this father's autobiography—effecting a restructured personal history—what would Francis have done with the raw material of history, specifically, damaging letters revealing that a hare named Wallace was outdistancing a tortoise named Darwin?

In 1902, as the result of the serious gaps in the first two volumes of *Life and Letters*, Darwin's friends—Lyell, Hooker, Huxley, and others —provided Francis with letters from his father which they had retained. "From this unused material we have been able to compile an almost complete record of Mr. Darwin's work," claimed Francis in the preface to the two-volume *More Letters of Charles Darwin*. Nonetheless, the most important missing links—Wallace's letters—never turned up.

This sorry state of affairs has a modern footnote. A copy of the wrapper Wallace put around the first eight letters he received from Darwin appears in the frontispiece of this book. The same copy used here first appeared in James Marchant's *Alfred Russel Wallace*, published in June 1916. Marchant presumably turned these eight letters and other material over to the British Museum. In 1978, in the course of my research, I went over the eight letters. To my surprise, I could not find the wrapper.

It is missing.*

---

* Alfred John Russel Wallace, Wallace's grandson, a gentle-mannered, soft-spoken individual who teaches mathematics at a Bournemouth technical school, expressed displeasure at the mention of Marchant's name. He said the Wallace family had given Marchant, who had been a friend of Alfred Russel Wallace, Wallace's papers *carte blanche* but that many of them were either lost, misplaced, or never returned. (See p. 344.)

Chapter 7

W HEN HE forced the issue and, in 1856, wrote Darwin for the first time, Wallace was in Macassar, the picturesque capital of the spider-shaped island of Celebes, now called Sulawesi, situated east of Sarawak and west of Ternate. The island's terrain runs the gamut from jungle-clad escarpments in the south to palm-studded, crystal-white beaches in the north—a contrast as dramatic as the people themselves, who range from the dark-skinned, seafaring Moslem Bugis and Macassarese in the south to the light-skinned Christian Minahahassans in the north.

Sitting within view of the walls of the great Dutch fort that commands the entrance to Macassar's harbor and dominates the seascape, Wallace, quill in hand, composed his first letter to the patriarch of Down House. That letter set the parameters of their future relationship. Although the letter has not survived, it is fair to assume that Wallace probably introduced himself as an insect collector and recalled that he had once casually met Darwin in the Insect Room of the British Museum before shipping out for the Malay archipelago. Darwin could hardly be expected to remember Wallace, and there was no reason why he should. Wallace also probably wrote that he had read and reread Darwin's *Voyage of the Beagle* with enthusiasm and respected Darwin as a naturalist.

Against this background Wallace, unaware that Lyell and Blyth had done the same thing before him, probably drew Darwin's attention to his Sarawak Law and asked: "What do you think of it?"

The shipping lanes between Macassar and Singapore, then as now, were heavily traveled, a seagoing shuttle of Buginese *praus*, European tramp ships, and Chinese junks collecting copra, spices, and other commodities. Wallace's letter probably reached Down before the end of January; most likely around New Year's Day.

Darwin did not reply.

G. H. Wells, writing under the pen name of Geoffrey West, made a trenchant observation about this period in his biography of Darwin, which was published on the eve of World War II. "Every line of the [Sarawak] essay revealed its author as running hard upon the track of Charles's ideas, a hare in pursuit of the tortoise," West wrote; " . . . there could be no doubt that he was on Charles's trail."

If this judgment is fair—and the facts support West's assessment—the pressure of the chase mounted when Darwin received Wallace's direct communication. And it increased as Darwin toyed with the idea of whether or not to reply to Wallace. Darwin probably had many new sleepless nights and fresh bouts of various illnesses, real or perceived, for by developing the when and where of the origin of species, Wallace pointed to the solution of the divergence problem, which had stalled Darwin for years: how grossly different species—the ant and the whale—evolved from the same primordial origins.

Darwin was right to believe that Wallace was hot on the trail. As Darwin procrastinated over whether to reply to Wallace's letter, Wallace solved the riddle of divergence the following year, in a 650-word note which appeared in the *Zoologist*, one of Darwin's favorite journals, and one to which he often contributed. Wallace's note bore a striking title: "Note on the Theory of Permanent and Geographical Varieties."

"As this subject is now attracting much attention among naturalists," said Wallace in a persistent effort to rouse interest in his Sarawak Law, " . . . I venture to offer the following observations."

What, he inquired, is a species? "The general adopted opinion is that species are absolute independent creations, which during their whole existence never vary from one to another." As for variations among species, he observed, naturalists did not consider such variations independent creations, treating them instead as "descended from a parent species," but nevertheless themselves fixed. Suppose this process went on *indefinitely*, asked Wallace, the varieties moving further and further away from the original species? In effect, Wallace told the scientific establishment, you cannot have your cake and eat it, too. Either species are absolute, independent, permanent creations, or they are the result of evolution, the offspring of related or parent species.

Although the note was not published until early 1858, it may have been part of the pressure which Darwin must have felt in 1855–56 as the challenge from Wallace grew larger in his imagination.

Essentially, Darwin was a man of integrity and character. A true scientist committed to the advancement of science, his interest was the enlargement of human knowledge. His conscience would not permit him to continue to ignore a reply to Wallace. Darwin, however, was not only as sophisticated and shrewd as Wallace was naive and innocent, but beyond this—and by his own admission—he suffered the fixation of priority.

On May 1, 1857, some four months after his probable receipt of Wallace's introductory letter, Darwin replied, commencing a correspondence that lasted until Darwin's death twenty-five years later. The first line of the letter is disingenuous. "I am much obliged for your letter of October 10th from Celebes, received a few days ago," wrote Darwin. If, indeed, Darwin had just received the letter, then it had been in transit for fully six-and-a-half months, twice the normal time for mail to travel from Macassar to Singapore to London, a major shipping artery.

"By your letter and even still more by your paper in the *Annals*, a year or more ago, I can plainly see that we have thought much alike and to a certain extent have come to similar conclusions," continued the master of Down House, confirming the supposition that Wallace had written Darwin for an opinion of the Sarawak Law. "In regard to the paper in the *Annals*, I agree to the truth of almost every word of your paper and I daresay that you will agree with me that it is very rare to find oneself agreeing pretty closely with any theoretical paper; for it is lamentable how each man draws his own different conclusions from the same fact."

The best defense is offense, strategists often explain, and Darwin took the offensive. He was Wallace's senior in years, the author of books and monographs, a member of learned societies, and he put down the youthful, uneducated, and impoverished Wallace gently.

"This summer will make the twentieth year (!) since I opened my first note-book on the question how and in what way do species and varieties differ from each other," Darwin said. In effect, Wallace was an upstart.

Then, in an apparent maneuver to forestall a challenger, Darwin disclosed that "I am now preparing my work for publication." He did not say, of course, that he had been forced into the work by Lyell and the Sarawak Law, but he did add that he hoped to complete the book in two years. As it developed, he never finished it. Given the hare's increasingly swift pace, the tortoise was compelled to write the abstract of his "big book"—the *Origin*. Many of his colleagues felt it doubtful that Darwin would have ever published anything on the evolution of species without Wallace's pressure, visible and invisible. There certainly would never have been an abstract.

In his reply to Wallace, Darwin skillfully avoided the species question. "It is really *impossible* to explain my views in the compass of a letter as to causes and means of variation in a state of nature," he wrote. "But I have slowly adopted a distinct and tangible idea—whether true or false, others must judge; for the firmest conviction of the truth of a doctrine by its author seems, alas, not to be the slightest guarantee of truth."

In conclusion, Darwin took refuge behind a familiar complaint—chronic poor health. "This is a very dull letter," he wrote, "but I am a good deal out of health, and am writing this, not from my home, as dated, but from a water-cure establishment."

If the reference to poor health was designed to discourage Wallace, the latter was too unsophisticated to appreciate the subtlety. Wallace had established his first link with a member of England's fabled ruling elite, and he lost no time in strengthening the fragile connection. Wallace's second letter, written September 27, 1857, is of course missing. But a fragment exists, and it is as explosive as it is revealing. It refers to the Sarawak Law and in it Wallace expresses delight that "my views on the order of succession of species [are] in accordance with your own; for I had begun to be a little disappointed that my paper had neither excited discussion nor even elicited opposition."

A fragment of the next sentence also exists: "The mere statement and illustration of the theory in that paper is of course but preliminary to an attempt at a detailed proof of it, the plan of which I have arranged, & in fact written, but which of course requires much [portion missing] libraries and collections, a labor which I look . . ."

Darwin must have verged on cardiac arrest. The Sarawak Law was only the announcement of Wallace's theory, and he was already at work on a "big book" about it. Darwin had not yet even publicly announced his theory. He had not yet resolved the keystone of the theory—the principle of divergence.

Little wonder that, as the London *Times* described it in Wallace's obituary notice more than a half century later, "Wallace was destined to cause [Darwin] considerable perturbation." There can be little doubt about it. Darwin was unnerved, and this time he did not delay a reply to this outrider of the theory of evolution.

Darwin dashed off a quick note to Wallace in an apparent bid to restrain him. Darwin's second letter was written three days before Christmas, 1857, three months after the mailing of Wallace's second letter—which had not taken a half-year to reach London as Darwin claimed the first letter had.

In his second letter, Darwin bought time.

"You say that you have been somewhat surprised at no notice having been taken of your paper in the *Annals*," Darwin wrote. " . . . But you must not suppose that your paper has not been attended to: two very good men, Sir C. Lyell and Mr. E. Blyth at Calcutta, specially called my attention to it."

Darwin was honest in letter and dishonest in spirit. His references to Lyell and Blyth were misleading, a misrepresentation. Blyth was elated by Wallace's paper and Lyell was so astounded that he opened his first species notebook and bounded off to Down House to get Darwin's reaction in person—forcing Darwin, as a consequence, to start his "big book."

None of this comes through in Darwin's second reply to Wallace. For that matter, Darwin again conspicuously avoided airing the question raised by the Sarawak Law—the origin of species, the origin of man himself. "Though agreeing with you on your conclusions in the [Sarawak] paper," Darwin said, "I believe I go much further than you." How much further? "It is too long a subject to enter on my speculative notions," he protested.

As for man, a subject which Darwin artfully sidestepped for fourteen years after the publication of *Origin*, he replied: "You ask whether I shall discuss Man; I think I shall avoid the whole subject, as so surrounded with prejudices, *though I fully admit that it is the highest and most interesting problem for the naturalist.*" (Italics added.)

The Sarawak Law had publicly proclaimed that man was an animal descended from preexisting, closely allied species. What species? The anthropoid ape? The orang-utan?

Both Wallace and Darwin were revolutionaries; Darwin, however, was the more conservative in developing his radical line of thought. He had more to lose. He was afraid to think the unthinkable—how would it effect Emma, a devout Christian? His children? His in-laws, the Wedgwoods? Their place in London society? For that matter, how would such ideas influence civilization itself? Darwin had exemplary cause for caution. The concept of man's descent from a preexisting, closely allied species, he felt, must develop slowly to win first scientific, then popular, acceptance. The theory could not be handed down engraved on a stone tablet.

Darwin was also a pessimist. Inwardly, he did not believe that the truth would necessarily make man free. Quite the contrary, given the sorry human condition—wars, slavery, and other ageless social evils—the development of a purely materialistic concept of human evolution might cast off all moral restraint and worsen that condition.

In contrast, Wallace was struck from a different mold. Whereas Darwin was cautious, slow-thinking, and inhibited, Wallace was impatient and uninhibited. Wallace was single. Neither he nor his family (a mother, a brother, and sister) were of high social rank. Wallace had nothing to lose. He, too, recognized the traumatic impact his theory of the origin of species would have on man and society.

But Wallace, unlike Darwin, was an unconditional optimist, a philosophical utopian. The truth, he felt, would free man for nobler things. Wallace's optimism was born of incurable innocence and naïveté. In the century that followed the two naturalists', the general acceptance of man's descent from a preexisting, closely allied species provided the rationale for a belief that evolution could be stage-managed and could lead to the perfectibility of mankind. Darwin's nephew, Sir Francis Galton—a founder of eugenics—was in the forefront of this movement. He envisioned the management of heredity *pro bono publico*. But the theory was distorted by ideological extremists of the "right" and "left" and gave rise to totalitarian political systems based on mass murder, systems that would have horrified and tormented Wallace, Darwin—and Galton.

After the initial exchanges of correspondence between Wallace and Darwin, Wallace received a letter from Henry Walter Bates, another of Stevens' "fly-catchers" and the same Bates with whom Wallace had collected beetles and birds in South America several years earlier.

Bates was in the Upper Amazon when the September issue of the *Annals* reached him. "I was startled at first to see you ready ripe for the enunciation of the theory," wrote an enthusiastic Bates on November 19, 1856, in a letter from Tunantins, a shabby Amazon river town. "You can imagine with what interest I read and studied it, and I must say it is perfectly well done. The idea is like truth itself, so simple and obvious that those who read and understand it will be struck by its simplicity; yet it is perfectly original."

Bates' letter took a year to reach Wallace, following the path of the equator from the rain forests of Brazil and the Guianas to the rain forests of the Malay archipelago on the other side of the globe. That the letter got through at all testifies to the incredible efficiency of the Victorian postal system.

Wallace was in Ambon, the most important of the Moluccan spice islands, when Bates' letter reached him. Ambon is half-Christian, half-Moslem, and possesses a harbor large enough to hold the ships of the world. It is a veritable paradise of fish-filled waters, clusters of coconut palms, spice trees, and wild orchids, a "comfortable" island without the rugged terrain and inhospitable temperature of Sarawak.* Wallace hastened to reply.

"To persons who have not thought on the subject much I fear my paper on the 'Succession of Species' will not appear so clear as it does to you," Wallace wrote Bates on January 4, 1858. "That paper is, of course, merely the announcement of a theory, and not its development. I have prepared the plan and written portions of a work embracing the whole subject, and have endeavoured to provide in detail what I have as yet only indicated."

Unlike Darwin, Wallace was by nature neither secretive, nor suspicious, nor possessive. He was the reverse: frank, open, unacquisitive. Priority meant nothing to him, and he told all who would listen— albeit they were few—among them Bates in the Amazon and the White Rajah in Borneo—about his grand theory on the origin of species. Although he had not yet completely worked out the theory—the missing link, the mechanism, was to come to him shortly thereafter—he had already published a paper and a note on the subject. Darwin had published nothing.

Wallace was in high spirits when he answered Bates. "I have been much gratified by a letter from Darwin," he wrote with pride, "in which he says that he agrees with 'almost every word' of my paper." Wallace then informed Bates that Darwin was working on a "great

* In the many years my wife Aggie and I lived on Java, I never visited Ambon without returning with baskets of orchids (largely *Dendrobium philanthopsis*.)

work" about his own theory. "He may save me the trouble of writing more on my hypothesis, by proving that there is no difference in nature between the origin of species and of varieties," Wallace wrote cheerfully, "or he may give me trouble by arriving at another conclusion; *but, at all events, his facts will be given for me to work upon.*" (Italics added.)

That was all Wallace wanted—neither glory nor gold—only "more facts to work upon." Wallace epitomized one of the ideals of Western civilization, the spirit of free, open inquiry, an uninhibited exchange of ideas.

Thus, it is against the backdrop of this thirty-one-month period between December 1855, when Darwin read and annotated Wallace's Sarawak Law, and June 1858, when Darwin received Wallace's complete theory of the origin of species—the Ternate Paper—that the conspiracy and cover-up had its origins.

When, in the familiar surroundings of his warm study at Down House, a shaken Darwin finished reading the contents of Wallace's Ternate envelope, Darwin must have envisioned more than twenty years of work reduced to a footnote in history. Given his medical record for periods of stress, he most probably also became violently ill.

Darwin did not respond directly to Wallace on the Ternate Paper. His Christmas letter of 1857 was the last letter Darwin wrote Wallace until after July 1, 1858—until the "delicate arrangement" had been concluded. And at that, Darwin wrote only a brief note (now lost) to accompany a published version of the results of the arrangement. The next time Wallace heard from Darwin in the round was not until 1859, the year *Origin* was published and, having established his priority, Darwin had achieved immortality and reduced Wallace to a passing reference in history.

Chapter 8

DURING the thirty-one months that elapsed between his reply to Wallace and the publication of *Origin*, Darwin acquired field for maneuver: an opportunity to clarify his own roiled thinking about the origin of species and to do so in the isolated, tranquil setting of rural Down.

Darwin's central problem was resolving the principle of divergence, explaining how the jellyfish, jaguar, and jay had evolved, by modification through natural selection from the same original source, into completely different species. As early as 1837, in his species notebook, Darwin conceived of evolution as a "tree of nature," not unlike a family tree, and observed that new species "branched" from the same trunk. The concept, which Wallace arrived at independently in his Sarawak essay, was novel, although, curiously, a clue is found in Genesis in the Garden of Eden, when God admonished Adam and Eve not to seek to unravel the mysteries of the Tree of Knowledge (the origin of species?). Before Darwin's time, evolution had been conceived of as an Aristotelian–Lamarckian ladder. On this ladder, life—rung by rung—evolved progressively into "higher," more complex forms.

But Darwin could not explain how the "branching" of the tree took place, how the great multitude of different species came into being on Earth. He was completely baffled and saw his first gleam of light in Wallace's Sarawak paper.

In 1857 the impact of Wallace's work apparently dawned upon him and Darwin began to work out his theory of divergence.

For Darwin, the right and proper course of action would have been to discuss his freshly developed thesis—based upon Wallace's work—with his dearest friends, Lyell and Hooker. But Darwin's vaulting pride would not permit him to do this. He was as obssessed with secrecy and priority as with the species question itself. Like ancient Nineveh, Darwin wanted posterity to claim, as it did, "I am, and there is none like me."

Darwin could not inform Lyell because Lyell would realize that Wallace was the primary source of Darwin's concept. As for Hooker, Darwin's confidant, Darwin kept him completely in the dark until June 8, 1858, during the critical month when Wallace's Ternate essay reached Down House. There is no explanation for this treatment of his closest friend.

Yet Darwin had to protect himself against the hare. He had to develop some sort of evidence that he had long possessed the secret of divergence, that it was such common knowledge as to be unworthy of discussion. And if he did not tell Lyell and Hooker, he would certainly not tell Wallace. Darwin, therefore, did not run before the wind with his principle of divergence. He tacked on a broad reach. He set forth his thesis in a private letter to a foreigner with whom he had a slight acquaintance, the American botanist Asa Gray.

In 1839 Gray visited England for the first time and through Hooker, who was ten years his senior, Gray was casually introduced to "Mr. Darwin, the naturalist." A dozen years later Gray revisited England, accompanied by his wife, lunched at Hooker's house, and met Darwin for a second time. "Mr. Darwin [is] a lively, agreeable person," wrote Jane Loring Gray in her diary. But the Grays spent no time with Darwin. Their principal contacts were Hooker; Robert Brown, the president of the Linnean Society, whom they "saw constantly at the British Museum"; and Nathaniel Wallich, a Dane by birth and a specialist in the botany of Wallace's Malay archipelago.

There matters rested between Gray and Darwin until 1855, the year Wallace announced his Sarawak Law.

Darwin that year was interested in the range of Alpine plants in North America and asked Gray, by then a prominent Harvard botanist, for an opinion. Darwin's first letter to Gray has the ring that must also have marked Wallace's first, lost letter to Darwin. "I hope you will remember that I had the pleasure of being introduced to you," Darwin wrote.

The early exchanges between Darwin and Gray are of minor historical interest. But on July 20, 1856—some dozen-odd weeks after Lyell visited Down and pressed Darwin for an explanation of Wallace's Sarawak Law—Darwin wrote Gray a letter of substance. In the same manner in which he had treated Wallace, Darwin—feeling it necessary to establish priority in the species field—observed that he had already been working nineteen years on the species question, and as an "honest man"—and odd phrase—Darwin said that he felt compelled to tell Gray of having arrived at the "heterodox conclusion there are no such things as independently-created species—that species are only strongly defined varieties."

Why should Darwin be so open, disarming, and informative? So out of character? Why should he reveal to an almost total stranger a position he did not reveal to Lyell for decades and artfully declined to reveal to such correspondents as Blyth and Wallace, fellow countrymen and naturalists working on the species question?

A. Hunter Dupree, in his definitive biography, *Asa Gray*, published by Harvard almost twenty years ago, skirts the question.

"In July 1857 [sic], Darwin, already deep in the business of writing his large book on species, felt he needed to let Gray in on his secret," Dupree wrote. "To [maintain] the stream of Gray's remarks, so valuable to him, required the risk of revelation."

This explanation is paltry. Surely Wallace's published paper and letter were of greater value to Darwin than Gray's remarks about the flora of North America. Moreover, Dupree's explanation is suspect. Dupree never saw the "valuable remarks" Gray mailed to Darwin because Dupree never saw Gray's letters to Darwin. Nobody has. They, too, have conveniently disappeared.

In 1893 Jane Gray edited two volumes of her late husband's letters, and apparently wrote the Darwin family for copies of his communications to Darwin. She received a plethora of correspondence but nothing from the historically critical period 1855–1858, when all signs pointed to Wallace running ahead of Darwin in resolving the species question.

Mrs. Gray must have thought the omission strange because she offered an astonishing explanation. "Unfortunately," she said, "Mr. Darwin destroyed all the [Gray] letters he received before 1862, except the one published in *Life and Letters*. . . ." That letter, incidentally, was written by Gray to Darwin in 1860, the year after publication of *Origin* and two years before 1862—the year in which Francis Darwin claims his father began preserving all correspondence.

Later in her 838-page collection of Asa Gray's correspondence, Jane

Gray repeated her claim about the destroyed correspondence—a claim she had probably gotten from Sir Francis. "As before stated," she said, "Dr. Gray's letters to Dr. Darwin previous to 1862 have been destroyed."

How, then, does Dupree know that Gray's remarks to Darwin were so "valuable" that Darwin had to wire Gray into his secret work? Dupree's statement is inconsistent with fact.

Then why did Darwin make Gray privy to his secrets? Was he setting Gray up as an escape hatch for the moment at which he would proclaim priority in the field?

This conclusion is strengthened by an event of the following year. Darwin revealed to Gray his doctrine of divergence on September 5, 1857, sixteen weeks after having received his first letter from Wallace—which he answered noncommittally although engaged on his "big book" as the result of Wallace's Sarawak Law. However, Darwin did not disclose his "discovery" of the doctrine to Hooker, his most intimate friend, until June 8, 1858, the month in which Darwin received Wallace's Ternate Paper; nor did he tell Lyell or Blyth, and certainly not Wallace.

Darwin spelt out his theory of divergence thusly: "I cannot doubt that during millions of generations individuals of a species will be occasionally born with some slight variation, profitable to some part of their economy," he wrote Gray. Through survival of the fittest, continued Darwin, each new variation would take the place of a less well-fitted parent species, and so on through millennia, giving rise to diverse species. "This sketch is *most* imperfect," Darwin said, "but in so short a space I cannot make it better. Your imagination must fill up the very wide blanks."

In that revealing September letter to Gray, Darwin also pleaded for secrecy. "You will, perhaps, think it paltry in me, when I ask you not to mention my doctrine," Darwin wrote. His reason was specious. "The reason is, *if any one*, like the author of *Vestiges*, were to hear of them, he might easily work them in, and then I should have to quote from a work perhaps despised by a naturalist . . . and this would greatly injure any chance of my views being received by those whose opinions I value."

This explanation is not only specious, it is a travesty of the truth. Darwin's reference to *Vestiges* was to a popular book on evolution, the most popular to appear before *Origin*. Written by Robert Chambers, a publisher and journalist, the subject was so "hot" that Chambers published it anonymously in 1844 for fear of injury to his reputation and business. The book was an immediate sensation and sales soared when gossip mongers whispered that Victoria's husband, Prince Albert, was the author! Darwin's contempt for *Vestiges of the Natural History of Creation* (its full title) reflected his sense of insecurity. Chambers was the Velikovsky of his day, the subject of considerable ridicule in the academic establishment. But even Francis observed that his father's copy of *Vestiges* bore signs of heavy reading. It was well-marked.

In his books, Chambers described Lamarck as "a naturalist of the highest character" but said that "I . . . go beyond the French philosopher." Chambers not only believed in the inheritance of acquired characteristics, the heart of Lamarckian philosophy, but that the laws governing nature are "the works of God," a view postulated by St. Augustine centuries earlier. In a sequel, also published anonymously under the title *Explanation* in 1845, the year after *Vestiges* created a storm, Chambers put forth the notion that "all orders of animals have not proceeded on a single line but in in a plurality of lines . . . ranged side by side." This postulate of lateral development is a conclusion now drawn by some contemporary scientists who, for example, believe anthropoid apes, such as the orang-utan, may not be linear but instead are collateral relatives of man, and that the parallel lines which gave rise to the great apes and man branched from the same tree of nature thirty million or more years ago. Chambers also professed that he did not seek to overthrow the Mosaic cosmogony but was "merely endeavoring to read aright another chapter in the mystic book which God has placed under the attention of his creatures."

Darwin's claim, in his letter to Gray, that *Vestiges* was "despised by naturalists" is nonsense. Wallace, for example, who lacked any sense of insecurity and felt at ease among original thinkers whatever their trade, described Chamber's work in a letter to a friend in 1847 as "an ingenious hypothesis strongly supported by some striking facts and analogies, but which remains to be proved by more facts and the additional light which more research may throw on the problem."

Whatever the case, why did Darwin pledge Gray to secrecy? Did Darwin fear Chambers, whose *Vestiges* was published more than a decade earlier, or Wallace, whose Sarawak Law had only recently shaken the scientific aristocracy and who had confided in Darwin that he planned to do a "big book" on his theory?

Despite the burden of truth upon him to have informed Gray about

Wallace's Sarawak Law and of its impact on him and Lyell, Darwin's letters to Gray contain not a single mention of Wallace. After all, as a handful of contemporary writers—such as the Linnean Society's Professor Pantin—have observed, Wallace's Sarawak paper was the most advanced thinking on the species question since Lamarck. Surely this merited a mention in the Darwin–Gray correspondence.

At this point it is worth observing that several of Darwin's friends and foes alike detected in him a slipperiness of character. Oxford botanist and geneticist C. D. Darlington has characterized Darwin precisely in this manner, accusing him of "failure to recognize or to relate his own ideas, his larger ideas, with those of others working in the same field; and [of possessing] a flexible strategy which is not to be reconciled with even average intellectual integrity. By contrast with Wallace," claimed Darlington, "Lyell, Hooker, Chambers or even Spencer, Darwin was slippery."

The *Pall Mall Gazette*, a popular periodical of the last century, put its finger on this Darwinian quality of laying claim to being the world's only evolutionist by ignoring or refusing to acknowledge the work of others, when it described Darwin as a "master [of] happy simplicity." Darwin's arch opponent, Samuel Butler, a literary giant of the Victorian period, the author of *Erewhon*, *The Way of All Flesh*, and other literary classics, was far more caustic. In *Athenaeum*, a magazine that catered primarily to intellectuals, Butler accused Darwin of plagiarism, notably, of disowning his grandfather Erasmus' contribution to his thinking on the species question. Darwin was aware of these attacks and in a private letter howled that Butler had accused him of "lying [and] deception." The Darwin–Butler controversy, one of the celebrated broils of the Victorian period, was omitted in its entirety by Francis Darwin in his father's life and letters.

So fervent an admirer of Darwin as the late Loren Eiseley, the science historian, waffled on Darwin and described in his *Darwin's Century* the character of Darwin with the delicacy and obfuscation of a diplomat in the delegate's lounge of the United Nations. Darwin, said Eiseley, possessed "a gift for being ambiguously inconspicuous." Happy simplicity is a better phrase.

This happy simplicity may explain why Darwin plucked Gray from nowhere as a confidant to attest later to the priority of his "discovery," even though *ex post facto*, since Darwin's revelations to Gray came in 1857, *after* Wallace had announced his Sarawak Law and had entered into correspondence with the reclusive master of Down House. In an historical sense, Darwin set Gray up as a straw-man.

Gray's reaction to what he may have perceived as Darwin's strange request to suppress an apparent advance in science is not known. His reply to Darwin, of course, is missing.

When the crunch came—probably much sooner than Darwin expected—in June 1858, in the form of Wallace's Ternate Paper, Darwin suddenly recalled his obscure letter to Gray on divergence and fortuitously discovered that he had kept a copy of the letter. At the right moment, like a prestidigitator pulling a rabbit from a hat, Darwin produced the letter as proof of his primacy.

Chapter 9

THE DEEPEST CRISIS in Charles Robert Darwin's life covered thirteen days, from June 18 to July 1, 1858. During that period, like Jacob in Genesis, he was "left alone; and there wrestled with a man until the breaking of the day." But in contrast to Jacob's night of struggle, Darwin's thirteen days were days of conspiracy and cover-up, the unfolding of the "delicate arrangement." The principals in the sorry business were Darwin, Lyell, and Hooker. Late in life, all three were openly and genuinely confused about the course of events as that June of 1858 dissolved into July. Certainly Lyell and Hooker were. Yet, no matter how they sought to rationalize their behavior, the evidence makes clear that they knew they had acted dishonorably. Subconsciously, they seem to have blocked the unhappy details of the affair from their thoughts. When history, that long-distance runner, caught up to them, the details of the affair emerged in bold relief.

The curtain was raised on Friday, June 18, when Darwin wrote to Lyell.

"Wallace . . . has today sent me the enclosed," Darwin said, "and asked me to forward it to you." Accompanying Darwin's letter was Wallace's Ternate Paper, spelling out more lucidly than ever before or since the concept of evolution and divergence through natural selection, a complete theory. To this day the paper reads with a freshness absent in Darwin's muddled *Origin*. Indeed, years later, Lyell complained to Darwin that when he was compelled to deliver a speech on the theory he used Wallace's paper as the basis of his remarks because of the clarity and forcefulness of Wallace's exposition as compared with Darwin's writings. And Lyell, like Darwin inherently decent, wrote Wallace similarly. "I have been reading over again your [Sarawak] paper . . . passages of which I intend to quote, not in reference to *your priority of publication*," said Lyell in a letter of April 4, 1867, "but simply because there are some points laid down more clearly than I can find in the work of Darwin itself." (Italics added.)

Lyell was hardly alone in his view. Darwin's other intimate friends, Hooker and Huxley, also complained that Darwin was "difficult" to read. Huxley said that *Origin*'s style was so obtuse that it "is one of the hardest books to master," and Hooker complained, "It is the very hardest book to read, to full profit, that I ever tried."

One explanation for Darwin's writing problem is that he lacked Wallace's confidence in the theory and that, as a matter of "happy simplicity," *Origin* was written in a heavy-handed, abstruse style open to conflicting interpretation. Wallace never wavered; he denounced, for example, Lamarck's theory of the inheritance of acquired characteristics as nonsense, and did so unconditionally. Darwin was not so sure, and toward the end of his life, although he repeatedly remarked how he detested Lamarck's ideas, he adopted, refined and employed them in later editions of *Origin*. Indeed, every new edition of *Origin* differed from its predecessor, like the evolution of a variety into a species, and, taken as a whole, the series of editions leaves the reader in a state of almost complete confusion, giving the impression of a muddled individual incapable of the commitment and clarity of a Wallace. This later gave rise to the quip, made by Darwin himself as well as by his contemporaries, that "Wallace is more Darwinian than Darwin." This should no longer cause surprise, for what we now accept as the "Darwinian" theory of evolution is truly Wallacean, not Darwinian—a point being slowly recognized in a small but increasingly influential circle within the scientific world.

Darwin was aware of his inability to write clearly for publication; he was too inhibited in public. But in private letters he was uninhibited, explosive, and direct. The uncertainties that plague his *Origin* do not clutter his letters.

"Some are born with a power of good writing, like Wallace," Darwin conceded. "Others like myself and Lyell have to labour very hard and slowly at every sentence." And on another occasion, Darwin confessed, "A naturalist's life would be a happy one if he had only to observe, and never write."

After the low-key opening of his letter of June 18 to Lyell, the dam containing Darwin's emotions burst: "Your words have come true with a vengeance," he wrote, ". . . that I should be forestalled."

Ambition, uncontrollable and uncompromising, surfaced. "So all my originality," Darwin said painfully, ". . . [is] smashed."

Darwin claimed that Wallace's manuscript caught him by surprise. "I never saw a more striking coincidence," he said. "If Wallace had my MS. sketch written out in 1842, he could not have made a better short abstract! Even his terms now stand as heads of my chapters." Darwin asked Lyell to return the Wallace manuscript and said that although Wallace had not asked Darwin to arrange for its publication, "I shall, of course, at once write and offer to send [it] to any journal."

Lyell's reply to this letter is also missing. But within a week Darwin wrote Lyell again and apologized for troubling him about "so merely a personal an affair." Darwin now appealed to Lyell on how to shield his "priority."

In support of his claim to priority Darwin cited his unpublished sketch of the 1840s which Hooker had read and emended. Like a magician, he also suddenly produced a copy of his 1857 letter on divergence to Gray—a letter which neither Lyell nor Hooker knew existed. Gray's letter was Darwin's escape route. Had he planned it this way in the event Wallace won the race?

"There is nothing in Wallace's sketch which is not written out much fuller in my sketch," Darwin averred; ". . . so that I could most truly say and prove that I take nothing from Wallace."

This statement, however, does not stand up to scrutiny. For one thing, the 1844 sketch makes no mention of the principle of divergence, a glaring omission as well in the 1842 sketch.

In Darwin's confused state of mind, which he implied in his letter, he added that he could write for Lyell a paper of about a dozen pages setting forth his views "but I cannot persuade myself that I can do so honorably." Such a paper, of course, would destroy Darwin's claim to priority and create an ugly situation in which Darwin could be accused of plagiarism, the charge which Samuel Butler had leveled at him, anyway.

Darwin told Lyell that he was in such a state of torment that "I cannot tell whether to publish now would not be base and paltry." Darwin concluded the letter by describing his predicament as a "trumpery affair" and drew Hooker into the developing drama by asking Lyell to forward his letter and Lyell's reply to Hooker first, so that Hooker could then return it to Darwin, "for then I shall have the opinion of my two best and kindest friends."

Darwin's guilt complex resurfaced on the last line of the letter, which Lyell fortunately retained. Here Darwin repeated his character-ization of the affair as "trumpery," a word meaning something showy and vain, and derived from the French *tromper*—to deceive. Darwin would have been more accurate had he described the situation as "trumped up," a more expressive phrase which means to devise un-fairly, to fabricate—a corruption of the French word *triomphe*, to triumph.

In a hastily penned postscript beneath his signature, as if in after-thought, Darwin promised, "I will never trouble you or Hooker on the subject again."

The promise was short-lived. Darwin spent another tormented, sleepless night. And on the following morning, Saturday, June 26, he had no sooner risen than he got off a third letter to Lyell. In it he con-fronted reality. "It seems hard on me that I should be thus compelled to lose my priority of many years standing," he said with bitterness, "but I cannot feel at all sure that this alters the justice of the case." And building the case against himself even more strongly, a testimony to his basic integrity, Darwin conceded that Wallace might justifiably say, "You did not intend publishing an *abstract* of your views till you re-ceived my communication. Is it fair to take advantage of my having freely, though unasked, communicated to you my ideas, and thus pre-vent me forestalling you?" For the second time Darwin used the word "abstract," and for a third time appealed to Lyell for advice. The fly was cast; would the trout rise to the bait?

Over the next three days Darwin received separate letters from Lyell and Hooker. Apparently the pair conferred and worked out a scheme to save Darwin's priority. Their letters were sent to Down and are among the vital documents of the thirteen-day period that have either been lost, misplaced, or destroyed, intentionally or not. Never-theless, Darwin's reply to Hooker, which the latter saved, is revealing.

"I have received your letters," Darwin wrote Hooker on June 29. "I can see that you have acted with more kindness, and so has Lyell, even than I could have expected from you both, most kind as you are."

"I cannot think now on the subject," Darwin added, "but soon will."

The reason Darwin's interest was momentarily diverted was that scarlet fever, rampant in that era, had struck Down House on June 26. Charles, his father's namesake and the Darwins' tenth and last child, who was one-and-a-half years old, was stricken. The boy, who had been born severely mentally retarded and never learned nor lived long enough to learn how to walk or talk, died two days later, on June 28— the day before Darwin wrote to Hooker. Emma, then forty-eight, and Darwin, one year older, were both saddened but also relieved by the turn of events. As Darwin unabashedly said in his *Autobiography*, he was "thankful." And Henrietta, who edited her mother's letters, observed, "The poor little baby was born without its full share of intelligence. Both my father and mother were infinitely tender towards him but, when he died in the summer of 1858, after their first sorrow, they could only feel thankful." Natural selection, the theory of the survival of the fittest in the struggle for existence, had taken its toll in the Darwin household.

But worse was ahead.

The day before tiny Charles's death, the baby's nurse contracted the disease, and their fourth child, the fifteen-year-old Henrietta who was later to edit her mother's papers, came down with diphtheria, another dread disease of the period. Her nurse then contracted it. The Darwin household was in turmoil.

When Darwin wrote Hooker that Tuesday, June 29, he said, "You shall hear [from me] soon, as soon as I can think."

That same night, as Darwin fought the internal threat of invisible microbes to his happy household, he could still think clearly enough to defend himself against the external threat posed by Wallace. The following morning, he rushed to his study for his original sketch of 1844 and a copy of his 1857 letter to Asa Gray. He had no difficulty locating both, a fair indication—Francis Darwin's later disclaimer notwithstanding—that Darwin kept a special file for important papers and letters on the species question.

Darwin's behavior that morning, as his son Charles's small, lifeless body awaited burial, was reproachful, and he knew it. "It is miserable in me," he wrote Hooker from stricken Down that sorrowful day, "to care at all about priority." But, obviously, he did care. Priority gnawed at his innards. His concern with priority belied the carefully coated veneer he had created of himself as a detached, modest, ambitionless man who had settled into an isolated, rural life-style and discouraged publicity, celebrity, and social contact. The truth is that he cared so greatly about priority that he did not dispatch the letter by mail to London's Kew Gardens, where Hooker lived, but posthaste by hand, to be delivered by a servant.

Thus, despite the swirl of crises around him—the death of a child and a household ravaged by scarlet fever and diphtheria—Darwin focused on the time factor in the race to neutralize Wallace. For his part, of course, Wallace was completely unaware of Darwin's dilemma. He was half a world away, in the Malay archipelago, fighting recurrent attacks of malaria accompanied by alternating periods of torrid fever and cold-numbing chills, oblivious to the confusion and uproar in Down and London, and continuing to ponder the origin of species while collecting, preserving, and shipping insect specimens to London for a bare living.

For Darwin, the time factor turned on a piece of luck. The previous month Darwin, like Lyell and Hooker a fellow of the Linnean Society, had been named to the Society's ruling council. And then, as now, the Society was one of the world's most important forums for the "cultivation of the science of natural history in all its branches." Named for Carl von Linné (Linnaeus), the Swedish botanist who developed the modern system of biological nomenclature, the group was founded in London in 1788 and received a royal charter fourteen years later.

A general meeting of the Society had been scheduled for June 17, but the organization's former president and then vice president, Robert Brown, the botanist friend of Asa Gray, died the week before. In respect for Brown, the meeting was cancelled. But under the Society's bylaws, the vacancy had to be filled within three months, and rather than put off the business, the members summoned a special meeting for July 1. In addition to the election of a new vice president, the papers scheduled to be read June 17 were rescheduled for presentation that night.

For Darwin, Brown's death was a windfall. It was imperative that Wallace be checkmated as quickly as possible and the July 1 Linnean meeting provided him with an unexpected opportunity and a prestigious forum.

Darwin's remarks about Brown after the latter's death are curious.

"[Brown's] knowledge was extraordinarily great, and much died with him, owing to his excessive fear of ever making a mistake," Darwin said. "He poured out his knowledge to me in the most unreserved manner, yet was strangely jealous on some points." On one occasion,

Darwin peered through Brown's microscope and when Darwin asked him what it was he was looking at or for, Brown quipped, "That is my little secret."

Darwin, whose views appeared in his *Autobiography*, then summed up Brown's character as though summing up his own. Brown, Darwin said, was "capable of the most generous actions [and] there is enough [in him] to make up for any degree of scientific penuriousness or jealousy."

On Wednesday, June 30—the day before the Linnean Society met—Darwin's servant had put in Hooker's hands Darwin's sketch of 1844 and a copy of his letter to Gray. Frances Hooker, Hooker's wife of seven years, was pressed into service to make a copy of the letter and excerpts from the sketch, no mean feat since the two documents were in Darwin's own atrocious, often illegible, hand. That same day and in the midst of these preparations as the hour for the meeting approached, Lyell and Hooker, apparently using Darwin's servant as courier, drafted and sent a joint letter to J. J. Bennett, the Linnean's secretary. The two linchpins of Britain's scientific aristocracy, its leading geologist and botanist, suggested to Bennett that in the interests of science Darwin's extracts and Wallace's monograph "be laid before the Linnean Society."

Their letter wrongly implied bonds of friendship between Wallace and Darwin and described them as "two indefatigable naturalists." They said Wallace wrote his Ternate Paper "for the perusal of his friend and correspondent Mr. Darwin." They added: "These gentlemen having, independently and unknown to one another, conceived the same very ingenious theory to account for the appearance and perpetuation of varieties and of specific forms on our planet, may both fairly claim the merit of being original thinkers in this important line of inquiry."

"Neither of them having published his views . . ." continued Lyell and Hooker, "both authors having now unreservedly placed their papers in our hands, we think it would best promote the interests of science that a selection from them should be laid before the Linnean Society."

The Lyell–Hooker joint letter to the Linnean Society reeks of half-truths and outright deception. For one thing, they gave the impression of lengthy association between Darwin and Wallace, the "friend and correspondent [of] Mr. Darwin." Actually, Wallace and Darwin had exchanged two letters and Darwin never recalled having even been introduced to Wallace. More substantively, the Lyell–Hooker letter said that neither Wallace or Darwin had yet published his views. But Wallace had already twice published his views on the species question, in *Annals* and the *Zoologist*, with their devastating effect on Darwin and their consequence of forcing Lyell to open his own species notebook.

Nor had Wallace placed his paper unreservedly either in Darwin's or Lyell's hands. True, he had asked Darwin to show the paper to Lyell. But to Hooker, Darwin's most intimate friend? The thought never crossed Wallace's mind. Nor did Lyell and Hooker plan to present both points of view completely. Wallace's Ternate Paper was to be given complete, with beginning, middle, and end, a total theory, and in fact was presented in its entirety. Darwin's contribution consisted of extracts, not abstracts. Indeed, Lyell and Hooker were so unfamiliar with the Gray letter that they misdated it and referred to it in their letter to Bennett as "an abstract [extract] of a private letter addressed to Professor Asa Gray, Boston, U.S., in October, 1857. . . ." The letter actually was dated September 5, 1857.

The date is trivial. Transcending everything else is that Hooker and Lyell had an ulterior motive for presenting Darwin's fragments with Wallace's complete paper. They sought not merely to promote science, but to promote and protect Darwin's claim to priority. This was what the whole affair was about, and they knew it.

Bennett immediately acquiesced to their proposal. If two of the nation's most prominent scientific figures proposed putting an item on the agenda, the secretary would hardly stand in their way.

Lyell and Hooker were now confronted with a problem in saving Darwin's priority during the formal presentation of Wallace's paper and the extracts from Darwin's 1844 sketch and 1857 Gray letter. Academic integrity—and, more simply, what was just fair play and cricket—required that Wallace's Ternate Paper be read without a dropped line, and read first because it presented a total theory. Darwin's extracts should either have served as a footnote or should have been read after the presentation of Wallace's monograph.

Unknown to the fellows of the Linnean Society, of course, was that Hooker and Lyell were engaging in a devious, unethical ploy. It was the arrival of Wallace's paper in June that had forced Darwin to act. Clearly, Wallace's paper should be read first. But there was a catch. If it were read first, it would dilute Darwin's claim to priority. And in history, the Linnean meeting would then be remembered—and remembered it would be, of that Lyell and Hooker were sure—as the setting of the "Wallace–Darwin" communication and not, as it is now known, the other way around. Slightly more than a century later Gerhard Wichler, a Darwinian enthusiast, pinpointed and slid quickly over the core of the affair in his *Charles Darwin, The Founder of the Theory of Evolution and [sic] Natural Selection.* In this scholarly work, Wichler wrote: "He [Darwin] felt it his duty to publish the treatise, which Wallace had sent him in confidence, as soon as possible. But the day of publication would also decide the priority date. Wallace would be the founder of the theory of selection."

As it developed, Lyell and Hooker judiciously skirted the awkward situation by altering the order in which the papers were presented.

They first introduced excerpts from Darwin's incomplete sketch of 1844, then a fragment from the Gray letter and, finally, Wallace's complete paper.

Later, even Darwin professed amazement at their order of presentation. "I had thought that your letter and mine to Asa Gray," protested Darwin to Hooker in a letter of July 13, 1858, "were to be only an appendix to Wallace's paper." A brief explanation is necessary here. Darwin referred to his unpublished sketch of 1844 as a "letter" from Hooker because he, Darwin, had sent it to Hooker around that year for comment and Hooker had written comments in the margin before returning it to Down shortly afterwards.

In their letter to the Linnean Society, moreover, Lyell and Hooker sought to dispel any notion that priority for Darwin lurked behind their request that the items be placed on the agenda in the order they proposed—Darwin first, then Wallace—or that the order of presentation was designed to provide Darwin with priority over Wallace.

In their joint letter to Bennett at the Society, Lyell and Hooker explained that Darwin proposed to obtain, as quickly as possible, Wallace's consent to publish the Ternate Paper and that neither Lyell nor Hooker objected "provided Mr. Darwin did not withhold from the public" excerpts from his own sketch.

But this was specious. In the first place, contacting Wallace "as quickly as possible" would involve, at a minimum, six months. Second, what right did either Lyell or Hooker have to offer no objection to the publication of a scientific paper by someone outside their immediate circle? As for denying Darwin's priority as a factor in their odd position, Lyell and Hooker claimed in their letter to Bennett that, "In adopting the present course . . . we have explained to him [Darwin] that we are not solely considering the relative claims to priority of himself and his friend, but the interests of science generally."

The Lyell–Hooker letter provided no hint of the turmoil behind it— the problem of Wallace's priority and Darwin's anguish. But it is to the distastefulness of the affair that Lyell's and Hooker's later genuine haziness over what transpired during those thirteen days in June can be attributed.

In 1875, at the age of 78, Lyell, for example, mistakingly recalled that it had been Hooker who gave him Wallace's paper, not that Darwin had sent him the paper and that he, Lyell, had sent it to Hooker.

"[Wallace] requested Mr. Darwin to show this essay to me should he think it sufficiently novel and interesting," Lyell recalled. "It was brought to me by Dr. Hooker, who remarked how complete the coincidence of Mr. Wallace's views and those contained in one of chapters of Mr. Darwin's unpublished work. Accordingly, he suggested that it would be unfair to let Mr. Wallace's essay go to press unaccompanied by [Darwin's] older memoir on the same subject."

Hooker was equally confused over the course of events.

In 1906, at the age of 89, as if to purge himself of dishonor, Hooker provided this account of what happened: "After writing to Sir Charles Lyell, Mr. Darwin informed me of Mr. Wallace's letter and its enclosure . . . explicitly announcing his resolve to abandon all claim to priority for his own sketch," Hooker said. "I could not but protest against such a course. . . . I further suggested the simultaneous publication of the two [Hooker did not know of the existence of the Gray letter] and offered—should he agree to such a compromise—to write Mr. Wallace fully informing him of the *motives* of the course adopted." (Italics added.) Darwin, according to Hooker, replied that he was "disposed to look favorably on my suggested compromise, but that before making up his mind he desired a second opinion as to whether he could honorably claim priority, and that he proposed to apply to Sir Charles Lyell for this."

Then Hooker said that he had no recollection of receiving the answer which Darwin, in his letters of June 26 and 27, 1858, had asked Lyell to forward to Hooker.

"It cannot fail to be noticed," Hooker said pointedly, "that all these inter-communications between Mr. Darwin, Sir Charles Lyell, and myself were conducted by correspondence, no two of us having met in the interval between June 18 and July 1st . . . and no fourth individual

[Wallace?] had any cognisance of our proceedings.* In making this statement, Hooker appeared to have mixed motives. On the one hand, he sought to dispel the notion of a plot against Wallace, and, on the other hand, out of feelings of guilt, he confessed that Wallace was not privy to the "delicate arrangement."

But Hooker then touched off a land mine.

"It must also be noted that for the detailed history [of the thirteen days] there is no documentary evidence beyond what Francis Darwin has produced. . . . There are no letters from Lyell relating to it, not even answers to Mr. Darwin's of the 18th, 25th and 26th June; and Sir Leonard Lyell has at my request very kindly but vainly searched his uncle's correspondence for any relating to this subject. . . ."

Hooker continued: "There are none of my letters to either Lyell or Darwin, nor other evidence of their having existed beyond the latter's acknowledgement of the receipt of some of them. And, most surprising of all, Mr. Wallace's letter and its enclosure have disappeared."

The land mine Hooker exploded in public was the mystery of the missing letters. Many historians, before and since that meeting, have ignored the situation. But Hooker put it on the record for all time, his surprise that all the critical correspondence to Darwin during the fateful thirteen days had vanished, Sir Francis' weak explanations, and those of Darwinian fanciers, notwithstanding. Hooker's implication was that someone had committed an act of foul play.

The latter observation requires explanation, for not only had Wallace's Ternate envelope and the wrapper around the first eight letters he received from Darwin disappeared—as well as the note Darwin had received from Wallace and forwarded to Lyell—but the original, handwritten, and apparently twenty-page manuscript on "foreign stationery paper" in which Wallace set out the "Darwinian" theory of evolution had also mysteriously disappeared.

Fortunately, Wallace's Ternate Paper was read aloud into the Linnean record at that July 1 meeting of 1858, and transcribed. Otherwise, the contents of the Ternate paper itself might have vanished!

---

* Curiously, at Down House today, in the former drawing room that was converted by Darwin in 1858 into a dining room, there is a painting presented by the Darwin Museum in Moscow that depicts a Soviet artist's conception of the scene at Down House that historic June day when Wallace's Ternate Paper arrived. The painting shows Darwin holding aloft Wallace's letter and reading it aloud to Lyell and Hooker. Artistic license notwithstanding, the scene is a revisionist fake in its entirety. Neither Lyell nor Hooker, the record shows, visited Down at any time during the critical thirteen-day period.

Chapter 10

THE SUMMER of 1858 was unusually and unbearably hot. Thursday, July 1, was unspectacular except for being a bit on the cool side. Victoria went horseback riding, accompanied by the Duke and Duchess of Brabant. The steamship *North Star* arrived from New York in eleven days and six hours, a spectacular record which the captain attributed to remarkably calm seas.

The politics of the day had a familiar, desultory ring. The Irish Question was debated hotly inside and outside Parliament. The Indian Mutiny and a memorial to soldiers who fell in the Crimean War were other topics of the day. The inscrutable East was as inscrutable as ever—to Westerners. A dispatch from Hong Kong reported that in Canton "nobody knows who is in power, or what is power, whether Chinese or European, where begotten, where nourished." There was the usual trouble in the Balkans, this time between Turks and Montenegrins. In Paris Prince Napoleon was nominated Minister for Algeria and the Colonies. Disraeli had domestic matters in mind. In Parliament he held forth on the "sewage question," the pollution of the Thames.

In lighter affairs, Madame Tussaud announced that at a Baker Street bazaar she would unveil a full-length portrait of the new "President of the United States of America." Admission price: 1 shilling. The President, of course, was the Pennsylvania Democrat inaugurated the year before, James Buchanan. In cricket, the Gentlemen crushed the Players 158 to 103 in what was enthusiastically described by the press, despite the lopsided score, as an exciting match. Mary Ann Oulds was summoned to court again for "ill-treating her husband." A notorious husband-beater, she had this time threatened him with a carving knife. Mesmerism was very much in vogue—the psychoanalysis of the era—and the celebrated clairvoyant, Miss Ellen Dawson, could be consulted only by appointment, or so she advertised. Other advertisements guaranteed to restore gray hair "to its original colour."

On the cultural scene, the Royal Italian Opera Company scheduled a performance that night of von Flotow's *Martha*. The highlight of the evening was a reading by Charles Dickens of excerpts from his works.

A fairly routine July 1 for Victorian England.

Yet the day was destined to go down as one of the great watersheds in the history of Western civilization as the fellows of the Linnean Society—that is, those who had not already run off to the country to escape the heat—gathered at Burlington House, Piccadilly, that summer evening to elect a successor to Brown, the secretary who had died the previous month. They also listened to the papers that had been scheduled to be read at the canceled meeting. Perhaps to their surprise, the agenda listed a new item. Put on the calendar by Bennett that very day, it read as follows:

> On the Tendency of Species to form Varieties; and on the Perpetuation of Varieties and Species by Natural means of Selection. By Charles Darwin, Esq., F.R.S., F.L.S., & F.G.S., and Alfred Wallace, Esq. Communicated by Sir Charles Lyell, F.R.S., F.L.S., and J. D. Hooker, Esq., M.D., V.P.R.S., F.L.S., &.

The nub of the theory—Wallace's Ternate Paper, buttressed in part by the Darwin extracts—was that all species are derived from one or several simple original forms and, in the course of millions upon millions of years, evolved into different species by gradual change as the result of their survival in nature as varieties or mutants. In sum, in the struggle for existence, favorable varieties waxed, unfavorable ones waned.

That the Lyell–Hooker "communication" to Bennett was written June 30 and either reached Burlington House late that same day or early the following morning, the day of the meeting, and that the topic was immediately inscribed on the meeting agenda, testifies to the puissance of Lyell and Hooker in matters scientific. It is doubtful that any other fellow of the Linnean Society wielded such authority within the establishment. Darwin, perhaps; Wallace, most assuredly not. The modest "Esq." tagged after Wallace's name tells the Wallace story eloquently. Wallace's profile in the scientific aristocracy was so low as to be barely visible. Lack of formal education aside, although Wallace had spent ten years hunting species in the jungles of South America and Asia, often at great personal peril, he still did not belong to a single scientific body!

There is another extraordinary aspect to the Linnean proceedings that evening. Neither Lyell nor Hooker had ever seen the 1857 Gray letter until the day before, when Darwin's servant delivered a copy of it to them. Why did Darwin insist on including an excerpt from this obscure letter in the meeting proceedings, and why did Lyell and Hooker go along with the ploy? Inadvertently, perhaps, Francis Darwin provided the reason. "The fact that there is no set discussion on the principle of divergence in the 1844 Essay makes it clear why the joint paper [sic] read before the Linnean Society on July 1, 1858, included a letter to Asa Gray, as well as an extract from the Essay of 1844," he said.

The proceedings were published in the Society's journal in August. Darwin was given a set of page proofs before publication and made enough alterations in the text to serve as the basis for innumerable Ph.D. theses. These corrections in content and style only served to sharpen the contrast between Darwin's work and that of Wallace, which, untouched, stood out in high relief. "The extract from my MS. and the letter to Asa Gray had neither been intended for publication, and were badly written," Darwin protested later in a private letter in answer to criticism that the excerpts were difficult to read. And, Darwin added, "Mr. Wallace's essay, on the other hand, was admirably expressed and *quite clear*."

Darwin, however, failed to add that Wallace never received a set of either the galleys or the page proofs of the published record of the meeting. Wallace, therefore, never had the opportunity to correct a single word, much less a phrase, in his manuscript. Indeed, Wallace was completely out of the picture. He did not even entertain an inkling that his paper was being read before the Linnean Society or that it would be published. As Thomas Huxley crisply expressed it, "Wallace was far away in the Malay archipelago."

The turnout at Burlington House that summer evening was sparse. Only twenty-eight fellows were identified by name as present, plus two visitors. Darwin, who normally avoided public meetings, was also absent. Given the circumstances at disease-ravaged Down, his absence on this occasion was hardly surprising. The Wallace–Darwin papers were read aloud, and the reaction is illuminating.

The botanist and nephew of philosopher Jeremy Bentham, George Bentham, who had been elected vice president in place of the late Robert Brown, had planned to read a paper on the fixity of species. He was quick to recognize the revolutionary implications in the Wallace–Darwin papers and immediately withdrew his own. Years later Bentham recalled "the day his [Darwin's] celebrated paper [sic] was read at the Linnean Society." By then the Darwin myth had taken hold within the scientific establishment. Bentham did not recall that Darwin's "paper" consisted of two fragments and that Darwin shared the occasion with Wallace, an indication of how quickly the winds of history shift from accuracy. "Most fortunately my paper had to give way to Mr. Darwin's and once that was read," Bentham elaborated, "I felt bound to defer mine for reconsideration."

At least Bentham was quick-witted enough to appreciate that Wallace and Darwin had shattered for all time the complacent theory of the permanence of species, of their immutability through eternity.

Thomas Bell, President of the Linnean, zoologist and pioneer in dental surgery, failed to appreciate the significance of the occasion. In his annual address later that year he described 1858 as a bust, scientifically. "It has not, indeed, been marked by any of the striking discoveries which at once revolutionize, so to speak, the department of science which they bear," Bell said. Carried away by oratory, Bell lamented that a Bacon or a Newton "is an occasional phenomenon, whose existence and career seems to be especially appointed by Providence, for the purposes of effecting some great important change in the condition or pursuit of man."

On July 2, the next day, Hooker wrote Darwin that after the meeting the species question was "talked over with bated breath; Lyell's approval, and perhaps in a small way mine, as his lieutenant in *the affair*, rather overawed the Fellows, who would otherwise have flown out against the doctrine." (Italics added.) Although it was Hooker who apparently concocted the Linnean arrangement, he was quick to describe himself only as Lyell's lieutenant in the dirty business, just as Darwin had earlier sought to shift blame for embarking on his "big book" from his own shoulders to those of Lyell.

As observed earlier, Darwin did not record the date of the Linnean meeting in his pocket diary, although he presumably reserved the little book for the most important dates of each year. The omission must have been deliberate. The same may be said for Lyell. For a man who had opened his own scientific journal in 1855 after reading Wallace's Sarawak Law, and threw into it all sorts of scraps of information and news about the species question, it is incomprehensible that Lyell's scientific journals should contain a July 2, 1858, reference only to a Professor van Beneden who "thinks that naturalists will, & perhaps must, begin with a severe analysis of species making. . . ." There is no notice of the previous night's proceedings, nor any hint whatever of the trials and tribulations of the thirteen days preceding it.

The only reasonable explanation for the omissions in Darwin's and Lyell's private diaries is the dogging of both men's consciences by their devious behavior of the previous fortnight.

Yet for all intents and purposes, on the surface at least, Wallace's Ternate Paper, backed by Darwin's excerpts and the weight of the Lyell–Hooker letter, scarcely caused a stir. To his own mind, Bell was right, and most people in 1858 probably agreed with him: the year was scientifically drab. Neither the *Times* nor any other London newspaper reported the meeting. And with one notable exception, both scholars and lay public seemed unaware that July 1 had been an awesome watershed, marking the demise of one age and the beginning of another in the history of mankind.

"Our joint productions excited very little attention," observed Darwin himself in his *Autobiography*, "and the only published notice of them which I can remember was by Professor Haughton of Dublin, whose verdict was that all that was new in them was false, and what was true was old."

Yet here again, Darwin misrepresented the truth. That observation was not at the heart of the Reverend Professor S. H. Haughton's commentary on the Linnean meeting.

Indeed, it is historically fascinating that the "only" published remark about the meeting to make a lasting impression on Darwin was also the most dispassionate, truthful, and revealing—and the most damaging to Darwin. Haughton's objectivity in the affair is unimpeachable. He was unaware of the developing plot and was not in touch with Darwin, Lyell, or Hooker in the month leading up to July 1. He had never heard of Wallace. He had no ax to grind.

Darwin's recollection of Haughton's commentary may be partly explained by his guilt feelings for his behavior and partly by a compulsion to tell the truth even when it hurt his own interests—but also to tell that truth in such an offhanded, slippery manner, and with such "honest simplicity," that it threw others off the track.

Haughton's remarks have been lost in history, but are available to anyone interested in testing Darwin's priority and prepared to ferret them out. The Haughton annual report and analysis is buried on page 137 of Volume III of the *Journal of the Geological Society of Dublin* which was published by M. H. Gill, Dublin printers, in 1860. The same volume also contains the minutes of the 1857–60 meetings of what later was renamed the Royal Geological Society of Ireland, and includes Haughton's annual review of 1858 as president of that Irish society.

In that role, Haughton exchanged journals with Bell, his Linnean counterpart. But whereas Bell wrote off 1858 as a lost year, Haughton wrote off Darwin but not Wallace.

"Mr. Darwin's paper is simply an application of Malthus's doctrine of population to organic species, and a consequent demonstration that none but the healthiest, the most vigorous, and the best provided of a species can survive; and that the weakest must 'go to the wall,' " said Haughton. He concluded: "To this there can be no objection, except that of want of novelty."

But—which is why it is so seemingly inexplicable that Haughton's commentary, like a Sarawak leech, fastened itself so firmly to *Darwin's* mind—Professor Haughton recognized in Wallace an original, revolutionary, and dangerous doctrine of evolution, one to which Haughton took strong exception.

"Mr. Wallace, in his paper, adopts the same line of reasoning, and *carries it one step further.* . . ," Haughton wrote. (Italics added.) Correctly, he quoted Wallace as saying: " 'We believe we have now shown that there is a tendency in nature to the continued progression of certain classes of varieties further and further from the original type— a progression to which there appears no reason to assign any definite limits. . . .' "

Haughton was troubled by Wallace's assumption of limitless evolution.

"The possibility of departing *indefinitely* from the original type is here assumed," Haughton complained, "and must be regarded as an hypothesis contrary to our experience, and at variance with all we know of other departments of nature."

This observation suggests that Haughton was familiar with the theory except for the Wallace conclusion that evolution was interminable.

In point of fact, as later demonstrated by the Eiseleys, Darlingtons, and other historians of evolution, William Wells, forty-five years earlier, had delivered a paper before the Royal Society of London in which he observed that "amongst men, as well as among other animals, varieties of a greater or less magnitude are constantly occurring." Wells attributed this to natural selection and the survival of the fittest.

But there had been other precursors, too. In 1831, Patrick Matthew, a Scottish botanist, published a conclusion similar to Wells' in an obscure book entitled *On Naval Timber and Aborculture*. In my own research, I discovered that Haughton was also a friend and correspondent of Edward Blyth, who was a correspondent of Darwin's, the same Blyth who had tipped off Darwin about Wallace's Sarawak Law. It is worth speculating that Haughton and Blyth probably discussed the species question in their own correspondence.

In his analysis, Haughton spelled out his understanding of evolutionary theory.

"According to the law on which the Creator has formed the universe," he continued, "it appears to me that the propagation of special varieties is simply a provision to guard against the destruction of the species by any, the least, change; and that it is unphilosophical [i.e., unscientific] in the highest degree to assume an unlimited amount of change to be possible."

Given Haughton's brushoff of Darwin's thoughts as conventional thinking, and his attack on Wallace for developing an unconventional theory, there arises the disturbing question of whether any of the thirty-odd persons in attendance at the Linnean meeting drew a similar conclusion—that Wallace displayed more originality, more profundity, than Darwin. Did they then ignore Wallace because he was an unlettered, unknown quantity outside their elitist scientific and social circles?

Haughton ended his analysis of the meeting—"the only published notice" Darwin could remember—with the line Darwin recorded in his *Autobiography*. "This speculation of Messrs. Darwin and Wallace would not be worthy of notice were it not for the weight of authority of the names under whose auspices it has been brought forward [Lyell and Hooker]," Haughton said. "If it means what it says, it is a truism; if it means anything more, it is contrary to fact."

Immediately after the July 1 meeting, Lyell and Hooker reported to Darwin on the outcome. Their letters are also missing. If Sir Francis

Darwin's explanation is accepted, his father burned them as "unimportant." Fortunately, both Lyell and Hooker retained Darwin's replies to their letters.

Darwin was overtaken by guilt.

His reply to Hooker mirrored a sense of horror. "Thank you much for your note, telling me that all had gone prosperously at the Linnean Society," Darwin wrote Hooker on Monday, July 5. "You must let me once again tell you how deeply I feel your generous kindness and Lyell's on this occasion.

"But," he continued, "in truth it shames me that you should have lost time on a mere point of priority." In truth, of course, priority was the core of the affair. And in a second letter to Hooker, Darwin returned to the same theme. "I always thought it very possible that I might be forestalled, but I fancied that I had a grand enough soul not to care," he said. "But I found myself mistaken and punished."

Darwin then claimed that he had written "half a letter to Wallace to give up all priority to him" and, had it not been for Lyell's and Hooker's intervention (solicited by Darwin)—"your quite extraordinary kindness," as Darwin quaintly phrased it—he would have dispatched the letter to Wallace. Instead, Darwin said, he tore it up.

Darwin expressed an intense need to restore his honor. "You said you would write to Wallace," he wrote. "I certainly should much like this, as it would quite exonerate me: if you would send me your note, sealed up, I would forward it with my own, as I know the address, etc."

But no matter how deep swirled the crises around him, the death of one child and the serious illness of another, the unveiling of *his* theory of evolution by an unknown rival, Darwin, although passing off the objective as Hooker's and Lyell's, never lost his bearing and continued to plot a true course toward his destination—priority. Thus, troubled though he was by the delicate arrangement, Darwin requested that Hooker conspire for him to receive page proofs of his excerpts before publication, and expressed some confusion as to whether the Gray excerpt would be printed at all. "I suppose not," he said, although he must have been aware that the proceedings of the Society were printed in their entirety in the organization's journal.

Once again, Darwin took the opportunity to slough off the coil of responsibility for the affair. "I am quite indifferent [to what is published]," he claimed, "and place myself absolutely in your and Lyell's hands."

Apparently Hooker's wife, Frances, also wrote Darwin a note, probably inquiring about the state of the family. Henrietta and the two nurses had recovered from the trials of diphtheria and scarlet fever, and Darwin appreciated Hooker's wife's concern. Frances Hooker's letter is lost, of course, but she saved Darwin's note to her husband.

"I am . . . in truth ashamed to think that she should have had the trouble of copying my ugly MS.," Darwin said. "It was extraordinarily kind of her."

Despite any misgivings, Darwin clearly was relieved at the outcome of the affair. "I am more than satisfied at what took place at the Linnean Society," he also wrote Hooker. His priority was not only protected, but Lyell and Hooker had linked their names to its defense, and had stage-managed the proceedings in such a way that Darwin's excerpts took precedence over Wallace's complete theory of the origin of species.

Darwin wrote Lyell along the same lines on July 18.

"I have never half thanked you for all the extraordinary trouble and kindness you showed me about Wallace's affair," he said. (Curiously, it was Wallace's affair, not his.) Darwin also repeated his elation with the outcome. "Hooker told me what was done at the Linnean Society," Darwin wrote, "and I am far more than satisfied."

Once more he repeated to Lyell his confession that he was a prisoner of priority, the irresistible desire to be first. "I certainly was a little annoyed to lose all priority," he admitted, "but had resigned myself to my fate."

He was quite relieved, too, in another sense. The species question which had haunted and troubled him for almost a generation was now out in the open. The inference that man evolved from preexisting species was open to serious discussion, hopefully, unclouded by prejudice. "I look at this as so very important," Darwin said, "that I am almost glad of Wallace's paper for having led to this." But the transcending reason for the rush to Burlington House that first of July, 1858—the continued ascendancy of Charles Robert Darwin in his area of interest—has come in with the tide of history.

And what was the primacy he established? Not the theory of evolution, with which Darwin's name, to the exclusion of almost everyone else's, is associated in the popular, educated mind. From Lucretius to Lamarck, from the Roman to the Victorian empire, before and beyond, evolution was hardly a novel concept. No. The trio had engaged in a conspiracy to protect a different priority, the concept of descent and divergence by modification and natural selection through preexisting, closely allied species—Wallace's origin of species—what is today commonly called the "Darwinian" theory of evolution.

Now that the "miserable . . . trumpery affair" was successfully concluded, Darwin sought to justify his own and his friends' behavior. No matter how heinous is a conspiracy, the participants—especially if it is successful—are apt to develop a plausible rationale for gilding it. "I do not think that Wallace can think my conduct unfair in allowing you and Hooker to do whatever you thought fair," Darwin wrote to Lyell. The message was clear: Lyell and Hooker bore historical responsibility for the cover-up. Darwin did not "allow" Lyell and Hooker to act independently. On the contrary, Darwin gave a demonstration of his penchant for "happy simplicity." In this instance, he appeared helpless, informed powerful friends of his impending doom, pointed subtly in the direction of a solution, let his friends solve the problem by dubious means, and went along with the solution—claiming it, of course, as theirs.

In 1859, in a letter to Wallace, who was and remained until very late in his life oblivious to what had happened, Darwin wrote, ". . . I had absolutely nothing whatever to do in leading Lyell and Hooker to what they thought a fair course of action."

Chapter 11

IN AUGUST the Linnean Society published Wallace's Ternate Paper and the extracts from Darwin's essay and letter to Asa Gray. To this day nobody knows who read the Wallace proofs or, for that matter, what happened to the original manuscript. Intentionally or otherwise, it was discarded, lost, or destroyed. Thus, nothing now exists of the postmarked envelope that Wallace mailed from Ternate, the manuscript it contained, or the note from Wallace to Darwin that accompanied it.

Conceivably, Darwin could have destroyed the contents of Wallace's envelope and said nothing about it. But for Darwin to have done so would have been out of character. Darwin was committed to the advancement of science, and his commitment was genuine. It was a commitment from which he could not free himself, his obsession with priority notwithstanding, for in his mind the commitment to science and the need for priority were not mutually exclusive.

For more than a hundred years many of the bits and pieces that make up the Darwinian conspiracy and cover-up have been available to both students and scholars. With an occasional exception proving the rule, the failure of these groups to put the puzzle together is inexplicable. Consistently, the "miserable affair," as Darwin phrased it, has been poorly handled by historians, especially those who should know better. Library shelves practically groan beneath the weight of biographies and studies of Darwin, yet most of them have either fostered or perpetuated the myth of "Darwinism."

The myth-making began immediately after the Linnean Society meeting. For example, Lyell, addressing the British Association in Aberdeen some months later, disclosed that Darwin was presently engaged in writing a book on the "mysterious subject" of the origin of species after twenty years of observation and experiment, and that Darwin appeared to throw light on the subject in a manner "for which *no other hypothesis* has been able, or has even attempted to account." (Italics added.) The statement is astounding, the more so since it was Wallace's Sarawak Law that had provoked Lyell himself into opening a species notebook a scant three years earlier, and since it had been Lyell, through Darwin, to whom Wallace had forwarded his Ternate Paper marking the greatest advance on the species question since Lamarck.

Leonard Huxley—son of Thomas Huxley—in his biography *Life and Letters of Sir John Dalton Hooker*, published in 1918, unabashedly described the Linnean episode as "arranged" and then blithely paid tribute to Wallace as one who "genuinely waived all claim to priority." Being out of contact on the other side of the world that fateful year, Wallace, of course, was in no position to waive or not to waive priority.

Other misstatements also abound in the writings of the younger Huxley. For example, Huxley said that Darwin "first confided Wallace's unexpected letters [to] Hooker" and also claimed that it had been Hooker who suggested "the obtaining of Lyell's judgment." But the record shows that Darwin had first approached Lyell, and that it was Darwin who suggested to Lyell that the latter brief Hooker on the affair.

Like his son Leonard, Thomas Huxley—who should have known better if he read the Linnean proceedings—also muddied the waters. In *Darwinia*, published in 1896, some thirty-eight years after the Linnean incident, Huxley senior claimed that Wallace had "forwarded [the] memoir embodying his views to Mr. Darwin, for communication to the Linnean Society." This, of course, contradicts directly the Darwin, Lyell, and Hooker exchanges.

In 1885 Grant Allen, in his *English Worthies*, claimed that "the elder naturalist [Darwin] never strove for a moment to press his own claim to priority against the younger [Wallace]. . . ." This view has been widely accepted ever since.

In *Pioneers of Evolution*, Edward Clodd, an intimate colleague of Henry Walker Bates with whom Wallace had first trekked through the Amazon, contributed his own fable as the nineteenth century drew to a close. Referring to the roles of Lyell and Hooker at the Linnean meeting, Clodd wrote that the meeting "was arranged by them, not as considering claims of priority, which have too often been occasion of unworthy wrangling, but in the interests of science generally." Wryly, he added, "Darwin came out well in this business."

In America, the myth deepened appreciably by the eve of World War I and was enriched further during and after World War II.

Henry Fairfield Osborn, president of the American Museum of Natural History, wrote in 1913 that it was "through the persuasion of the great botanist Hooker" that Darwin consented to present his views alongside those of Wallace on July 1, 1858. "All the finest points of Darwin's character were displayed at this time," Osborn said, adding, "In a naturalist like Darwin the ego entirely disappears."

Osborn's views were so popular that they were republished in the Roaring Twenties. And in that same decade, in the very Dutch East Indies where Wallace worked out and wrote up his theory, the *Encyclopedie van Nederlandsche-Indië* claimed that at the Linnean meeting "a short outline of Darwin's theory" was presented. Of course, there was no "outline," short or long.

With the passage of time the Darwin–Wallace legend was also transformed into a "collaboration" between the two men. In 1954 biologist Garrett Hardin stated in a college text that "Lyell and Hooker put their heads together and came up with a solution that would save both his [Darwin's] honor and his claim to priority: they would present both Wallace's paper and a brief one by their friend—who must write it immediately—to the Linnean Society. . . . And that is how it came about that the theory of evolution by natural selection was announced jointly by Charles Darwin and A. R. Wallace in July, 1858." Darwin, of course, never wrote a paper for the meeting. Interestingly, Hardin sighted the surfacing skim ice when he fleetingly observed that there was a conflict between Darwin's "honor and his claim to priority."

The farther observers drop back from the front lines, as journalists are often aware, the greater the distortion. And so it appears in the Wallace–Darwin story. Thus, the late Michigan University zoologist Marston Bates, in his 1960 *The Forest and the Sea*, puts the situation in these terms: "Wallace hit upon the idea of evolution through natural selection quite independently of Darwin and the idea was first presented to the world in papers written jointly and read before the Linnean Society, June 30, 1858—a momentous date in the history of ideas." Written jointly? And so momentous that the wrong date is given?

The work of entomologist Herbert Ross is another example of inaccuracy through distance. "By prearrangement," claimed Ross, "Darwin and Wallace read their papers in London at the same meeting of the Linnean Society in 1858." Ross is the author of several books on evolutionary theory, biology, and entomology. Neither Wallace nor Darwin was present, and there was no prearrangement, of course. As for "papers," there was only one paper—Wallace's.

One of the most inaccurate accounts of the episode appeared in Gertrude Himmelfarb's *Darwin and the Darwinian Revolution*, published in 1959 and brought out in new editions in 1962 and 1968. The *Yale Review*, to cite one reviewer, hailed this book as "the dramatic story of how the theory was first made public," described Dr. Himmelfarb as possessing "a firm grasp of her subject," and praised her for "an illuminating contribution to an understanding of it."

According to Himmelfarb, Lyell's "genius for compromise intervened to salvage [sic] something for Darwin out of the wreck of his hopes," and—striving for the summit of innaccuracy—she continued, "after Wallace heartily agreed to it, Darwin consented to the joint publication of both papers"! Himmelfarb also expressed contempt for Wallace's low caste. "Unlike Huxley, he [Wallace] showed no intellectual talent, and, unlike Darwin, he had not even the primitive interest in nature that the biographer can point to as a premonition of scientific distinction."

Her commentary is scandalous. When the concept of natural selection was put forward by Wallace and Darwin, Huxley, the intellectual, for example, boldly confessed publicly that he had been "extremely stupid not to have thought of that!" And he added, ". . . none of us had suspected that the road to the heart of the species problem lay through them, until Darwin and Wallace dispelled the darkness, and the beaconfire of the *Origin* guided the benighted."

As for Wallace's lack of "primitive interest in nature," as early as 1847, at the age of twenty-four, Wallace proposed to a friend, in a letter that still exists, that they set out for the Amazon with a view "toward solving the problem of *the origin of species*." (Italics added.) A dozen years later, the last four words were to make up the title of Darwin's celebrated work.

The 1959 centenary marking the publication of *Origin* resulted in other monumental scholarly bloopers. Among the best is a 471-page tome published by The Johns Hopkins University press, *Forerunners of Darwin: 1745–1859.** The chief editor (there were two others), Hiram Bentley Glass, in a short preface, observed that "this volume is devoted to the forerunners who made Charles Darwin's achievement possible." In an oversight of indescribable proportions, despite fleeting references to Wallace in the volume, Wallace's name is omitted from the index. For the reader, Glass holds out hope for the future. "Perhaps another centennial," he wrote, "will produce a more ambitious and definitive work."

In 1962, Gerhard Wichler, the German historian and enthusiastic Darwinian, in his *Charles Darwin* observed that in the Ternate Paper Wallace not only cogently developed the mechanism for evolution—natural selection—"but he went further. . . . The principle of 'Divergence' was expressed quite clearly, i.e., that the superior variety always annihilates the inferior archetype. . . ." But, inexplicably, Wichler concluded that "thus Darwin was no longer the only scientist who could explain the missing intermediate forms." Yet no evidence exists of the date on which Darwin discovered the critical principle of divergence, and a case can be made that Wallace beat him to it.

Some well-known historians of science have even taken liberty with fact, among them Loren Eiseley. Thus, wrote Eiseley in 1958: "When Wallace sent his theory to Down . . . there occurred that mutual nobility of behavior so justly celebrated in the annals of science—a tolerance and recognition of their two claims which led to the reading of their preliminary papers jointly before the Linnean Society in 1858—a new world had opened up for man." How can a unilateral act turn into an act of "mutual" nobility? Nor—again—had there been any Darwin paper.

But the legend that Darwin wrote a paper for the Linnean Society's meeting persists to the present. *Scientific American* magazine devoted its September 1978 issue wholly to the subject of evolution, and in his written introduction to the issue, Ernst Mayr—zoologist, leading scholar in evolutionary theory, and one of the most powerful figures in the American scientific establishment—cited the Linnean meeting,

---

* Darwin, as late as 1861 in the third edition of *Origin*, sought to stifle criticism that he had unfairly laid claim to the theory, by citing among his forerunners Lamarck, Saint-Hillaire, W. C. Wells, W. Herbert, Patrick Matthew, Herbert Spencer, M. Naudin, *even* Robert Chambers of *Vestiges*, and, of course, Wallace, among others.

adding that "Alfred Russel Wallace . . . had come independently to the concept of natural selection and had set his ideas in a manuscript he mailed to Darwin; his paper was read at the meeting along with Darwin's." In Mayr's presentation, the Wallace paper is presented as an afterthought.

In 1964 Mayr, in the introduction to the Harvard facsimile reproduction of the first edition of *Origin*, felt constrained to defend Darwin against charges that in failing in 1859 to append a bibliography to his abstract *Origin*, he had "not give[n] credit to his precursors."

"Nothing in Darwin's character would support the accusation of plagiarism or of a deliberate attempt to conceal his intellectual debt to various precursors," Mayr wrote. "Yet, there is little doubt that Darwin was guilty of a good deal of naivete and a lack of generosity." Mayr conceded that Darwin omitted his sources and did not write *Origin* in a scholarly manner but, Mayr added, "the situation was aggravated because *Origin* was rushed into publication. . . ." Mayr, however, failed to give the reason for Darwin's sudden "rush" into publication.

In his 1970 *Darwin*, a volume in the Norton Critical Editions, editor Philip Appleman contended that Wallace's discovery of the theory of evolution through natural selection, including the principle of divergence, "prompted Darwin to allow [!] a brief account of his ideas to be given before the Linnean Society." Yet in the same volume, history of science professor Charles Coulston Gillispie of Princeton University confessed, ". . . I shall in the interests of economy perpetuate the injustice which makes Wallace's role in the history of science little more than an object lesson in the agonizing generosity of creative minds."

Nor are the fables cited earlier surrounding the Linnean meeting limited to the West. In the Soviet Union, Darwin is a hero of sorts and Moscow boasts a Darwin Museum. Yet the 1973 *Soviet Encylopaedia* both sustains and embellishes upon Western myths, observing, for example, that "Darwin, at a meeting of the Linnean Society in London, first read a lecture that contained the basic precepts of the theory of natural selection [and] at the same meeting A. Wallace delivered a report expressing views that coincided with Darwin's."!

But even Eiseley, the enthusiastic Darwinian, echoed the puzzlement of the Jane Loring Grays, Leonard Wilsons, and others over the disappearance of critical correspondence in the Darwin collection.

"Though Darwin's life is far more elaborately documented than that of many world figures," said Eiseley, "there are, nevertheless, some annoying gaps in the huge mass of private papers." Given the extent and nature of the vanished material, the adjective "annoying" is bland indeed.

And like the salmon, an occasional scholar boldly swims against the current. Charles C. Gillispie was one.* Barbara Beddall of Connecticut is another. In the *Journal of the History of Biology*, in 1968, Beddall expressed the conviction that the Linnean affair was not "particularly noble."

"However just Darwin's claim to priority," she wrote, "he was a gainer, not a loser, from the decision [of Lyell and Hooker]." Wallace, she observed, had no opportunity to be either noble or generous. And she is frankly skeptical of Francis Darwin's explanation about the disappearance of the material relating to the incident. "Darwin was meticulous . . . ," Beddall said. "It seems surprising that all the material relating to the most dramatic (not to say traumatic) moment in his life should disappear."

Nevertheless, after July 1, 1858, the tortoise raced against the hare— and won. While Wallace pursued his "fly-catching" in the Malay archipelago, fought recurrent attacks of malaria, and continued in his mind to refine his theory of natural selection, Darwin performed a *tour de force*. He was a man in a hurry, and in thirteen months, after thirteen years of procrastination, wrote *The Origin of Species*, an abstract of his still unfinished, unpublished "big book." Darwin's achievement was remarkable, and shook Western civilization to its very roots.

In Rome, Pope Pius IX placed the book on the *Index Expurgatorius* and in Britain Cardinal Manning organized a society "to fight this new, so-called science that declares there is no God and that Adam was an ape." The Jews were rattled. "Darwin's volume is plausible to the unthinking person," Rabbi Hirschberg, an American, sputtered, "but a deeper insight shows a mephitic desire to overthrow the Mosaic books and bury Judaism under a mass of fanciful rubbish."

Protestants were equally alarmed. The Bishop of Oxford, writing in *Quarterly Review*, charged that the concept of interminable natural selection "attempts to limit the power of God . . . contradicts the Bible . . . [and] dishonors Nature." And free-thinkers were equally up in arms. "The one motive of the whole book is to dethrone God," a leading iconoclast of the day, Geoffrey Spurgeon, declared.

* Although he has since turned downstream, see p. 345.

Years later, in 1905, in the tiny village of East Aurora, New York, in a volume handset in an old-fashioned print shop, a popular writer, Elbert Hubbard, expressed astonishment that "the Church of England, the Catholics, the Non-Conformists and the Jews are aroused and standing as one man."

"Peculiar spectacle," Hubbard mused.

Darwin, author of the *Origin*, was the eye of the storm, but, above the din, voices were raised. "Who," they asked, "is Wallace?"

Alfred Russel Wallace in 1848 on the eve of his departure for the Amazon at the age of twenty-five, in search of what he termed, in a letter to his companion Bates, "the origin of species." Wallace, who was forced to go to work at the age of fourteen, financed his expedition with his meager savings. (Courtesy of the New York Public Library. Reprinted by permission.)

Henry Walter Bates, like Wallace self-taught, published his first scientific paper at seventeen and journeyed into the Amazon with Wallace in search of Wallace's "origin of species." Bates promulgated the theory of mimicry in nature which Wallace later refined and singled out as dramatic proof of the theory of evolution by natural selection. (Courtesy of the Royal Geographical Society of London. Reprinted by permission.)

Charles Darwin in 1854 at the age of fifty-four, a leading figure in the scientific aristocracy. This daguerrotype was made a year before Wallace published his Sarawak Law, belatedly recognized as the most significant development in evolutionary theory since Lamarck. In 1858 Wallace produced his Ternate Essay, a complete formulation of the theory of the origin and divergence of species by natural selection. Darwin had not yet worked out a complete theory. (The American Museum of Natural History. Reprinted by permission.)

Sir Charles Lyell, a founder of modern geology and confidant of Darwin, warned Darwin as early as 1856 that he, Darwin, was being overtaken by Wallace in developing a theory of evolution. Two years later Lyell played a central role in "a delicate arrangement" aimed at forestalling Wallace in the event Wallace ever made a claim to priority for the theory of natural selection. (The American Museum of Natural History. Reprinted by permission.)

Sir Joseph Dalton Hooker, the greatest botanist in England and intimate friend of Darwin, a co-conspirator with Lyell in the "delicate arrangement." The coup to protect Darwin, who had never published a line on evolutionary theory, was stage-managed at the Linnean Society, London, July 1, 1858, an epic watershed in the course of human history. (The American Museum of Natural History. Reprinted by permission.)

Thomas Henry Huxley, the brilliant, acerbic essayist and anatomist who became the major publicist of the startling theory of evolution by natural selection. Huxley was not privy to the "delicate arrangement," as his son Leonard described it, of Darwin, Lyell, and Hooker. (Courtesy of the Picture Collection, the New York Public Library. Reprinted by permission.)

A copy of Wallace's "Sarawak Law," written in 1855 at a hill station near Kuching, the present-day capital of Sarawak, a state of Eastern Malaysia, situated on the island of Borneo. The law postulated that "every species has come into existence coincident both in space and time with a pre-existing closely allied species." Wallace implied the law included man. He was the first scientist to undertake a field study of the anthropoid ape, the orangutan, which, translated from the Malay, means "forest man." (Courtesy of the Royal Geographical Society of London. Reprinted by permission.)

A letter from Wallace to the secretary of the Royal Geographical
Society, September, 1858. Unknown to Wallace, the "delicate arrangement" staged by Lyell, Hooker, and Darwin had run its course the
previous July. Wallace's Ternate Paper, which contained the first full
statement of the theory of evolution by natural selection, had been
skillfully slipped into the dustbin of history. (Courtesy of the Royal
Geographical Society of London. Reprinted by permission.)

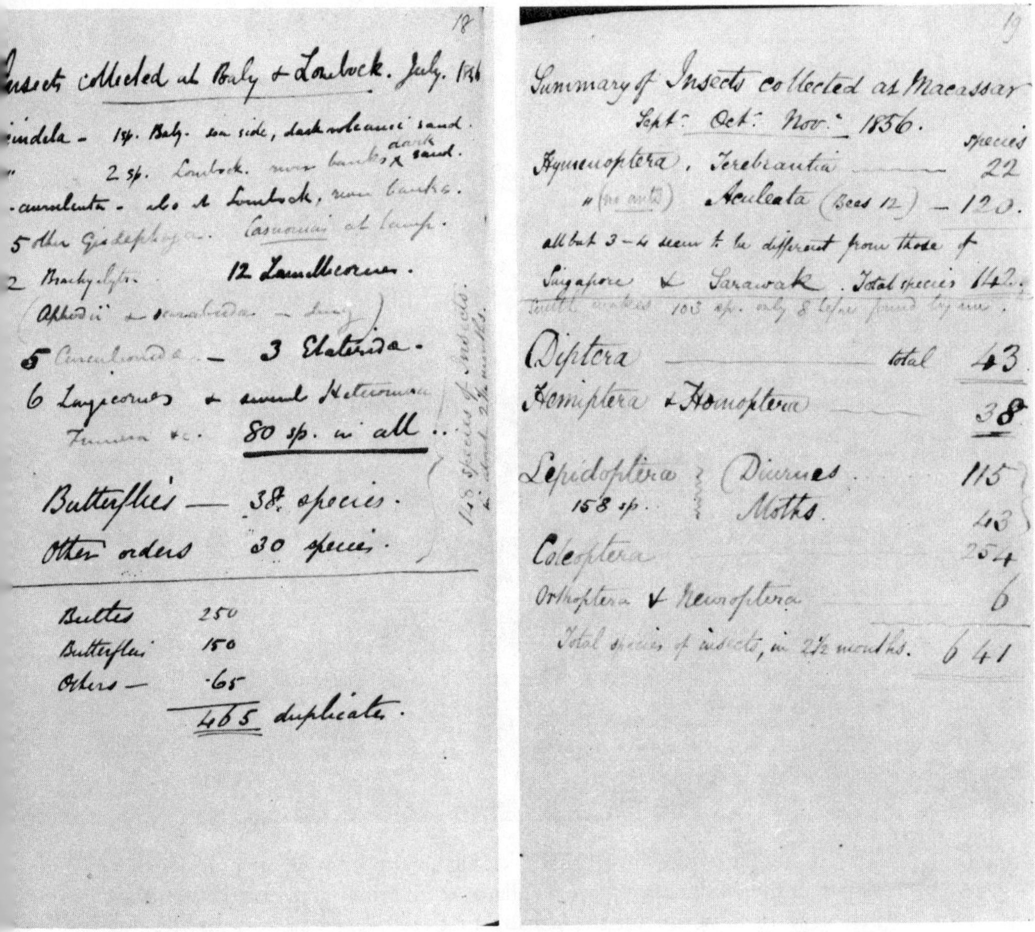

[Page 18 — handwritten]

Insects collected at Baly & Lombock. July. 1856

Cicindela - 14. Baly. sea side, dark volcanic sand.
" 2 sp. Lombock. river banks, dark sand.
aurulenta - also at Lombock, river banks.
5 other Geodephaga. Casnonia at lamp.
2 Brachyelytra. 12 Lamellicornia.
(Aphodii & cremabridae - many)
5 Curculionidae - 3 Elateridae.
6 Longicornes & several Heteromera
Femora &c. 80 sp. in all...

Butterflies — 38 species.
Other orders 30 species.

Beetles   250
Butterflies 150
Others — 65
465 duplicates.

[margin: 143 species of insects in 2½ months.]

[Page 19 — handwritten]

Summary of Insects collected at Macassar
Sept. Oct. Nov. 1856.   species

Hymenoptera, Terebrantia ——— 22
" (no ants) Aculeata (Bees 12) — 120

all but 3 — 4 seem to be different from those of
Singapore & Sarawak. Total species 142.
until unknown 103 sp. only 8 before found by me.

Diptera ——————— total 43
Hemiptera & Homoptera ———— 38
Lepidoptera ⎰ Diurnes. 115
158 sp. ⎱ Moths. 43
Coleoptera 254
Orthoptera & Neuroptera 6
Total species of insects, in 2½ months. 641

Two pages from Wallace's Malay journal. Wallace spent eight years among the islands of Malaysia, Indonesia, and Singapore in quest of a theory for "the origin of species." He financed his expeditions by selling insects to museums and collectors, sometimes at a penny apiece. (Courtesy of the British Museum [Natural History]. Reprinted by permission.)

The author, in white bush jacket, riding in the bow of an Indonesian out-rigger in the Moluccas, where Wallace, recovering from a malarial attack in February 1858, wrote out the world's first *complete* statement of the theory of the origin and divergence of species by natural selection. Wallace mailed it to Darwin who received it months later. At that time Darwin had never published a word on the subject. Darwin hurriedly wrote and published his instantly celebrated *The Origin of Species* the following year. The Moluccas are the Spice Islands of antiquity that Columbus went in search of in 1492.

Darwin in 1881, a year before his death, guilt-ridden over his treatment of Wallace in the Linnean affair, made peace with himself by arranging for Wallace to receive a pension from Victoria for his contributions to science. The pension was for £ 200, less than the amount Darwin spent annually for meat at his Georgian mansion in Down, Kent. (The American Museum of Natural History. Reprinted by permission.)

Wallace in the winter of his life, hailed as the greatest tropical naturalist of the Victorian age, chided as "more Darwinian than Darwin," was destined to slip into almost complete obscurity after his death. (Courtesy of the Picture Collection, the New York Public Library. Reprinted by permission.)

PART II

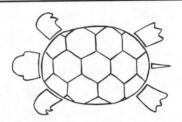

The Green Infernos

God knows, if admirable zeal and energy deserve success, most amply you deserve it.

> Darwin, in a letter to
> Wallace, January 25, 1859

In future histories of science, the Wallace–Darwin episode will form one of the few bright points among rival claimants. . . .

> Erasmus Darwin, in a letter
> to his niece, Henrietta,
> March, 1871

His [Darwin's] conduct has been most liberal and disinterested.

> Wallace, in a letter to
> his brother-in-law,
> Thomas Sims, 1860

Chapter 12

Alfred Russel Wallace's roots, as in the case of most people, are obscure. "Our family had but few relations," he remarked, "and I myself never saw a grandfather or grandmother." According to his modern descendants, however, he took pride in the distinctive spelling of his middle name, omitting the customary second "l," although Wallace did not know the origin of the unusual spelling.

Like all Wallaces, he considered himself descended from one of the many branches of the family of Sir William Wallace—which branch is unclear—who drove the English from Scotland in 1297 but eight years later was betrayed into their hands and put to death in the Tower. Wallace's matrilineal ancestry is equally blurred and romantic. His mother's family, the Greenells, possessed an old seal which indicated that their surname was a corruption of the French Grenaille and that the family was probably of French origin, perhaps descended in a somewhat mythical way from Raymond of Toulouse, whose Protestant followers, the Huguenots, fled France in 1685 as a result of religious persecution.

Whatever their genealogical origins, Thomas Vere Wallace, 35, and Mary Anne Greenell, 20, met and married in 1807. Within three years they had two children and, as Alfred Russel Wallace wryly quipped in his memoirs, "the prospect of a large family."

The Wallaces were doting parents and devout members of the Church of England—indeed, their reliance on Providence almost amounted to fatalism. They also shared a green thumb and a love for books but, as Alfred himself observed, "the family displayed no special talent, either literary, artistic, or scientific."

In his youth Thomas Wallace had been apprenticed to a solicitor but he does not appear to have ever practiced the law. Somehow he acquired a piece of property which provided him with a respectable middle-class income of £500 ($2,500) annually. With marriage and "the prospect of a large family," Thomas engaged in sundry business ventures with a view to amassing his fortune. His attempts at commerce were disastrous. It appears he was suited to little, except his family, gardens, and the library. He possessed a taste for the arts and started an illustrated magazine that foundered after a few issues. Wallace's bookkeeper was a scoundrel who misappropriated funds allocated for ink, paper, and printing. Undaunted, Wallace made plans to launch a second magazine, but this scheme also came to grief. Other business ventures ended in similar calamities, piling up insurmountable debts.

In 1818, as the family's financial situation worsened, the Wallaces and their children, now six in number, moved to Usk, a small market town near the Welsh border, embracing a square mile and a few hundred people. Like Down, it has barely changed in character since then. For the Wallaces, Usk's chief distinctions were threefold: the ruins of a Roman fort; an English castle built in the 13th century to contain the marauding Welsh; and, above all else, a low cost of living. "In such a remote district, rents were no doubt very low and provisions of all kinds very cheap," Alfred Wallace surmised, "—probably not much more than half London prices."

The Wallace cottage was a two-chimney affair, and overlooked the Usk, a fine stream which linked Wales and England, emptied into the Bristol Channel, and was noted for its trout and salmon fishing. Here among the chalk hills of Monmouthshire, the senior Wallace subsisted on tutoring children in reading and writing, and operating a small subscription library. The Wallace table was largely homegrown.

In this atmosphere of penury and domestic tranquility—the days at Usk were among the family's happiest—the eighth of the couple's nine children, a boy, was born on a wind-tossed January 8, 1823, not long after Napoleon died at St. Helena, Beethoven wrote his last symphony, and the first trade union was permitted to organize in England. Eight days later the baby was christened Alfred Russel.

He had entered the world during a tempestuous period, as the

Industrial Revolution gathered irresistible momentum (it would send a man to the moon in slightly more than a century) and set the pace for the scientific and technological breakthroughs which Wallace later termed "this wonderful century"—a phrase he used for the title of a book in 1898.

As a result of the family's straitened circumstances, the nine children (only Alfred and three others survived beyond the age of twenty-two) were farmed out early as apprentices, one boy to a surveyor, one to a carpenter, another to a trunk maker, and so on. "It will be seen that we were all of us very much thrown on our own resources to make our way in life," Alfred said.

Alfred was abnormally tall for that period (he attained six feet in height by the age of sixteen and grew another two inches before he reached his majority) and with his flaxen hair and freshwater-blue eyes the Welsh-speaking people of the countryside bestowed upon him, by the age of three, the sobriquet, "little Saxon."

Alfred Wallace's height compounded an innate shyness and he appeared hardly cut from an heroic die. He was, for one thing, accident prone. On one occasion, at the age of four, he was swept down a hill by a stone lawn roller and into a pond where he would have drowned. On another occasion, he was playfully pushed by a friend into a swimming hole, before he had learned to swim, and went under several times before his brother John, five years his senior, plucked him out. "It was, I think, the first year if not the first time, I had ever bathed," he recalled merrily.

Wallace's first recollection of a journey—a trip to London—was also associated with a possible watery end. To reach the capital, the family boarded a gaff-rigged ferryboat and sailed across the Severn, the broad-mouthed river that washed the bank of the Darwin estate at Shrewsbury, where Charles Darwin had been born twenty years earlier. "It was the first time I had ever been in a boat," Wallace said. "It was a little awful to me, and I think we were all glad when it was over and we were safe on land again."

Obviously, Alfred Russel Wallace was not the kind of boy to rove afar, and he was certainly not cast from the adventurous, any more than the heroic, mold. Wallace himself was aware of his deficiencies and frequently spoke of his "want of confidence," "want of assertiveness," and "want of physical courage." He considered himself cowardly.

In his childhood he also survived a bout with scarlet fever, the scourge which struck Down House that memorable June when Darwin received Wallace's manuscript from Ternate. Wallace recalled the illness in detail.

As he dressed one morning, he suddenly felt weak and faint. "I remember little more but heat and horrid dreams till one morning when all the family came to look at me, and I had something given me to drink all night," he said. The physician observed that this was the crisis and that the boy should be spoon-fed port wine at short intervals. "If I was not dead before morning," he recalled the doctor telling his parents, "I might recover."

At Hertford, his mother's village, to which the family moved when Alfred was five, he received his first formal education. At the age of seven, he began attending the Hertford Grammar School for a period of seven years, the full extent of his formal education.

There was no busing in those days and he rose at six each morning, walking the half mile to the neighborhood schoolhouse. Three days a week pupils remained in school until five and during the winter, when darkness fell in midafternoon, each student brought his own candle to class, usually stuck in an empty ink bottle, to illuminate his writing table.

Like his father, Alfred Wallace excelled in reading and writing. Astonishingly—in the light of what was to come—his two most painful subjects were Latin and geography. Yet he was to become expert in the Latin designations for living things: varieties, species, genera, families, orders, classes, phyla, and kingdoms. As he sheepishly admitted, Latin had come in handy, since it "enabled me to understand the specific descriptions of birds and insects in that tongue." As for his dread of geography, he was destined to become the first European to penetrate the upper reaches of the veiled Rio Negro, a major tributary of the dark Amazon, and to explore, a hemisphere away from that, the rugged mountains, retreating ridge behind ridge into the interior of New Guinea where, Wallace later observed, "the foot of civilized man never trod." Yet in school, he recalled, "When I had to learn the chief towns of the provinces of Poland, Russia, Asia Minor, and other parts of Western Asia, with their almost unpronounceable names, I dreaded the approaching hour."

But as reflected in his two-volume autobiography, published in 1905 when he had reached the age of eighty-two, Wallace gazed back on those few years of schooling with undeniable pleasure. He was a born student and never shed his enthusiasm for learning. Moreover, for a time he boarded out at the school, in the company of about thirty boys, and the routine, he confessed, was "pretty good."

The school breakfast, at 8 A.M., consisted of a mug of milk mixed with water and a thick slice of bread with butter. A boy could have an egg if he brought it himself, "but comparatively very few had such luxuries," Wallace recalled later. Dinner was served at 1 P.M. and consisted of a hot joint of meat. On Saturdays a treat was served, a hot meat pie, well-seasoned and with plenty of gravy (Wallace, throughout his life, had a weakness for the gravy boat). Dinner was washed down with a half pint of beer. Supper, consisting of bread and cheese and another mug of beer, was served at eight in the evening. Among the less attractive aspects of boarding school, however, were the boxing of ears for infraction of rules and flogging with a cane for serious breach of discipline. "These punishments were usually deserved," Wallace said candidly, "but not always."

Cricket and baseball—curiously, he used that latter word although, since Abner Doubleday, there has been endless debate over the origin of baseball—were among his favorite sports and Wallace would be surprised today if he toured the spring training camps of American baseball clubs and viewed their pitching machines. "I once saw a curious bowling [pitching] machine which it was thought might advantageously take the place of a human bowler . . . the ball could be made to pitch on any spot desired," Wallace recalled in his memoirs. "It was thought that it might be used for practice but it never came into general use, and is now, perhaps, wholly forgotten."

It was during this formative period that the naturalist within him stirred. At dinner his father often talked about the progress of his garden and on one occasion mentioned that a rare plant, the *bee-orchis*, was occasionally discovered in the region. "Once, during the time we lived at Hertford, someone showed us the flower," Alfred said, "and I remember looking at it as something so strange as to be almost uncanny, but as I never found one myself I did not think more of it." It was a hesitant step into the future, but not a full step.

Gradually, however, he acquired, by his father's table talk and during solitary rambles in the adjoining fields, a rudimentary introduction, "with my fellow-creatures . . . with nature."

"I began to feel the influence of nature and to wish to know more of the various flowers, shrubs, and trees I daily met with but of which, for the most part, I did not even know the English names." he said. "At that time I hardly realized that there was such a science as systematic botany, that every flower and every meanest and most insignificant weed had been accurately described and classified, [or] that there was any kind of system or order in the endless variety of plants and animals which I knew existed."

At this juncture, Chance, the fickle goddess, intervened.

At the age of twelve, Alfred and his father were walking down Hertford's main street when they ran into a friend of the family. The father and the woman chatted amiably for a few moments when the boy overheard her say, "We found quite a rarity the other day—the *Monotropa*." The boy was puzzled by the reference. He pondered over the remark and wondered what a *Monotropa* looked like. Alfred asked his father—fathers know everything, or should—about it. Thomas Wallace could only tell his son that it was a rare plant.

"I thought how nice it must be to know the names of rare plants when you found them," the boy mused. As his Chinese friends in Singapore later told him, a journey of a thousand *li* begins with one step. This was Alfred Russel Wallace's first step. His curiosity aroused, it was never stilled.

When Wallace was thirteen his parents could no longer afford to maintain him at school, but they succeeded in working out an arrangement with the headmaster to keep him at his books for another year. In lieu of tuition, young Wallace tutored his classmates in writing and reading while he continued to study Latin and algebra as a pupil.

His abnormal height had already made him feel self-conscious. The mixed role of student/teacher made him feel even more so and compounded his bashfulness. Worse, his parents could not afford to keep him in new clothes and his mother patched up his jackets like quilts, causing him great personal embarrassment. He felt "loss of face," an odd phrase for someone who would spend almost a decade in the Far East where "face," maintaining one's respect, was magnified into a way of life. Thus, as he matured, Wallace developed the temerity of the mouse deer—"the love of solitude," is the way he described it.

Wallace spent Christmas week, 1836, as he approached his fourteenth birthday, at home. The family's fortunes, he learned with heartache, had taken still another turn for the worse. Wallace was compelled to quit school. He was packed off to his brother John, then nineteen, an apprentice carpenter in London who put in a ten-hour day, six days a week, at 30 shillings ($6) a week. Willy-nilly, the tall, slim Alfred Russel Wallace, shy and retiring, who had taken to wearing eyeglasses and who would have liked to do nothing better than to lock himself

up in his room and read books or take solitary walks through the countryside—making of England a giant Sandwalk—was thrown into the
rough and coarse world of the working class.

Wallace bid his parents farewell early in the new year of 1837, the
year an eighteen-year-old girl ascended the throne and ushered in the
Victorian Age. When he journeyed to London, Wallace also journeyed
into history—and more than a generation would pass before he would
again have a roof to call his own.

Chapter 13

LONDON OVERWHELMED the open-eyed teenager: the Tower; Old Bailey; Westminster Abbey; London Bridge (which, despite the nursery rhyme his mother recited, was not falling down); the Thames' roadstead, crowded with ships and flags of every description. In the company of John, the youngster often spent the evenings window-shopping. The newly invented plate-glass window in store fronts fascinated him. "A wonder!" he exclaimed. The brothers also spent their evenings at the Hall of Science, a workingman's club whose members were chiefly followers of Robert Owen.

Even in his day, like Saint-Simon, Fourier, and Blanc, Owen was held up to ridicule, in the words of British historian Alexander Gray, as a "queer, visionary, Utopian socialist." The human degradation accompanying the onrushing, uncontrolled Industrial Revolution appalled Owen. He was horrified by the abuse of child and woman labor in the mills and mines, the intolerably long working days, the abominable, filthy working conditions. Raw capitalism, in Owen's eyes, reduced human beings to hulks in the struggle for survival and many wound up as debtors and petty criminals who rotted away in the hulks.

Owen preached socialism, and his brand was unusual. The core of his philosophy was that each individual, whether slave or slave owner, was the product of circumstances. No individual could be faulted; each man must be pitied. But, he argued, transform the environment into a paradise and man will find paradise on earth as in heaven (assuming there was a heaven, which Owen doubted).

Imaginative and naive, Owen mixed his socialist theory with practice. He competed against the captains of industry at their own game, spoke their language, and beat them. At New Lanark, Owen operated his own cotton mill—at a handsome profit. The mill was, comparatively, a worker's paradise, and Owen viewed it as the wave of the future. In a sense it was.

Many of his concepts would hardly seem revolutionary today. Owen campaigned for higher wages for workers on the ground that increased pay boosted purchasing power, and profits. He raged against child labor by observing that "judicious farmers will not prematurely put their young beasts of burden to work."

But Owen also staunchly opposed class warfare and forecast that such conflict would simply perpetuate class evils in a new form, giving rise to what the Yugoslavian dissident Milovan Djilas, in our time, has termed the "new class" in so-called Marxist societies. He denounced Malthus, the economist and pessimist who contended that population increased geometrically and food supply only arithmetically and that, therefore, exploding populations ended in chaos. Famine, war, pestilence and vice, Malthus pointed out, fortuitously held population growth in check but added that, given these horsemen of the Apocalypse, a happy society was beyond mankind's reach. Owen, the limitless optimist, rebutted Malthus with the view that an educated, intelligent, and industrious society would produce more food and luxuries than it could consume and that a great society was within man's grasp.

Owen genuinely believed that through love, faith, and charity, obviating the need for hope, the productivity of workers would rise astonishingly and "saturate the world in wealth." Owen also called for the creation of communes, a faint echo of the late Mao Tse-tung's comical vision of every home equipped with its own backyard furnace for making steel.

These Owenite beliefs sat well with the impressionable, fourteen-year-old Wallace, and above all Owen's fundamental conviction that character was shaped by environment. Although much of the talk at the Hall of Science was over his head, it was here that Wallace heard for the first time the name of Malthus, a name which was fated to change his life, as it would Darwin's. Indeed, it would change man's view of himself in the world.

Wallace not only came to share Owen's belief in Utopian socialism, but also Owen's strong passion for justice, an abhorrence of all forms of tyranny, all compulsion, all unnecessary interference with civil liberties. For the remainder of his life Wallace was a Utopian socialist. He believed that the character of each individual is formed by circumstance, first by heredity and then by environment. This was a concept of pure determinism that flew in the face of the Victorian Age. For whatever a person's environment, the Victorians held, the individual could rise above it through hard work, thrift, and perseverance. Ironically, the Alfred Russel Wallaces of the period rose above their environment and provided the Victorians with shining examples in support of their thesis.

"I have always looked upon Owen as my first teacher in the philosophy of human nature," Wallace said later, "and my first guide through the labyrinth of social science." Wallace revered Owen as more than a social reformer. He considered him "the real founder of modern socialism."

Not only was Wallace's brand of socialism out of joint with the popular *laissez-faire* economic philosophy of his youth, but also with socialist theory late in his life, notably the "scientific" socialism propounded by Marx, who branded the Utopian socialists dreamers who painted "fantastic pictures of a new society."

Wallace's ideas also ran against those of the Church of England, the established official religion. Like Owen, he spoke out against the Church on the ground that revealed religions dispensed rewards and punishments on the basis of a premise that the individual was responsible for his own failings when, according to Owen's theory, people were products of circumstance. Thus, as evangelism swept the mid- and late-Victorian periods, Wallace swam against the current. Wallace, like Darwin, developed into a religious skeptic and moved away from the Church of England; he developed into a free-thinker who solemnly believed that "the only true religion is that which preaches service to humanity and brotherhood of man."

Wallace's youthful brush with socialism and agnosticism at the impressionable age of fourteen influenced the molding of his character.

In the summer of 1837 Alfred's parents decided that surveying offered their son a brighter future than carpentry and he was shipped off to Barton-by-the-Sea, opposite the Isle of Wight, to his brother, William, a land surveyor.

William was fourteen years Alfred's senior, and single. He lived the life of the road, putting up at inns or in the homes of workers or shop-keepers. At his brother's side, Alfred mastered the rudiments of sur-veying and mapping, including the use of the pocket sextant, and also received his first introduction to science, in geology. As a child at Usk, he and his friends often found strange objects embedded in chalk for-mations. The children believed that they fell during thunderstorms and called them "thunderbolts." But Alfred's brother enlightened him. The "thunderbolts," William laughed, were fossils, molluscan belemnites, and William showed the boy vast accumulations of fossilized oysters and other fragments of worlds of the past. Alfred was fascinated.

Life on the road was rough, often boisterous. When the brothers lodged at a pub, Alfred confessed, "I had an opportunity of seeing a good deal of drunkenness"—and undoubtedly much more. Some scenes belonged to Falstaff. They were, Wallace said, "of an outrageously gross character," and occasionally William begged those around them to exercise more restraint "so as not to injure the morals of youth."

On the road the gangling, awkward, bespectacled lad developed a normal, healthy interest in the fairer sex, but his meekness held him back from close encounters. In his memoirs, he dropped hints about "good-looking village girls," and recalled a period on the road when he and William befriended a Mr. Worthing, a man of fifty or sixty whose wife was perhaps twenty years younger, "rather middle size and very quiet and agreeable." Wallace's eyes also ranged over her sister, who was "younger, smaller and more lively." In Wales, he noted dis-consolately, "the girls are often exceedingly pretty when about fifteen to twenty" but hard work thereafter aged them rapidly, a phenomenon he would later observe in the tropics, and by twenty-five a Welsh girl would often be mistaken for being nearer forty.

During their travels the brothers were frequently invited to Sunday teas. Young Wallace made little headway at these functions. He was ill at ease, his tongue usually furled, and he discovered that he was a poor conversationalist. "I should have enjoyed [the teas] more than I did had it not been for my excessive shyness," he said, "which was aggravated by the fact that I was growing very rapidly and my clothes, besides being rather shabby, were too small for me."

But the outdoor life of a surveyor slowly pushed him, with the force of a silent, deep-running current, into a totally unforeseen direction—toward the real world of nature.

He came to wonder about the origin of species. A typical incident illustrates this gathering leeway. In a tavern one evening he overheard a young farmer complain of the poor wheat crop he had gotten from his best field.

"What did you do to this field?" a prosperous farmer and local authority asked.

"I ploughed it," the young man said hesitatingly, "—twice."

"Ah," said the doyen of the pub, "that's where you lost your crop."

At the bar, all the farmers nodded solemnly in agreement.

The oracle had spoken, and that was the end of it. But in his own mind young Wallace questioned the true cause for the poor crop. Other factors, he thought, must have influenced the harvest, just as circumstance influenced character: the kind of seed, the mode of sowing, the quantity and type of manure, the condition of the soil, and more. "I should have liked to have asked about this at the time," he said, "but I was too shy."

Between jobs, the young Wallace spent his free time hiking across the moors and hills. During these walks, the mystery of nature "occupied me chiefly and became more and more the solace and delight of my lonely rambles." Like Darwin, Wallace acquired intimacy, and deepening insight, into an extraordinarily diversified natural world, a world alive with seemingly endless varieties of life.

In 1841, four years after joining his brother William as a surveyor's apprentice, he heard of and quickly obtained, for a shilling ($.20), a paperback, "the title of which I forgot," on botany. The book stunned him. He beheld a new world and embarked on a voyage of discovery from which he never returned. The tiny volume contained an outline of the structure of plants and a short description of the most common of the natural orders of British plants (*Cruciferae, Caryophalleae, Leguminosae, Rosaceae, Umbelliferae, Compositae, Scrophularineae, Labiatae, Orchideae*, and *Glumaceae*). "This little book was a revelation to me," he said later, "and for a year was my constant companion."

His Sundays were now spent in the field in search of specimens. And like a child collector who joyously, unaided, identifies an outlandish postage stamp, Wallace was delighted when he identified a *Cruficer*, an *Umbellifer*, and a *Labiate*.

He not only identified various plant orders, but gently dismantled his specimens and taught himself their various parts and organs. Then it struck him: life was not a crazy quilt. "I began to realize for the first time the order that underlay all the variety of nature," he said.

The more he taught himself, the less he knew and the more impatient he became, especially when he found a curious-looking plant. He felt a compulsion to learn everything there was about botany. But he did not know where to turn. "I had no one to help me," he said. One day, at Neath, in Glamorganshire, Wales, he stumbled across several old copies of the *Gardeners' Chronicle* (which Darwin subscribed to and scrupulously read and filed). Wallace's pulse quickened. One issue advertised an 1838 fourth edition of John Lindley's *Elements of Botany*. The price, 10 shillings, 6 pence ($2.60), "rather frightened me," Wallace said, "as I was always very short of cash." But he was seized by an uncontrollable desire and ordered a copy from the local bookseller, a Mr. Hayward.

When the slim, pocket-sized volume arrived, the excited Wallace could barely control himself.

"I opened it with great expectations," he said. But the great expectations collapsed immediately. The book was devoted to systematic botany, but there was hardly any reference to British plants. Not a single British genus was described, and the book did not even state which orders contained British species nor was there any indication of their general distribution or whether they comprised few or many genera or species. The inclusion of all the natural orders, however, coupled with handsome woodcuts, enabled Wallace at once to classify a number of plants that had puzzled him. But Wallace was deeply chagrined, and the book had been so expensive.

He returned to the bookshop and asked the proprietor if he knew of any book that would help him identify British plants. To Wallace's great delight, Hayward cited London's *Encyclopaedia of Plants*. It cost several pounds, far beyond Wallace's meager resources. But Hayward recognized in the eighteen-year-old boy an unusual enthusiasm and agreed to lend him a copy. For the next several weeks, young Wallace spent his leisure copying out the characteristics of every British species listed in the tome. Since Lindley's volume had broad margins he found room to cram the orders into the margins in a neat hand. When the lists overflowed the margins, he copied the orders and species on sheets of thin paper and interleaved them at the proper places. The task was awesome and Wallace copied out not only the information on every British flowering plant but also on ferns and the genera of mosses, as well as the main divisions of lichens and fungi. Then he returned the book to Hayward and "with increased ardour" returned to his lonely rambles in search of specimens. "This was quite a new experience for me," he said enthusiastically. But sometimes, even with his lists, he could not decide to which of two or three species a particular specimen belonged. He often wondered how allied species come about.

Despite its shortcomings, Lindley's *Elements* must also have stimulated Wallace and probably had a most profound impact on this formative period of his life. Lindley relied heavily on such forerunners of evolutionary theory and botany as Jussieu, Ray, and de Candolle. Wallace came across the speculation that "as nature never passes from one extreme to another, except by something between the two, so she is accustomed to produce creations of an intermediate and doubtful condition, which partake of both extremes."

"If true," Wallace read on hurriedly, "[this] would obviously go to the annihilation of all definitions of natural history; for if every object is admitted to pass into some other object by an insensible gradation, it would be necessary to admit also that no real limits are to be found between one thing and another and that absolute distributions can have no existence."

But, as Lindley observed, "this speculation will probably find few advocates at the present day."

Wallace also now began to collect seed catalogs and, at Swansea, attended a flower show and viewed his first orchid, an *Epidendrum fragrans*. Although horticulturists consider it one of the less attractive varieties, it generated in Wallace "a thrill of enjoyment which no other plant in the show produced."

This was also his first encounter with the tropics, although much later he would learn that the orchid is not necessarily a tropical plant; it can, for example, be found among the foothills of the Himalayas at elevations of five thousand feet. But to Wallace, the orchid came to symbolize the equatorial world, and his interest in orchids thereafter could not be restrained. In the *Gardeners' Chronicle*, with rising excitement, he read an article by Lindley in which the botanist described the *Dendrobium devonianum* as "too delicate and beautiful a flower for earth." To Wallace, the orchid acquired "a weird and mysterious charm," and he suddenly yearned to visit the tropics, a longing that was as ridiculous for him to contemplate as man journeying to the moon.

Wallace soon found that by identifying plants in the field he lost considerable time. Accordingly, he built a herbarium, collecting specimens and drying them out between absorbent papers and a couple of boards, weighting the latter with books or stones.

Wallace's brother William took a dim view of these proceedings.

"You're wasting your time," he said. Wallace's parents apparently felt likewise; nobody ever made a living collecting and drying plants and uppermost in the Wallace family's thoughts was economic survival. But the lad observed that he pursued his hobby on his free time. William was stumped; even he could not suggest how his younger brother could spend his leisure more profitably.

No matter how many jobs they contracted, Sunday was always free and Wallace spent it, collecting box in hand, scouring the moors for specimens. In the evenings he returned with his box "full of treasures."

"At times, I experienced the joy [of] discovery of a new form of life," he said. These discoveries stirred his imagination and, increasingly, he wondered about the origin of living things.

He viewed his specimens objectively and subjectively. Unlike much of the dryness of contemporary scientific inquiry, a delightful subjective quality appeared in many of Wallace's finds. Thus, he referred to the eye-bright as "charming," the cow-wheat as "strange-looking," the foxglove as "lordly." But he never lost his objectivity, his sense of scientific inquiry. The more he collected the more he came to understand, he wrote, that his specimens "formed parts of a great natural order, and that under all their superficial diversity of form there was a similarity of structure which, when once clearly understood, enabled me to locate each fresh species with greater ease."

Truly, he had made of England and Wales his own Sandwalk.

"This," he said, "was the turning point of my life."

Chapter 14

THE MORE ENGROSSED Wallace became with his herbarium, the less was he aware of his brother William's struggle for economic survival. "I was ignorant of it at the time," Wallace remarked later, ". . . [but] he was often hard pressed to earn enough to keep us both in the very humble way in which we lived."

Rarely did the brothers discuss money matters and during the years Alfred served as William's apprentice, apart from a brief stint working for a watchmaker, the youngster rarely possessed more than a few shillings as pocket money. Each Christmas, however, the brothers visited their parents and Alfred received a new set of clothes—"an absolute necessity," he said—and a present of perhaps ten shillings ($2), sometimes a pound ($5).

These cheery, Bob Cratchit-style family reunions, with the Yule log crackling in the fireplace and the goose hung high, ended in 1842, shortly before Alfred's twentieth birthday. The following year his father died at the age of seventy-two and the destitute family scattered. Alfred's mother took a job as housekeeper; Fanny, the sole surviving sister, landed a job as governess in, of all places, the American South, first Georgia, and then Alabama; and the surviving four boys continued "in trade," as the aristocracy snobbishly phrased it. William and Alfred worked as surveyors; John, as a carpenter; and Herbert, as a trunk-maker.

The same year his father died Alfred attended a lecture at Neath on Linnaeus' classification of plants. But the presentation, by a respected botanist, was so insipid that Wallace felt a compulsion to sit down and try his hand at an essay on the same subject. The result was his first attempt at a scientific paper. Like Darwin's paper the year before on the species question, Wallace's article was never published. But it was a healthy exercise and the manuscript, which he retained through life, displayed an independence of mind which later became a hallmark.

In his essay, Wallace conceded that any classification, however artificial, was better than none and that Linnaeus had made a tremendous contribution to science when he substituted generic and specific names for the short Latin descriptions of species used before him, and by classifying known plants by means of a few well-marked and easily observed characteristics. But Wallace severely criticized Linnaeus for over-indulging in unnecessary, albeit impressive, gobbledygook. Wallace had a strong dislike for jargon and this distaste grew stronger as he became more immersed in biology.

"I am very much disinclined to use technical terms wherever they can be avoided," he explained. "This is especially the case when a subject is elaborately divided up under various subordinate groups and sub-groups, each with a quite new technical name. This often seems to me more confusing than enlightening. . . ." His view, however, never sat well with the academic and scientific communities, and Wallace was later criticized for deliberately avoiding technical words, although he was quite familiar with the conventional jargon.

In 1844, the year after his father's death, Wallace attained his majority, but the timing was poor. The surveying trade was depressed and since William, who had many contacts among engineers, could barely find work, the younger Wallace felt it unfair to hang like a monkey on his older brother's back, getting a free ride. The twenty-one-year-old Wallace set out on his own in search of work and landed a job as an English teacher at £30 ($150) a year, plus room and board, at the Reverend Abraham Hill's Collegiate School in the Midlands manufacturing town of Leicester. It was a happy landing.

"I had a very comfortable bedroom, where a fire was lit every afternoon in winter," he said, "so that with the exception of one hour with the boys and half an hour at supper with Mr. and Mrs. Hill, my time after four or five in the afternoon was my own."

He spent his free time building up his herbarium and reading every book about travels in the tropics that he could find at the Leicester town library.

His taste in reading was a harbinger of things to come. He was enthralled by Humboldt's *Personal Narrative of Travels in South America*, Prescott's *History of the Conquests of Mexico and Peru*, and Darwin's *Voyage of the Beagle*. He observed that "perhaps the most important book I read" was Malthus' *Principles of Population*. Significantly, Wallace did not regard Malthus as an economist. He considered him a "biologist philosopher" and later acknowledged that Malthus' "main principles remained with me as a permanent possession." For Wallace, as for Darwin, Malthus was the key that opened the secret door that led to the discovery of the origin of species.

During this carefree period Wallace also attended several lectures on mesmerism, then riding a popular wave as the answer to "painless surgical operations." The Reverend Hill was similarly fascinated by mesmerism's possibilities and permitted young Wallace to try his hand at hypnosis in school. The whole student body turned out for the demonstration. "I found that I succeeded after one or two attempts in mesmerising three boys from twelve to sixteen years of age," he said. Thereafter, Wallace himself was mesmerised by mesmerism and related subjects such as phrenology and spiritualism, although this interest would not surface for years.

Leicester played yet another critical part in his life. It was there that he met his Hooker.

At the town library he heard, for the first time, of Henry Walter Bates.

Two years Wallace's junior, Bates was very much like Wallace in temperament: unassuming, retiring, and softspoken. He was also usually in poor health, his circulation being poor and face disfigured by blotches.

Like Wallace, Bates enjoyed lonely rambles in the Leicester area, collecting insects and studying nature intently. Like Wallace, too, Bates was a young man of modest means. A native of Leicester, he was the son of a family of hosiery manufacturers and was being trained for a business career.

Bates, like many boys, had begun to collect butterflies in school, but soon shifted to the collecting of beetles. Nor was this interest, as in most cases, a passing, youthful fancy. Soon Bates filled all the drawers in his room with specimens and began to teach himself their classes and orders. His brother Frederick recalled, "I well remember he could give you the names of all the wild flowers that were within our rambles [and] like most collectors he commenced with the lepidoptera, but soon abandoned these for coleoptera."

When Bates captured his first Tiger beetle (*Cincindela compestris*) he bounded home in exultation like Agamemnon returning victorious from Troy. Bates' family background, however, dictated his entry into trade but, as Edward Clodd, a friend and admirer, expressed it, the young Bates found the counting house "uncongenial."

"As often as he could," Clodd recalled, "he escaped from the desk to the open air."

By the time Wallace caught up with him—a chance meeting at the Leicester town library—Bates was an accomplished, self-educated entomologist whose first published paper, written at the age of eighteen, had appeared in the prestigious *Zoologist*, one of the many journals to which Darwin subscribed. The short piece, dated January 3, 1843, was entitled, "Note on the Coleopterous Insects frequenting damp places." Coleoptera is the Latin name for the order of insects known as beetles, chafers, weevils, fireflies (which in reality are not flies but soft-bodied beetles), and ladybugs. Some beetle families, among them the scarab beetle which formed the cartouche or seal of Egyptian pharaohs such as Tutankhamen, are now known to embrace more than 30,000 species.

"During the past year I paid particular attention to the marshes, banks of streams, rivers and pools in our neighborhood in my researches after Coleopterous insects," wrote Bates in the *Zoologist*, "and from the success I met with, I am inclined to think such localities are not examined with the industry they deserve." The note then went on to identify some of the insects taken in the neighborhood of Leicester.

For a self-taught entomologist, Bates put on an astonishingly professional display of technical ability, and reported finding such rarities as the *Chalaneius nigricornis* and *melanocornis, afrum, consimile,* and *Simposoni*. Bates was not trying to befuddle laymen: he was writing for peers.

When Wallace and Bates accidentally met in 1845 at the Leicester library—neither recalled the exact date—they peered into a looking glass and immediately recognized kindred spirits. A fast friendship developed.

Bates invited Wallace to his lodgings on Queen Street to inspect his collection, and Wallace jumped at the opportunity.

Wallace had expected to view some fifty different specimens "or at the outside a hundred, a very liberal allowance." But he was stunned. Bates' collection embraced hundreds of different varieties and Bates gleefully estimated that probably one thousand different kinds of beetles dwelt within a ten-mile radius of the town. Wallace was dumfounded

—and became an instant convert to beetle collecting. "I obtained a collecting bottle, pins, and a store-box," he said.

If his walks across the moors in search of different plant specimens had opened a new world to him, collecting beetles opened a galaxy. The existence of thousands of varieties of beetles in the British Isles alone puzzled as well as amazed Wallace. How could there be so many? How did it come about? Thoughts such as these again moved him to speculate about the origin of species. But Wallace was also enamored of beetles at a subjective level. "It is a melancholy fact that many of our fellow creatures do not know what is a beetle!" he wrote in his 1856 notebook. "They think cockroaches are beetles! Tell them that beetles are more numerous, more varied and even more beautiful than the birds and beasts and fishes that inhabit the earth, and they will hardly believe you."

Curiously, Darwin shared Bates' and Wallace's fascination and fondness for beetles. During his days at Cambridge, Darwin recalled, no pursuit gave him "so much pleasure as collecting beetles" and many was the glass of wine he raised at college with the toast, *"Floreat Entomologia!"*

"I will give proof of my zeal," Darwin said in his *Autobiography*. "One day on tearing off some old bark, I saw two rare beetles, and seized one in each hand; then I saw a third and new kind, which I could not bear to lose, so that I popped the one which I held in my right hand into my mouth. Alas! It ejected some intensely acrid fluid, which burnt my tongue so that I was forced to spit the beetle out, which was lost, as was the third one."

And late in life, Darwin wrote his neighbor, Sir John Lubbock, "I feel like an old war-horse at the sound of the trumpet when I read about the capturing of rare beetles—is not this a magnanimous simile for a decayed entomologist?—it really almost makes me long to begin collecting again."

As Wallace became enthralled by beetle collecting, he obtained through a Leicester bookseller, at a discount as a teacher at the Reverend Hill's school, a copy of James Francis Stephen's *Manual of British Coleoptera*. Again, fate had put Wallace and Darwin on a parallel track. The first time Darwin had ever seen his name in print was in one of Stephen's catalogs.

"No poet ever felt more delighted at seeing his first poem published than I did at seeing, in Stephen's *Illustrations of British Insects*, the magic words, 'captured by C. Darwin, Esq.,' " Darwin said, adding, "It seems, therefore, that a taste for collecting beetles is some indication of future success in life!" Stephen wrote that the object of his book, which was published the same year as Darwin's *Voyage of the Beagle*, 1839, "is to render a knowledge of the delightful science of entomology more generally accessible by enabling the student (at a reasonable cost) to obtain the names of his insects, and thereby register more conveniently any facts that he may observe with respect to their economy etc." Stephen's insect collection contained 100,000 specimens.

At Leicester, in Wallace's words, "I came of age."

But he attained more than his legal majority. He was entrapped by beetlemania, and it provided him with a delightful, inexpensive, and thought-provoking hobby.

Wallace, of course, continued to long for the tropics, in particular, for the great rain forest of South America. But, we can surmise, he knew in his heart that this was an idle dream and nothing would ever come of it. Everyone had unfulfilled fantasies. This was part of life. There was no point being discouraged and frustrated. He could still read about the handful who had fulfilled *his* dream, and he stuck to his Humboldts, Prescotts, and Darwins.

Then, early in February 1846, Wallace received an unexpected jolt. William died. His brother was returning from a business trip to London, riding, as usual, a wretched open-air, third-class carriage, the only rail transportation he could afford. William contracted pneumonia. He was dead within a week.

William's ledgers revealed that a "considerable amount" was owed to him by contractors for work done the previous two years and Wallace, thinking of his mother's plight, felt constrained to assume the leadership of the family. He resigned from the Reverend Hill's staff, with an air of misgiving, and set out to wind up his brother's affairs.

Looking back on his sojourn at Leicester, Wallace later remarked, "My year spent at Leicester must be considered as perhaps the most important in my early life."

For Wallace, William's death coincided with an unexpected windfall —"railroad mania"—for in making the rounds collecting, or trying to collect, the monies due his brother's estate, he was told that at Swansea civil engineers wanted all the surveyors they could get, and that they paid two guineas ($8.40) a day, an unheard of figure. "This, Wallace said, "I could hardly credit."

But the information was accurate and, more astounding yet, the contractors were in such dire need of experienced surveyors that the company offered to pay expenses on the road. Wallace was swept up by the sudden, wild flurry of railway speculation late that year, and rode the boom hard before it collapsed as swiftly as it had begun.

At the height of the mania, plans for 1,263 new railways were drafted, having a proposed capital of £563 million ($2.8 billion). But the sum required to be deposited at the Board of Trade was so much larger than the total amount of gold in the Bank of England and notes in circulation at that time that the public got frightened, panic ensued, shares in the new lines collapsed overnight, and even established railroads found their stock greatly depreciated. Wallace himself estimated that not one-tenth of the lines proposed during the boom were ever built and that the money "wasted" on engineers, lawyers, and surveyors amounted to millions of pounds.

By January 8, 1848, his twenty-fifth birthday, with the collapse of the railroad boom, Wallace had quietly squirreled away what to him was a fortune, £100 ($500). But during this period of money-making the species question rarely left his mind. Indeed, as with Darwin, it had come to haunt him. Wallace could not understand how so many different varieties and subvarieties of beetles could possibly have originated. They came in so many curious markings, colors, and shapes. Yet clearly they were structurally related to one another. Did they all troop aboard the Ark before the Flood? Implausible. But, if not the productions of a special act of Creation, where did they come from? The clue, Wallace thought, lay in their variations. But how did these come about in nature?

Coincidentally, in the same year that Wallace amassed his "fortune," Dr. Robert Waring Darwin died at the age of eighty-two. Charles Darwin's share of the family estate came to slightly more than £40,000 ($200,000)—including a portfolio of railway stocks. And, while Wallace mused about the origin of species, he may have surveyed, at two guineas a day or less, the beds of Darwin's newly acquired holdings.

Chapter 15

DURING THE TWO YEARS that Wallace built up his savings, he maintained a regular correspondence with Bates. The two ardent beetle collectors also swapped coleoptera specimens like baseball cards, and in the summer of 1847, while Wallace surveyed a new rail bed near Neath, Bates fled the brewery and the hosiery businesses for a week and visited his friend. They talked entomology, and they talked about "the origin of species."

Wallace's letters to Bates during 1845 through 1847, saved by Bates' wife, attest to Wallace's burning interest in the species question.

In a letter dated November 8, 1845, Wallace asked Bates for his reaction to the sensation of the period, Robert Chambers' *Vestiges*. The letter was written barely a year after Darwin wrote out his incomplete and unpublished essay on evolution, the excerpts of which Wallace forced to light fourteen years later at that historic meeting of the Linnean Society.

Chambers had brought out *Vestiges* only the year before, anonymously because of its controversial thesis. The book openly challenged the popular view that species were special acts of Creation, fixed and as permanent as the stars.

The author was roundly denounced, however, by the scientific élite, including Darwin. Judging from Wallace's letter to Bates, the latter also took a dim view of *Vestiges*. "I have rather a more favorable opinion of the *Vestiges* than you do," Wallace wrote his friend.

Vestiges was one of those irritating books that took the reader on a roller-coaster ride—at one moment brilliant, sublime, and penetrating, at another inane and absurd. Chambers viewed organic life as a series of small progressions, the simplest and most primitive form of life giving birth to the species next above it, and that type producing the next highest, "and so on to the very highest." And Chambers added: "Nor is man himself exempt from this law." He pointed out that "at one of the last stages of his foetal career, [man] exhibits an intermaxillary bone, which is characteristic of the perfect ape; this is suppressed, and he may then be said to take leave of the simial type, and become a true human creature."

"Man, then, considered zoologically, and without regard to the distinct characters assigned to him by theology," Chambers adduced, "simply takes his place as the type of all types of the animal kingdom, the true and unmistakable head of animated nature upon this earth."

The suggestion that man had descended from an ape ruffled many a Victorian feather. Chambers, however, sought to soothe these ruffles. Thus, he continued: "But the idea that any of the lower animals have been concerned in any way with the origin of man—is this not degrading?" and answered his own question by adding that "degrading is a term, expressive of a notion of the human mind, and the human mind is liable to prejudices which prevent its notions from being invariably correct."

Creative Providence, the author contended, ordered that evolution should be so.

"It has pleased Providence to arrange that one species should give birth to another, until the second highest gave birth to man, who is the very highest," Chambers said. "Be it so, it is our part to admire and to submit."

Unfortunately, Chambers' book is marred by political prejudices, some hilarious. For example, Chambers apparently disliked the color yellow, and therefore arbitrarily concluded that the most dangerous animals were yellow-coated. "Is this not true of tigers?" he asked. It followed, therefore, that among the races of mankind the Chinese, because of their skin pigmentation, were also dangerous. Moreover, claimed Chambers, the Chinese were on an evolutionary rung beneath that of Europeans. This could easily be proven by the Chinese language. Chinese, Chambers said, was so deficient in consonants that "this people can scarcely pronounce our speech in such a way as to be intelligible."

This conclusion led to another: "The Chinese, strange to say, though they early attained to a remarkable degree of civilization, and have preceded the Europeans in many of the most important inventions, have a language which resembles that of children, or deaf and dumb people."

Given the many heresies his book contained, Chambers may have been playing to the popular prejudice of the period to make his heresies more palatable, for in the course of writing *Vestiges*, the first Anglo-Chinese opium war was in full swing and a fleet of twenty British warships, accompanied by twenty-eight transports, landed troops on the China coast. In *Vestiges*, Chambers made his contribution to the war by raising the spectre of the "yellow peril." At least, the reader would conclude, the author was a patriot.

Unlike Darwin and other members of the scientific world, including Bates, however, Wallace was able to sort out the wheat from the chaff in Chambers.

The central weakness in *Vestiges*, Wallace felt, was the author's failure to explain the mechanics of evolution. Thus, for example, how did beetles modify their structure and evolve into so many different varieties?

Nevertheless, Wallace caught glimmers of scientific truth in *Vestiges* and on December 28, 1845, wrote Bates that he felt the book contained an adroit thesis and striking observations, but that they "remained to be proved."

In the back of Wallace's mind, a "wild scheme," as he later called it, began to take shape—a plan to search for the *vera causae* of evolution.

Wallace also wrote Bates that he had concluded—like Lawrence, Pritchard, and other scientific writers of the period whom he had been reading—that the different races of mankind were not produced by external causes, but resulted from the development of certain distinctive peculiarities in an individual, which thereafter became propagated through an entire race. For example, he wrote, "I should say that a peculiarity not produced by external causes is a characteristic of 'species' and not mere 'variety'. Thus, if the theory of the *Vestiges* is accepted, the Negro, the Red Indian, and the European are distinct species of the genus Homo."

Then, warming to his case, Wallace explained: "An animal which differs from another by some decided and permanent character, however slight, which difference is undiminished by propagation and unchanged by climate and external circumstances, is universally held to be a distinct *species*; while one which is not regularly transmitted so as to form a distinct race, but is occasionally reproduced from the parent stock (like Albinoes), is generally, if the difference is not very considerable, classed as a *variety*. But I would class both these as distinct species, and I would only consider those to be varieties whose differences are produced by external causes, and which, therefore, are not propagated as distinct races."

As Wallace later observed—as if he subtly put forward his own priority on the species question—these letters to Bates contained "some very crude ideas" and incontrovertibly demonstrated that "at this early period . . . I was already speculating upon the origin of species."

On April 11 of the following year, 1846, in another letter to Bates, the names of Darwin and Lyell crop up in Wallace's correspondence for the first time as the paths of Darwin and Wallace, unknown to either, neared each other.

Wallace expressed enthusiasm in his letter to Bates for Lyell's *Principles of Geology*, published in 1833, which obliterated the Reverend Ussher's specious chronology and introduced the concept that the age of the earth stretched back in time for perhaps millions of years. "I was much pleased to find that you so well appreciated Lyell," Wallace wrote Bates. As for Darwin, Wallace recalled reading the *Voyage of the Beagle* at the Leicester town library, and said that he had just reread it.

"As the journal of a scientific traveller, it is second to Humboldt's *Personal Narrative*—as a work of general interest, perhaps superior to it," Wallace said. Wallace also noted that Darwin "is an ardent admirer and most able supporter of Mr. Lyell's views." Thus, when Wallace was moved to send his Ternate Essay—containing the first completely worked out theory of evolution based on origin and divergence by natural selection—to Lyell, he may have recalled Darwin's *Beagle* and that it was dedicated to Lyell. Accordingly, Wallace used Darwin as a conduit to Lyell, for in terms of the mid-nineteenth-century pecking order in science, Lyell was on the top rung.

But while sophisticated in addressing himself to the complexities of nature, Wallace was, like his father, simplistic in politics and naive in dealing with people. And, he confided in Bates, one of the reasons that he so admired Darwin was that Darwin was "so free . . . [of] egotism."

Wallace ended the letter with the plaint of the specialist living in isolation. "I know not a single person in this little town who studies any one branch of natural history," he wrote from Neath, "so that I am quite alone in this respect."

The next year, 1847, Wallace's "wild scheme" acquired a new dimension. A business trip on behalf of his brother William took him to London and in a spare moment he hurried to the Insect Room of the British Museum.*

He was overwhelmed by the vast array of beetles and butterflies on display. "I begin to feel rather dissatisfied with a mere local collection; little is to be learnt by it," he wrote Bates. "I should like to take some one family and study it thoroughly, principally with a view to *the theory of the origin of species*." (Italics added.)

The species question had now become an obsession. Species, Wallace was convinced, were neither a special act of Creation nor the result of random chance. Their origin was founded on natural laws. "I firmly believe that a full and careful study of the facts of nature will ultimately lead to a solution of the mystery," Wallace said.

That autumn Wallace was given the push that put him and Bates, in the words of contemporary entomologist Robert Usinger, "among the foremost scientific explorers of their time." By now the siren call of the tropics was growing stronger and, unlike Odysseus, Wallace did not stuff his ears against it; his reading listed increasingly toward the tropical Americas, from the Amazon to Yucatan.

A few months after Bates' visit to Neath and Wallace's trip to London, John Murray—who later published Darwin's *Origin*—brought out *A Voyage Up the River Amazon* by William H. Edwards. Wallace hastened to procure a copy and upon opening the 210-page journal— "this little book," he dubbed it—began to read it with irrepressible excitement.

The preface along was orgastic. Edwards, an American, expressed astonishment that "in these stirring times, when all Anglo-Saxondom is on the *qui-vive* for novelty, and the discovery of a new watering-place is hailed with more enthusiasm than the discovery of a new planet . . . it has been a matter of surprise to me that those who live upon the excitement of seeing and telling some new thing have so seldom betaken themselves to our Southern continent."

Discussing the Amazon, Edwards called it "the mightiest of rivers . . . and the garden of the world." The river, he raved, rolled majes-

---

* The Insect Room had recently been transferred from Montague House to the newly built home of the British Museum at Great Russell Street, an impressive building with a portico of forty-four Ionic columns. In 1881 the collection was shifted to the British Museum (Natural History) on Cromwell Road, a massive structure patterned on the style of an eleventh-century Rhenish Romanesque church and situated across the road from the Victoria and Albert Museum.

tically through primeval forests of boundless extent, concealing yet bringing forth the most beautiful and varied forms of animal and vegetable existence. In the course of a year of danger and high adventure, said Edward, he had ascended the Amazon to a higher point than any American before him and "as an amusement," Edwards collected specimens of different plants, insects, and birds "in the hope that they might not be unacceptable to the naturalist."

Edwards made no pretense of being a scientist, but was simply astonished by the rich diversity of life in the rain forest.

Wallace could barely restrain himself when he read about "all sorts of vegetables and insects, particularly beetles" and how Edwards obtained a specimen of the *Phanaeus lancifer*, a coveted beetle; how Edwards "observed great swarms of butterflies of every size and color"; and how one day he discovered "a small monkey, as white as snow, and undoubtedly an Albino."

Above all, Wallace's pulse quickened when he read about the Amazonian island of Marajo, "a little world of itself, differing from aught else in its appearance, its productions, its birds, and its animals." Could the great mystery of species be unraveled there?

And repeatedly, Edwards observed that living costs in the region were cheap. The largest and finest oranges in the world, for example, cost twelve cents a bushel. There was danger in the interior, of course, notably from "water boas" (the anaconda) and cannibals, ague (malaria), and black vomit (yellow fever). And there were the perils of the sea in reaching South America. A Portuguese barque, Edwards cited as an example, had left Brazil for Lisbon during his stay and only one day out of the mouth of the Amazon was struck by so terrible a squall that she was thrown on her beam's ends. The vessel capsized and the passengers, trapped in their cabins, went down, as did the captain. Only a mate and seven seamen, who, without food or water, had drifted on the ocean past the Brazilian bulge and into the shark-laced waters of the Caribbean to land on the coast of the Guianas, had been saved.

Wallace was probably chilled when he read this passage, mindful of the two occasions on which, as a child, he had almost drowned and of his fright at crossing the Severn in a ferryboat. Yet the perils of the sea could not dampen the call of the tropics. Wallace's urge to visit the Amazon gained irreversible momentum. The "wild scheme" incubating within him suddenly matured. The £100 pounds he had saved, the windfall, his "fortune," was burning a hole in his pocket. He would mount an expedition up the Amazon. But let Bates tell the story as he set it out in 1863 in the preface to his two-volume masterpiece, *The Naturalist on the River Amazons.**

"In the autumn of 1847 Mr. A. R. Wallace," Bates wrote in prim Victorian style, "proposed to me a joint expedition to the river Amazons, for the purpose of exploring the natural history of its banks; the plan being to make for ourselves a collection of objects, dispose of the duplicates in London to pay expenses, and gather facts, as Mr. Wallace expressed it in one of his letters, 'towards solving the problem of *the origin of species*,' a subject on which we had conversed and corresponded much together." (Italics added.)

The scheme was mad. But Bates leaped at the opportunity. If the choice was between beetles and business, there was no choice.

As Wallace later described Bates' reply to his proposal, "Bates . . . at once agreed."

* Correctly, perhaps, Bates insisted on referring to the region as the "Amazons." In his view there were two Amazons, the river and the rain forest.

Chapter 16

EARLY in the new year of 1845 Bates and Wallace met in London to draw up plans for the joint venture. Wallace had just turned twenty-five; Bates, twenty-three. Studying a map of what was known of the region, they hit upon a "five-year-plan" which would take them up the Amazon and into the unexplored reaches along its tributaries. They lost no time in mounting the outlandish, if not reckless, scheme. Together they visited London's principal insect and plant collections at the British Museum and Kew Gardens, respectively; took copious notes on whatever they viewed; purchased pins, collecting boxes, scientific books, a sextant, Kater's compass, shotguns, and other supplies. With foresight, Wallace bought several pairs of spectacles (he would lose or break most of them).

By a curious coincidence, as Wallace termed it, William Edwards, the author of the book that was sending them off pell-mell into the Amazon, was in London and they visited the American at his Regent Street hotel. Edwards turned out to be in his late twenties, not much older than they were, plied them with information and, Wallace said, "kindly gave us letters of introduction to some of his American friends in Pará"*—which, since renamed Belém, was the principal port of entry at the mouth of the Amazon, some twenty miles upriver.

* Nearly forty years later, in 1887, Wallace spent four days with Edwards as his house guest at Coalburg, W.Va., where Edwards, who had become a lepidopterist, showed Wallace his fine collections of North American butterflies and elaborate drawings of the larvae at every moult. "We had only met once in forty years," Wallace commented, "but . . . felt quite as old friends. . . . [He] made my visit a very agreeable one."

Edward Doubleday, in charge of the British Museum's butterfly collection, also encouraged the prospective explorers in their plan. "He assured us that the whole of northern Brazil was very little known, that some small collections they had recently got from Pará and Pernambuco contained many rarities and some new species, and that if we collected all orders of insects, as well as land shells, birds, and mammals, there was no doubt we could easily pay our expenses," Wallace said. The nature of Wallace's scheme was, no doubt, a novelty to Doubleday.

Many historians have observed that Darwin, Hooker, Huxley, and Wallace shared a common beginning as scientists. They began their careers as explorers. Darwin landed in the Galápagos from the deck of H.M.S. *Beagle*; Hooker explored Antarctica aboard H.M.S. *Erebus* and H.M.S. *Terror*; and Huxley reached New Guinea aboard H.M.S. *Rattlesnake*. But there is a singular difference between Wallace's first exploration and those of Darwin, Hooker, and Huxley. Wallace commanded no personal wealth (beyond his "fortune" of £100), and received neither a government subsidy nor a foundation grant. He had no gunboat, much less even gunboat diplomacy, to back him. His accomplishments, and those of Bates, were therefore all the more extraordinary and enterprising.

Wallace and Bates also scouted around London for an agent and lucked into Samuel Stevens, whose older brother J. C. Stevens was a "natural history auctioneer" in Covent Garden. Young Stevens, an enthusiastic collector of coleoptera and lepidoptera who operated from a small office near the British Museum, quickly became a lifelong friend of the pair. "During the whole period of our business relations," said Wallace, ". . . I cannot remember that we ever had the least disagreement about anything whatsoever."

Stevens, wrote Wallace, spared no pains to dispose of Wallace's duplicate specimens to the best advantage, took charge of Wallace's private collections, insured each collection as it was dispatched, kept Wallace supplied with bank drafts and with such stores as he required, and, "above all, wrote me fully as to the progress of the sale of each collection, what striking novelties it contained, and gave me general information on the progress of other collectors and on matters of general scientific interest."

At the suggestion of Edwards, Doubleday, and Stevens, the would-be adventurers also practiced shooting and skinning animals and a week before leaving England—at the invitation of Bates' parents, who had abandoned all hope that their son would follow the family's tradition as hosiery manufacturers—Wallace and Bates paid a farewell visit to Leicester.

At Liverpool, on April 20, 1848, according to Wallace, and April 26 according to Bates' journal, the two boarded a 192-ton, square-rigged barque, her mizzen gaff-rigged, fittingly named *Mischief*. The young Englishmen quickly discovered they were the only passengers.

The captain no sooner ran up the Blue Peter, a signal flag announcing the vessel's departure, and put to sea when the wind rose and attained gale strength. The sea ran higher and higher, the wave crests grew, spindrift enveloped the vessel, and part of her bulwarks were washed away. "All this time," Wallace remarked gloomily, "I was in my berth prostrate with sea-sickness."

But a week later they caught the trade winds and the sea flattened out. To his surprise, Wallace gained sea legs and, with them, a new outlook on the main. "The exquisite blue of the water by day and vivid phosphorescence often seen at night were a constant delight, while our little barque, with every sail set, and going steadily along day and night at ten knots an hour was itself," Wallace said rapturously, "a thing of beauty and perpetual enjoyment."

Within a month the Atlantic shed her blue coloration, turned green, then olive, and finally olive-yellow as the vessel approached the mouth of the Amazon. "One morning we saw on the horizon the long, low line of the land," Wallace recalled as vividly as a first love, "and on the next, when we came on deck before sunrise, found ourselves anchored opposite the city of Pará." The journals of both Wallace and Bates agreed that *Mischief* anchored in Pará's roadstead on May 26. The barque had made excellent time.

"The air was excessively close, the sky overcast, and sheet lightning played almost incessantly around the horizon," Bates said as he recalled the moment, "an appropriate greeting on the threshold of a country lying close under the equator!"

Until Wallace and Bates journeyed through the largely trackless Amazon, explorers had ignored the great South American rain forest and river whose majesty and grandeur defy description. The only notable expeditions could be counted on the fingers of one hand, the French mission of Charles de la Condamine a century earlier, and the German expedition of J. B. von Spix, the zoologist, and Karl von Martens, the botanist, shortly before Wallace and Bates were born. The latter two trod through vast tracts of virgin terrain comparable to that of Stanley and Livingstone a generation later in equatorial Africa.

How vast a tract encompassed the Amazon would have stupefied both Wallace and Bates had they an inkling beforehand, just as the region continues to strain the credulity of contemporary travelers. Nowhere on earth is there a more extensive, unbroken, and massive tropical rain forest nor so awesome a river as in the Amazon. The river itself stretches for more than four thousand miles and boasts more than one thousand tributaries.* The rain forest embraces slightly more than two million square miles, an area large enough to shade the whole of Europe.

In the popular mind, even today, the Amazon is thought of as exclusively Brazilian. Yet its forests and tributaries cross the frontiers of nine surrounding states, notably the three Guianas—Surinam (formerly Dutch Guiana); Guyana (formerly British Guiana); French Guiana, known in Wallace's day as Cayenne—and Venezuela, Colombia, Ecuador, Peru, and Bolivia, in addition to Brazil.

For sheer magnitude, the Amazon River can only be described in superlatives. Its channel is so deep that ocean-going vessels venture almost 2,500 miles upstream. One-fifth of the world's fresh-water supply surges down the river, and the strength of the discharge is so great that it carries out into the Atlantic for upward of two hundred miles, accounting for Wallace's observation of the ocean's changing color pattern as *Mischief* drew closer to the river's mouth; in point of fact, the Amazon discharges enough fresh water in one day to flood the whole of Texas.

Only superlatives, too, serve to describe the region's flora and fauna. The Amazon possesses (or possessed**) the world's largest butterflies, largest beetles (up to six inches in length), largest rodents (four feet in length); more than half the world's 320 different species of hummingbirds; two thousand different species of fish, including the murderous piranha which grows to a length of two feet; and one hundred

---

* The length of the river is still debatable; it may be the longest river in the world, a title currently held by the joint Mississippi–Missouri–Red Rock. In 1953 French explorer Michel Perrin claimed to find the source of the Amazon in the snow-crowned peaks of the Peruvian Andes and in 1970 an American National Geographic expedition, supporting the French claim, pinpointed the source as Mt. Huagra in Peru; but so far nobody has found the link between Huagra and the Pacific to fulfill the late Perrin's dream of proving that the Amazon is a natural canal between the Atlantic and Pacific oceans.

** Today, in the name of development, the Amazon is being systematically ravaged. In 1974 José Piqué Carneiro resigned as director of the Brazilian Foundation for the Conservation of Nature and exploded, "They are turning the Amazon basin into a desert, destroying its forests, rivers, and animal life." He accused the government of "crimes against nature" and stressed that he was not opposed to "progress" but that progress and preservation must go hand-in-hand, a theme that Wallace was among the foremost to press as the Industrial Revolution took its deepening toll of nature in the winter of his life.

different species of snake, including the forty-foot anaconda and the poisonous bushmaster and fer-de-lance. But this is barely an introduction.

Untouched by the Ice Age, the Amazon is more than a million years old, an enormous greenhouse where temperatures hover near ninety degrees Fahrenheit and trees rise two hundred feet from the compost-matted, dark and dank jungle floor on which a greater variety of insect life exists than anywhere else on earth except in the Malay archipelago. Unlike the jungles of equatorial Africa and Asia, the Amazon's is unique. Even jungles normally consist of stands or, a mixture of stands of, a single kind of tree. Not so in the Amazon, a botanical wonderland where hundreds of different kinds of trees press against one another within a single acre in the grim, perpetual struggle for the survival of the fittest. Scant wonder that this battlefield has been called a green hell.

Wallace's Amazon was sparsely inhabited by warring Indian tribes who dwelt in a Stone Age culture, armed themselves with curare-tipped darts for their blow guns and, like the head-hunters of Borneo, dried heads and hung them in the rafters of their bamboo-stilted, thatched-roofed houses. The first Spanish explorer to journey upriver, Francisco de Orellana, in the mid-sixteenth century, named the river Amazon when he observed, or thought he observed, Indian women fighting alongside their men. The behavior of the women recalled to him the legends of Periclean Greece about a race of women warriors—the Amazons—who cut off their right breasts so they could better handle their bows.

This, then, was the Amazon of Wallace and Bates in 1848 when they rushed ashore as *Mischief* off-loaded. Like the mosquito flying into a nudist camp, however, the pair didn't know where to begin.

Pará produced cultural shock. The town was a backwater of neglect and decay. Garbage filled the streets and mangy, stray dogs were as common as the ticks they carried. Apathy, indolence, and lack of am-bition—the absence of the Puritan work ethic—appalled both youths. Shortly afterwards, however, Wallace quietly admitted that this im-pression "soon wears off, and some peculiarities are seen to be dependent on the climate." The heat was stifling, especially after their sea voyage; the humidity high; and pestilence, notably yellow fever, malaria, and dysentery, diseases of unknown origin, hung heavy in the air.

The inhabitants, it seemed, spent most of their time sleeping, gambling, or drinking. Neither Wallace nor Bates, fresh from their orderly, pristine England and Wales, had ever encountered such a varied mixture of races—blacks, whites, and browns—and, Wallace observed in wonder, "between these a hundred shades and mixtures, which it requires an experienced eye to detect."

During their initial week at Pará, after renting a *rochina* or country house at the outrageously high price of twenty milreis ($11) a month, they wandered into the forests on the fringe of town and were downcast. They did not see a single hummingbird, parrot, or monkey. All the fabled stories of the Amazon as an equatorial zoological-botantical garden seemed gross exaggeration, a myth.

"On the whole," Wallace confessed, "I was disappointed."*

And an equally disappointed Bates wrote in his journal, "The number and beauty of the birds and insects did not . . . equal our expectations."

---

* My wife, Aggie, a native of Surinam, laughed merrily when she read this passage in Wallace's journal. "The reason is quite simple," she said. "There is no wild life around any jungle village or town because the people hunt, cook, and eat everything that walks, flies, crawls, or swims."

Chapter 17

FIRST IMPRESSIONS are sometimes misleading and, for Wallace and Bates, the Amazon was a case in point. The farther afield they moved from "civilized" Pará, the more deeply they became entrapped and enmeshed in what Bates movingly described in his journal as "this uproar of life."

Within weeks they collected two hundred different species of butterflies; within a month, 1,300 different species of insects; within a year, 284 different species of birds. Before they got done with Pará's environs, Wallace and Bates had built a collection of seven hundred different kinds of butterflies! By constrast, the total number of butterflies in the British Isles did not exceed sixty-six and all of Europe supported only 321.

In early August they shipped to Stevens their first collection, four hundred butterflies, 450 beetles, and four hundred "others." "In all," a pleased Wallace recorded, "1,300 insects." The figure was inflated by fifty: hardly worth a quibble. The Amazon was an El Dorado, not the El Dorado of the Spanish conquistador, motivated by greed, and in search of gold and glory (in the name of God, of course), but an El Dorado of flora and fauna.*

Bates, in one assessment, estimated that before he was done in the Amazon he alone collected 14,712 different species of insects, birds,

---

* H. M. Tomlinson, in his 1912 classic about the Amazon, *The Sea and the Jungle*, read Wallace and Bates avidly and described the region as "Elysium for the entomologist."

reptiles, and other creatures. Eight thousand of them—more than half —had never before been seen in Europe.

Within a fortnight of their landing, Wallace and Bates also had a taste of the terrors that awaited them in the interior. "Having laid down my collecting box in the verandah during half-an-hour's conversation," Wallace said, "I was horrified to find, on opening it to put in fresh capture, that it swarmed with small red ants, who had already separated the wings from near a dozen insects, and were dragging them in different directions about the box; others were at the process of dismemberment, while some had buried themselves in the plumpest bodies, where they were enjoying a delicious repast."

The attack, however, was a lesson for both collectors, and they never forgot it during their South American sojourn. Henceforth they kept their eyes even wider open in the jungle. "I had great difficulty in making them quit their prey," Wallace said, "and gained some useful experience at the expense of a half a successful day's captures, including some of the splendid *Epicalias* which I so much prized."

On June 23, after a month at Pará, the pair made their first trek into rain forest, walking to the nearby rice mills at Magoary, which were operated by friends of Edwards. Their initial impression of the jungle was unforgettable. "Its striking characteristics were the great number and variety of the forest-trees, their trunks rising frequently for sixty or eighty feet without a branch, and perfectly straight; the huge creepers, which climb about them, sometimes stretching obliquely from their summits like the stays of a mast, sometimes winding around their trunks like immense serpents waiting for their prey," Wallace recorded. ". . . Our great treasure was the beautiful clearwinged butterfly, with a bright violet patch on its lower wings, the *Haetera esmeralda*, which we now saw and caught for the first time."

Within six months of scouting Pará, Magoary, and other towns and villages on the periphery of the mouth of the Amazon, both Wallace and Bates were anxious to move upriver. On December 3, 1848, Bates complained in his journal that the forests around Pará "are no longer novel to me . . . I want to be off to witness other novelties." Wallace was like-minded, and off they went while from London Stevens sent the cheering news of sales, "the completest satisfaction seeming to have resulted on all sides," he wrote them.

In the interior Wallace and Bates engaged in so many adventures and made so many discoveries that their notebooks contained enough material for several books, which they finally did write. In 1853 Wallace produced *A Narrative of Travels on the Amazon and Rio Negro,* which covered his four years of travel in the basin, and Bates, who spent an additional seven years in the rain forest, published in 1864 a two-volume account of his own travels entitled *The Naturalist on the River Amazons.* As testimony to the durability of their works, both, more than a century later, are still in print.

Life in the Amazon for Wallace and Bates was a far cry from the Sunday social teas and boisterous pubs of Neath and Leicester. The pair rose at six each morning and dressed in colored shirts, long pants, common boots, and wide-brimmed hats. They often breakfasted an hour later, usually on farinha, the staple in most Amazonian river towns (later, among the Indians, they ate fish and yams liberally sprinkled with searing peppers). They then outfitted themselves for the day's work. Over their left shoulder they each carried a double-barreled gun, one barrel loaded with No. 10 shot for small finch-like birds and the other with No. 4 for larger birds.* In their right hands they held nets. Promptly at eight they started for the jungle and, Wallace recalled, "we continued hard at work till about two or three in the afternoon." Each man also carried a large leather satchel with two pockets, one for an insect box, the other for large specimens (birds, lizards, snakes, and so forth). Their game bag also included primitive paraphernalia for the preservation of species, including wrapping paper (for packing delicate birds), wads of cotton, and powdered plaster and a damped cork for entomological specimens the size of a flea or smaller. On their shirts, like fly fishermen, they wore patches or pincushions into which they stuck a cluster of pins in assorted sizes.

En route back to their *rochina,* tired, sweaty, grimy, their faces and hands often badly bitten by *pium,* a jungle gnat, they halted momentarily at the nearest clear stream for a midafternoon bath, and immediately upon reaching their base of operations refreshed themselves with large slabs of watermelon. "We then changed our clothes, dined, set out our insects, and in the cool of the evening took tea," Wallace said.

Tea.

They were Englishmen to the core, and that final cup of tea made their day. They were English in other ways, too, reminiscent of the aphorism about mad dogs and Englishmen in the noonday sun. Wherever they went, people wondered aloud who in their right mind would

---

* Not being a hunter, I asked a friend who hunted what he would shoot with No. 10 shot. He looked at me in wonderment and, not knowing why I asked, laughingly replied, "Butterflies!"

run around the jungle with a butterfly net, in midday no less, other than a pair of lunatics. This was the conviction of the sophisticated town people along the Amazon's banks and, in the jungle interior, the opinion of the less inhibited and more direct Indians. The Indians simply considered the two "albinos" as possessed. But by whom or what they were possessed was questionable. The Indians were closest to the truth. Wallace and Bates were possessed, possessed by the desire to unlock the mystery of the origin of species.

For two years Wallace and Bates worked in tandem, moving steadily upriver but always clinging to the banks of the Amazon which, even in its greatest isolation, psychologically still served as an umbilical cord linking them to the mouth of the river, and civilization. By the spring of 1850 they found themselves a thousand miles up the Amazon in the sleazy, seedy river port of Barra—present-day Manaus—whose morals, Wallace observed, "are perhaps at the lowest ebb possible in any civilized community." At Barra, slavery and prostitution, and worse, were commonplace.

At this point in their peregrinations, they split up. On March 26 Wallace went off alone, traveling northwest, following the tributary Rio Negro, while Bates turned south and traced the river Solimoens. As Wallace expressed it, they each found it "more convenient to explore separate districts and collect independently."

A suspicion later circulated that the decision to break up the team was the result of a disagreement or friction. But as the late Professor Poulton, a friend of Wallace, observed, "There are no grounds for these conclusions." Nor were there. Wallace and Bates continued to stay in communication in the Amazon and they maintained regular correspondence when Bates remained behind and Wallace wound up in the Malay archipelago on the other side of the globe. After their eventual return to London, they remained steadfast friends.

Stevens may have had a hand in their decision to split up. The country was so vast, so rich in specimens, that it was obvious that better results would be obtained for science, and the marketplace, if the two collectors explored different biological sectors.

In 1915, in a conversation with Poulton, Wallace's son William, named in memory of Wallace's surveyor brother, reinforced this impression. "It is probable that they had to consider the commercial aspect of collecting," William Wallace said, adding that, while he grew up, he never heard his father utter an unkind word about Bates.

Another factor may also have entered into their decision. By op-

erating independently, each enjoyed a greater opportunity to earn
scientific distinction. Despite their shy and retiring characters, and their
unaggressiveness, their exploits in the Amazon made plain that both
were men of action and, therefore, not lacking in ambition and drive.
They were not cut in the colorful pattern of other great Victorian
explorers or adventurers such as Austin Henry Layard, who unearthed
Biblical Nineveh, or Henry Morton Stanley, who discovered the "lost"
Dr. David Livingstone, or such swashbuckling folk heroes as General
"Chinese" Gordon. But they shared with these romantics those intan-
gibles found in pathfinders—individualism, imagination, perseverance,
enthusiasm, resourcefulness, and a taste for exotic places.

Once they agreed to go their separate ways, the life-styles of both
Wallace and Bates changed abruptly. In the interior they were compelled to travel alone or in the company of a few Indians, who had
never before gazed on a European.

Wallace usually traveled by canoe. He took with him a watch,
pocket sextant, Kater's compass, insect and bird boxes, shotgun and
ammunition, and salt, beads, fishhooks, calico, and coarse cotton cloth
as gifts for Indians he met on the way. As for any Europeans he might
meet, he carried letters of introduction from Brazilian officials and
friends in Pará. One such letter, in florid, diplomatic Portuguese, recommended him to his host's "friendship and protection in the scientific
enterprise which [he has] undertaken, in order to obtain those natural
productions which render our province a classic land in the history of
animals and plants." As for Wallace's Indians, they were less encum-
bered. They carried blow guns and quivers of poisoned arrows, paddle,
knife, and tinderbox.

The farther afield Wallace and Bates traveled, the more intense were
their hardships. They were attacked not only by insects but by pestilence. Both were repeatedly ravaged by ague. Like the Indians, they were
forced to live off the jungle. In his journal Bates complained bitterly
that he was so tired of turtle as a staple that he often preferred to go
hungry. Wallace was more adventuresome; he tried everything, from
alligator meat to red ants, a favorite of many Indians. Above all, Wallace and Bates were isolated physically, intellectually, and spiritually.
Gradually the green paradise turned into the *inferno verdes* of Portuguese explorers.

"Jaguars I knew abounded here, deadly serpents were plentiful, and
at every step I almost expected to feel a cold gliding body under my
feet, or deadly fangs in my leg," Wallace said. ". . . But to turn back

or to stop were alike useless . . . and so [I] pressed on, with a vague confidence that after all nothing disagreeable would happen."

Nobody enters a jungle, alone no less, in search of danger. Danger, or "disagreeableness" to use Wallace's casual word, is unavoidable. Nor does one have to tangle with a big cat or boa constrictor to find "disagreeableness." Ticks, mosquitoes, leeches, and mildew will serve very nicely. Moreover, the deeper the two adventurers traveled into the interior and the longer they stayed, the more frayed their clothes and the more decayed their boots. Day by day, increasingly, they were exposed to the horrors of the rain forest. "The torments I suffered when skinning a bird or drawing a fish, can scarcely be imagined by the unexperienced," Wallace wrote. "My feet were so thickly covered with little blood-spots produced by their bites [the *piúm*] as to be of a dark purplish-red colour, and much swelled and inflamed. My hands suffered similarly, but in a less degree, being more constantly in motion."

Both Wallace and Bates, separately, were also attacked by vampire bats, a chilling experience long before Bram Stoker's popularization of such lycanthropic tales as those of the Carpathian mountains and Count Dracula. The Amazon's bats through evolution had developed the skill to bleed without giving pain, as if their victim were under anesthesia, and they attacked repeatedly during the night until the victim's loss of blood became serious. Wallace usually escaped these attacks because he kept himself wrapped up through the night, but he did report that "I myself have been twice bitten . . . in neither case did I feel anything, but awoke after the operation was completed: in what way they effect it is still quite unknown." In one Indian village, a girl was so badly drained of blood by bats in the course of sleep that "fears were entertained for her life."*

Bates spent at least one night fighting off the vampires. "I was aroused about midnight by the rushing noise made by vast hosts of bats sweeping around the room," he said. "After I had laid about well with a stick for a few minutes they disappeared [but] the next night several got into my hammock; I seized them as they were crawling over me, and dashed them against the wall. The next morning I found a wound, evidently caused by a bat, on my hip. This was rather unpleasant." Un-

---

* Specialists in tropical medicine now believe that the progressive weakness and eventual death brought about by loss of blood from a vampire bat bite is actually a growing paralysis resulting from paralytic rabies. Most vampire bats suffer from rabies and die from the disease. An adult vampire consumes an average of fifteen pints of blood a year.

pleasant, disagreeable—these were the restrained, understated Victorian code words for horror and terror.

In the jungle interior there were no newspapers, no books, no companionship. The evenings especially, Wallace admitted in a rare moment, "were dull and dreary." But there were diversions, and in the jungle fastness he discovered the existence of Indian girls and said, "I might at any moment have had my choice of a half a dozen." On one occasion, the Indian maidens were apparently especially attractive to his restless eyes and, he confessed, "I tried to persuade one of the brown damsels of the village to come and make my fire and cook for me, but," he continued, "strange to say, not one would venture."

Compounding the dangers and inconveniences of the rain forest were the usual follies of travel. Once, Wallace narrowly averted accidentally shooting himself to death. "My gun was lying loaded on the top of the canoe, and wishing to shoot some small birds . . . I drew it towards me by the muzzle . . . The hammer, however, lay in a joint of the boards, and as I drew the gun towards me it was raised up, and let fall on the cap, firing off the gun, the charge carrying off a small piece of the underside of my hand near the wrist, and, passing under my arm within a few inches of my body, luckily missed a number of people who were behind me," Wallace said. "I felt my hand violently blown away, and looking at it, saw a stream of blood, but felt no pain for a few minutes." He wrapped up the hand and proceeded upriver as if the incident had been little more than tripping on a cobbled pavement along London's Tottenham Court Road.

There is in that paragraph a profound insight into Wallace's character, an insight over which a reader is likely to gloss. At the time of the incident he was traveling with a group of Indians. Most writers in Wallace's day, Darwin, for example, and, indeed, most travelers and historians today, would refer to the Indians as "natives," and despite protestations about the dictionary meaning of the term, consciously or subconsciously, would employ the word pejoratively. Wallace, it should be noted, referred to them as *people*. Unlike Darwin, who observed the genus *Homo* as a branch of nature's tree and yet its species and varieties as a Lamarckian ladder, climbing up the scale from black to brown to yellow to white, Wallace considered different races as simply different twigs of the same branch. To him, color was a scientific fact, with no hierarchical significance.

In the wilderness of the Amazon Wallace was called upon to exploit his childhood training as carpenter, watchmaker, and surveyor. "Being now in a part of the country that no European traveler had ever before visited," Wallace said lightly, "I exceedingly regretted my want of instruments to determine latitude, longitude and height above the sea." Yet ingeniously, singlehandedly, with a few primitive instruments, he surveyed, for example, the Uaupés. In 1908, more than half a century later, the Royal Geographical Society mounted a full-scale expedition along the river's banks, employing compass traverse supplemented by astronomical observations. After a year of mapping, Dr. Hamilton Rice, the expedition's leader, concluded with a touch of astonishment that Wallace's "work still holds good."

In London the sales by Stevens, and the work of Wallace and Bates in notes to the *Zoologist*, the *Proceedings of the Entomological Society*, and other journals were beginning to attract modest attention. Among those who expressed interest was Sir William Hooker, the eminent director of Kew Gardens and the father of Joseph Dalton Hooker, Darwin's most intimate friend (and later his father's successor at Kew Gardens). Sir William's passion was the palm tree, and he wanted as many dried examples of fronds as he could lay his hands on. In a letter to Sir William, Wallace reported that he and Bates had acquired new specimens. "We hope you will find the contents of the box," Wallace wrote hesitatingly, "worth £10 and the freight."

Thus, fate played a curious trick on Alfred Russel Wallace. During the railroad boom he labored for Darwin; in the green labyrinth of the Amazon, he labored for the father of Darwin's confidant.

Darwin and Hooker, no less Wallace, would have been confounded to know that their paths converged daily and that in a decade all three would emerge stage center as principal characters in one of the greatest dramas in scientific annals.

Chapter 18

IN THE AMAZON, despite privation and peril, Wallace never lost sight of his objective: "solving the problem of the origin of species." To Wallace the flora and fauna of the region were a constant "thrill," an endless source of "admiration and wonder." In the heart of darkness shafts of light occasionally broke on the species question. Transfixed, Wallace found evolution "ever new and beautiful, strange and mysterious." It was in the Amazon that he and Bates each registered major scientific breakthroughs.

Wallace was the first biologist to recognize that the earth was an intricate latticework of territorial rights and that the minutest insect on one slope of a hill may differ in detail from a related species on the opposite slope. He found this oddity also true of more complex living organisms and for the first time, during his travels in the Amazon, introduced the phrase that he later expanded into his celebrated Sarawak Law —"closely allied species." His discovery of "the limiting range of species" founded a new discipline, zoogeography or biogeography.

At Santarem, on one side of the river, Wallace captured a lovely butterfly which exhibited an exquisite sky-blue shade, while on the opposite bank of the selfsame source he found "a closely allied species" indigo-blue in color and with slightly different markings.

Before embarking for the Amazon, Wallace had confided in Bates his plan "to take some one family to study thoroughly, principally with a view to the theory of the origin of species." In the interior he focused on the beautiful and rare butterfly, *Papilio*. Wallace studied every variation on the *Papilio* theme. The *Papilio* became to him what the *Cirripedia* or barnacle was to Darwin.

"I have often sat down within a few of them [*Papilio*], and have caught with my fingers a single specimen of the rare *Papilio agesilaus* from among a hundred of the commoner species," he wrote in a paper for the journal of London's Entomological Society.

In the monograph he broke new ground and startled his scientific audience. He divided the *Papilio* into thirty-eight different species and classified them, not only on the basis of different characteristics, but geographically. Nobody had ever thought of that before. Thus, Wallace identified some *Papilio* as those that habitually frequented the banks of rivers, some as those found on open ground, and others which rarely abandoned the forest.

Wallace also impressed on naturalists the absolute necessity of identifying the precise location at which a specimen was found. Geography, he was convinced—and rightly so as it was later borne out—provided a clue to the modification of species into subvarieties and varieties and, finally, their emergence into new species. The mechanism, however, still eluded him, just as the problem of divergence continued to elude Darwin. Wallace recognized that climate (frigid, temperate, and torrid zones) and terrain (oceans, deserts, and mountains) were factors in the geographic limitation of species. This was manifest. But he also discovered, magnifying glass in hand, that species in the same region "are broken up into yet smaller groups, and that almost every [biological] district has peculiar animals found nowhere else."

The boundaries among these species, invisible to Wallace's mind but not his eye, were explained by Malthus' theory that the population of a region is ultimately brought into line with its surroundings, either by preventive checks or catastrophic checks, and that—which is at the heart of Malthusian doctrine—while food is produced arithmetically, population grows geometrically. Like Darwin, Wallace had read Malthus, but he did not yet appreciate the relationship between Malthusian doctrine and the origin and divergence of species through "natural selection."

Thus, without realizing it, Wallace saw in the jungle Malthus' theory at work and recorded examples in his *Travels on the Amazon*. "Brilliant scarlet and yellow macaws flew constantly overhead, while screaming parrots and paraquets were passing from tree to tree *in search of food*," he wrote. (Italics added.) The search for food was a clue to the origin of species. In other passages the clue turned up in different form, as in the case of plants struggling for light and life. "At every bend we could see before us a flock of elegant white heron, seated on some dead tree overhanging the water," Wallace wrote as he moved upriver by canoe. Suddenly, the channel of the tributary narrowed and "the scenery was now much more gloomy, the tall trees closed overhead so as to keep out every sunbeam."

As for Bates, his monumental contribution to science was his observation of the role of mimicry. He took meticulous notes in the Amazon on the resemblance in external appearance—shape, color, and other properties—of butterflies of widely different families. "I was quite unable to distinguish them on the wing," he confessed, "and always on capturing what I took for an *Ithomia* and found when in the net to be a *Leptalis* mimicking it, I could scarcely restrain an exclamation of surprise." In the endless struggle for survival, mimicry for some species became—through natural selection—a first line of defense against predators.

Wallace termed Bates' discovery of mimicry a "wonderful" advance for science. Like the geographical limitation on species, Wallace suspected that mimicry among different species was also a clue to the species question.

In this fashion, Wallace and Bates exploited their collections of insects and other species to gather "facts . . . to illustrate the modifications which all species undergo in nature." *How* these modifications occurred was an enigma. But for clues to this the two studied the different color shades and feather and scale patterns of birds and insects, observing the slightest modification in tone or structure which they recognized as varying, Wallace said, "in accordance with the slightest change in the conditions to which species are exposed."

Both Wallace and Bates also realized that on the filament membranes of a butterfly's wing—just as the Assyrians recounted their history on cuneiform tablets—nature told her story of the modification of species, of evolution.

The Amazon convinced both Wallace and Bates that species were in a fluid state, the Mosaic cosmogony notwithstanding, and that the evolution of species was governed by "the laws of nature."

At dusk each day before they split up, and in correspondence afterwards, the two naturalists analyzed their observations, particularly the meaning of the geographical limitation on species and the role of mimicry in a species' struggle for survival. In limitation, Wallace recognized a hint of common ancestry and, by the same token, in mimicry, evidence of divergence and mutability.

Like Darwin, Wallace knew that he held in his hands the pieces of an immense jigsaw puzzle. Each piece interlocked, but putting the pieces together was another matter; the puzzle of nature was still too complicated. Yet Wallace, like Darwin, kept playing with the pieces. It was not until eight years later, in 1858, in the distant Moluccas on the other side of the planet, that Wallace solved the puzzle, fitting into place the last piece—the principle of divergence—*before* Darwin. As the master of Down House glumly put it, "I was forestalled in only one *important* point, which my vanity has always made me regret." (Italics added.)

Thus, in the Amazon Wallace caught his first true glimpse of the process of evolution. As one of his editors commented in 1875 when a new printing of *Narrative on the Amazon* was published, "[Wallace's] assemblage of fact form the broad basis for induction as to the causes and modes of transformation of species."

Behind every observation, Wallace, in the deepest recesses of his mind, also plumbed what he described as "the highest and most interesting problem for the naturalist"—the origin of man.

Already at this early stage Wallace and Darwin approached the question of human origin with completely different outlooks. As James Marchant observed during World War I, in editing Wallace's letters, "At no time did the study of man from the metaphysical or psychological point of view appeal to Darwin as it did to Wallace." The contrast between them is dramatically illuminated by their first, independent encounters with man in his natural state.

"The most unexpected a sensation of surprise and delight was my first meeting and living with man in a state of nature—the absolute uncontaminated savage," Wallace wrote. ". . . And the surprise of it was that I did not expect to be all so surprised." Wallace's denizens of the rain forest were completely naked and carried tools or weapons of their own ingenious manufacture. "But more than all, their whole aspect and manner was *different*," Wallace said. ". . . In every detail they were original and self-sustaining as the wild animals of the forest, absolutely independent of civilization." (Italics added.) In another passage, Wallace observed that in nature man "walked with [a] free step," with an air of independence, unencumbered and uncluttered by the weight of civilization.

As in the passage about the accident with his rifle, Wallace's views of man were uncolored by bias. He saw different races of man as simply *different*. He held back from making value judgments.

Wallace's Amazon journal is dotted with such nonjudgmental observations about the aboriginals of the forest. For example, in the matter of the Indian diet, he observed that Europeans thought nothing of eating *Crustacea*, i.e., lobster, crab, and other such animals, but they were loath to eat locusts, butterflies, and worms. Wallace, however, saw nothing morally wrong about eating insects, simply a *different* cultural outlook, and in a note to the Entomological Society, he observed that the Amazon's Indians feasted on six different orders. The gourmet platter consisted of *Hymenoptera* (bees, wasps, ants), *Neuroptera* (nerve-winged insects such as hellgrammites), *Homoptera* (aphids and scale insects), *Coleoptera*, *Aptera* (wingless insects), and *Annelida* (elongated, segmented insects such as earthworms).

Wallace's note recounted his dining on the great-headed red ant (*Oecodoma cephalotes*) whose acquaintance he had made within a fortnight of his arrival at Pará when they attacked his collecting box en masse. "They are eaten alive," he said casually, "the insects being held by the head as we hold a strawberry by its stalk, and the abdomen being bitten off, the body, wings and legs are thrown down on the floor, where they continue to crawl along apparently unaware of their loss of their posterior extremities." Wallace found that they had a bitter taste, and preferred them slightly roasted or smoked, sprinkled with a little salt.

"The method of capturing and devouring insects is exactly the same as that which everyone has seen adopted by the monkeys at the gardens of the Zoological Society," he added, focusing attention on the origin of man.

In contrast to Wallace's nonjudgmental approach, Darwin's outlook on man in his natural state was colored by prejudice. Like Wallace, Darwin was also surprised by his own reaction and then opted for Lamarck's ladder of evolution. "Nothing," he wrote after his first encounter with primitive man in Tierra del Fuego, at the tip of South America, "is more certain to create astonishment than the first sight in his haunt of a barbarian, of man in his *lowest* and most savage state." (Italics added.) Darwin was chilled. "Could our progenitors have been men like these—men whose very signs and expressions are less intelligible to us than those of the domesticated animals; men who do not possess the instinct of those animals, nor yet appear to boast of human reason, or at least of arts consequent on that reason?"

"I do not believe it is possible to describe or paint the differences between savage and civilized man," Darwin added. "It is the difference between a wild and tame animal."

The contrast between the Wallace and Darwin outlooks is evident. Wallace considered forest man as "different"; Darwin, on the "lowest" rung of the evolutionary ladder. And since Darwinism, not Wallaceism, came to dominate the thinking of European man after the Linnean Society meeting of 1858, a subtle form of scientific racism insinuated itself into Western thinking. For while "Darwinism" rocked the pulpits of Victorian England, it also provided Western imperialism and colonialism with a scientific veneer, a biological rationale, the mission to "civilize" races—"natives"—on low rungs of the evolutionary ladder. A typical example of post-Darwinian thinking is found in the work of an early Darwinian, H. C. Chapman. Like many Darwinians, Professor Chapman viewed man's evolution as starting with the lower monkeys and ascending from them, through the higher apes and the lower races of mankind, to the higher forms. In a style of writing and thinking reminiscent of Chambers' *Vestiges*, Chapman concluded that "the skulls of the chimpanzee, Idiot, Negro and Kalmuck [are] a series of ascending forms."

The Amazon was rich in different species of monkey and to Wallace the "greatest treat was making my first acquaintance with the monkeys." One morning, as he walked alone in the forest, he heard a rustling of leaves and branches "as if a *man* were walking quickly among them, and [I] expected every minute to see some Indian hunter make his appearance, when all at once the sounds appeared to be in the branches above, and turning up my eyes there, I saw a large monkey looking down at me, and seeming as much astonished as I was myself." (Italics added.)

Among the Indians, monkey was a favorite food and on one occasion Wallace had monkey fried for breakfast. He was with a hunting party when the monkey was brought down. "The poor little animal was not quite dead, and its cries, its innocent-looking countenance, and delicate little hands were quite childlike," he observed. Apparently Wallace did not entertain thoughts of cannibalism when the monkey was cut up and fried for breakfast the following morning. "There was about as much of it as a fowl, and the meat somewhat resembled rabbit, without any very peculiar or unpleasant flavour," he said.*

For someone struggling with the species question, there is scant wonder that in the Amazon Wallace's thoughts continually turned on the descent of man. How could it be otherwise in a land of monkeys? "During my residence there I had many opportunities of becoming acquainted with their habits and distribution," he said. Among the twenty-one species he observed, a third of them with prehensile tails, his favorite was the popular big-bellied monkey *Logaothriz humboldti*, which the Brazilians called *barraidugo*. This species had a pleasant disposition, thick woolly fur, a long prehensile tail, and a grave countenance "more resembling the *human* face than [that] of any other monkey," Wallace said. (Italics added.) He acquired three of them as pets and they sailed with him for England on his return voyage.

During this period, in 1852, Wallace's first note appeared in the *Proceedings of the Zoological Society*. It combined his two great interests, the geographic limitation of species and the origin of man. "On the accurate determination of an animal's range many interesting questions depend," Wallace wrote. "Are the very *closely allied species* ever separated by a wide interval of country? What physical features determine the boundaries of species and of genera? Do the isothermal lines [geographical distribution of temperature] ever accurately bound the range of species, or are they altogether independent of them? What are the circumstances which render certain rivers and certain mountain ranges the limits of numerous species, while others are not?" (Italics added.)

Questions, questions, questions—but no answers. Significantly, his paper was followed in that same issue of *Proceedings* by a note from Thomas Huxley on the anatomy of the zebra. Clearly, the scientific aristocracy had the opportunity to encounter the disturbing questions raised by Wallace, and perhaps wonder who Alfred Russel Wallace, Esq., might be.

---

* In 1978 my brother-in-law, Ronald de Keyzer, a sea captain and former assistant harbormaster of Paramaribo, Surinam's main port, visited Connecticut for the first time and remarked, with a laugh, that "Indians still prefer monkey to a T-bone steak." He added: "I used to shoot them for the Indians in the interior and I'd eat them, too, until one day the Indians prepared a platter of monkey meat and on the top placed the cooked head of the animal. I've never eaten monkey again."

Chapter 19

ALTHOUGH Wallace and Bates separated ways and scoured the Amazon independently for "facts" upon which to develop laws of evolution, they occasionally touched base with each other in the riverine towns along the Amazon and its tributaries. Despite the incredible length and breadth of the basin, when it came to rumor, gossip, information, and misinformation, the region was like the globe itself, a very small place. With butterfly nets in hand, Wallace and Bates blended into the local setting as "the odd couple." Everywhere, Bates wrote in his journal, people concluded that he and Wallace were collecting birds and butterflies for "patterns for light-coloured calico prints." The textile and fashion industries were as notoriously competitive then as now and, obviously, this is why the pair kept secret the nature of their mission to the Amazon.

Wallace and Bates usually encountered each other at Barra, especially during the "uninviting weather," as Wallace characterized the rainy season, when violent sheets of water fell daily.

From Barra, Wallace shipped off new specimens to London and caught up on letters from Stevens and from home. His mother had moved in with Fanny, who had returned to England on the eve of his journey to South America and had married Thomas Sims, the eldest son of the Sims with whom Wallace and his late brother, William, lodged at Neath during a surveying job. Brother John, the carpenter, who had introduced the young Wallace to the Utopian socialism of Robert Owen, had quit England and set off for California and the

Gold Rush. Herbert, the trunk maker and baby of the family, had floundered, unsuited for trade.

"Frankly," Wallace admitted, "I knew very little of him [Herbert]." The boy had been seven-and-a-half when Wallace left home at the age of fourteen to find work, and Herbert was only eighteen-and-a-half when Wallace left for the Amazon. But Wallace recalled the aid John and William had given him, and he felt a special responsibility toward his youngest brother. Specimen collecting in the Amazon seemed to be a profitable venture—as observed earlier, first impressions may appear misleading—and Wallace proposed to Herbert that he come out and join him "to see if he has sufficient taste for natural history to become a good collector."

Apparently naturalists, or biologists, to use the term now applied to this species of scientist, are born, not made. Herbert took up his brother's challenge, but for him natural history was tasteless. He arrived at Pará in 1850 and early the following year, after a brief stint upriver, was back in Pará eager to grab the first ship for England. "It was now clear that my brother was not fitted to become a good natural history collector," Wallace concluded reluctantly; he had "little interest in birds or insects."

Wallace, meanwhile, pressed ahead alone, like Bates. The geographic limitations on the evolution of species tantalized him and filled his mind. What was the governing law? He constantly addressed himself to that question. "There must be some boundary which determines the range of each species," he wrote, "some external peculiarity to mark the lines which each one does not pass."

Adventures went hand-in-hand with scientific inquiry. Wallace's notes, published and unpublished, read like chapters from Edgar Rice Burroughs. One evening, toward dusk, Wallace took a gun and strolled beyond his Indian camp. "I heard the scampering of small animals," he recorded, "and the whizzing flight of ground birds, clearing the path for their dreaded enemy."

Twenty yards ahead of him appeared "a large jet-black animal . . . which took me so much by surprise that I did not at first imagine what it was," he said.

It was a jaguar, the lord of the Amazon.

Involuntarily, Wallace raised the shotgun to his shoulder and then remembered that both barrels were loaded with such small shot "that to fire would exasperate without killing." Wallace froze on position. The big cat turned his head, gazed on Wallace with a yawn, and slipped off into the jungle.

"This encounter pleased me much," Wallace said. "I was too much surprised, and occupied too much with admiration, to feel fear. . . . I was, however, by no means desirous of a second meeting, and, as it was near sunset, thought it most prudent to turn back towards the village . . . [and] my Indians."

But toward the middle of 1851, three years after he and Bates, in great enthusiasm, landed at Pará, Wallace's jungle idyll was beginning to collapse around him. Some 1,500 miles from the mouth of the Amazon Wallace had his first bout with "fever" or ague. From the human standpoint, the true lord of the jungle was not the jaguar but the mosquito.

Malaria, as usual, won the first round, leaving Wallace debilitated. "I began taking doses of quinine, drinking plentifully cream-of-tartar water," he said, "[but] at times I could hardly muster resolution to move myself to prepare them."

Isolation—the utter loneliness of having no one to talk to—also weakened his resolve and enthusiasm. "One feels the want of a friend or attendant," he said.

To his dismay, he discovered that he could not shake the invisible malarial parasite in his blood system. Shortly after the first attack, he said, "I was again attacked with fever." Gradually, the disease took its toll. The attacks occurred in sequences of two days. "I took quinine for some time without any apparent effect," Wallace said, "till, after nearly a fortnight, the fits and weakness ceased, and I only suffered from extreme emaciation and weakness."

After another brief respite at Barra, the pernicious assaults were renewed. They became almost a daily affair, lasting from noon to night. Wallace was also attacked by another silent killer, dysentery, and was so weakened that "I could with difficulty stand alone or walk with a stick down to the river-side."

Yet he pressed forward into the unmapped rain forest in quest of "facts," although admitting in an aside that "I was so weak that I had great difficulty getting in and out of the canoe." Spruce, the English botanist who had befriended Wallace and Bates and was destined later to have a profound influence on Wallace's personal life, entered this notation in 1852 in his diary: "I had sad news two days ago from my friend Wallace. . . . He writes me by another hand that he is almost at the point of death from a malignant fever, which has reduced him to such a state of weakness that he cannot rise from his hammock or even feed himself. The person who brought me the letter told me that he had taken no nourishment for some days except the juice of oranges and cashews."

Even a Wallace, despite persistence and perseverance, was compelled to adjust to realities. He could not go on. As Gregory Sohns has expressed it in a different context, "the mind that craves knowledge and responds to the beauty of the world can be racked with anxiety and driven to despair." With his health declining rapidly and his anxiety rising as quickly, Wallace renounced his five-year-plan and in September 1852 painfully recognized that another year in the Amazon would probably be his last—above ground. He estimated that it would take almost a year to work his way downstream and back to Pará. "I determined to return to England a year before the time I had fixed upon," he said.

Once the decision was made, Wallace was delirious. "What a paradise did that distant land seem to me!" Wallace exclaimed as his mind was flooded with thoughts of England and the cricket on the hearth. "How I thought of the many pleasures, so long absent—the green fields, the pleasant woods, the flowery paths, the neat gardens,— all so unknown here!"

Immediately he began to retrace his steps down the Rio Negro to the Amazon and in mid-September arrived at Barra, where a batch of letters awaited him, some of them three months old. One letter shut out the sun and encapsulated him in the gloom of the jungle. The British vice consul at Pará wrote that before Herbert could book passage for England, he had come down with "black vomit," and that there "[is] little hope of his recovery." Another letter, dispatched several days after the first, by a different correspondent, reported that a large vessel, heavily laden with valuable cargo, had foundered in a storm at the entrance to the Amazon. But there was no mention of Herbert's fate.

"From no one could I obtain a word of information about my brother, and so remained in a state of greatest suspense," Wallace said. "Had he recovered, he would himself, of course, have written, but on the other hand, it was strange that none of the English residents in Pará had sent me a line to inform me of his death, had it occurred."

Unknown to Wallace, Bates had returned to Pará with a large collection of specimens, and, in a state of depression, induced by the same fever and isolation upriver, had also decided to yield up the Amazon and return to England. Bates reached Pará in time to nurse Herbert as the virus destroyed his liver cells and distributed the bile pigment throughout his body, turning his skin and eyes yellow. Bates remained at Herbert's side for four days until, at the age of twenty-two, the youngest Wallace died in his arms. Bates himself then came down with yellow fever and was in no position to write Wallace. For that matter, yellow fever swept the town and nobody had the time, strength, or thought to write Wallace as Pará struggled for survival.

There was a third reason, in addition to fevers and isolation, that influenced Bates' decision to abandon the Amazon. An entry in his journal, dated March 30, 1851, recites the melancholy situation down to the last penny.

"I find I have taken 7,553 specimens of insects, which at 4d [$.20] each will bring £125 17s 18d and my expenses have been . . . 600 milreis, or £67 10s," he wrote. "Stevens's commission is 20 per cent, and commission for remitting money, with freight of boxes, etc., is about 5 per cent, thus leaving the produce of my collection, £94 9s."

In sum, after a year and eight months in the interior, Bates' net profit was £26 19s ($125)!

But at Pará, where he survived the attack of yellow fever and thereby developed a lifelong immunity, Bates' batteries were re-charged. Instead of fleeing the jungle, he rushed back into it—for another seven years. A letter from Stevens produced the astonishing turnabout. It contained, a jubilant Bates shouted, "better news than ever."

Stevens had succeeded in driving up the market for specimens, many of them unique in Europe. Bates' Barra collection, for example, which he thought would bring £40 ($200) had fetched £70 ($350), the collection he amassed at Ega, his upriver base of operations after parting with Wallace, which Bates calculated at £20, brought £34 18s, and so on. An overjoyed Bates promptly reinvested his "fortune" in another expedition into the interior to study mimicry and its rela-tionship to the origin of species.

But there was, perhaps, more than money involved. A new *Callithea* which he had captured at Ega, Stevens reported, had been "named *C. Batesii*!" A species had been named after him and like Darwin, who had written that no poet ever felt more delighted at seeing his poem published than he had upon first seeing, in *Illustrations of British Insects*, "the magic words, 'captured by C. Darwin, Esq.,' " Bates was in ecstasy. He had achieved a place in the sun, albeit a modest place, yet a place, the torque that turns *all* pathfinders, whether in jungle or on ice floe, whether peering through microscope or telescope, whether combing through historical papers or clearing an archaeological dig.

Ego? Ambition? The pursuit of immortality? An irrepressible thirst for the meaning of meaning? A combination of these? Whatever it was, this was the motivating force that drove Bates back into the horrors of the rain forest. He left in the middle of June.

Two weeks later, on July 2, 1852, a gaunt, bearded, haggard, exhausted, and almost unrecognizable six-foot-two-inch figure emerged from the interior and landed at Pará after a perilous voyage down the Amazon during which, Wallace said, "I had fits of ague, and was still very weak and quite unable to make any exertion." Ironically, Wallace and Bates had passed each other, within hailing distance, during the night. The next time they met would be in London a decade later.

Wallace found Pará a disaster area. "The yellow fever, which the year before had cut off thousands of the inhabitants," he recorded, "still attacked new-comers, and scarcely a ship was in port but had a considerable portion of her crew in the hospital."

At Pará Wallace learned of Herbert's death, and of Bates' struggle to save the boy's life. The British consulate kept an unsealed, unmailed letter which the lad had written his mother. "When I arrive in England I have my plans," Herbert wrote, "which I can better tell than write."

More than ever beset by melancholy, Wallace wanted out. He wanted to be done with the Amazon, with its pestilence, vermin, and interminable terrors. For the first time in years, he was in luck. *Helen*, a 235-ton, two-masted vessel, square rigged on both masts and with a boom mainsail, was loading and planned to sail for England in a matter of days. Wallace promptly booked passage and made arrangements with Captain John Turner, the brig's master and half-owner, to store aboard his immense collections of insects, birds, and reptiles as well as a live deck cargo consisting of numerous parrots and parakeets, a forest wild-dog, and several uncommon species of monkey, including three *Logothrix*, whose "countenances more resemble the human face than those of any other monkey."

When Wallace met him, Turner was in the midst of storing cargo, about 120 tons of baled rubber, and several tons of cocoa and other commodities, including balsam. The latter was packed in small kegs and embedded in damp sand as a precautionary measure; balsam, like damp cotton, is liable to burst into fire as a result of spontaneous combustion induced by the motion of a vessel at sea.

On July 12, as Captain Turner made ready to weigh anchor, another boat-load of balsam kegs was hoisted aboard. Since there was no sand handy in which to pack them, they were buried in rice-chaff to prevent them from knocking around. This shipment was stored under the cabin floor where Wallace's crates were stowed, including his collections of *Lepidoptera* and *Coleoptera*—the finest specimens ever pinned in the New World—boxes of bird, reptile, and other skins, and crates of geological rock specimens from the Uaupés and other unexplored tributaries of the Amazon.

As *Helen* took the outgoing tide downstream and into the broad Atlantic, Wallace was engulfed by a sense of relief. He had gotten out of the Amazon alive, and he looked forward to the voyage. The sea air would restore his health and the cruise would give him breathing space to go over his notebooks and take a new look at the "facts" he had collected—"facts" which, he was confident, held the secrets of the origin and diversification of species.

"[I] bade *adieu*," Wallace said in a relaxed mood, "to the . . . waving palm trees of Pará."

Chapter 20

AFTER A WEEK AT SEA, Wallace fell victim to a renewed attack of malaria and, he said, "at first thought I had got yellow fever after all." He remained confined to his small, comfortable cabin in "rather weak" condition.

Helen encountered light air but calm seas and made relatively good time. On August 6 Captain Turner shot the rising sun, as sailors term a sextant bearing, and took a fix. The vessel was at latitude 30° 30′ north, longitude 52° west, well into the North Atlantic, north of the Tropic of Cancer and west of the Bermudas. To a landsman, the ship might as well have been in the middle of nowhere with a thousand miles or more of sea in every direction.

At nine in the morning the captain knocked politely on Wallace's cabin door and imperturbably informed his only passenger, as if he were extending an invitation to tea, "I'm afraid the ship's on fire."

On deck Wallace saw a wisp of smoke rising from the f'oc'sle. The smoke thickened appreciably as he watched but there appeared to be more smoke than fire. The fore hatch was opened to get at the blaze but no fire was found. Thereupon Captain Turner calmly walked aft and lifted the aft hatch in search of the fire's origin. The captain had apparently never heard of Lavoisier and what sailors now call the "fire triangle." A fire requires three elements: combustible material, a spark, and oxygen. Inadvertently, the captain had created a circulating passage of air through the ship's bilges. With the vessel underway, air that had been scooped up through the forward hatch vented aft, producing the effect of a whirring fan. That was all the balsam kegs required to complete the triangle.

In short order, the kegs bubbled like boiling cauldrons. Smoke enveloped the ship and the heat became unbearable. In thirty minutes, Wallace recalled, "fire burst through the cabin floor . . . and up through the skylight."

While some crew members poured buckets of water into the holds, others manned the bilge pumps. The situation, however, was rapidly getting out of hand.

Captain Turner did not hesitate. He ordered the long boat, which was lashed on deck, launched, and the captain's gig, suspended from transom davits, lowered. The two planked wooden boats had not seen service in a long spell and the equatorial sun had opened up their caulked seams. "Very leaky," Wallace commented as both boats were quickly half-filled with water and had to be constantly bailed with buckets and mugs to keep afloat. The cook was sent to the galley forthwith for corks to plug up the seams.

Meanwhile, the crew threw two casks of biscuit and a cask of water, a barrel of raw pork, a few tins of preserved meats and vegetables, and some wine (!) into the boats. The captain grabbed his chronometer, sextant, charts, and a compass. Wallace raced to his cabin and snatched up a "small box . . . which [was] luckily at hand." The box contained a set of pencil drawings of different palm species, together with notes on their distribution and characteristics; a collection of sketches, drawn to scale, of fishes, with notes on their color, dentition, and scale structure;* and a Portuguese folio notebook containing his Rio Negro diary and notes made while mapping both the Rio Negro and Uaupés. Everything else, the labor of four years, was smoldering and burning in the hold beneath the cabin. Wallace also grabbed his watch and a purse containing a few sovereigns, the only money he possessed.

At noon all hands were ordered into the boats. Wallace was directed into the captain's gig and in the grand tradition of the sea—on occasion not so grand, depending on the company flag or the ship's nationality—Captain Turner was the last person to abandon ship.

* The notes on fishes, for example, consisted of four volumes of drawings, 201 pages in all, describing 215 different species of fish. Each volume was entitled, *Notes on Fishes of Rio Negro*. The drawings and notes were in pencil; many pages were water-damaged and the notes too faint to be read. A typical entry reads: "Curious position of the vent is in the fish under the throat." These and other Wallace papers are now in the British Museum (Natural History).

"I had to let myself down into the boat by a rope, and being rather weak, it slipped through my hands and took the skin off all my fingers," Wallace recounted later in a letter to his friend, Richard Spruce, the English botanist whom he had met in the Amazon and who was still at Pará. "Finding the boat still half full of water I set to bailing, which made my hands smart very painfully."

Many of the parrots, monkeys, and other animals aboard were already burned or suffocated, but several had retreated to the bowsprit out of reach of the rapidly encroaching flames. "The animals appeared to wonder what was going on," Wallace said, touched by the poignant scene, "and quite unconscious of the fate that awaited them."

The captain and crew made a valiant effort to get some of the animals into the boats, and failed. As the flames caught the base of the bowsprit, some of the creatures panicked and jumped into the fire. One parrot escaped. "He was sitting on a rope hanging from the bowsprit," Wallace said, "and . . . [fell] into the water, where, after floating a little way we picked him up."

On the shimmering sea, the gig and long boat lay near the burning ship and the sailors looked on in horror as the flames leapt up the shrouds and the sails caught fire. The scene awed Wallace. "A most magnificent conflagration," he said, as if he had been watching a Horatio Hornblower motion picture.

But the impression of magnificence dissolved as quickly as the vessel vanished from the scene. All Wallace could see was the distant horizon making a perfect circle around the gig (or officer's long boat as distinguished from the crew's) and the crew's long boat.

For the next three days, until the planks swelled tight, the crew and their passenger bailed in shifts around the clock to stay afloat. Captain Turner estimated their position as seven hundred miles east of the Bermudas. Since *Helen* had been following the familiar track of West Indian vessels, captain and crew were optimistic about being picked up shortly.

"I cannot attempt to describe my feelings and thoughts during these events," Wallace wrote Spruce. "I was surprised to find myself very cool and collected."

And this was the Wallace who, as a lad, was frightened crossing the River Severn in a ferry.

The first three days passed uneventfully, then another three. And still another three. With each passing day a measure of optimism was displaced by a measure of pessimism.

On August 13, after a week in the open boat, Wallace reported "my hands and face were much blistered by the sun and exceedingly sore and painful." It was only then that the full impact of the catastrophe, like a nightmare in slow motion, unwound in his own mind. "I began to think that almost all the reward of my four years of privation and danger was lost," he said.

Wallace's first thoughts, oddly enough, were about his financial straits. For Alfred Russel Wallace, life was an endless struggle for economic survival. "What I had hitherto sent home had little more than paid my expenses," he said, as had Bates before him, "and what I had with me in the *Helen* I estimated would have realized about £500."

Exhibiting mild hysteria, he laughed at himself and said, "I remember thinking it almost foolish to save my watch and the little money I had at hand."

The true dimensions of the tragedy knocked him down like a squall. *All* his new and strange species, literally hundreds of them, were irretrievably lost. So were his sketches, drawings, daily journal, and three massive notebooks, the whole of which, he realized, "unlike any pecuniary loss, can never be replaced."

In a passage in *A Narrative of Travels on the Amazon and the Rio Negro*, written the following year, the emotional dam burst:

> With what pleasure had I looked upon every rare and curious insect I had added to my collection! How many times, when almost overcome by ague, had I crawled into the forest and been rewarded by some unknown and beautiful species! How many places, which no European foot but my own had trodden, would have been recalled to my memory by the rare birds and insects they had furnished to my collection! How many weary days and weeks had I passed, upheld only by the fond hope of bringing home many new and beautiful forms from those wild regions . . . ! And now everything was gone, and I had not one specimen to illustrate the wild scenes I had beheld!

But Wallace recognized that regrets were useless and sought to drive these maddening thoughts from his mind. Philosophically, he resigned himself to bear his fate with patience and equanimity, and "to occupy myself with the state of things which actually existed."

In the gig, however, the state of things grew more precarious daily. As the first week blended into the second, the captain and crew almost despaired of seeing another vessel, "our circle of vision being so limited," Wallace said. Moreover, it was now mid-August and, they knew, the start of the hurricane season.

On August 17, after ten days and nights in the open boats under a merciless sun and sea, Captain Turner saw the long boat tack. "She must see a sail," he exclaimed.

"Looking round," Wallace said, "we saw a vessel coming nearly towards us, and only about five miles distant."

By eight that evening, "much rejoiced," as Wallace described the setting, they were safely aboard a West Indian man bound for London, the *Jordeson*, an old, lumbering brig that should have been beached years earlier. They had been picked up two hundred miles east of the Bermudas and it was doubtful that they would have ever made a landfall.

The remainder of the voyage to England, however, was anything but a tea party. In that era it was common to send rotting, unseaworthy merchantmen to sea in the expectation that they would founder. This was especially true of sailing vessels as the Age of Steam gradually replaced the Great Age of Sail. In this manner, the ship owners at least collected insurance. The *Jordeson* belonged to this class of ship. She was short on provisions (why waste good money, the investors thought, if she may go under) and with her crew now doubled, everyone was placed on strict allowance of bread, meat, and water. The sea biscuits were dry and coarse, and the meat wormy, "of the very worst quality I had ever eaten or even imagined to exist," Wallace said. He wrote Spruce later that aboard the *Jordeson* the food "beats even Rio Negro fare!"

The *Jordeson* averaged two or three knots, about the speed of Nelson's ships of the line at Trafalgar, and she was probably built during the Napoleonic wars.

With the innocence of the landlubber, Wallace once noted that he had never been at sea during a gale and that "I had some desire to witness the phenomenon." Before he got to England, he went through three whole gales, with winds howling from forty-eight to sixty-three knots (fifty-five to seventy-three miles an hour), and had lost all his desire. Each time the ocean turned into a mass of boiling foam, the crest of waves carried spindrift over the decks, the ship rolled and hobbyhorsed, strained and creaked, her bowsprit plunging under the water. Fires were banked in the ship's stoves as the sea broke continually over the galley, and bad leaks developed forward, forcing the crew to abandon their bunks and man the bilge pumps day and night.

Some half century later, in his autobiography, Wallace admitted that in both his *Narrative* and his letter to Spruce "some of the most alarming incidents to a landsman are not mentioned." Wallace was in a state of terror, and one example will suffice here.

Following their rescue at sea, the captain of the *Jordeson* had turned over the only berths in his cabin to Captain Turner and Wallace while he himself slept on a sofa in fine weather and on a mattress on the cabin floor during storms. On the worst night of one storm, Wallace said, "I saw him, to my surprise, bring down an axe and lay it beside him." Wallace was puzzled and inquired about the ax. "To cut away the masts in case we capsize," the master patiently explained to the astounded landlubber.

That night a great sea smashed the cabin skylight and water poured into the cabin, captain and mattress awash, sloshing from side to side with the ship's roll. "Now, I thought, our time has come," a chilled Wallace recalled, "and I expected to see the captain rush up on deck with his axe. But he only swore a good deal, sought out a dry coat and blanket, and then lay down on the sofa as if nothing happened."

On September 29, seventy days after Wallace left Pará—his outbound trip had taken only twenty-nine—the *Jordeson* lumbered into the English Channel. Home safe, at last. But she immediately encountered another gale and again narrowly escaped foundering. The storm was the worst in years and buffetted the Irish, Welsh, and English coasts. The London *Times* described the winds as "a perfect hurricane" and the seas as "fearful." The American ship *Mobile*, which had put to sea for New Orleans the day before, foundered, and forty passengers and thirty crewmen were lost. Thirty fishing smacks were also caught in the sudden storm and four went to the bottom. Mr. Brockman, second mate of Her Majesty's paddle-wheel steamer *Wildfire*, which safely made port, reported the vessel had "encountered very boisterous weather."

Wallace must have wondered what tricks the fates were playing on him.

On October 1, *Jordeson* dropped the hook off Deal. Wallace wrote in his newly kept log: "Oh glorious . . . day!"

And glorious it was as Wallace and the two captains bounded ashore and dined at the nearest inn. "Oh, beef-steaks and Damson tart," Wallace exclaimed again, "a paradise for hungry sinners."

During the voyage Wallace had vowed to himself "fifty times [that] if I once reach England, never to trust myself more on the ocean."

But as the chalk cliffs of Dover hove into view, his resolution faded. In the Amazon, Wallace had failed to solve "the problem of the origin of species." The species question now possessed him as never before. The clues to the mystery rattled around in his head like bits of glass in a kaleidoscope. Out there, somewhere, some place unspoiled and untrod by "civilized" man, where nature was still in her true state, lay the missing pieces.

On October 5, 1852, Wallace arrived in London and in the lengthy account of the voyage that he mailed to Spruce that week, confessed, "I am already only doubtful whether the Andes or the Philippines are to be the scene of my next wanderings."

Chapter 21

BEEFSTEAK and Damson tart notwithstanding, Wallace was in sorry condition. His ankles were so swollen that he walked with difficulty. The only clothes he possessed were on his back, and they were worn thin. The elongated, emaciated, bespectacled, and bearded figure gave the appearance of a scarecrow.

Stevens proved a friend as well as agent and, Wallace recalled with warmth, "[he] took me first to the nearest ready-made clothes shop, where I got a warm suit, then to his own tailor, where I was measured for what clothes I required and afterwards to a haberdasher's to get a small stock of other necessaries." Since Wallace knew no one in London, Stevens' mother put him up as a houseguest until he got his bearings.

With foresight, Stevens had insured Wallace's collection on his departure from Pará and Wallace now collected "about £200" for his losses. After four harrowing years in the jungle, he was twice as rich as when he started out, a misleading statistic if there ever was one.

Sovereigns and guineas jingled in his pockets, and Wallace prided himself as a man of means. He was determined "to make up for lost time," to enjoy the comforts of London for six months before setting out again in quest of the origin of species. But the rest and rehabilitation program stretched into a year and a half.

As he wished to be with his mother during his home leave (he had written to her regularly from the Amazon as circumstances permitted), Wallace rented a house in Upper Albany Street "so that we might live together," the "we" including Fanny and her husband Thomas Sims, with whom Wallace hit it off well since Wallace took a keen interest in the "rapidly advancing art of photography." The house was situated close to the Zoological Society, within easy access of Stevens' Bloomsbury office and close by the British Museum.

The family settled in during Christmas week and enjoyed a gala Yuletide dinner, featuring roast beef, Yorkshire pudding, and the gravy boat awash. The happy setting recalled to Wallace Christmases past when his father was alive.

With the scanty material that survived the sinking of the *Helen*, Wallace embarked on several ambitious projects, putting quill to ink pot "to write an account of my travels, as well as a few scientific papers." Much of the material, of course, was culled from memory. Under the circumstances, the results were spectacular. He completed two books by October 1853—within ten months of his return. One volume planted his foot in the literary world and the other in the scientific community.

The first was *Narrative on the Amazon*, which was brought out by Reeve and Company. The print run was a modest 750 copies and when Wallace returned from the Malay archipelago in 1862 he was disappointed to learn that only five hundred copies had been sold and that "there were consequently no profits to divide." Yet the book acquired increasing popularity over the years. Macmillan obtained the rights to the unsold copies and reissued them with a new title page in 1870; Ward, Lock & Company published a second London edition in 1889, and in New York, Harper's followed suit with the first American edition. In 1939, a São Paulo house brought out a Brazilian edition, *Viagens pelo Amazonas e rio Negro*; thirty years later two American reprint publishers, Haskell House and Greenwood Press, reissued the second edition; and in 1972 Dover brought out an American paperback.

Despite its poor sales, Wallace's editor considered the book "well received," and its in-print longevity attests to its classic character. Some of the critics, however, were unhappy with it. "I was a *little* disappointed in Wallace's book," Darwin wrote a correspondent. "Hardly facts enough." Considering that most of the "facts" went to the bottom of the Atlantic, as Wallace himself recounted in the volume, the judgment was harsh and unjust.

Wallace's second book was based on the tin he rescued containing drawings and notes on palm trees. No publisher, however, would risk capital on it and, like his father before him, Wallace plunged into publishing at his own expense. *Palm Trees of the Amazon* ran 137 pages and included forty-eight plates. To Wallace, the graceful palms were "the most striking characteristic" of tropical plant life. They had replaced orchids.

The volume on palms atttracted the attention of Kew Gardens and Hooker, especially since it contained drawings and technical descriptions of several new palm species. It is interesting to speculate whether Hooker drew the book to Darwin's attention, as he did with almost everything else of scientific interest. Since Darwin was familiar with Wallace's *Narrative*, he probably read *Palms*.

In *Palms*, Wallace tantalized the botanical community. "I was often unable to see any difference between trees which the Indians assured me were quite distinct, and had widely different properties and uses," he wrote. "More close examination, however, convinced me that external characters did exist by which every species could be separated from those *most nearly allied* to it, and I was soon pleased to find that I could distinguish one palm from another, though barely visible above the surrounding forest. . . ." (Italics added.) This passage contains the haunting refrain of "closely allied species" which was later to be the centerpiece of Wallace's Sarawak Law.

The Amazon collections Stevens sold had won Wallace modest recognition in London's small scientific circle. The Zoological Society gave him a pass to their gardens and he was a welcome visitor at their meetings and those of the Entomological Society. He lectured at the Royal Geographical Society about his explorations of the Upper Amazon and made a distinctly favorable impression. He also spent a good deal of time examining insect and bird collections in the British Museum and was also a regular visitor to Kew Gardens and to the Linnean Society. But even in his wildest moment, Wallace never remotely suspected that one day his name and that of Darwin would be inextricably linked for all time as the result of a Linnean Society meeting.

One evening Wallace attended a lecture by Thomas Huxley at the Zoological Society—the first time he had laid eyes on this engaging, articulate giant who later served as the cowcatcher of the "Darwinian" revolution. Wallace was too timid to introduce himself.

Huxley spoke on parasites, blithely thrusting his prepared remarks aside and plunging into the subject in an intense, freewheeling manner. "I was particularly struck with his wonderful power of making a difficult and rather complex subject perfectly intelligible and ex-

tremely interesting to persons who, like myself, were absolutely
ignorant of the whole group," Wallace said later. ". . . I was amazed,
too, at his complete mastery of the subject, and his great amount of
technical knowledge of a kind to which I have never given any
attention, the structure and development of the lower [i.e., less com-
plex] forms of animal life."

Huxley was then twenty-eight, two years Wallace's junior, but
Wallace felt that a person of his intellectual vigor and knowledge must
be quite older. "Many years afterwards," said Wallace, who enjoyed
telling jokes on himself, "I was surprised to find that he was really
younger."

It was during this interregnum in England—between two great
voyages of exploration abroad—that Wallace was introduced to Darwin
in the Insect Room of the British Museum. "I saw him once for a few
minutes in the British Museum before I sailed," Wallace recounted in
1887 in a letter to a correspondent. Darwin never recalled the meeting, although this is not to fault him. Wallace was still relatively
unknown.

Wallace found himself being drawn into London's scientific aristocracy because of his *Palms* and *Amazon* and his attendance at scientific
meetings. But he felt uncomfortable. He had the queasy feeling that
he did not belong. His extreme temerity, excessive shyness, and in-
ordinate modesty, his "lack of conversational powers," as he expressed it
(Wallace was miserable at making small talk), inhibited his entry into
Victorian society. And there was another consideration. Science was
still the pursuit of the independently wealthy—the Darwins, Lyells, and
Hookers. As the late Loren Eiseley wrote in *Scientific American* some
twenty years ago, "the Wallaces were struggling exceptions." Huxley
was inimitably more brusque. "Science in England does everything,"
Huxley said, "—except pay."

But Lancelot Hogben, the former senior lecturer at Trinity College,
Cambridge, who later acquired an international reputation as a science
historian, considered Wallace's lack of money and scholarly credentials
a boon. "[His] mentality was never cramped by an academic training," Hogben wrote in 1918. For that matter, despite his academic
background, Darwin's mind also was never cramped. Neither Wallace
nor Darwin permitted themselves to become captives of a given
discipline, its prejudices, fashions, and jargon.

Yet despite his doubts, and aside from a short holiday in Switzerland with a childhood chum, George Silk, "where I enjoyed my first visit to snowy mountains and glaciers," Wallace was a fixture in London and in constant attendance at meetings of learned societies. In effect, he was taking informal courses in botany, entomology, zoology, geology, and other disciplines. And while he crammed, Wallace never forgot about the species question, and the next best place to attack the problem.

His attendance at these sessions revealed enormous, inexplicable gaps in the natural history of the Malay archipelago. The first naturalist to study the region, the Frenchman Sonnerat, did so only as late as 1776, the year of the American Revolution, and a scant fifty years before Wallace's birth.

During the Napoleonic wars, Sir Thomas Stamford Raffles, the polymath statesman, explorer, administrator, naturalist, linguist, founder of Singapore, and Lieutenant Governor-General of Java, picked up Sonnerat's thread. Raffles concentrated on Java. He wrote a two-volume history of the island and its peoples, the Bantamese, Sundanese, and Javanese; compiled the first Malay-Javanese-English dictionaries; established at Bogor, Java, the world's first tropical botanical garden, and buried his wife there, amidst majestic palms and jungle cover. But, as in the case of Wallace's tragedy at sea, most of Raffles' collection of flora and fauna went to the bottom when the vessel carrying it to England foundered off the west coast of Sumatra.

The Malay world thus remained largely an empty page. "To the ordinary Englishman," Wallace realized, "this is perhaps the least known part of the globe."

After returning to England, in his first letter to Spruce, Wallace hinted that his thoughts were turning toward the Philippines, which embrace the northern part of the Malay archipelago. In London, this trend of mind crystallized. "I had obtained sufficient information," he remarked after attending several scientific meetings, "to satisfy me that the very finest field for an exploring and collecting naturalist was to be found in the great Malay Archipelago."

The richest variety of fruits and the most precious spices are indigenous there: the islands produce such monstrous flowers as the *Rafflesia arnoldii*, which is three feet wide and weighs twenty-four pounds! The great green-winged Ornithoptera, which Wallace later dubbed "the prince among the butterfly tribes"; the "man-like orang-utan," whose origin sparked Wallace's curiosity as had no mammal other than man himself; and the bird of paradise, which had never been exhibited in Europe, were other features of its giddy, divergent forms of life.

As Wallace dipped into the existing literature on the archipelago, he was astounded to learn that some of the islands were subcontinents, larger than either France or the Austrian Empire. Patently, the islands served as stepping stones between Australia and the Asian mainland, and as a natural barrier between the Pacific and Indian oceans. Wallace wondered whether the islands were mountain ranges in the process of creation, rising from the sea, or a chain of peaks, sinking beneath the waters.

Goodrich's *Universal History*, published in 1851, comprising two volumes and 1,193 pages, devoted only one page to the Malay archipelago, so little was known about it. But Wallace was accustomed to blank pages since Goodrich devoted less than a page to the Amazon and the Guianas. Like Edwards' thin volume on the Amazon, the Goodrich tomes excited Wallace's imagination. "It seems like a new world," Goodrich wrote of the Malay region, "for its vegetable as well as animal kingdom is unlike that of all other countries."*

It was left to Alfred Russel Wallace in 1854 to open up this new world to science.

As in the case of his venture into the Amazon, Wallace, shy as he was, did not think small. He now envisioned a massive, lengthy assault on the Malayan islands, and he outlined his idea to Sir Roderick Murchison, the president of the Royal Geographical Society, and Dr. Norton Shaw, the organization's secretary, whom he had met while attending scientific meetings.

Wallace planned to make Singapore, the seat of British power in East Asia, his base of operations and then sally forth "to visit in succession Borneo, The Philippines, Celebes, Timor, the Moluccas and New Guinea . . . remaining one or more years in each as circumstances may determine." Wallace thought in terms of an expedition of six years, and more.

Murchison and Shaw took a liking to the modest young man and, recognizing that he was hardly a person of independent means, they

---

* Presently, although the region is inhabited by almost 200 million people and enjoys extensive communications, it is still, for the biologist, clouded in enigmas. Charles Robequain, the contemporary French geographer, described it thus: "A wealth of living species unique in tropical islands. . . . The insect life is probably the richest in species in the whole world. . . . The same may be said of the bird life."

advised him to try to get a free passage to the islands aboard a Royal Navy vessel, *à la* Darwin, Hooker, and Huxley. Murchison also encouraged Wallace to put his project on paper so that the Society could formally submit it to the Admiralty and Foreign Office. Wallace readily accepted the advice and in a fifty-five-line letter, written on legal-sized paper, which is still in the archives of the Society, he outlined his plan in the third person, declaring, "[My] chief object is the investigation of the Natural History of the Eastern Archipelago in a more complete manner than has hitherto been attempted."

In the proposal Wallace revealed that he had been in contact with Sir James Brooke and that the White Rajah of Borneo had not only approved the scheme but that "he had little doubt of success in exploring the great Island of Borneo."

Wallace cited the expense of the journey, noting that as a result of the foundering of the *Helen* "he finds himself unable to make the necessary outlay" for executing the project. He appealed to "Her Majesty's Government to grant him a free passage to any convenient port in the Archipelago."

As evidence of his ability, Wallace referred to his explorations in the Amazon "where alone and unassisted he penetrated several hundred miles beyond any former European traveller.

"During his travels in South America he relied entirely on his duplicate collections in Natural History to pay his expenses," Wallace explained, "and he shall follow the same plan in his proposed journey."

Murchison was a man of influence and the Admiralty and Foreign Office, more likely for strategic than for scientific reasons, found the plan attractive, since it would supply them with information on a remote region of Asia, particularly during a period of Russian expansionism in many parts of the Orient. Accordingly, the Foreign Office obtained letters from the governments of Spain and Holland granting him permission to visit their East Indian possessions "for scientific purposes." On August 27, 1853, the Foreign Office also authorized Wallace to "apply to the Admiralty when he is ready to proceed in his scientific expedition to the Eastern seas in order that he may be informed whether an opportunity then exists for a passage in one of Her Majesty's Ships to Singapore."

Wallace wasted no time and announced that he was prepared to leave immediately, but the Admiralty advised him that the only ship available was a man-of-war bound for Trincomalee, the Royal Navy station in Ceylon. Wallace turned down the offer on the ground that "the journey from Trincomalee to Singapore and from Singapore to Borneo would entail considerable expense and loss of time."

There followed much correspondence about switching targets from the Malay archipelago to East Africa or Australia, but the Royal Geographical Society and Wallace both expressed greater interest in the East Indies.

In this manner the months slipped by. Impatient, in November Wallace wrote the Lords of the Admiralty, restating that "I shall be now at any time in readiness to accept a passage to Singapore, Batavia [the capital of the Netherlands East Indies] or any other port in the Eastern Archipelago."

In January 1854, shortly after his thirty-first birthday, the last he would spend with his mother, sister, and brother-in-law until 1863, the Admiralty notified Wallace that the twelve-gun brig H.M.S. *Frolic* was Singapore-bound. Wallace hurried to Spithead where *Frolic* was anchored with a number of other warships. It was his first time on a fighting ship and he found the vessel maintained in "Bristol fashion," all spit and polish, and the accommodations nonexistent.

The captain, a Commodore Nolloth, slung a cot in his cabin for his passenger and provided him with the luxury of a small table. Wallace was pleasantly surprised to discover the captain "very kind and of rather scientific and literary tastes." *Frolic* expected her sailing orders daily. But the ship rode at anchor into mid-February and when the order arrived, the vessel was dispatched to the Crimea. The British fleet had entered the Black Sea on January 3, five days before Wallace's birthday, and on March 28 England would declare war on Russia.

A disappointed Wallace bade farewell to *Frolic* and returned, downcast, to London. The chance of procuring passage on a Royal Navy ship was remote as long as war clouds gathered. But in London Murchison and Shaw had good news for him. The Royal Geographical Society was so enthusiastic about his work in the Amazon—Wallace's *Narrative* and *Palms* were being widely read by members—that the Society presented him with a ticket to Singapore aboard a Peninsular and Oriental steamer, first-class, no less. In return, the Society expected a stream of reports, sketches, and maps of *terrae incognitae* that he explored. Beyond scientific curiosity, Britain was a burgeoning empire and, in the case of the Malay archipelago, the world's largest, the Admiralty maintained an ongoing interest.

After splitting up with Bates in the Amazon, Wallace realized that working alone was hardly an ideal situation. There was simply too much research involved, not only in capturing species, but in preserving them, cataloging them, shipping out the collections, and so forth. On top of everything, he had to worry about his health, transport, supplies, finances, the hiring of local guides for trekking off into unexplored jungle, and other needs. "I made an inward vow never to travel again in wild, unpeopled districts without some civilized companion or attendant," Wallace said. For some time he thought of acquiring a young assistant for the Malay project, but this was out of the question if he travelled by warship. When the Society presented him with a commercial P. & O. ticket to Singapore, however, Wallace reconsidered the question of an assistant.

Charles Allen, a sixteen-year-old youth, the son of a carpenter who had done handiwork for Wallace's sister Fanny, had expressed an interest in learning the "insect trade" and his family expressed willingness to pay the boy's passage as Wallace's apprentice. Allen was of small build and was commonly taken to be thirteen or fourteen. In Allen, Wallace saw himself at the same age, floundering around in search of a future. Wallace took him on as an assistant.

Alfred Russel Wallace now set off to explore the maze of islands and atolls that made up the Malay world. Like Melville's Ishmael, Wallace clearly loved "to sail forbidden seas and land on barbarous coasts."

Chapter 22

ON APRIL 20, 1854, at the tail end of the northwest monsoon which sweeps down the Gulf of Siam and the South China Sea, Wallace's vessel tied up along the Singapore Harbour Board's wharf. Never before had he beheld such an array of ships, not even on the Thames when a boy: high-stemmed Chinese junks and low-lying sampans; spice-laden Javanese *praus* with lateen sails; three-masted American whalers with huge black cauldrons on their decks; European gunboats, both sail and steam.

Unlike the streets of Pará, where lassitude and indifference reigned, Singapore's alleys and byways bustled. Unlike Pará, where, under Latin rule, different races blended into one another, the peoples of the British crown colony largely retained their distinctive racial and cultural characteristics. The setting was, Wallace said, "so strange": half-naked coolies and fat, neat Chinese merchants, both wearing plaited pigtails signifying obeisance to the Manchu emperor in China and "all as pushing and full of business as any Londoners"; handsome, dark-skinned Tamils or *klings* from South India, who always asked double what they would take and with whom Wallace found it "amusing to bargain"; short, black-haired, beer-colored Malays and Indonesians in sarongs, the patterns of their wraparounds denoting the island from which they came, a *kris* or curved dagger with polished wooden handle tucked into the sarong's folds; the *pukka sahib* English in their white linens and pith helmets, the latter considered absolutely *de rigueur* for Europeans living in tropical Asia; sailors of every color and description, motley crews made up of Laskars and New Englanders who would feel at home aboard the *Pequod*; and, inevitably, ladies of the morning, noon, and night.

All were bound together by the profit motive, and by the law, order, and security symbolized by the British flag, which hung listlessly in the sultry heat from the staff atop Government House. They were also held together by a *lingua franca*, Bazaar Malay, which Wallace, who was no linguist, picked up easily. Within a year he was surprised to report that "I can talk to them all in the common language of the place."

A month after his arrival, in a letter home, Wallace wrote, "I am so busy with insects now that I have no time for anything else." He sent a thousand beetles to Stevens and considered this only an opener. "I have as many other insects still on hand, which will form part of my next and principal consignment."

"Singapore," he reported with satisfaction, "is rich in beetles."

Within days, he and Charles Allen had fallen into a routine. They rose at half-past five, took a cold *mandi* or dip (pouring buckets of water over themselves), and sat on their *serambi* sipping thick, black Java, the real thing, concocted with a heavy dose of sugar and served in demitasse cups. Then the pair sorted out the insects of the day before and set them out to dry. While Charles mended insect nets and refilled pincushions, Wallace catalogued the specimens, wrote up his log, and mapped the day's strategy. They breakfasted at eight, usually on *bebek telor* or duck eggs (among Malays the duck egg is considered superior to a chicken egg simply because it is larger). The eggs had a bluish tinge and were often rubbery in consistency.

At nine the bearded Wallace and his beardless assistant were off into the jungle which covered much of the island's 224 square miles. At two in the afternoon, sometimes three, they returned with fifty or sixty beetles, "some very rare and beautiful," Wallace observed, and perhaps a few butterflies. The divergence of species in the Malay jungle, as in the Amazon, continued to amaze him. In his treks into the rain forest of Southeast Asia he already knew, based on his experience in South America, that by shifting his location in the same area he could expect to find different species, and he suspected that this divergence of species among insects was not simply a random evolution, but one based on geography. Wallace was more convinced than ever that in nature he observed a continuous process of evolution unfolding itself in obedience to definite laws, a vast aggregate of original productions perpetually working out their own redistribution. But what were these laws?

Looking backward, Wallace's observations are so patently obvious and commonplace today that it is embarrassing, in surveying the development of man, to think that such a pedestrian conclusion slightly more than one hundred years ago was novel. Wallace's observations may be likened, within the context of another discipline—archaeology —to the attitudes of the "antiquarians" of Wallace's period casting aside potsherds as valueless, broken pieces of pottery. Today potsherds are acknowledged to be the time-prints of faded civilizations.

After returning to their base, Wallace and his aide took another *mandi*, changed from sweat-streaked clothes into fresh linens, and worked on their latest acquisitions. Charles did flies, wasps, and bugs. Wallace, enraptured by beetles, would not trust his assistant with his precious friends (nor would a Darwin or Bates have). At four they dined. The food could be anything, an Indian curry one day, Chinese fried rice the next, a Malay rijsttafel the day after.* Then they crated their collections and discussed the day's events until retiring around eight or nine, sleeping under a *klambu* or thick cotton mosquito net which shut off the already stifling air.

In July Wallace crossed the narrow Strait of Johore and trod on the Asian mainland for the first time. "Here the birds are abundant and most beautiful," he said, "more so than on the lower Amazon." At Malacca, once the seat of Portuguese power in the East, where a large Portuguese community still dwelt, Wallace wrote, "[I] find myself almost back in Brazil." But the west coast of the Malay peninsula was no Amazon. "Monkeys of many sorts are abundant," Wallace reported; "in fact, all animal life *seems* more abundant than in Brazil." He also ascended nearby Mt. Ophir, thought by some to be the Ophir of the Bible, mentioned in Genesis and believed to be Solomon's source of gold, monkeys, sandalwood, and ivory.

"The walk was hard work, thirty miles through jungle in a succession of mud-holes, and swarming with leeches, which crawled all over us, and sucked when and where they pleased," he wrote. Even so, Wallace studied the terrifying bloodsuckers with scientific de-

---

* The food of the Malay archipelago to this day is an unending source of inspiring gallimaufry. Agnes de Keijzer Brackman, in her miniclassic, *The Art of Indonesian Cooking*, published in Singapore a decade ago and still in print after two editions and several printings, describes the daily fare in the region as an "exciting blend of Moslem, Hindu and Buddhist influences . . . a melding of Malay-Arab, Indian and Chinese culinary arts."

tachment. "All are small," he observed, "but some are beautifully marked with stripes of bright yellow. They probably attach themselves to deer [sambar] and other animals which frequent the forest paths, and have thus acquired the singular habit of stretching themselves out at the sound of a footstep or of rustling foliage."

Here he also had his first grim battle with fever since leaving the gladed Amazon. "At Malacca I had a strong touch of fever, with the old Rio Negro symptoms," he said. But in Southeast Asia, unlike South America, he learned, the treatment was extremely large doses of quinine daily for a week and in less than a fortnight he had sufficiently recovered to go back into Asia's version of the Amazon's green inferno. "I never took half enough quinine in America to cure me," he said. But despite the heavy doses of quinine, Wallace never truly threw off the fever and the longer he remained in the region the more frequent and debilitating were the attacks. In the end, it drove him from the islands.

Biology in this era, like archaeology, was a happenstance thing. One afternoon while moving through the jungle armed only with a shotgun, Wallace spied a magnificent butterfly. "It was large, handsome, and quite new to me," he said. But it eluded his net. Wallace, however, noted that the butterfly had settled on the dung of a carnivorous animal, perhaps a sambar or tiger, and Wallace lay in wait for the butterfly's return, as if stalking big game. To Wallace's delight, the butterfly returned to the dung heap, and he netted it.

"It was an entirely new species," Wallace observed, and in London elated entomologists christened it *Nymphalis calydonia*. During eight years in the Malay world, Wallace never saw another and it was only after twelve years had elapsed that a second specimen, caught in Borneo, reached Europe. The manner in which Wallace obtained this rarity, he said later, "indicates how fragmentary and imperfect a traveller's collection must necessarily be."

Wallace, in his first letter to Norton Shaw, the secretary of the Royal Geographical Society, reported that in Singapore and the adjoining Malay peninsula "[I] made an extensive collection of insects, a great proportion of which are new to science and of very great interest to the entomologist." The letter exuded unrestrained optimism about the future.

Wallace had cause for optimism: by autumn he had built up a substantial collection of specimens and in Singapore had met the White Rajah of Borneo. Sir James Brooke "received me most cordially," said Wallace. Several Jesuit missionaries in Singapore, with whom he had made friends, were planning a journey to Cambodia and Wallace considered joining them. But the meeting with Brooke and the presence of the orang-utan in Borneo preempted all thoughts of Cambodia. In Wallace, a fantastic theory was taking shape.

"To my mind the evolution of species had taken place by natural succession and descent—one species becoming changed either slowly or rapidly into another," he wrote. He still did not understand the mechanics, but within a year he would set out this conviction as the Sarawak Law. Little wonder that he was especially anxious to see the orang-utan or *mias*, as the Dyaks called him, in his natural setting. As Wallace later expressed it, "We have every reason to believe that the orang-utan, the chimpanzee, and the gorilla have also had their forerunners." Although he did not say so, in his mind was surely the origin of the most interesting of all species, man. Logic demanded that man also have "forerunners."

"With what interest must every naturalist look forward to the time when the caves and tertiary deposits of the tropics may be thoroughly examined, and the past history and earliest appearance of the great man-like apes be at length made known," he wrote a half-century before Dubois unearthed "Java Man" among the islands and a century before Leakey made his discoveries of still earlier manlike creatures in Tanzania's Olduvai Gorge.

Wallace was interested in the orang-utan for another reason. The geographical distribution of animals, which he first observed in the Amazon, fascinated him as much as the question of the origin of species itself. Laws, he was convinced, governed distribution. "It is very remarkable that animals so large, so peculiar, and of such a high type of form as the orang-utan, should be confined to so limited a district—to two islands," he said. The islands were Borneo and Sumatra.

Against this background, Wallace opted for Borneo over Cambodia and left for the mysterious island at the end of October.

On the eve of his departure for Sarawak, as the northwestern region of Borneo is called, George Silk, his boyhood chum, wrote cheering news that there was a reference to Wallace in a scientific journal. A buoyed Wallace could not conceal his delight. "That ought to make my name a little known," he chuckled. In point of fact, he was becoming "a little known." Sir William Hooker at Kew Gardens, for example, was so enthusiastic about Wallace's *Palms* that he contacted

Stevens and wrote Wallace for specimens of Malayan flora. But, Wallace confessed, while Hooker's "remarks are encouraging . . . I cannot afford to collect plants."

"I have to work for a living," he explained to Silk, "and plants would not pay unless I collect nothing else, which I cannot, being too much interested in zoology."

Through Stevens, his agent, Wallace also learned that Darwin wanted "curious varieties" of ducks and there is a suggestion in Wallace's correspondence with an acquaintance in 1889, seven years after Darwin's death, about procuring such varieties for Darwin, raising the possibility that some of Wallace's specimens found their way into Down House. However, despite a search through existing files in the British Museum and elsewhere, I could find no evidence to support this speculation. Nevertheless, given Darwin's catholic interests and Stevens' wide contacts within the scientific community, it is likely that Stevens transacted business with Darwin and that Wallace and Bates were, therefore, two of Darwin's sources of supply for exotic new species.

On November 1, 1854 Wallace landed on the marshy coast of Borneo, at the mouth of the Sarawak River, and entered the independent domain of the swashbuckling White Rajah. Wallace discovered the region to be virtually unpopulated; to this day, the island, which covers 287,000 square miles and is a thousand times larger than crowded Singapore, is, like parts of the Amazon, relatively uninhabited. Torrid temperatures, terrible terrain, and disease (dengue, malaria, and other ailments), serve as natural checks against the spread of *Homo sapiens*.

Whatever the case, Wallace also found Borneo a beetle lover's horn of plenty; indeed, Darwin and Bates later envied him. In the four months Wallace spent traveling in and around Singapore before his visit to Borneo, he had obtained 320 different kinds of beetle. In less than a fortnight in Sarawak he doubled that number, acquiring an average of about two dozen new species daily. One day he collected seventy-six varieties, an astounding total, and exclaimed, "thirty-four are new to me!"

Before Wallace left the island-continent, he had amassed a collection of two thousand different kinds of beetles. With the pride of a poet, as Darwin described it, Wallace learned that many of the new species now bore his name, such as the *Ectatorhinus wallacei* and the *Cyriophalpus wallacei*. Actually, Wallace soon found himself with such a burgeoning collection of new insect species that he took to naming them himself. One, a beautiful and rare butterfly, he christened in honor of the White Rajah, *Ornithoptera brookeana*. It had long and pointed wings, was a velvety black in color, with a band of brilliant green dots extending across the wings from tip to tip, and possessed a neck-collar of vivid crimson.

Rare, indeed. Wallace later recalled capturing only "two or three" others of the same species. Each, it developed, was a male and it was not until a decade later that scientists captured a female. She resembled the male but was less brilliant in color.

Above and beyond the excitement of the chase, however, Wallace brooded over the origin of the species he hunted. For example, he captured the first tree-frog and upon examining it found that the toes were unusually long, and fully webbed with immense membranes, thereby developing the characteristics of wings. "This I believe is the first instance known of a 'flying frog,'" he said, adding that "the variability of the toes, which have been already modified for purposes of swimming and adhesive climbing, have been taken advantage of to enable an allied species to pass through the air like the flying lizard." But how this modification came about continued to baffle him.

It was at this point, as a houseguest of the White Rajah in a bungalow at the foot of Mt. Santubong, recovering from yet another bout of fever, that Wallace formulated his Sarawak Law or, as he termed it, "my paper on the succession of species." It was his first hard, firm, published work on the species question. *The Annals and Magazine of Natural History*, as recounted earlier, published it in September that year, 1855.

The Sarawak Law was the law declaring that "Every species has come into existence coincident both in time and space with a pre-existing closely allied species"; it was the Law that caused a flurry of excitement within Darwin's confined circle, literally driving Sir Charles Lyell to open his own "species book," while Darwin took notes on different sections of Wallace's paper, at one point asking, "Can this be true?"

Indeed, in this century, as early as World War I, Lancelot Hogben, the controversial historian, discussed the Sarawak Law glowingly. "This was the *first* great attempt to deduce any general ideas from the phenomena of [animal] distribution," said Hogben, "and certainly the *first* effort to coordinate the results of organic geography with the knowledge of fossil remains." (Italics added.)

It was at this juncture, too, that Wallace confided in a letter to

Bates that "I have prepared the plan and written portions of a work embracing the whole subject, and have endeavored to prove in detail what I have as yet only indicated."

There was, of course, no visible reaction to his Sarawak Law and a year later, in a bold stroke doubtlessly arising from frustration, Wallace initiated his celebrated correspondence with Down House, drawing Darwin's attention to the Law.

Darwin's reply "gratified" Wallace, but it also provided him with a grossly misleading impression of Darwin's activities at that time. Darwin had taken his time about replying, waiting more than a half year to do so. Then he claimed that after twenty years of work on the species question, "I am now preparing my work for publication." The innocent Wallace could only have concluded that Darwin was eons ahead of him and was about to announce to the world a complete theory on the origin of species. Wallace had no notion of how the Sarawak Law had badly shaken Darwin, rocked Lyell, and pushed Lyell and Hooker into forcing Darwin to get to work on his book before he lost his cherished "priority"—even though Darwin still could not account for the incredible divergences in the productions of nature. As it turned out, Wallace was among the last to know of Darwin's plight and it would only partly come to light after Darwin's death in 1882, more than a generation after they began their correspondence.

Chapter 23

IN THE two-and-a-half year period between Wallace's announcement of the Sarawak Law and his mailing Darwin the world's first
complete theory of the origin and divergence of species, Wallace
underwent a series of adventures and misadventures in the Malay world
that made the perils of the Amazon almost comparable to a stroll
through London's Hyde Park.

One incident, which occured at Ambon, in the eastern half of the
archipelago, illustrates the point. Wallace tells the story:

> One night about nine o'clock I heard a curious noise and rustling
> overhead, as if some heavy animal were crawling slowly over the thatch.
> The noise soon ceased, and I thought no more about it and went to bed
> soon afterwards.
>
> The next afternoon just before dinner, being rather tired with my
> day's work, I was lying on the couch with a book in my hand, when
> gazing upwards I saw a large mass of something overhead which I had
> not noticed before. Looking more carefully I could see yellow and
> black marks, and thought it must be a tortoise-shell put up there out
> of the way between the ridge-pole and the roof. Continuing to gaze, it
> suddenly resolved itself into a large snake, compactly coiled up in a
> kind of knot; and I could detect his head and his bright eyes in the very
> centre of the folds.

The noise of the previous evening was now explained: a python had
slithered up one of the house's columns and settled under the thatched

roof "within a yard of my head . . . and I had slept soundly all night directly under him," Wallace said.

Wallace bounded out of the bamboo hut and summoned help. An Indonesian from the nearby island of Buru, where there are many snakes, took command. He approached the job lightheartedly. The man made a noose of rattan and with a long pole in the other hand poked at the snake which began slowly to uncoil itself. The man hurriedly slipped the noose over the serpent's head and hauled it down from the rafters and out of the house as the great beast thrashed wildly, breaking furniture. Outside, the Buru man fearlessly grabbed the python's tail and dashed its head against a tree while others standing nearby, hatchets in hand, dispatched it.

"It was about twelve feet long and very thick," Wallace said easily, "capable of doing much mischief and of swallowing a dog or a child."*

But Wallace was not in the Malay archipelago—like a "white hunter" in a Hemingway tale—through boredom and in search of adventure for want of something to do in life. He was there for scientific purposes; adventure was incidental, an occupational hazard. During the period between his Sarawak and Ternate papers, Wallace emerged as the preeminent tropical naturalist of the Victorian age. He published twenty-three scientific notes and monographs in that brief span alone while assiduously building up the largest collection of different species of insects ever pinned by a single individual in the annals of science. His articles appeared in the *Zoologist, Transactions of the Entomological Society, Journal of Botany*, and *Chambers' Journal*, among others, his most popular outlet being the *Annals and Magazine of Natural History*. And throughout this hectic period, amid bouts of recurring malaria and dysentery, Wallace lay awake under his mosquito net night after night thinking out the theory of evolution now almost universally ascribed solely to Darwin.

Wallace's scientific notes appeared in Darwin's favorite journals, and Darwin was probably aware of the lengthening shadow Wallace, the intruder, cast over Darwin's private preserve, the species question. Within the privacy of Down House, a troubled Darwin, suffering a wide variety of real and imagined illnesses, must have studied and re-

---

* In 1959 Wallace's descendants found the snake's skin among his bric-a-brac and presented it to the Linnean Society. It now adorns a wall at Burlington House, the Society's London headquarters.

studied each line of Wallace's articles for clues on the question, the more so after Lyell and Hooker (and Blyth) had independently called his attention to the Sarawak Law. For that matter, Lyell and Hooker— certainly the latter through his father, Sir William—must have become increasingly aware of Wallace's presence. And the grand triumvirate in the scientific aristocracy, Lyell, Darwin, and Hooker, must have been perplexed. None of them could recall the pattern and color of Wallace's school tie, or even what he looked like.

For a self-educated former surveyor, who had dabbled in carpentry, watchmaking, and teaching, Wallace's published pieces were a measure of his originality, maturity, imagination, and sophistication in matters of science (in political and financial affairs Wallace was as naive as ever). He wrote on a broad spectrum of subjects: "Botany of Malacca," "Note on the Sexual Difference in the Genus *Lompatera*," "On the Orang-Outang [sic] or Mias of Borneo," "Correction of an Important Error affecting the Classification of the *Psittacidae*," "On the Habits etc. of a Species of *Ornithoptera* Inhabiting the Aru Islands," and "Note on the Theory of Permanent and Geographical Varieties."

Indeed, during this period Wallace turned out scientific papers at the rate of almost one a month, not counting his earth-shattering Sarawak Law and Ternate Essay. And he did so without the advantages of a comfortable study or laboratory, library, or even contact with like-minded scientists. He was forced to carry on alone, most of his observations in his head or jotted down in pocket notebooks. Many of these notebooks are lost; three concerning the Malay archipelago— tattered, worn, and faded—are now in the library of the Linnean Society.

On some of the islands of the archipelago, New Guinea, for one, Wallace lived in "miserable, crazy and filthy hovels, utterly destitute of anything that can be called furniture; not a stool, or bench, or board to be seen in them." On such occasions, he used a crate for a writing table and a box for a chair. He slept on the floor. Yet, as Wallace would be the first to admit, it is misleading to think of the archipelago in such primitive terms. One of the astonishing aspects of the East Indian or Indonesian islands to this day is that life-styles in the insular chain ride a cultural trapeze. One island boasts the comforts of a Bermuda; another is a Devil's Island.

In Macassar, the capital of the southern Celebes, Wallace might as well have been in Down.

"Macassar was the first Dutch town I had visited and I found it prettier and cleaner than any I had yet seen in the East," he said in appreciation.* "The Dutch have some admirable local regulations. All European houses must be kept well whitewashed, and every person must, at four in the afternoon, water the road in front of his house. The streets are kept clear of refuse, and covered drains carry away all impurities into large open sewers, into which the tide is admitted at high water and allowed to flow out when it has ebbed, carrying the sewage with it into the sea."

On Bali, the enchanted Hindu island, as famous for its dancing, painting and sculpture as for its terraced rice fields and barebreasted women, Wallace was stunned by the beauty. "I was both astonished and delighted," he wrote. ". . . I had never beheld so beautiful and well-cultivated a district out of Europe."

But Aru was an island of loathing and dread, something out of Edgar Allen Poe. In a letter dated "August, 1857" to Norton Shaw, the secretary of the Royal Geographical Society—and still preserved in the vaults of the Society—Wallace described Aru unendearingly as an island of horrors, thick-matted jungle, black marshes, swarms of mosquitos at night and leeches by day, and stifling air around the clock. Out of touch with an orderly, if not more civilized world, Wallace's letters and notes, like the letter to Shaw, sometimes bore vague dates, since he frequently lost track of time, days intermingled with days, weeks with weeks, and sometimes even months got mixed up, especially after an attack of fever kept him bedridden for numberless days.

"This is horrid country," he informed Shaw. "I leave as soon as I can enroute for N. Guinea." As he soon discovered, New Guinea, where the Americans and Japanese fought it out in World War II, proved more inhospitable than Aru. As the Malays or Indonesians would say, it was a case of escaping the mouth of the crocodile only to fall into the mouth of the tiger.

Between Bali and the Celebes, on one hand, and Aru and New Guinea on the other, Wallace often found plateaus of comfort, islands out of Robert Louis Stevenson. Pythons notwithstanding, Ambon, a truly lovely island with a magnificent bay, was a splendid example. "My abode is merely a little thatched hut, consisting of an open verandah in front and a small dark sleeping room behind," said Wallace.

* Strangely, in the Dutch archives in Holland, *Algemeen Rijksarchief*, I found only one document relating to Wallace's eight-year sojourn among the islands, a September 23, 1861, letter in which Wallace asked for permission to visit Sumatra and Bangka "for the study of natural life." The Netherlands Indies government promptly approved the request.

"It is raised about five feet from the ground, and is reached by rude steps to the center of the verandah. The walls and floor are of bamboo, and it contains a table, two bamboo chairs, and a couch. Here I soon made myself comfortable, and set to work hunting for insects among the more recently felled timber, which swarmed with fine *Curuculionidae*, *Longicorns*, and *Buprestidae*, most of them remarkable for their elegant forms or brilliant colours, and almost all new to me."

"Only the entomologist," he added, "can appreciate the delight with which I hunted."

Wallace's originality of thought and frankness in print kept pace with his literary output and movements among the islands. Shortly after the publication of the Sarawak Law, he openly took issue with Lyell's view that the same species should be found on islands sharing the same climate and vegetation. Wallace said this was simply not so, and he cited Borneo and New Guinea as a striking case in point. The natural productions of these islands were completely dissimilar. If, as Wallace contended, new species were the offspring of preexisting, closely allied species, the farther apart the islands, even if they shared a similar climate and vegetation, the more likely different species would evolve. Wallace himself was not yet sure of why this was so, but he clearly recognized the existence of a natural mechanism, and was determined to ferret it out.

Lyell, of course, still clung to the dogma of special creation, although in compelling Lyell to open his first species notebook, the Sarawak Law demonstrated that Wallace had badly shaken his belief in Genesis.

In another paper, published in the *Zoologist* in 1858, on the eve of his discovery of the mechanism that produced different species, Wallace openly questioned the Biblical story of creation. A species, he said, is "every group of individuals presenting permanent characters, however slight."* And, since most scientists were prepared to admit that subvarieties and varieties were not special acts of creation, Wallace argued forcefully that it was ridiculous to consider the formation of species as one-time, creative acts.

In that early definition of species, Wallace employed the word "permanent," but later he discarded it. Evolution for him was an interminable, unpredictable thing. In the millennia to come, the creatures of our era, including man, may well have become fossilized curiosities,

* In the Wallace–Darwin age, and to a lesser extent today, biologists use the noun "character" in a special sense for the adjective "characteristic."

the conversation pieces of creatures yet to come into existence on this planet.

To compound Wallace's hardships in this period, Charles Allen, his apprentice, proved another Herbert; in a word, a misfit. Allen was uninterested in biology and—worse in Wallace's eyes—hopelessly disorganized. After a year in the field, Allen still could not master the pinning of insects, the skinning of birds, or the preservation of specimens. He was all thumbs. Wallace grew more exasperated with him each month and after a year and a half among the islands, Allen quit in disgust and wound up comfortably in Singapore, where he settled down, married, and raised a family. Wallace rarely bore a grudge—it was not in his nature—and he and Allen parted on good terms. Indeed, on occasion Allen would sally forth from Singapore and rejoin Wallace for brief periods, returning to the British crown colony with Wallace's latest collections for shipment to England.

Wallace's mother, however, conspired with Stevens to send out a replacement. Wallace was wary. Since his sister Fanny knew the candidate-apprentice, Wallace wrote her from Borneo on June 25, 1855, and asked her to "let me know what you think of him."

This letter reveals more about Wallace's trials in the field than anything he ever wrote in his published works.

"Do not tell me merely that he is 'a very nice young man,'" the thirty-two-year-old, gaunt Wallace wrote. "Of course he is. So is Charles a very nice boy, but I could not be troubled with another like him for any consideration whatever. . . . Another with a similar incapacity would drive me mad."

What qualities did Wallace seek in an apprentice? For Fanny's benefit, Wallace spelled them out:

> I have written to Mr. Stevens to let me know his character, as regards *neatness* and *perseverance* in doing anything he is set about. From you I should like to know whether he is quiet or boisterous, forward or shy, talkative or silent, sensible or frivolous, delicate or strong. Ask him whether he can live on rice and salt fish for a week on an occasion— whether he can do without wine or beef, and sometimes without tea, coffee or sugar—whether he can sleep on a board—whether he likes the hottest weather in England—whether he is too delicate to skin a stinking animal—whether he can walk twenty miles a day—whether he can work, for there is sometimes as hard work in collecting as in anything. Can he draw (not copy)? . . . Does he write a good hand? Can he make anything? Can he saw a piece of board straight? . . . Your affectionate brother.

Apparently the apprentice-elect failed to meet Wallace's standards, for the lad never left England. Fortunately, in Sarawak, on the lookout for a bright, bushy-tailed new assistant, Wallace hired a young Malay, Ali. The youth helped Wallace master the Malay language, was attentive, cooked well, and soon learned to shoot birds, skin them, pin insects, and do other chores. He was also a superb seaman: almost all of Wallace's expeditions to different islands involved travel either aboard an Indonesian *prau* or a *kora-kora* with outriggers. Wallace and Ali became inseparable companions. They parted in 1862 when Wallace left for England and, as a gift, Wallace presented the young man with his two double-barreled shotguns and his stores—ammunition, tools, and other goods—"which made him quite rich." Ali married a Moluccan girl and, like Allen before him, settled in Singapore. There he cast aside his sarong and *kris* and adopted the European style of dress. In his memoirs, Wallace referred to Ali as "my faithful companion."

Chapter 24

BUT the dreadful discomfort Wallace put up with and the constant battle he waged against malaria and dysentery, from island to island, were far outweighed by the compensations. Wallace studied the orang-utan in its natural habitat; gazed in wonder on his first bird of paradise; and admired butterflies, beetles, and other productions of nature, never before seen by western man. The constant discovery of new species altered his perception of man and man's place in the universe. "All living things," he concluded, "are not made for man."

This philosophical outlook colored his future writing. In his day, with Evangelicalism riding high, the Victorian era positive and forward-looking, Wallace thought the unthinkable: man was not at the center of the world, any more, as Copernicus proved, than the Earth was at the center of the universe.

Wallace's outlook is reflected in his reaction to his first glimpse of the bird of paradise, in Malay, *burung rajah* or king of birds. Portuguese sailors first reported the existence of these birds to Europeans but such tales were thought to be sea stories. The Portuguese called them "birds of God." Occasionally a mutilated skin was brought back to Europe as evidence and Linnaeus classified them in his system, but his description was incomplete.

"The emotions excited in the mind of a naturalist, who has long desired to see the actual thing which he has hitherto known only by descriptions, drawing, or badly-preserved external covering—especially when that thing is of surpassing rarity and beauty—require the poetic faculty fully to express them," Wallace wrote. His agitation was heightened by the facts of the situation: he saw his first bird of paradise on Aru, that "horrid" island, in the midst of an almost un-visited sea, deep in the recesses of a wild, luxuriant forest. "I thought of the long ages of the past, during which successive generations of this little creature had run their course—year by year being born, and living and dying amid the dark and gloomy woods, with no intelligent eye to gaze upon their loveliness; to all appearance such a wanton waste of beauty."

The loveliness and beauty of the bird exceeded all his expectations. But as he gazed on this wonder of evolution, resplendent with fan-tastic colors, Wallace involuntarily shuddered. His discovery of their habitat, he realized, spelled their doom.

At this moment, Wallace emerged as one of the earliest conserva-tionists in modern history. ". . . Should civilized man ever reach these distant lands, and bring moral, intellectual and physical light into the recesses of these virgin forests," he forewarned, "we may be sure that he will so disturb the nicely-balanced relations of organic and inorganic nature as to cause the disappearance, and finally the extinction, of these very beings whose wonderful structure and beauty he alone is fitted to appreciate and enjoy."

"This consideration," he philosophized, "must surely tell us that all living things are not made for man."

In that passage, Wallace read the future. When he returned to England with the first captive birds of paradise ever viewed in the West, Europe's fashion industry went wild. Between the mid-Victorian period and the Roaring Twenties, a million birds of paradise were slaughtered, the bird's feathers eagerly sought by women to adorn their hats. In 1924, by international agreement, the export of the glorious birds from the Aru Islands, the Moluccas, and New Guinea was banned.

The first bird of paradise he saw (Wallace identified eight different species, three new to science) was the color of bright cinnabar, "with a gloss as of spun glass." Like all birds of paradise, the creature was about the size of a thrush. The head was rich orange, the breast pure white, and a brilliant band of green separated the colors of the body from that of the head. "Yet this comprised only half of its strange beauty!" Wallace exclaimed.

Springing from each side of the breast were tufts of magnificent greyish feathers, each terminated in a band of emerald green. The two middle feathers of the tail were divided like slender wires into a broad, double curve. Near the end of each tail, which curled spirally inward, hung a pair of glittering buttons. These two ornaments, the breast fans and the spiral tipped wires, were unique. They do not appear once in the more than eight thousand other different kinds of birds known to exist on Earth.

Wallace had never before seen such incredible majesty in nature.

If the birds of paradise had stirred thoughts about their future survival within Wallace, his first encounter with the orang-utan prompted thoughts of "there but for the grace of God, go I."

Wallace spied his first orang-utan at Simanjun, some thirty-five miles as the crow flies from Kuching, the White Rajah's capital, except that the crow does not fly in Borneo and Wallace was forced to go by dugout, a journey of more than a hundred miles through dense jungle and swamps.

"I was out collecting insects, not more than a quarter of a mile from [camp]," Wallace wrote, "when I heard a rustling in a tree nearby, and, looking up, saw a large red-haired animal moving slowly along, hanging from the branches by its arms. It passed on from tree to tree till it was lost in the jungle, which was so swampy that I could not follow it."

In one of his unpublished notebooks on Borneo, Wallace quoted an "old man who knows much about the *mias*." "It has no enemies," the old man said. "No animal dare attack it but the alligator and the boa constrictor." The orang-utan, he said, always slew the alligator by sheer strength, pulling open the jaws and ripping up its throat. As for the snake, if the boa attacked, the *mias* seized it and bit it in two. "There is no animal in the jungle as strong as he," the old man repeated.

Some fifteen years later, when Wallace returned to his notes and incorporated them into his *The Malay Archipelago*, with a deepening knowledge of zoology and the Malay language, he amended the old man's statement to read "crocodile" for alligator (there are no alligators in Asia; all are in the Americas) and boa to python (there are thirty-five different species of boa in the Americas; three in Asia).

It was during his sojourn at Simanjun that Wallace lived with the Dyaks in a longhouse "in which were several great baskets of dried human heads," the trophies of past generations of head-hunters. But this induced no cultural shock in Wallace; on the contrary, in sharp contrast to Darwin, Wallace considered the "uncivilized" peoples among whom he dwelt to be more civilized in many respects than his "civilized" countrymen, with their sweat shops, child labor, pollution, gallows, and hulks tied up along the Thames.

"The more I see of uncivilized people, the better I think of human nature on the whole, and the essential differences between civilized and savage man seem to disappear," he wrote home, assuming a posture radically at odds with the way Darwin and many colonial-minded Victorians saw "natives."

In Borneo, in pursuit of the orang-utan, Wallace found himself among Chinese and Malays, as well as Dyaks. To this day these three peoples blend into the Sarawak junglescape. Wallace was amused by the popular conception of these people.

"The Chinese are generally considered, and with some amount of truth, to be thieves, liars, and reckless of human life, and these Chinese are coolies of the lowest and least educated class, though they can all read and write," Wallace said, reflecting on the Yellow Peril popularized by Chambers and others. "The Malays are invariably described as being barbarous and bloodthirsty; and the Dyaks have only recently ceased to think head-taking a necessity of their existence."

Wallace wrote these words in the interior of Sarawak, a two-day journey from Kuching, the White Rajah's capital, whose racially mixed government ruled only with the consent and support of these different peoples.

"Yet," Wallace continued, "I can safely say that in any part of Europe where the same opportunities for crime and disturbance existed, things would not go on so smoothly as they do here."

Wallace slept with open doors, and went around completely unarmed. The Chinese, he discovered, were a "loyal, quiet, honest, decent sort of people." The Malays were pleasant and friendly; the Dyaks, a delight.

In the name of the advancement of science, Wallace shot dead several orangs and shipped their skeletons and skins to England for research. Killing was distasteful to Wallace, as it is to many naturalists, and both Wallace and Darwin shared strong feelings of tenderness toward living creatures. They revered life as sacred, yet for the sake of knowledge they killed and killed.

Darwin's torment over the destruction of life is reflected in his admission that he could not recall, except in one instance, ever taking more than one egg from a bird's nest, and although he was an ardent fisherman, he said he never "spitted a living worm, though at the expense, probably, of some loss of success." As for Wallace, on one occasion he empathized with a young naturalist who quit biology on the moral ground that it was wrong to kill wondrous and beautiful living creatures. Wallace said he understood. And to another correspondent, who wrote him similarly, Wallace replied, "We are [both] lovers of nature, from bugs up to humans."

Yet the shy, retiring Wallace, the man whom one was likely to describe as the type that "could not kill a fly," killed daily. In the name of science Wallace sought to rationalize his dilemma. He argued that living creatures other than man possess no awareness of the future. Therefore, when an insect is killed, said Wallace, the insect's life ends with a finality lacking in the death of a human being, the latter an acquisitive creature with a sense of time who lives not only for today but also for tomorrow and whose death is, accordingly, the most painful for all living things. But Wallace's arguments for the taking of life failed to convince him.*

In killing orangs in Borneo, Wallace felt an especially deep guilt. One explanation may stem from the man-like appearance of the creature, another might be that Wallace was the first scientist to study the social habits of the anthropoid ape—more than a century before George Schaller's work among gorillas and Jane Goodall's life among the chimpanzees—and that, therefore, he could not help but see even more clearly the vague, confused link between man and the *mias*.

"It is a singular and very interesting sight to watch a *mias* making his way leisurely through the forest," Wallace wrote. Comparing him with man, Wallace noted that the *mias* walked along large boughs in a semierect attitude "which the great length of his arms and the shortness of his legs cause him naturally to assume; and the disproportion between these limbs is increased by his walking on his knuckles, not on the palm of the hand, as *we* should so." (Italics added). The orangutan, Wallace recorded, never jumped or sprang, nor ever hurried

---

* Scientists to this day wrestle with their consciences whenever they kill to advance man's knowledge. Christiaan Barnard, the man who made history with his heart transplants, openly wept in an interview in 1958 when he recalled the moment he removed the beating heart of an ape for transplant. "Working with animals gives me tremendous emotional pain," Barnard, in the spirit of a Wallace and a Darwin, said. ". . . I don't think I could be forced to take out the heart of a chimp again." Referring to his killing of a baboon and a chimp, he added, "At first I said, 'Human life is more important.' But then I went to see [them], God, they were so much like human beings!"

himself. "Yet he manages to get along almost as quickly as a person can run through the forest beneath," he said.

Wallace confirmed Dyak stories that the orang-utan or forest man slept in a tree house nightly, about twenty to fifty feet from the ground, "probably," Wallace surmised, "because it is warmer and less exposed to wind than higher up." Moreover, the orang-utan did not rise from his bed until the sun was high in the sky and the dew on the leaves had dried. Wallace also observed that the orangs "do not seem much alarmed at man, as they often stared down upon me for several minutes, and then only moved away slowly to an adjacent tree."*

During his travels in Sarawak, Wallace killed seventeen *mias*, and adopted one.

"I must now tell you of the addition to my household of an orphan baby," he wrote his mother. ". . . Don't be alarmed: I was the cause of its mother's death."

Wallace recounted how he had fired at a large orang in a tree and "down fell this little baby—in its mother's arms." He added, "I have preserved the mother's skin and skeleton, and am trying to bring up her only daughter, and hope some day to introduce her to fashionable society at the Zoological Gardens."

When the mother fell mortally wounded, the baby somersaulted out of the mother's arms and into a swamp "the consistency of pea-soup, and when I got it out it looked pitiful," Wallace said. "It clung to me very hard when I carried it home, and having got its little hands unawares into my beard, it clutched so tight that I had great difficulty in extricating myself."

The little innocent was not yet weaned and Wallace got a large-mouthed bottle, made two holes in the cork stopper, and inserted a large quill.

He filled the bottle with rice-water and the baby sucked up the nourishment. "I fitted up a box for a cradle with a mat for it to lie upon, which I had washed and changed every day," he wrote.

"I feed it four times a day, and wash it and brush its hair every day which it likes very much, only crying when it is hungry or dirty. In

* The orang-utan has learned about man the hard way, and today avoids him. In three journeys in Borneo as a foreign correspondent, in 1951, 1954, and 1964, including the interior, I never saw an orang. Presently, the *mias* is on the endangered species list and in Sarawak experts estimate that there are fewer than three thousand orang-utans today outside captivity.

about a week I gave it rice-water a little thicker, and always sweetened it to make it nice. I am afraid you would call it an ugly baby, for it has a dark brown skin and red hair, a very large mouth but very pretty little hands and feet. It has now cut its two lower front teeth, and the uppers are coming.

"I can safely say, what so many have said before with much less truth," said Wallace pridefully, " 'There never was such a baby as my baby,' and I am sure nobody ever had such a dear little duck of a darling of a little brown hairy baby before." After five weeks the baby suffered from an attack of diarrhea and Wallace gave it a small dose of castor oil. The baby appeared to recover but a fortnight later suffered a relapse. Wallace recognized the familiar symptoms, the same as he, Bates, and other *Homo sapiens* succumbed to in the tropics. "The symptoms were exactly those of intermittent fever . . . ," he said.

The baby, which, oddly enough he never named, lost all appetite, lingered for three more weeks, and died. "I much regretted the loss of my little pet," a grieving Wallace said. ". . . For several months it had afforded me daily amusement by its curious ways and the inimitably ludicrous expression on its little countenance."

As Wallace cradled the baby in his arms, the species question loomed ever larger in his mind. It drove away other thoughts. The baby, like himself, he was convinced, had evolved from a preexisting, closely allied species. The Sarawak Law, he was convinced, "absolutely necessitates the former existence of a whole series of extinct genera filling up the gap between the isolated genera which in many cases now alone exist." His concept of evolution, like that of Darwin at distant Down, converged on an essential point. As Wallace put it, a theory of evolution implied "a great lapse of time."

But the mechanism of change—the how—continued to elude Wallace's grasp. Yet there must have been a subconscious glimmer because he later observed that the mechanics were not only unknown but "appeared almost inconceivable."

The problem of divergence, as in the case of Darwin, also troubled Wallace and remained unresolved. "The great difficulty was to understand how, if one species was gradually changed into another, there continued to be so many quite distinct species, so many of which differed from their nearest allies by slight yet perfectly definite and constant characters," he said. "One would expect that if it was a law of nature that species were continually changed so as to become in time new and distinct species, the world would be full of inextricable distinct species, a mixture of various slightly different forms, so that the well-defined and constant species we see would not exist."

Thus, the problems confronting Wallace and Darwin were broadly similar in 1855 through 1858. In addressing themselves to the question of the origin of species, a central issue was not only how new species came into being but how they remained different, not reverting to type but diverging forever.

During this formative phase of Wallace's journey through the Malay archipelago his itinerary staggers the imagination: 1855—Singapore and Borneo; 1856—Bali, Lombok, Celebes, Ke; 1857—Aru, New Guinea, Timor, Banda, Ambon; 1858—Ternate, Gilolo, Kaioa. Frequently he retraced his steps and revisited an island, as in the case of Sarawak, which he visited in 1855 and again in 1856. Before he was done with the Malay world, Wallace undertook ninety-six separate collecting expeditions into the remotest regions, traveling largely by boat and covering upward of fifteen thousand miles by sea, almost equal to a voyage half way around the world.

On Friday, January 8, 1858—fittingly, Wallace's thirty-fifth birthday—a mail boat put into Ternate, one of the many conically shaped volcanic islands that dot the Moluccas or Spice Islands, as they were called in Marco Polo's time. The decayed battlements of a Portuguese fort, resembling the one Wallace had seen at Malacca on his first trip into the Malay world, overlooked the palm-thronged bay, and the water might have come from Hans Christian Andersen's imagination, "as blue as the petals of the loveliest cornflower, and as clear as the purest glass." The fragile network of coral reefs in the lagoon sparkled under the bright equatorial sun.

With a European ship in port, Wallace dashed off a letter to Bates, and raved about the prospects of collecting in the Moluccas, particularly around Ternate. He disclosed a plan to jump off for Gilolo, present-day Halmahera, ten miles east of Ternate, "perhaps the most perfect entomological *terra incognita* now to be found." Not a single insect had ever been caught, pinned, and classified on the island. As for Ternate itself, Wallace wrote, "I think I shall stay in this place two or three years, as it is the centre of a most interesting and almost unknown region." And stay three years he did.

Although today's average literate person has no more inkling of Ternate's whereabouts than of Wallace's name, after Wallace's sojourn in the Moluccas the world was never the same. In this remote area of the world, Wallace unlocked the secret of the origin of species—descent *and* divergence through natural selection. Darwin notwithstanding, Wallace was the first to develop fully a coherent thesis to explain evolution. His impact on history is incalculable. The fascinating, unanswerable question—raised by Darwin's intimate friends themselves—is whether Darwin would ever have written *Origin* had there never been a Wallace.

Chapter 25

WALLACE no sooner settled down at Ternate than he suffered violent paroxysms of intermittent ague, or malaria. Despite large doses of quinine, Wallace was unable to throw off the debilitating, recurrent attacks. During these bouts he was often in a state of physical and mental disarray.

Wallace seesawed between chills and fever. First his bones ached intolerably and his teeth chattered uncontrollably. Despite room temperatures in the nineties and higher, he felt entombed in a new Ice Age. Just as suddenly, the chills abated. Now his brow burned and his body felt like hot charcoal as he was enveloped by high fever. The bamboo bed on which he normally slept was drenched in perspiration. These frequent relapses after reaching Ternate were proof positive, if any were needed, that Wallace had developed a dangerous, chronic form of the disease.

A remarkable aspect of malarial attacks is their unpredictability and duration. An attack can last for minutes, hours, or days, and may end as abruptly as it began.

Until World War II and the emergence of modern drugs, the East Indies produced ninety-three percent of the world's quinine supply to combat malaria. After the war, the development of DDT put an end to the malarial reign of terror, although DDT-resistant anopheles mosquitoes have since then evolved as the species has struggled for survival in new environment. As recently as a generation ago, however, malaria was widely considered by the World Health Organization as mankind's greatest killer, afflicting an esitmated 300,000,000 people and killing 3,000,000 annually.

In Wallace's day little was known about malaria except that "ague" was associated with marshy, swampy terrain. It was not until near the turn of the century that a French biologist, working in Algeria, identified the causative parasite; that British investigators, working in India, pinpointed the mosquito as the vector or carrier of the parasite; and that Italian scientists singled out the female anopheles as the transmitter. Since then, thirty-five different species of anopheles mosquito have been identified, from the jungles of the Amazon to those of the Malay world. Wallace must have had a clinically splendid parasitic mixture in his bloodstream.

Like the vampire bats of the Amazon which Wallace and Bates fought off, the female anopheles requires a dinner of blood to produce the fertile eggs that preserve her species. By comparison, the male of the species is a Caspar Milquetoast, a vegetarian who feeds only on plant juices.

Wallace's rambling letters and notebooks provide evidence of his deteriorating health during this period. For example, a page in one Malay notebook reads, "January 20, 1858, Gilolo." Yet his first letter to Bates from Ternate, cited earlier, bears the postscript, "Ternate, January 25, 1858," with the news that he planned to leave for Gilolo in a few days. In his memorable *The Malay Archipelago* Wallace reported the date of his return to Ternate from Gilolo as March 1.

The confusion in dates, is, under the circumstances, explicable, and in the preface to his book on the Malay world, Wallace apologized to his readers. His journeys to different islands, he explained, were regulated by the monsoons and the availability of transport—Dutch schooners, Bugis *praus*, Moluccan *kora-kora*, and other assorted vessels. "I visited some islands two or three times at distant intervals," he wrote, "and in some cases had to make the same voyage four times over." As a result, he said, in providing an account of travels in the archipelago he abandoned chronological sequence because "it would have puzzled my readers." It may as well have puzzled him. "They would never have known where they were," he went on; ". . . [the book] would have been hardly intelligible."

It must also be borne in mind that Wallace made these journeys more than a century ago, when many islands of the archipelago were *terra incognita*, if not literally, then figuratively; indeed, Wallace liked to twit his friends in London by identifying the place he was at and then challenging his correspondent or the Royal Geographical Society to find the spot on their maps. "By-the-by, you do not yet know where I am," Wallace wrote a friend, "for I defy all the members of the Royal Geographical Society in full conclave to tell you where is the place from which I date this letter." In this instance the letter was dated "Bessir, September 1, 1860."* Taunting the experts was always a Wallace delight.

Austen Henry Layard, a contemporary of Wallace and the discoverer of ancient Nineveh—which in Genesis was the capital of the first empire after the Flood—also suffered and survived, as did many of Britain's empire builders in this period, from the ravages of malaria. "I was still suffering from my attack of fever," he wrote on one occasion, "and those who have had the advantage of experience in these matters know that one of the results of fever is a considerable excitement of the brain, consequent audacity and no small additional loquacity, only limited by physical debility."

In a phrase, a malarial attack sometimes left Layard "high." The same may be said of Wallace.**

In 1898, in Wallace's first public account of the events surrounding his Ternate Paper, he observed that ever since he had read Chambers' *Vestiges* he had been convinced that the development of species was the outcome of evolution but, he noted, "no one had set forth the various kinds of evidence that rendered it almost a certainty."

Even Wallace's Sarawak Law, belatedly now hailed as the longest leap forward in biology after Lamarck, fell short of explaining the origin of descent and divergence among species. "I had no conception of how or why each new form had come into existence with all its beautiful adaptations to its special mode of life," Wallace confessed. It was a problem that preyed upon his mind. At Down House, Darwin went through similar agony. Darwin had worked out the mechanism

---

* Bessir is a village encircled by palms on the southwest island of Waigiou, at the northwest tip of New Guinea; the island is almost cut in half by an extraordinary, finger-shaped bay.

** This explanation is necessary because H. Lewis McKinney, op. cit., p. 17, who appears never to have visited the Malay archipelago nor to have suffered from malaria, has accused Wallace, alternately and repetitiously, of "mendacity," "deception," and "lying" about where he was when the solution to the species question struck him. McKinney has contended that the solution came to Wallace on Gilolo and not Ternate, as Wallace said. According to McKinney, the reason for this was that Ternate was better known than Gilolo (!). McKinney's accusation is ludicrous. See also p. 343.

of the origin of species, but could not come up with a theory to explain the origin of diversity.

In a 1905 account of events surrounding the Ternate Paper, as noted earlier, Wallace recalled that ". . . the exact process of the change and causes which led to [evolution] were absolutely unknown and *appeared almost inconceivable*." (Italics added.) The last three words indicate that the idea may have stirred in Wallace's mind earlier and fleetingly, that the idea was more of a falling star than a comet whose brilliance would light up the heavens.

The star may have fallen shortly before Wallace returned to Ternate on March 1, perhaps in February during an excursion to Gilolo. It was on the latter island, a few hours' journey by outrigger from Ternate, that his first serious attacks of recurrent malaria in the Moluccas hit him, and hit him hard. Whatever the case, on March 1 an exhausted Wallace was back at Ternate.

"At the time in question," Wallace reminisced, "I was suffering from a sharp attack of intermittent fever, and every day during the cold and succeeding hot fits had to lie down for several hours, during which time I had nothing to do but to think over any subjects then particularly interesting me."

Since the incident marks a watershed in the world's history, with the consequences still unfolding more than a century later, here is Wallace's version of the episode, written at the age of seventy-five, as it appeared in his book. *The Wonderful Century.*

> During one of these fits, while again considering the problem of the origin of species, something led me to think of Malthus' *Essay on Population* (which I had read about ten years before [actually thirteen]), and the "positive checks"—war, disease, famine, accident, etc.—which he adduced as keeping all savage populations nearly stationary.* It then occurred to me that these checks must also act upon animals, and keep down their numbers; and as they increase so much faster than man does, while their numbers are always very nearly or quite stationary, it was clear that these checks in their case must be far more powerful, since a number equal to the whole increase must be cut off by them every year. While vaguely thinking how this would affect any species, there suddenly flashed upon me the idea of *the survival of the fittest***—that the individuals removed by these checks must be, on the whole, *inferior* to

* "All savage populations" wryly suggested all peoples.
** The term, of course, is Herbert Spencer's and it was at Wallace's urging that Darwin used it increasingly in his writing after 1866.

those that survived. Then, considering the *variations* continually occurring in every fresh generation of animals or plants, and the changes of climate, of food, of enemies always in progress, the whole method of specific modification became clear to me, and in the two hours of my fit I had thought the *main points of the theory*. (Italics added.)

Again, the last several words are significant. They suggest that the inspiration came either on Gilolo or Ternate toward the end of February or early March and that Wallace worked out the details in his mind before putting the whole theory to paper. In the aftermath of a fresh seizure, perhaps around March 6, Wallace wrote it out. He was then on Ternate, of course, but the first inkling of inspiration may have come shortly before, when he was still on Gilolo.

At the meeting of the Linnean Society which observed the fiftieth anniversary of the reading of Wallace's paper and the extracts from both Darwin's unpublished 1844 essay and his letter to Asa Gray, Wallace provided additional insight into his discovery of the theory of the origin of species. Lyell's work, he said, had had a more profound influence on the solution of the species question than Malthus'. "Along with Malthus," Wallace told the 1908 meeting, "I had read, and been even more deeply impressed by, Sir Charles Lyell's immortal *Principles of Geology*, which had taught me that the inorganic world—the whole surface of the earth, its seas and lands, its mountains and valleys, its rivers and lakes, and every detail of its climatic conditions—were and always had been in a continual state of slow modification."

"Hence," Wallace continued, "it became obvious that the forms of life must have become continually adjusted to these changed conditions in order to survive."

In 1908, portly and sporting a full white beard, his unlined face belying his eighty-five years, Wallace may have laughed to himself when he cited fossils as convincing proof of Lyell's thesis. As a small boy at Hertford, it will be recalled, when he occasionally found fossils in chalk formations—"thunderbolts," his companions had labeled them— a young Wallace believed that the fossils had fallen to earth during thunderstorms.

When the malarial attack abated, Wallace repeatedly thought through *his* startling theory of evolution. Why did some members of a species die while others live? The reason was as manifest as the rising sun on a cloudless morning. The reason was so obvious that Huxley, Bates, and others later kicked themselves in public and expressed astonishment and embarrassment that since recorded history the world's greatest thinkers had been blind to the rising sun.

Suddenly a new world opened up in Wallace's mind, and before his very eyes: from the effects of disease, the most healthy species escaped; among enemies, the strongest, the swiftest, or the most cunning members of a species survived; from famine the best hunters or those with the best digestion matured.

"I seemed to see the whole effect of this," Wallace said, "that when changes of land and sea, or of climate, or of food supply, or of enemies occurred—and we know that such changes have always been taking place—and considering the amount of individual variation that my experience as a collector had shown me to exist, then it followed that all the changes necessary for the adaptation of the species to the changing conditions would be brought about; and as great changes in the environment are always slow, there would be ample time for the change to be effected by the survival of the best fitted in every generation."

This was the principle behind divergence which mystified Darwin after his discovery of natural selection.

Wallace was also "higher" than he had ever been, or would ever be again. He trembled as he waited for the last phase of the latest attack of malaria to dissipate "so that I might at once make notes for a paper on the subject." He was afraid that the theory would dissolve in his mind, as a dream.

That night Wallace, sitting in a thatched-roof hut, made his precious notes and on two succeeding evenings in the first week of March he wrote out the theory "carefully." His style was as limpid as the mythical waters of Hans Christian Andersen. When Wallace completed the paper, he wrote above it, "On the Tendency of Varieties to Depart Indefinitely from the Original Type," and at the end of it, "Written at Ternate, February, 1858"—his location when he wrote it, not where he first contemplated the "almost inconceivable."

In Wallace's Ternate Paper the pieces fell together effortlessly to form a complete picture of evolution: descent and divergence by modification through natural selection.

Wallace's paper consisted of 3,764 words, the equivalent of fifteen double-spaced pages of typewritten copy. His cogent style overcame the problem of how to present the complex subject simply, but not simplistically. At the very moment Wallace drafted his paper, Darwin's "big book" had reached 500,000 words and there was no end in sight as the master of Down House grappled unsuccessfully with the riddle of divergence. It was as if Darwin sought to write himself out of his problem.

Wallace's lucidity speaks for itself. Here are excerpts from the Ternate Paper:

> The life of wild animals is a struggle for existence. . . .
>
> By a careful consideration of all the circumstances we may be enabled to comprehend, and in some degree to explain, what at first sight appears so inexplicable—the excessive abundance of some species, while others closely allied to them are very rare. . . .
>
> Even the least prolific of animals would increase rapidly if unchecked, where it is evident that the animal population of the globe must be stationary, or perhaps, through the influence of man, decreasing. . . .
>
> A simple calculation will show that in fifteen years each pair of birds would have increased to nearly ten millions.*
>
> It is evident, therefore, that each year an immense number of birds must perish—as many in fact as are born; and as on the lowest calculation the progeny are each year twice as numerous as their parents, it follows that, whatever be the average number of individuals existing in any given country, *twice that number must perish annually,*—a striking result. . . .
>
> Wild cats are prolific and have few enemies; why then are they never as abundant as rabbits? The only intelligible answer is that their supply of food is more precarious.
>
> It appears evident, therefore, that so long as a country [biological district] remains physically unchanged, the numbers of its animal population cannot materially increase. If one species does so, some others requiring the same kind of food must diminish in proportion. The numbers that die annually must be immense; and as the individual existence of each animal depends upon itself, those that die must be the weakest—the very young, the aged, and the diseased—while those that prolong their existence can only be the most perfect in health and vigour—those who are the best able to obtain food regularly, and to avoid their numerous enemies. It is . . . "a struggle for existence," in which the weakest and least perfectly organized must always succumb.

Wallace now took another long leap forward. He laid bare the theory of divergence, the law governing the incredible, immense diversity of living things, from snakes to salmons to simians. If the population of a species in a given area is kept stationary by checks and balances,

* In *Natural Selection*, a collection of his essays published in 1871, Wallace amended that statement with this footnote: "This is under estimated. The number would really amount to more than two thousand millions!"

and if the comparative abundance or scarcity of the individuals of several species is due to their compromises with nature and resulting habits, "we shall be in a condition to proceed to the consideration of varieties, to which the preceding remarks have a direct and very important application."

Again, to quote directly from the Ternate Paper:

> Most or perhaps all the variations from the typical form of a species must have some definite effect, however slight, on the habits or capacities of the individuals.
>
> Even a change of colour might, by rendering them more or less distinguishable, affect their safety. . . .
>
> If, on the other hand, any species should produce a variety having slightly increased powers of preserving existence, that variety must inevitably in time acquire a superiority in numbers.
>
> Now, let some alteration of physical conditions occur in the [biological] district—a long period of drought, a destruction of vegetation by locusts, the irruption of some new carnivorous animal . . . it is evident that, of all the individuals composing the species, those forming the least numerous and most feebly organized variety would suffer first, and, were the pressure severe, must soon become extinct. . . .
>
> The superior variety would then alone remain. . . .
>
> The *variety* would now have replaced the *species*. . . .
>
> Such a variety *could not* return to the original form; for that form is an inferior one, and could never compete with it for existence. . . .
>
> Here, then, we have *progression and continued divergence* deduced from the general laws which regulate the existence of animals in a state of nature, and from the undisputed fact that varieties do frequently occur. . . .
>
> Now the scale on which nature works is so vast—the numbers of individuals and the periods of time with which she deals approach so near to infinity, that any cause, however slight, and however liable to be veiled and counteracted by accidental circumstances, must in the end produce its full legitimate results.

Wallace displayed none of Darwin's tendency to accept Lamarckism; indeed, as Darwin grew older, he gravitated back to the cardinal principle of Lamarckism—that acquired traits may be inherited. Wallace's paper on "the tendency of varieties to depart indefinitely from the original type" destroyed Lamarck for all time, with one glaring exception.*

---

* In the Soviet Union, during Stalin's reign of terror, Russian biologists and geneticists were forced to accept Lamarck's doctrine for ideological reasons, as evidence of the validity of Marxist-Leninist theory; those who failed to do so faced imprisonment, exile, or execution.

Perhaps the most ingenious example of Lamarck's theory was his suggestion that the giraffe acquired its long neck through inheritance, each giraffe trying to reach the foliage of more lofty trees. The giraffe's progeny then acquired this trait and the neck of the species grew longer and longer, claimed Lamarck. Wallace considered the theory nonsense, arguing that "any varieties which occurred among its antitypes [forerunners] with a longer neck than usual *at once secured a fresh range of pasture over the same ground as their short-necked companions, and on the first scarcity of food were thereby enabled to outlive them.*" The giraffe had evolved through natural selection.

In conclusion, Wallace wrote, as he sat at his rude bamboo table in Ternate:

> We believe we have now shown that there is a tendency in nature to the continued progression of certain classes of *varieties* further and further from the original type—a progression to which there appears no reason to assign any definite limits. . . . This progression, by minute steps, in various directions, but always checked and balanced by the necessary conditions, subject to which alone existence can be preserved, may, it is believed, be followed out so as to agree with all the phenomena presented by organized beings, their extinction and succession in past ages, and all the extraordinary modifications of form, instinct and habits which they exhibit.

Wallace probably leaned back when he finished the paper and sighed audibly, the exhilaration that had enveloped him as he wrote fading. For the first time since the species question had taken hold of him— preying on his mind night and day from Leicester to the Amazon to the Malay archipelago—he must have felt inwardly relaxed and at peace with himself.

"The more I thought it over," said Wallace later, "the more I became convinced that I had at length found the long-sought-for law of nature that solved the problem of the origin of species."

Now that he had put his novel, revolutionary theory to paper, a theory that would shake the earth, what should he do with it? He could send it off to any one of a number of journals. Certainly the *Annals and Magazine of Natural History*, which had published the Sarawak Law, would have been an obvious market. But less than a year earlier Wallace had received his first letter from no less a celebrity than Charles Darwin, the greatest naturalist of the day, whose *Voyage of the Beagle* Wallace had read in his youth and admired. Indeed, that book had helped set him off on the path he was now following. Moreover, in that first letter of May 1, 1857, Darwin had confided in Wallace, a complete stranger. Didn't Darwin reveal that, after twenty years of work on the species question "I am now preparing my work for publication." Darwin, of course, did not reveal that he had finally begun work on the project as a result of the publication of Wallace's Sarawak Law. By now, Wallace probably thought, Darwin's book was on the verge of being printed—was, possibly, already in print.

And barely a dozen weeks earlier, on December 22, Wallace had received a second letter from Darwin. In it Darwin said he was troubled by the distribution of species on islands "and any facts on this subject would be most gratefully received." Wallace was sitting among the world's largest collection of islands. Darwin, a man of stature and influence in the scientific hierarchy, had asked for help, for Wallace's help, for "facts." Facts! Wallace had been doing nothing else but collecting facts on the species question, in both hemispheres no less, and for almost a decade. Wallace was understandably flattered that Darwin, whom he revered, had asked for assistance.

Wallace's course was as clear as his Ternate Paper. This was Wallace's grand opportunity to lift himself from relative scientific obscurity. The great Darwin beckoned; unknown to Wallace, so did history.

A Dutch mail boat was scheduled to leave Ternate on March 9. Wallace acted immediately, perhaps impulsively. "[I decided] to send it to Darwin by the next post," he said, "which would leave in a day or two." (The Ternate Paper, reasoned Wallace, would reach Down House toward the end of May or, at the latest, the first week of June, assuming, of course, no ship foundered en route to England.)

"I wrote a letter to him in which I said that I hoped the idea would be as new to him as it was to me, and that it would supply the missing factor to explain the origin of species," Wallace recalled.

It is interesting, and pointless, to speculate how the course of history might have been changed had Wallace not sent his manuscript to Darwin. Would Darwin have ever finished his "big book?" His closest friends, Lyell and Hooker, doubted it. In point of fact, Darwin never completed the giant volume, since Wallace's manuscript forced him into writing an abstract.

Whatever the precipitating factor, Dunkinfield H. Scott, the president of the Linnean Society at the turn of the century, described Wallace's decision to send his manuscript to Darwin "a most happy inspiration." Incontestably it was—for Darwin.

In any event, Wallace handed the Dutch master of the boat his envelope and sent the Ternate Paper on its way to Down via Singapore, Southampton, and London.

By March 25 Wallace had fully recovered from his intermittent bouts of malaria and he immediately booked passage to the north coast of New Guinea aboard a trading schooner. The skipper of the vessel promised to drop him ashore and pick him up "three or four months later." Thus Wallace became the first European to live alone on that huge, magnificent island, parts of whose interior today are still *terra incognita* and whose people, the Papuans, continue to live largely in a Stone Age culture.

"The weather had been unusually wet and the place was unhealthy," Wallace said. He had four companions on the trip, his Malay assistant Ali, two Moluccans, and a Javanese. "Three . . . had fever as well as myself," wrote Wallace, "and one of my hunters died."

Chapter 26

FOR THE NEXT HUNDRED DAYS, until his manuscript reached Down, Alfred Russel Wallace stood alone in the world as, in our time, Neil Armstrong stood on the moon in 1969, and Charles A. Lindbergh sat, isolated in the cabin of his tiny airplane over the vastness of the mid-Atlantic less than a generation earlier. Wallace was the first individual in history to set out a complete view of man as a creature of evolution, descended from a closely allied species in both time and space, his descent *and* diversity modified by the process of natural selection. Unknown to the thirty-five-year-old Wallace, this was the supreme moment of his life. There were no trumpets, no flags, no headlines, nothing to show for it except the new way he looked at the living world around him.

To most persons, as Wallace later put it, nature appears calm, orderly, and peaceful. They see the birds singing in the trees, he said, the insects hovering over the flowers, the squirrels climbing among the treetops, and all living things in possession of health, vigor, and the enjoyment of a sunny existence. But the average individual does not see, and hardly ever thinks of, the means by which this beauty, harmony, and enjoyment are brought about. He or she does not see the constant, daily search for food, the failure to obtain which means weakness or death; the unremitting effort to escape enemies; the ever recurring struggle against the forces of nature. "This daily and hourly struggle, this incessant warfare," Wallace observed, "is nevertheless the very means by which much of the beauty and harmony and enjoyment in nature is produced, and also affords of the most important elements in bringing about the origin of species."

On January 4, 1858, only a few weeks before the theory came to fruition in his mind, Wallace wrote Bates that "I have prepared the plan and written a portion of a work embracing the whole subject."

If Wallace had begun his own "big book," and there is no reason to doubt his word, he presumably halted in midstream, and whatever he wrote out is either lost or was destroyed by Wallace himself. Darwin's *Origin*, published the following year, preempted Wallace, and from Wallace's point of view, happily so. As Wallace put it to Bates, Darwin "may save me the trouble of writing more on my hypothesis."

Like Darwin, Wallace did not feel he was fully equipped to execute the ambitious project of providing irrefutable scientific evidence in support of the preposterous theory of man's descent from a closely allied species. Like Darwin, he was afraid to kill God (although history has demonstrated since then that the theory of natural selection did not kill God; on the contrary, it deepened the mystery of the inexplicable, in us and above us). And like Darwin, Wallace also felt that he lacked the stamina and fortitude to stand against the hysterical outcry, the hostile outpouring, that was certain to follow publication of the theory. The queen descended from an ape? For to the popular Victorian mind, and in fact, the essence of the Wallace–Darwin theory is that man is related to a monkey.

Of course, Wallace had no idea of what Darwin was writing about and it was possible that Darwin would put forth a theory of evolution which, like Lamarck, Wallace would demolish easily. If Darwin failed to understand either descent or diversity in nature, Wallace was prepared to complete a "work embracing the whole subject," as he confided to Bates.

But whatever Darwin's direction, Wallace stood to gain by Darwin's work. Even if he disagreed with Darwin's conclusions, Wallace knew that Darwin would provide him with additional "facts" about the species question. In this light, Wallace, Darwin, Lyell, and Hooker were driven as scientists by a Baconian compulsion to amass "facts." In the last analysis, they realized, the theory that varieties transformed themselves into species would fall or stand on a presentation of incontrovertible "facts." Each knew that their countrymen mistrusted philosophers, and that the practical English could be persuaded to accept a point only by establishing the "facts" of the case.

Thus, inwardly, Wallace was delighted that Darwin had tackled the awesome task of the "big book." What a relief, if Darwin's theory proved to be similar to his own.

But Wallace had to get on with making a living. There were still more "facts" to collect, more specimens for Stevens, his London agent, to sell. "In the Amazon . . . there is work for fifty collectors for fifty years . . . ," Wallace wrote Bates' brother, Frederick. "Here it is the same with the islands. I could spend twenty years here were life long enough."

Wallace no sooner posted his Ternate Essay to Darwin than he was off to New Guinea, and again the advancement of science went hand-in-hand with danger and discomfort.

For the first three days on the dark, brooding island-continent, after being put ashore by a Dutch schooner, Wallace and his men were "fully occupied from morning to night building a house" about two hundred yards from the beach. "I [soon] found myself fairly established as the only European inhabitant of the vast island," he said. His headquarters were at Dorey, present-day Manokwari. The Papuans viewed Wallace and his party of Malays, Moluccans, and Javanese with a mixture of surprise, as well as suspicion and curiosity. "We slept at first with loaded guns beside us," wrote Wallace, and a "watch set." But after several days, "finding the people friendly, and feeling sure that they would not venture to attack five well-armed men, we took no further precautions." The latter point is revealing and amusing. Again, as with the Indians of the Amazon, Wallace did not refer to the first Papuans he met as "natives," but as *people*. And as for the latter comment, the Papuans, ignorant of gunpowder, would not have considered the party "well-armed."

The Papuans, especially those from the interior, fascinated Wallace, just as had the first Indians he had met in the vastness of the Amazon. The Papuan men, women, and children went completely naked. They were, like the animals around them, productions of natural selection. But they astonished Wallace in many ways, most notably by their rudimental love of art. "If these people are not savages, where shall we find any?" he asked. "Yet they have all a decided love for the fine arts, and spend their leisure time in executing works whose good taste and elegance would often be admired in our schools of design!"

The color of the Papuans was "generally black," he observed, not the coffee tint of the average Malay. Papuan hair was short, matted, and frizzy. Thus, the Papuans possessed Negroid facial characteristics. All this should hardly have surprised Wallace. The first Europeans to view the peoples of the island, in the sixteenth century, made the same observations and christened the place New Guinea because they felt it so closely resembled the Guinea of Africa's west coast.

Unlike the Amazon, however, where the legend of El Dorado enticed explorers and adventurers, "in Netherlands New Guinea it was not the lustre of gold that attracted travellers," the Dutch scholar H. J. P. Bylmer wrote, "but a brilliance less tangible and more sublime: snow." In the Malay world, eternal snow glistened only in New Guinea and it was not until 1907 that the first European expedition attempted to reach the snow, and failed, since the jungle interior was so formidable.

But Wallace was in search of species, not snow. And he found another entomological lode. One exciting discovery was a new genus of "curious . . . novel . . . horned flies," the horns protruding from beneath their eyes. "I obtained four distinct species," Wallace said joyfully. Nobody in the West had ever seen such creatures and, in London, W. W. Saunders, the entomologist, named one of the flies *Elaphomia wallacei*. Whatever his destiny, one thing was assured: Wallace's name in science was becoming imperishable, like the stars above him on a clear, black New Guinea night.

Wallace was in his glory. He averaged forty-nine new species daily and said triumphantly, "On the 31st of May [1858], I took 78 distinct sorts, a larger number than I had ever captured before." He found them among dead trees and under rotted bark.

While clambering around the jungle, Wallace slipped and fell badly, injuring his ankle. "As usual with foot wounds in this climate," he recorded, "it turned into an obstinate ulcer." The ankle swelled and the wound became infected. Wallace was immobilized in his bamboo and thatched-roof hut for a month. He leeched and lanced the wound repeatedly, and applied poultices. "I was almost driven to despair—for the weather was at length fine, and I was tantalized by seeing grand butterflies flying past my door, and thinking of the twenty or thirty new species of insects that I ought to be getting every day. And this, too," he added, "in New Guinea! . . . a country which no naturalist had ever resided in before—a country which contained more strange and new and beautiful natural objects than any other part of the globe."

That was one of the worst months Wallace spent in the islands; to add to his torment, his men were constantly down with fever and dysentery, and the only reading matter he had brought with him was Smollett's *Tristam Shandy*, which he read three times.

On June 26 of that year, the day that Darwin put on his letter to Lyell a postscript saying that after sleeping overnight on Wallace's Ternate Paper he had decided that "it would be dishonourable in me now to publish," one of Wallace's men died from malaria and dysentery. He was buried on the white beach, beside a brown and green palm tree, overlooking the blue Pacific.

On July 6, five days after the conspiracy had run its course at the Linnean Society, the Dutch schooner reappeared in Dorey harbor and picked up the emaciated Wallace and his remaining party for the return voyage to Ternate. For five days the vessel resembled Coleridge's painted ship on a painted ocean. The best wind was a sultry three knots and as the schooner finally drew within view of Ternate, a gale struck and forced it to beat almost endlessly to reach the island. "Such is the annoyance of travelling these seas," Wallace wrote in an unpublished notebook now in the possession of the Linnean Society. "Sixteen and 17 days for a voyage of about 500 miles, and each way in the favourable monsoon!"

An August entry added: "I was heartily glad to find myself again at home in Ternate, enjoying milk to my tea and some small variety in my bill of fare. . . . I was indeed pretty well knocked up by this New Guinea voyage."

In September, after recruiting his health, Wallace made preparations to explore another biological *terra incognita*, the large, nearby island of Batchian. Shortly before his departure, however, a Dutch mail boat anchored in Ternate's roadstead. It carried the letter from Hooker explaining what had happened at the Linnean Society, and folded within the letter was the note Darwin had asked Hooker to forward to Wallace with Hooker's explanation. The letter and note are missing, as are Wallace's replies. But strong circumstantial evidence suggests that Wallace was delighted by the communications, surprised that his paper had been read before such a prestigious body as the Linnean, and grateful to Darwin and Hooker for all they had done, as far as he could see, on his behalf.

Fortuitously, a letter from this period, addressed to his mother on October 6, 1858, has survived:

"I have received letters from Mr. Darwin and Dr. Hooker, two of the most eminent naturalists in England, which has highly gratified me," Wallace wrote. "I sent Mr. Darwin an essay on a subject on which he is now writing a great work. He showed it to Dr. Hooker and Sir C. Lyell, who thought so highly of it that they immediately read it before the Linnean Society."

As far as Wallace knew, Darwin was still working on his "big book," as he had been for some twenty years. Apparently it was still not yet in print. Wallace had no way of knowing that Darwin had abandoned the project because of Wallace himself. He did not know that Darwin was now racing to establish his own priority, prodded by Lyell and Hooker, by publishing an "abstract." The communications from Darwin and Hooker provided no hint of the bolt of lightning from Ternate that struck Down, of the panic it unleashed in Darwin, of the rescue operation plotted by Darwin, Lyell, and Hooker, or of the "delicate arrangement" that had unfolded at the Linnean following Brown's death.

As John W. Judd, a Fellow of the Royal Society and dean of the Royal College of Science, later aptly observed, "Little did Wallace think, in the absence of all knowledge on his part of Darwin's own conclusions, what stir would be made by his paper when it arrived in England!"

Wallace was a babe in the woods, but he was an elated babe. His theory of the origin of species had won the recognition of the power brokers of the scientific establishment. Wallace had drawn the attention of England's most distinguished scientists, men of wealth and social station. Wallace was flattered and pleased. "This," he wrote his mother, "insures me the acquaintance of these eminent men on my return home."

After sending off replies to Darwin and Hooker, Wallace embarked for Batchian, where he saw "quantities of a black, short-tailed ape resembling that of the Celebes but probably a distinct species" and where he discovered "a completely new specie of Bird of Paradise . . . a great prize—it had two white feathers sticking out from each shoulder."

In a free moment on Batchian, Wallace wrote George Silk, his boyhood friend. "You cannot, perhaps, imagine how I have come to love solitude," he wrote. ". . . I find it favorable to reflection." Darwin would have been in complete agreement.

Playfully, Wallace urged Silk to get a copy of the Linnean's *Journal of Proceedings* for August and to read the last article and the accompanying remarks of Lyell and Hooker. "As I know neither of them," Wallace wrote, "I am a little proud."

The Ternate Essay had been recognized on merit; the author's school
tie and social ties, his politics and religious beliefs, had not entered into
its evaluation.

Wallace was so delighted with Batchian that he spent six months
there. "Four or five different kinds of ants attack everything not isolated by water, and one kind even swims across that; great spiders lurk
in baskets and boxes, or hide in the folds of mosquito curtains; centipedes and millipedes are found everywhere," he said.

"I have caught them under my pillow and on my head; while in every
box, and under every board which has lain for some days undisturbed,
little scorpions are sure to be found snugly ensconced, with their formidable tails quickly turned up ready for attack or defense."

Yet these companions in nature, Wallace complained, "all combined
are not so bad as the irritation of most mosquitoes." Unknown to him,
the mosquito was the carrier of the debilitating, murderous malarial
parasite.

The mosquitoes were an unending source of torment. By comparison,
he observed, "you may live a long time among scorpions, spiders, and
centipedes, ugly and venomous though they are, and get no harm from
them." "After twelve years of living in the tropics," he added, "I have
never yet been bitten or stung by either [scorpions or spiders]." In
truth, in the jungles of the Amazon and Indonesia, Wallace had led a
"charmed life," or as the Malays would put it, Wallace was *bakar tidak
basah*, he was scorched but never burned.

On April 12, 1859, a Dutch government boat arrived at Batchian
from Ternate with rice for the island's garrison of *Koninklijk Neder-
landsche Indies Leger*, Dutch colonial troops composed largely of Am-
bonese and Menadonese. The boat was a *kora-kora*, with freeboard almost awash, four tons burthen, equipped with five bamboo outriggers,
twenty rowers, and a gaff-rigged mainsail.

Wallace clambered aboard with his butterfly net and insect boxes
for the return voyage to Ternate, joining a group of passengers that
included three Javanese soldiers, two recently released Moluccan con-
victs, a Dutch schoolmaster's wife and her servant, and a Chinese trader.
"We all had to sleep together in the cabin, packed pretty close," Wallace said, "but they very civilly allowed me plenty of room for my
mattress, and we got on very well together."

As the boat slipped through the green-blue Molucca Sea, two sailors
incessantly beat wooden drums while the rowers, stripped to their

waists, wearing only a sarong with the inevitable *kris* tucked into the folds, swung the oars to the beat during periods of calm. "The passage would have been agreeable enough but for the dreadful tom-toms," Wallace complained wearily, ". . . making a fearful din the whole voyage."

There was a small galley forward where each passenger boiled his rice, mixed with one of several fiery pastes called *sambal*, and brewed his coffee. Everyone, of course, brought his own provisions and arranged mealtimes as convenient. Thus, the smoke from the charcoal brazier, the odor of freshly brewed coffee and spices, and the inescapable fragrance of cloves wafted aft throughout the trip. An individual can travel blindfolded around the world and recognize the Indonesian islands by the aroma of cloves, particularly since Indonesians are heavy smokers and mix this spice with their tobacco.

En route, the *kora-kora* put into a islet for fresh provisions, plantains, bananas, and other stores. That night, retiring for the evening, Wallace lay down on his mattress and snuffed out his candle. Next to his bedroll was a box with his handkerchief atop it. "[I] put out my hand to take it," he said, "and I quickly drew back on feeling something cool and very smooth, which moved as I touched it."

Wallace cried out for a light. In the glow of a coconut oil lamp, the terrified passengers and crew observed a snake neatly coiled on Wallace's handkerchief. "It was now necessary to catch or kill him immediately, or he would escape among the piles of miscellaneous luggage," Wallace said, adding a customary touch of understatement, "and we should hardly sleep comfortably."

One of the Javanese soldiers offered to catch the snake and wrapped a cloth around his hand. But at the last moment he broke into a cold sweat and hesitated. Wallace acted with dispatch. He seized a chopping knife "and carefully moving my insect nets, which hung just over the snake and prevented me getting a free blow," brought it down swiftly across the snake's back, cutting it in two, while Ali, his companion, crushed the serpent's head with a blow from the handle of his *kris*.

On examination, Wallace found the snake had large poisonous fangs. "It is a wonder that he did not bite me when I first touched him," he said.

And this was the shy, unadventuresome Wallace who dreamed only of the quiet English countryside.

On returning to Ternate, Wallace was in welcome receipt of not one, but two letters from Darwin. The first was dated January 25, 1859;

the second, April 6. Both are now in the manuscript collection of the British Museum. The tone, structure, and content of the letters are characteristically Darwinian, and reinforce the *Pall Mall Gazette*'s description of Darwin as the "master of happy simplicity." Both letters exhibit guile, glibness, and guilt mixed with integrity and honor, a pastiche of Darwin's character.

It is from these two Darwinian communications that we learn about the contents of the letters, now lost, which Wallace had written to Darwin and Hooker after learning, on his return from New Guinea, of the event that transpired at the Linnean Society on July 1. Darwin's letter of January 25 is explicit.

"Permit me to say how heartily I admire the spirit in which they were written," Darwin wrote of Wallace's letters. "Though I had *absolutely* nothing whatever to do in leading Lyell and Hooker to what they thought a fair course of action," Darwin claimed, "yet I naturally could not but feel anxious to hear what your impression would be." The italics are Darwin's.

Why should Darwin be so "anxious" about Wallace's reaction when he bore *absolutely* no responsibility for the actions of Lyell and Hooker? Clearly, Darwin misled Wallace about his concern for priority. That damning sentence also reveals the doubt gnawing at Darwin about the propriety of the "Wallace–Darwin episode," as Darwin's son Erasmus called it. The English writer, Dorothy L. Sayers, who created the character of Lord Peter Wimsey in the 1920s, expressed it nicely in *Clouds of Witness*. "He had accused him of cheating at cards," Miss Sayers wrote about a member of her English drawing-room set. "In that kind of society . . . such a misdemeanor as cheating at cards was regarded as far more shameful than such sins as murder and adultery."

For the first time, Darwin informed Wallace that he had abandoned his "big book" and had embarked upon an abstract of it. But Darwin did not offer an explanation. Wallace did not, and could not, know of the awesome impact of the Sarawak Law and Ternate Paper on Darwin. Darwin dropped a hint, but it must have been inexplicable to Wallace. "I owe indirectly much to you and them [Lyell and Hooker]," Darwin said, "for I almost think that Lyell would have proved right and I should never have completed my larger work, for I have found my abstract hard enough with my poor health; but, now, thank God, I am in my last chapter but one."

Darwin again felt it necessary to impress upon the younger Wallace, as he had before, how long and hard he had worked on his theory of evolution, subtly reinforcing his claim to priority against the one person who could dispute it.

"Everyone whom I have seen has thought your paper very well written and interesting," Darwin said. "It puts my extracts (written in 1839, now just twenty years ago!), which I say in apology were never for an instant for publication, in the shade."

Darwin ended on a note of warmth and good will. "God knows," he wrote Wallace, "if admirable zeal and energy deserve success, most amply you deserve it."

The April letter is very revealing about this traumatic period in Darwin's life. In it, Darwin informed Wallace that he had turned the first part of the abstract over to Murray, the publisher. And while Darwin said he had mentioned Wallace in the abstract, he added, "You must remember that I am now publishing only an Abstract, and I give no references." Darwin also reported, with happy simplicity, that Hooker "is a *full* convert" to the new theory of the origin of species. Similarly, Sir John Lubbock, Darwin's neighbor. And in that letter Darwin made his first concession regarding the theory as a joint production.

"Huxley is changed and believes in mutation of species," Darwin wrote; "whether a *convert* to us, I do not quite know." The italics, again, are Darwin's; perhaps they are misplaced. They should have read "a convert to *us*."

In Darwin's first three letters to Wallace, the salutation read, "My dear sir." The fourth communication, the note Darwin enclosed with Hooker's letter, is missing. But the fifth Darwin communication, the April letter, postmarked at Down, is addressed to "My dear Mr. Wallace."

Oceans and continents apart, their intimacy was growing. Fate had linked the names of Darwin and Wallace forever—that is, as long as man survives on this planet; for if the Wallace–Darwin theory of descent and divergence is correct, man will pass in time from the scene and emerge as a new species. To paraphrase Pericles, the Earth is not the sepulchre of great men, it is the sepulchre of extinct species.

Darwin had a fondness for postscripts and, more often than not, a brief aside disclosed more of his true feelings than the body of a letter. The April letter bears an extraordinary postscript. In full it reads as follows:

P.S.—You cannot tell how I admire your spirit, in the manner in which you have taken all that was done about establishing our papers. I had actually written a letter to you, stating that I could *not* publish anything before you had published. I had not sent that letter to the post when I received one from Lyell and Hooker, *urging* me to send some MS. to them, and allow them to act as they thought fair and honorably to both of us. I did so.

Chapter 27

ON NOVEMBER 24, 1859, the day Murray published *Origin*, Wallace was slogging through the jungle-blanketed island of Ceram in the Southern Moluccas. Ceram was a disappointment.

"[I] found no rare birds or insects," he recalled in exasperation. ". . . Beetles were scarce." Worst of all, the island was infested with a variety of gnat which resembled the *pium* of the Amazon.

"All the time I had been in Ceram I had suffered much from the irritating bites of an invisible *acarus*, which is worse than mosquitoes, ants, and every other pest because it is impossible to guard against them," he said.

"[The] . . . journey in the forest left me covered from head to foot with inflamed lumps, which, after my return to Ambon, produced a serious disease, confining me to the house for nearly two months—a not very pleasant memento of my first visit to Ceram, which terminated with the year 1859."

While the theory of the origin of species was uppermost in Wallace's mind, the need to earn a living was always close behind it. As a child of impoverished circumstances, the matter of livelihood repeatedly bobbed up in his notebooks and personal letters. A letter to Silk, written from Batchian, is a sample.

"Malays and Papuans, beetles and birds are what now occupy my thoughts," Wallace wrote, "mixed with financial calculations and hopes for a happy future in Old England, where I may live in solitude and seclusion, except for a few choice friends."

Wallace did not know it, but his dream was kindred to Darwin's life-style.

As for money, Wallace's Malay ledgers provide a poignant insight into his plight.

In September 1978, *Scientific American* (founded in 1845, the year Bates introduced Wallace to beetle collecting at Leicester) devoted an entire issue to the single topic of evolution, and described the idea as one of the most consequential in intellectual history. "First proposed in 1858 by Charles Darwin and Alfred Wallace to explain the marvelous diversity of living things," the journal said, "evolution has motivated and organized the work of the life sciences ever since."

It identified Wallace as "a young English naturalist doing fieldwork in the East Indies." This description was as accurate as it was misleading, especially for contemporary readers, since it conjured up the image of Wallace living on the handout of a private foundation or government endowment, or perhaps working as a graduate student on a Ph.D. thesis.

In contrast, a typical entry in Wallace's journal, dealing with butterflies, moths and beetles, including duplicates collected by Wallace at Wahai, on the north coast of Ceram,* tells the story poignantly. It read:

362	pinned at 2c.	Total:	$ 7.24
81	bad specimens at 1c.		.81
150	in papers at 2c.		3.00
166	sorts at 8c.		13.28
			$24.33

And so the ledger went. The value of the Ceram collection came to $345.56. The calculations were in Straits dollars, a currency still in vogue today in Singapore and Malaysia; the exchange rate was then about three Straits dollars to the American dollar. Wallace's Wahai collection came to U.S. $38.93.

Unlike Darwin, who was a superb businessman, parlaying his railroad portfolio, savings, and royalties into more than a million dollars by the time of his death, Wallace was a commercial misfit, like his father before him. On one occasion, however, Wallace collected a pot of gold

---

* Ceram's jungles provided cover for the separatist movement of the "Republic of the South Moluccas" in the 1950s. Its followers have conducted an intermittent campaign of terror in The Netherlands in the 1970s. During a visit to the island in 1954, I was offered, in the interior, roasted bat for lunch by a platoon of Indonesian soldiers but, not as adventuresome as Wallace, declined.

at the end of the scientific rainbow. That was in 1858, the most important year of his life, when, like the species theory, everything fell into place. Stevens, his agent, sold Wallace's Aru collection for £1,000.

"This makes me hope I may soon realise enough to live upon and carry out my long cherished plans of a country life in Old England," he said. Aru, it will be recalled, was the island Wallace described as "horrid." In that miserable place, he collected nine thousand insects, 1,600 of them different species, many new to science.

But Ceram had a glorious compensation—Captain van der Beck was one of those cosmopolitan Dutch who are found almost everywhere on the globe, a master of different languages, customs, and anecdotes, at home in the most remote areas. "I rather regretted leaving [Ceram]," Wallace said, "because my host was one of the most remarkable men and most entertaining companions I had ever met with." Van der Beck spoke French, Malay, and Javanese as well as his native Dutch; and English with the trace of an accent, but fluently, and with a complete knowledge of the idiom in which Wallace often tried to puzzle him but failed. Van der Beck was also at ease in German and Italian, modern Greek, Turkish, Russian, colloquial Hebrew, and Latin. "He used to sing a Hebrew drinking-song, which he had learned from some Jews with whom he had once travelled, and astonished by joining in their conversation," Wallace recalled; "and he had a never-ending fund of tale and anecdote about the people he had met and the places he had visited."

On Wallace's return to Ternate early in 1860, he found a letter from Darwin which had been written the previous November 13, on the eve of the publication of *Origin*. "I have told Murray to send you by post (if possible) a copy of my book," Darwin wrote, "and I hope that you will receive it at nearly the same time with this note."

Darwin's openness was startling, and the attachment between him and Wallace, distantly placed as they were in space and social status, was closing fast. "I should very much like to hear your general impression of the book," Darwin said, "as you have thought profoundly on the subject and in so nearly the same channel with myself."

Now that *Origin* was on the press and his priority assured, Darwin's character altered radically; his obsession for secrecy, his mistrust of even close friends, much less strangers, evaporated. Wallace's reaction to the Linnean affair had stamped him, in Darwin's mind, as a gentleman as well as a brilliant scientist. A friendly, solicitous Darwin emerged, and in his letter, written from Ilkey Wells, a water-cure establishment, eleven days before *Origin*'s publication date, a frank Darwin said, "I do not think your share in the theory will be overlooked by the real judges, as Hooker, Lyell, Asa Gray, etc."

Darwin also asked Wallace when he intended to return home, and extended hands of friendship and assistance. "I suppose that you will be thinking of returning soon with your magnificent collection and still grander mental materials," Darwin said. "You will be puzzled how to publish. The Royal Society Fund will be worth your consideration."

This letter alone from Darwin was worth all the suffering Wallace underwent in the Amzon and Malay archipelago.

Wallace occasionally thought of home, and sometimes longed to return to England, but there was still work to do—and a living to earn. Unlike the *pium* and *acarus*, money matters were a plague from which he would never escape. Underlying every financial thought was the question of how to earn a livelihood when he returned. He certainly could not live on scientific article sand monographs, or as a "fly-catcher." The truth was that Wallace had no job prospects at all, any more than poor Bates, who was still roaming the Amazon. But the offer of help from Darwin raised Wallace's spirits and gave him hope for the future.

Shortly before *Origin* was published, Wallace heard from Stevens of Bates' safe return from the Amazon after eleven years, and Wallace hastened to write his companion in the ecstasies and terrors of the jungle. The letter was written from Ceram November 25, 1858, the day after *Origin*'s publication. "Allow me to congratulate you on your arrival home with all your treasures; a good fortune which I trust is this time reserved for me," Wallace wrote Bates, thinking of his own ill-fated voyage of the *Helen*.

Stevens had told Wallace that Bates planned to write a book on the Amazon and Wallace encouraged his former partner. "I hope you may undertake it and bring it to a glorious conclusion," Wallace said. Then he disclosed for the first time that he, too, contemplated a book, the subject being the Malay archipelago.

Bates' return to England—"much depressed in health and spirit," said Bates later—probably also stirred within Wallace visions of his native land, of the English countryside immortalized by Constable.

So did letters from home. Thomas Sims, Wallace's brother-in-law, frequently expressed the family's concern about Wallace's health. "[Sims] urged me very strongly to return home before my health was seriously affected," Wallace recalled.

In a lengthy, eloquent reply to one of the Sims' appeals, Wallace made known his decision to carry on among the islands.

"Your ingenious arguments to persuade me to come home are quite unconvincing," Wallace wrote. "I have much to do yet before I can return with satisfaction of mind; were I to leave now I would be ever regretful and unhappy. That alone is an all-sufficient reason."

". . . But I am engaged in a wider and more general study," he continued, "that of the relations of animals to space and time, or in other words, their geographical and geological distribution and its causes."

Then Wallace came to grips with life as he saw it. "As to health and life, what are they compared with peace and happiness?" he asked. He summed up his philosophy as "work with a purpose, and the nobler the purpose the greater the happiness."

Wallace also raised his "pecuniary" problem, which he characterized as both weighty and powerful. And, for once, he was realistic. "I have not yet made enough to live upon, and I am likely to make it quicker here than I could in England," he said. "In England there is only one way in which I could live, by returning to my old profession of land surveying. Now, though I always liked surveying, I like collecting better and I could never now give my whole mind to any work apart from the study to which I have devoted my life."

In his letters Sims had apparently sought to put down Wallace, as many scientists did later and still do, by branding him a dilettante and "an enthusiast."

But Wallace relished the label. "So far from being angry at being called an enthusiast (as you seem to suppose) it is my pride and glory to be worthy to be so called," Wallace replied jubilantly. "Who ever did anything good or great who was not an enthusiast? The majority of mankind are enthusiasts only in one thing—in money-getting; and these call others enthusiasts as a term of reproach because they think there is something in the world better than money-getting. It strikes me that the power or capability of a man in getting rich is in *inverse* proportion to his reflective powers and in *direct* proportion to his impudence. It is perhaps good to *be* rich [Darwin?], but not to *get* rich, or to be always trying to get rich."

Wallace ended his sermon on a merry note: "Few men are less suited to get rich, if they did try, than myself!"

Another reason Wallace decided to continue exploring the Malay world may have been the publication of Darwin's *Origin*. It precluded his early return. Wallace apparently received his copy of the book early in 1860; the exact date is unknown. But he read it through "five or six times" and each time with increasing admiration. In a letter to Silk, he predicted that Darwin's *Origin* would live as long as Newton's *Principia*.

"It shows that nature is, as I before remarked to you, a study that yields to none in grandeur and immensity," Wallace commented. ". . . Mr. Darwin has given the world a *new science*, and his name should, in my opinion stand over that of every philosopher of ancient or modern times. The force of admiration can no further go!!!"

And in a letter to Bates, now resettled in Leicester, where Bates gloomily wrote that "I see little prospect of ever giving my narrative to the world," Wallace confided from Ternate that Darwin had saved him the trouble of writing his own "big book" on the origin of species.

"I know not how, or to whom, to express fully my admiration of Darwin's book," Wallace said. "To *him* it would seem flattery; to others self-praise." This is the closest Wallace ever came to raising a claim to priority.

"I could *never have approached* the completeness of his book," Wallace continued. ". . . I really feel thankful that it has *not* been left to me to give the theory to the world."

Wallace revealed to Bates in that same letter that in the Malay archipelago he was still working out the theory of geographical distribution which had first attracted his attention in the Amazon. "I am now convinced that insects, on the whole, do not give such true indication of zoological geography as birds and mammals, because, first, they have such immensely greater means of dispersal across rivers and seas; second, because they are so much more influenced by surrounding circumstances; and third, because the species seem to change more quickly, and therefore disguise a comparatively recent identity," Wallace wrote. ". . . This is strikingly shown here, where the insect-fauna from Malacca to New Guinea has a very large amount of characteristic uniformity while Australia, from its distinct climate and vegetation, shows a wide difference. I am inclined to think, therefore, that a preliminary study of, first, the mammals, and then the birds, is indispensable to a correct understanding of geographical and physical changes on which the present insect-distribution depends. . . ."

When he completed this phase of his research, Wallace made his second greatest contribution to science, and the one for which he is best remembered among scientists—the geographic distribution of animals.

As he wrote in *The Malay Archipelago*, "I have arrived at the conclusion that we can draw a line among the islands, which shall so divide them that one-half shall truly belong to Asia, while the other shall no less certainly be allied to Australia."* That line, to this day, is universally acclaimed as the Wallace Line. It runs between Borneo and the Celebes, between Bali and Lombok. The theory was completely worked out in *The Geographical Distribution of Animals*, which Macmillan published in 1876. This book founded the discipline of zoogeography.**

As for surrendering his claim of priority to Darwin, Wallace made clear in his letters to Silk, Bates, and Sims, his most intimate friends, that he was grateful that Darwin forestalled him and, perforce, he gladly abandoned all claim to priority. Wallace deliberately cast himself in the role of Darwin's shadow. But in history Darwin cast such a long and dark shadow that he has almost blotted out Wallace.

Wallace not only preferred seclusion, but developed a philosophical outlook, which he repeatedly put forward as he grew older, to explain his decision not to advance his priority. "I have long since come to see that no one deserves either praise or blame for the *ideas* that come to him, but only for the *action* resulting therefrom," Wallace said. "Ideas and beliefs are certainly not voluntary acts. They come to us—we hardly know *how* or *whence*, and once they have got possession of us we cannot reject or change them at will. It is for the common good that the promulgation of ideas should be free—uninfluenced by either praise or blame, reward or punishment."

Although they differed in many ways, the parallels between Wallace and Darwin are truly astonishing. Darwin also wondered why history

---

* It is interesting to speculate to what extent Indonesian folklore influenced Wallace's thinking about geographical distribution. Tales about *kantjil*, the mouse deer, who combines the wisdom and slyness of the owl and fox in Western fables, abound among the islanders. Some of the stories include shrewd scientific observations; for example, why there are no tigers in Borneo (*kantjil*, of course, outwitted them and they fled to Java and Sumatra).

** The Wallace Line today is, in the light of new discoveries, a scientific curiosity. But Wallace's impact on biogeography—and his fate to be usually mentioned in the same breath as Darwin—is perhaps best illustrated by the 1957 symposium, at Stanford University, of the American Institute of Biological Sciences and the American Association for the Advancement of Science. Twenty distinguished zoologists, biologists, geologists, and paleontologists attended the conference and a collection of their papers, edited by Carl L. Hubbs and entitled, *Zoogeography*, was dedicated to Wallace and Darwin, "two great zoogeographers . . . whose observations and reflections on the distribution of animals provided much of the evidence that led them, just one hundred years ago, to propose to the world the epochal concept of Organic Evolution, which unshackled the minds of men and helped inaugurate the Age of Science."

had left the discovery of so obvious a theory to Wallace and himself. Like Wallace, Darwin continually pondered the inexplicable.

"I have been speculating last night what makes a man discoverer of undiscovered things; and a most perplexing problem it is," Darwin wrote Horace, his ninth child. "Many men who are very clever—much cleverer than the discoverers—never originate anything."

Wallace's self-sacrifice did not sit well with his family, however, and Thomas Sims felt that Darwin, in the *Origin*, slighted, with happy simplicity, his brother-in-law's contributions to the theory. Darwin made no reference in his introduction to the Sarawak Law and never mentioned by name the Ternate Paper although, as one critic of the period has observed, in Darwin's first four paragraphs the words "I," "me," and "my" occurred forty-three times.

From Dili, the capital of the last Portuguese outpost in the Malay archipelago, situated on the island of Timor—perhaps best-known as the island where Captain Bligh landed after the mutiny on the *Bounty*—Wallace rebuked Sims.

"You quite misunderstand Mr. D's statement in the preface of his sentiments," Wallace wrote in 1861. But did Sims misunderstand? It appears that it may have been the other way around, that Wallace misunderstood. Wallace wrote, "His [Darwin's] conduct has been most liberal and disinterested."

Darwin not interested in the Sarawak Law and Ternate Paper? In the Linnean presentation?

In that letter to Sims, Wallace again demonstrated his innocence of events in England between publication of his Sarawak Law and the meeting of the Linnean Society on July 1, 1858, less than three years later. But how could Wallace possibly have known otherwise?

Wallace also confessed—as did Lyell, Hooker, Huxley and others in different circumstances—that *Origin* was "difficult" to read. "It was only on the *fifth* perusal that I fully appreciated the whole strength of the work," Wallace wrote, "and as I had been long before familiar with the same subjects I cannot but think that persons less familiar with them cannot have any clear idea of the accumulated argument by a single perusal."

The problem, of course, was that Darwin, in addition to having a heavy-handed style, hedged constantly, as though lacking full confidence in the theory of descent and divergence. For one thing, Darwin could not shed his belief in Lamarckism—that acquired characteristics may be inherited—and never would; for another, Darwin was concerned about the devastating impact the theory would have on Emma, his wife, their children, and his in-laws, the Wedgwoods. With happy simplicity, Darwin couched his theory obscurely.

Within a brief period the descent of man became the burning question in London. Hooker expressed himself cautiously in supporting the theory of the origin of species and Lyell hesitated in publicly accepting it, while Darwin continued to hide behind a "difficult" style. Wallace, upon returning to England, beat the drum hard for the theory, so hard and openly that he embarrassed Down House's inner circle. In a nasty, condescending letter to Darwin, Hooker wrote, "It is all very well for Wallace to wonder at scientific men being afraid of saying what they think. . . . Had he as many kind and good relations as I have, who would be grieved and pained to hear me say what I think, and had he children who would be placed in predicaments most detrimental to children's minds by such avowals on my part, he [Wallace] would not wonder so much."

In that small revolutionary scientific circle, Wallace was clearly the most audacious. In the end, Wallace did not give a fig for Victorian social values or public opinions. But when he was in the Malay world, shortly after his discovery, Wallace also expressed qualms about the impact of his unthinkable thoughts on his family, notably his mother.

In a postscript appended to the Ceram letter to Sims, Wallace, the Utopian socialist, sought to set his brother-in-law straight on the relationship among God, nature, and man.

"I have since wandered among men of many races and many religions," Wallace wrote. "I have studied man and nature in all its aspects, and I have sought after truth. In my solitude I have pondered much on the incomprehensible subjects of space, eternity, life and death. . . . I am thankful I can see much to admire in all religions. To the mass of mankind religion of some kind is a necessity. But whether there be a God or whatever be His nature; whether we have an immortal soul or not, or whatever may be our state after death, I can have no fear of having to suffer for the study of nature and the search for truth."

Again, there is that strange parallel between Wallace and Darwin. Wallace's view of religion closely resembled that of Darwin—Huxley invented the word "agnostic" to satisfy their indecision—and just as Darwin took pains to temper, if not conceal, his views from Emma, Wallace treated his mother similarly. In a Darwinian postscript to his postscript to the Ceram letter, Wallace implored Sims, "This is for yourself; show the *letter only* to my mother."

But the most important communication Wallace received during this period was a letter from Down House dated May 18, 1860. It contained Darwin's reaction to Wallace's feelings about *Origin*.

After chiding Wallace for "too high approbation of my book," Darwin, his conscience continuing to trouble him, repeated the theme of the letter he had written Wallace the year before. "Let me say how I admire the generous manner in which you speak of my book: most persons would in your position have felt bitter envy and jealousy," Darwin wrote. "How nobly free you seem to be of this common failing of mankind. But you speak far too modestly of yourself; you would, if you had my leisure, have done the work just as well, perhaps better, than I have done it."

For a man of great integrity, the Linnean affair was a blot on his honor which Darwin knew he could never obliterate. One day history would catch up with him; Darwin was too sophisticated to think otherwise no matter how mysteriously much of Darwin's pre-*Origin* correspondence has disappeared. In that damaging admission to Wallace, Darwin conceded that if Wallace had published first, he, Darwin, would have felt envy and jealousy. Darwin conceded that he, unlike Wallace, was neither noble nor free of the common failings which afflict much of mankind. It was a great admission, a significant concession to truth, by a complicated and troubled human being.

Darwin's admission speaks well for Darwin, as Wallace's behavior does for Wallace.

Chapter 28

THE YEARS ROLLED BY, and so did the multifaceted islands of the Malay world. In 1860 Wallace explored Waigou, revisited Ambon (his third trip), and worked his way back to Ternate. The following year he roamed across Banda and Buru, and then abandoned the eastern end of the archipelago and journeyed westward to Java, the most densely populated of the islands, nearly the size of England, and the center of Dutch power in the archipelago. "My retreat westwards," Wallace termed it. In 1862 he visited Bangka, known for its open-pit tin mines, and then Sumatra, a slumbering giant whose potential has yet to be developed.

Marco Polo, travelling these waters in the thirteenth century, and thinking of trade, described Java as the island of gold; Sumatra, of silver. But Wallace saw them in a completely different context. "Java," he exclaimed, "is probably the very finest and most interesting tropical island." Sumatra he dubbed "the very land of monkeys."

Travel became more comfortable, particularly on Java, with its good roads and *pasanggrahans* or guesthouses for travellers. Wallace was no longer obliged, like a snail, to carry his house with him—bed, kettles, and washbasin; tea, sugar, and curry powder; and half a hundred more odds and ends whose constant looking after, packing, and repacking "have been the standing plague of my life for the last seven years," he wrote in a letter home. And he added for emphasis that he had moved eighty times, about once a month, during that period and that on each occasion all of his articles had to be rearranged and repacked.

Wallace found Java dotted with lofty forests, smoldering volcanoes, great temple ruins, and, curiously, considering that archaeology was in its infancy—Austen Henry Layard having raised Biblical Nineveh to sunlight only a decade earlier—"the remains of extensive cities." On Java Wallace trod across ground where Dubois would find "Java Man" a generation later, one of the elusive missing links in the evolution of man. In Batavia, the canal-lined Dutch capital in the western half of the island, Wallace stayed at the charming, fabulous Hotel des Indes, "the gateway to Java," the world's first motel, which was foolishly torn down less than a decade ago to make way for steel, glass, and chromium.

Wallace's visit to Java coincided with the dry season and his collections were relatively unimpressive. But on neighboring Sumatra, a region of great jungles, swamps, escarpments, canyons, and lakes, he encountered another biological cornucopia, and he thought of Bates.

Wallace collected numerous *Papilio memnon*, a butterfly of deep black color with clear, ashy blue scales. The butterfly was commonplace and Dutch entomologists had done considerable work on it, but it was left for Wallace to make the great discovery that this species contained two different sets of females, one with and one without a tail.

"This peculiarity," he wrote, ". . . led me to discover that this extraordinary [tailed] female closely resembles (when flying) another butterfly of the same genus but of a different group (*Papilio coon*), and that we have here a case of mimicry similar to those so well illustrated and explained by Mr. Bates."

In Sumatra Wallace dabbled with genetics, using the *Papilio* as the subject of study, and he did so, remarkably, within the same time frame that Gregor Mendel, the Austrian monk, experimented with peas and founded the science of genetics, although Mendel's work would go unrecognized for more than another generation.

In discussing the existence of tailed and tailless *Papilio*, Wallace, the bachelor, drew an interesting analogy. Subconsciously, perhaps, he may have indulged in gatefold fantasy. Wallace wrote:

> Let us suppose a roaming Englishman in some remote island [Wallace?] to have two wives—one a black-haired, red-skinned Indian, and the other a woolly-headed, sooty-skinned Negress; and that instead of the children being mulattoes of brown or dusky tints, mingling the characteristics of each parent in varying degrees, all the boys should be as fair-skinned and blue-eyed as their father, while the girls should altogether resemble their mothers. This would be thought strange enough, but the case of these butterflies is yet more extraordinary, for each mother is capable not

only of producing male offspring like the father, and female like her-self, but also other females like her fellow wife, and altogether differing from herself!

But Wallace was distracted by the natural selection around him. The result was a short attention span. "My great fault is haste," he once said. "An idea strikes me, I think over it for a few days, and then write away with such illustrations as occur to me while going on."

In Sumatra, he had no sooner plumbed the mystery of the *Papilio* than he was captivated by Sumatra's monkey population. The monkeys swarmed about the Sumatran villages and estates, and filled the jungle with their incessant chattering. Wallace saw long-tailed monkeys, short-tailed monkeys, and some with no tails at all. He also viewed long-armed apes who never walked or ran upon the trees but traveled by their arms, swinging from bough to bough, easily and gracefully, as they still do.

Wallace was anxious to study and compare the orang-utan of Su-matra with that of Borneo, but the *mias* lived at the northern tip of the island, Atjeh, a region still independent of Dutch rule and inaccessible to Europeans.*

Despite his endless interest, however, Wallace in 1861 began to feel the first symptoms of weariness that overcame him in the Amazon. Repeated attacks of malaria and dysentery, and the hardships and priva-tions of constant travel, drained him of energy and—sometimes—even enthusiasm. From Sumatra, he confided to Bates that he was tiring but that "I am getting, however, some sweet little blue butterflies (*Lycaeni-dae*), which is the only thing that keeps up my spirits."

By the year's end, Wallace had reached the end of the tether.

On Christmas Eve, in a letter to Silk written from Lobo Rahman (Wallace misspelled it as "Roman"), "one of the places unknown to the Royal Geographical Society,"** he announced plans to quit the Malay archipelago in the new year. The decision surprised and delighted his friends and family.

"I really do now think and believe that I am coming home," he said with a touch of fatigue.

* The Dutch conquered the territory after a forty-year war which lasted into this century. Periodically, in Atjeh, as in the Moluccas, separatist movements struggle for independence from the centralized government located on Java. The most recent flare-up in Atjeh, on a miniscale, was in 1977–1978.

** Silk placed it in southwest Sumatra. Wallace was in east Sumatra. Both were correct, there are at least two Lobo Rahmans.

There was no way that Wallace could post a letter from Lobo Rahman and, as was his custom, he carried the letter around for weeks until he could find a link to the outside world. A postscript, dated Singapore, January 20, 1862, confirmed his decision. He told Silk that he expected to remain in Singapore another month, "then, ho! for England!"

Wallace had observed his thirty-ninth birthday a fortnight earlier; he was unmarried, he had no prospect for future employment, and he still had not saved enough money to live out his dream in his enchanted English countryside. But Wallace's head was bursting with ideas—the outlines of books and scientific papers—and his storage chests were bursting with specimens. In eight years in the Malay archipelago, Alfred Russel Wallace had registered astounding triumphs. He had collected 125,660 specimens, including 310 specimens of mammals; 100 reptiles; 8,050 birds; 7,500 shells; 13,100 butterflies; 83,200 beetles; and 13,400 "other insects." He had drawn the Wallace Line, founded the science of zoogeography, explored the fringes of genetics and social anthropology, and—above all—he had independently solved the riddle that had engaged man for millennia, that of the origin of species, their descent and divergence.

In an unpublished Malay notebook, Wallace outlined plans for his return to England. His treatment of the coleoptera collection was ambitious. He intended to print tags, sort out the collection's 83,200 specimens, tag each one, group them in display boxes family by family ("at first all the specimens from different localities being placed together"), then arrange the species geographically—something unheard of in science—and, finally, prepare a catalog.

He also worked up an outline for a book about the Malay archipelago and the geographical distribution of animals. As he had written Bates, "I have work to do for the rest of my life."

There may have been other considerations that entered into Wallace's decision to return home in 1862. Letters, occasional newspapers, and scientific journals filtering back from Britain indicated that the scientific revolution which he and Darwin had launched at the Linnean Society three years earlier had acquired a self-generating momentum, influencing every branch of science, the arts, theology, and even politics and economics. London was the place to be.

Darwin himself was so buried in the species problem that he was almost oblivious to the cultural and political worlds around him, with the exception of the American Civil War—which he apparently followed with great interest as a staunch supporter of the North—and the stock market tables in the *Times*. "I cannot endure to read a line of poetry. . . ," Darwin lamented. "I have also lost my taste for pictures or music."

In contrast to Darwin, Wallace retained a lively interest in everything—politics, economics, the cultural scene. Over a thirteen-year period, except for a brief interlude in London upon returning from the Amazon, Wallace had not read a daily newspaper on a regular basis, and he thirsted "for books and [art] collections and comforts."

The different approaches of Darwin and Wallace to the superstructure man had erected upon the real or natural world was a measure of how each of them saw the universe. Darwin, eternally and intensely pessimistic, sat isolated at Down, brooding and meditating in his Sandwalk, working out the consequences of the theory and the inescapable conclusion that man is a passing phenomenon, a byproduct of descent and divergence through natural selection—a never-ending process which in time would account for the emergence from man of a new species. The future frightened Darwin.

But while Darwin envisaged man's extinction as inevitable in the far distant future, Wallace remained the incurable optimist and Utopian socialist, who saw in his joint discovery with Darwin the secret of man's survival. "Can this theory be applied in any way to the question of the origin of the races of man?" he asked. "Or is there anything in human nature that takes him out of the category of organic existence, over whose successive mutations it has had such powerful sway?"

In man Wallace detected qualities which he felt were not the product of survival of the fittest. Man's social, moral, and intellectual faculties, his higher capabilities as compared with all other forms of life, Wallace believed, "checked"—his word—the process of natural selection. Man possessed an intelligent foresight that prepared him to cope with the future.

In man, the weaker, the dwarfish, those of less active limbs or less piercing eyesight, did not suffer the extreme penalty that befalls animals so defective in nature. While the law of natural selection accounted for man's descent, it no longer applied to man. Wallace would not put forth his ideas on the subject publicly until after his return home. They proved as lively then as now.

In the spring of 1862 Wallace was homeward bound, his thoughts once again centered on beefsteaks and Damson tarts.

PART III

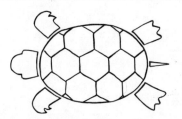

The Nobility
of Character

Never was there a more beautiful example of modesty, unselfish admiration for another's work, of loyal determination that the other should receive the full merit of his independent labours and thoughts, than was shown by Charles Darwin. . . .

Sir E. Ray Lankester, at the
Linnean Society, July 1, 1908

You are the only man I ever heard of who persistently does himself an injustice and never demands justice.

Darwin, in a letter to Wallace,
April 14, 1869

We cannot help asking whether Darwin underestimated his debt to his many precursors. Did he even, possibly, play down their importance so as to exalt his own originality? No one who understands Darwin's nobility of character, his single-minded candour, and his oversensitive care for truth, could entertain such a fantasy. It is enough to point to his magnanimous treatment of Wallace. . . .

Basil Willey, *Darwinism and the
Study of Society,* 1961

Chapter 29

WALLACE'S HOMEWARD JOURNEY, after the terrors of *terrae incognitae* in the Malay archipelago, offered comic relief; yet although Wallace later laughed about it, the situation at the time was hardly amusing.

In addition to notes and crates of specimens, Wallace brought along, as he had when he left the Amazon, a menagerie for London's Zoological Gardens. His companions included two birds of paradise, the first live specimens ever to reach the Western world. Wallace's main concern was feeding the creatures and he laid in a good supply of bananas. The vessel no sooner put to sea than he was surprised, and delighted, to discover that it was infested with cockroaches and that the birds ate roaches greedily. "Every evening I went to the storeroom in the fore part of the ship," he said, "where I was allowed to brush the cockroaches into a biscuit tin."

At Suez, a city of white, sunbaked houses, date palms, camels, donkeys, and docks, Wallace, with his notes and specimens, was off-loaded for the fast overland trip to Alexandria and the second half of the journey by sea to England (the Suez Canal would not be completed for another seven years). Although the short dash across the desert and the transfer from one ship to another were inconvenient, they obviated the necessity of doubling the length of the journey by sailing around the Cape of Good Hope at the southern horn of Africa.

At Alexandria, Wallace and his goods were reloaded aboard a newly built, London-bound "screw steamer." Wallace was impressed with the vessel when he boarded. Then he was mortified. "I found that the ship was free from cockroaches," he exclaimed. Wallace was panic-stricken, and when the vessel put into Valletta, Malta's principal port, for coaling, Wallace and his cargo disembarked and put up for a fortnight at a harbor inn to acclimatize the birds of paradise to the increasingly cooler weather, and to lay in a store of cockroaches. "I . . . found," he said with satisfaction, "that I could get unlimited cockroaches at a baker's close by."

Mary Anne Wallace embraced her son tightly on his arrival in London toward the end of a blustery March. Sister Fanny hugged him and brother-in-law Thomas Sims beamed approvingly. Beefsteaks and Damson tarts awaited Wallace at the house recently purchased by Sims, whose photographic studio in Westbourne Grove was working out profitably. The house, situated in the same neighborhood as the studio, was cold and damp when they returned home from the ship. Wallace put on several of Thomas' sweaters and tossed an afghan across his legs as his brother-in-law lit a log fire.

If Wallace's relatives were startled by his appearance, nobody said anything. Wallace was gaunt, his beard salt and pepper, his face drawn. But behind the metal-rimmed spectacles the crystal-blue eyes, alert and twinkling, were the same. So was his demeanor. Although he had spent years in the East, was accustomed to servants, had bargarined with Chinese traders and Malay pirates, dealt with sea captains, sultans, and rajahs both white and brown, his character was unchanged. The cheerful outlook on the world, the innate shyness, the touch of humility, were still there. He was their Alfred, all right. In one respect, however, he had changed: he often had a faraway look in his eyes and, when lost in thought, appeared to dwell in another world. He was still overwhelmed by his view of life and the origin of species.

In a letter he wrote his mother some months earlier, Wallace had expressed a desire to lodge with the family, and offered to bear the expenses. "I should prefer being a little way out of town [London]," he said. There were reasons: it would be "quieter [and] much cheaper than living close to town."

To his family, Alfred was a returning hero (and he was), but he was as impoverished financially as his father before him. "I must of course study economy," he explained in that letter of July 20, 1861, "as the little money I have made will not be all got in for a year or two after my return."

On the top floor of their house, the Sims' had reserved a large room for Wallace and he immediately set about remodeling it. Although he was a good carpenter, Wallace discovered that he "could not work long at a time without rest" and he hired a carpenter to put in shelving for his specimen collection. He also ordered a gross of cardboard boxes in three different sizes, and had thousands of tags printed.

A strange parallel between Wallace and Darwin now emerged. In Darwin's study at Down, to this day, the most prominent piece of furniture—it arrests the eye immediately—is the unusually high, upholstered chair equipped with casters and with a writing board affixed across the arms. In this contraption Darwin first read the Sarawak Law and the Ternate Paper. In this chair he wrote *Origin*. The chair was the epicenter of Darwin's world and, as Wallace's animistic companions in the Amazon and Malay archipelago would still say, to touch the chair is to touch Darwin's spirit.

For Wallace, a good chair was also a centerpiece of life. "As I reached home in a very weak state of health," Wallace said, "my first step was to purchase the largest and most comfortable easy-chair I could find." That chair is now long gone, but he also purchased a wood writing board, twenty-four inches long, fourteen inches wide.

Worn, ink-stained, and badly scarred, the desk slate, as the British call a writing board, today dominates the impressively long, polished table in the stately Council Room of the Royal Entomological Society of London.* It is the only slate on the table. And whenever the executive board of that august Society gathers, Wallace's spirit is there in that room.

Immediately after settling down at Westbourne Grove, Wallace wrote Darwin of his return and Darwin promptly invited him to Down. Wallace was in no condition to accept the invitation, and in a letter to Darwin dated April 7, 1862—the earliest believed to exist—Wallace wrote: "As I am being doctored a little, I do not think I shall be able to accept your kind invitation at present, but trust to be able to do so during the summer."

The following month Wallace broke out with a serious, and embarrassing, case of boils—"disagreeable though far from dangerous," he said—a malady from which Darwin constantly suffered. Wallace's case was so serious that he was confined to bed for ten days.

---

* A plaque identifies it as Wallace's "desk slate from 1865 to his death in 1913." It was presented to the Linnean Society in 1921 by Professor Poulton of Oxford, a personal friend of Wallace's and a former president of the Society.

One suspects that part of the trouble stemmed from unsanitary living conditions. Wallace's room, for example, was a mess. "I found myself surrounded by a room full of packing cases, containing the collections that I had from time to time sent home for private use," he said. Among other items, the room contained three thousand bird-skins and "at least 20,000 beetles and butterflies." Through the spring and into early summer Wallace spent most of his time unpacking, sorting, and arranging the mass of specimens. During this period his mother pampered him and the gravy boat overflowed at dinnertime.

Wallace was determined, before embarking on his "big book" about the Malay archipelago, to get his collections in order. He also had other priorities—to get a job, to meet Darwin, and to get married, not necessarily in that order of importance.

Bates, who had returned three years earlier after eleven years in the Amazon, apparently entertained similar objectives. He lost little time in getting married. In 1860 he proposed to Sarah Ann Mason of Leicester, "a young lady for whom he had kept a tender place in his heart during his long absence," as Bates' close friend, Edward Clodd, primly expressed it. They were married in January 1861, and raised a family of three sons and two daughters.

Eight years among the Malay islands without intimate companionship radically changed Wallace's outlook on marriage. He and Silk, his boyhood chum, for example, had agreed when very young that marriage was something to be approached warily and that the primary consideration was the intellectual relationship between the man and woman. But from Sumatra, on the eve of his departure for England, Wallace confessed to Silk that "my opinions have changed much on this point." As for matrimony itself, Wallace wrote, "I [now] believe a good wife to be the greatest blessing a man can enjoy, and the only road to happiness." But, he continued, he doubted if Silk would approve of his revised qualifications.

"I now look at intellectual companionship as quite a secondary matter," Wallace said. The highest priority, he explained, was an "affectionate" wife.

His firsthand observations in the remote parts of the world had altered his views on marriage in other ways, too, and in an unpublished notebook he blasted Samuel Johnson's smart-set claim that "marriage is not natural to man in a savage state." Wallace considered Johnson's statement "incorrect," as he politely phrased it, and wrote in his diary:

"The Indians of the Amazon and the Dyaks of Borneo never leave their wives."

Marriage, he now felt, was man's natural state, and what could be more natural for a naturalist?

Like Bates before him, Wallace, on returning to England, lost little time in the quest for an "affectionate" wife. Finding the bird of paradise, he discovered, was simpler and less painful.

George Silk played marriage broker and introduced Wallace to his small circle of friends, among them a "Mr. L—," as Wallace, in the grand Victorian tradition of honoring privacy, later put it in his memoirs. To this day, in neither his private correspondence nor the recollections of his grandchildren, is there an inkling as to Mr. L.'s full name other than Wallace's disclosure that Mr. L. was a widower with two daughters and a son at Cambridge.

Wallace and Mr. L. got along well and the latter frequently invited Wallace and Silk to join him at his house for tea or dinner. "On these occasions," Wallace said, "the young ladies were present." The daughters were unmarried and the eldest, about twenty-eight, caught Wallace's fancy. She was, he said, "very agreeable, though quiet, pleasant looking, well educated and fond of art and literature." But was she affectionate?

Wallace was captivated. "I soon began to feel an affection for her," he confessed, "and to hope that she would become my wife."

But as Wallace's Malay friends were apt to say, rice in the spoon does not always reach the mouth. The shy Wallace did not know how to telegraph his intentions. After a year of visits to Mr. L.'s house, he still lacked the courage to make known his interest in the young woman. At last, in desperation, he worked up enough boldness to write her a letter in which he described his feelings and asked if she could "in any way respond to my affection."

Miss L. was surprised, a fair indication of Wallace's abnormal reticence. "My undemonstrative manner had given her no intimation of my intentions," a confused Wallace said. Her reply was negative, and Wallace was crushed. He languished at home for days and finally showed the letter to his mystified mother and sister.

The Wallace women interpreted the letter differently. Miss L. had, they observed, expressly stated that despite her rejection of his suit she hoped that Wallace would not allow her refusal to break off his visits to her father. Fanny and his mother urged him to take heart and to resume his courtship by reappearing at Mr. L.'s table. "Make another offer later on," they counseled.

And so the "affair," if that is the proper word for it, dragged on through the remainder of 1862 and into 1863.

Wallace's relationship with Darwin fared appreciably better.

About four months after his return, Wallace had sufficiently recovered his health not only to begin his unanimated courtship of Miss L. but also to accept Darwin's invitation to Down. In the months before their historic meeting, Darwin was in the throes of another round of household turmoil, not unlike the tragedy that enveloped Down House when Darwin received Wallace's Ternate Paper. In the late spring and early summer of 1862, two of Darwin's sons came down with scarlet fever, eight-year-old Leonard critically.

Thus, although they lived about twenty miles apart, the first Wallace–Darwin meeting was put off repeatedly because of illnesses on both sides. Toward the end of July, the two greatest naturalists of the Victorian age met face-to-face for the first time, a true meeting that replaced their perfunctory encounter at the British Museum more than eight years earlier. Wallace, of course, had never forgotten the earlier, casual introduction to Darwin in the Insect Room of the Museum after his return from the Amazon.

There is no record of the exact date that Wallace traveled by diligence to Down; nor did either party record impressions of that first true encounter.

No doubt Parslow opened the imposing, massive front door to the Georgian mansion and led Wallace into the airy, cheery, sunlit living room, so spacious that it was uncluttered by Emma's baby grand piano, overstuffed chairs, a chaise longue, footstools, several tables, and a gilded mirror over the unlit fireplace. In the living room, Darwin's wife and one of their daughters joined them, either Henrietta, who was then nineteen, or Elizabeth, fifteen; there is no record of which one.

The Darwins chatted amiably with their visitor over cups of tea. Their subsequent correspondence makes it clear that the meeting was singularly successful. Wallace and Darwin hit it off admirably.

The starry-eyed, ill-at-ease Wallace probably found the famous author of *Origins* gracious, loquacious, witty, and friendly, qualities Darwin often exhibited when receiving guests on his own turf. It is fair to speculate that behind this screen, however, Darwin was also caught up by feelings of anxiety, guilt, caution, and wariness.

But if Wallace was captivated by Darwin's warmth and charm, as the evidence—his letters, autobiography, and other information—suggests, Darwin was surely taken aback by Wallace's demeanor. Wallace was a rare species. He was a man without a strain of envy or jealousy. He admired Darwin to the point of obsequiousness. For a man who had spent much of his life on his own, traveling in difficult terrain, exploring regions never before trod by Europeans, facing perils that lesser men would shrink from, Wallace was hardly a dashing, ambitious, adventurous figure. Darwin was accustomed to the scientific and academic worlds, riven by controlled and open jealousies and pomposity. Wallace was almost too good to be true. He put himself down and was embarrassed to talk about his accomplishments. After a short interval, Darwin probably invited Wallace into his study to view his collections and papers. There Darwin quickly discovered a different person. One-to-one, in scientific matters, Wallace was no longer meek and shy. His vigorous originality, conceptual boldness, alertness of mind, and soaring imagination surged to the fore.

Wallace's first visit to Down was marked by a white stone near the house, a Darwinian custom reserved for special occasions. Stones were set out for Hooker, Lyell, and Huxley, and, later, for Bates, who was invited to Down shortly after Wallace's visit and probably at Wallace's suggestion.

Darwin must have been relieved to find Wallace unambitious, inoffensive, and engaging. Wallace, after all, was the only individual who could challenge Darwin's priority, accuse him of deception in his handling of the "delicate" Linnean episode, and express indignation and anger over Darwin's slighting of him in *Origin*.

Wallace never harbored these feelings or, if he did, he never expressed them.

On August 8, 1862, Wallace wrote Darwin a brief note expressing the hope that Leonard had recovered from his illness "and that you are therefore enabled to follow your favourite investigations with a more tranquil mind." Wallace also informed Darwin that he himself planned to take a few weeks of rest at Devonshire before completing the formidable task of cataloging his specimens. Wallace closed the letter on a note of intimacy. "Present my compliments to Mrs. Darwin and Miss Darwin," Wallace said. If the Miss Darwin was the older sister, Wallace probably had taken special note of her.

In that same letter, as in all their correspondence, they touched on the species question, the subject that enraptured and bound them like compasses to a pole. Wallace threw in some comments about ostriches and cassowaries.

Darwin replied a fortnight later and reported that Leonard "became frightfully worse after you were at Down . . . and my wife took the scarlet fever rather severely. I have had a horrid time of it," Darwin said.

Then the letter turned to a discussion of ostriches and bustards.

Wallace returned from Devonshire at the end of September and found a copy of the third edition of *Origin* awaiting him, perhaps the most famous of the six editions published in Darwin's lifetime. In it, Darwin answered those critics who had charged him with ignoring his precursors, and incorporated an "Historical Sketch" of evolutionary theory in which he traced his forerunners from Aristotle through Lamarck to the contemporary views "on the origin of species . . . propounded by Mr. Wallace and myself."

Referring to the July 1 meeting at the Linnean Society, Darwin spoke warmly of Wallace: ". . . the theory of Natural Selection is promulgated by Mr. Wallace with admirable force and clearness." Belatedly, Darwin had sought to straighten out the history of the species question and dispel the impression that he claimed to be the world's only icebreaker in the field.

Wallace considered Darwin's sketch "very interesting," and wrote Darwin that it "shows that the time had quite come for your book."

The following year Wallace's health improved considerably, although he was still troubled by recurrent attacks of malaria, while Darwin's constitution was in as bad a state as ever. "I am very sorry indeed to hear you are still in weak health," Wallace wrote Darwin January 14, 1863, less than a week after Wallace observed his fortieth birthday. ". . . I am now in much better health but find sudden changes in weather affect me very much, bringing on ague and fever fits."

Before the year ended both men had abandoned Victorian formality and addressed each other as "Dear Wallace" and "My dear Darwin."

Not only was Wallace's health gradually restored—he was never sick another day in his life—but he began to put on weight, his beard filled out, and his face regained its unlined, cherubic youthfulness. Wallace also made splendid headway sorting out his collection of specimens, had begun working on his epic, *The Malay Archipelago*, and maintained a furious pace writing scientific papers.

The papers ranged over a wide field, as usual, from "List of Birds from the Sulu Islands" to "Notes on Genus Iphias" to "Some Anomalies in Zoological and Botanical Geography." Interestingly, he also wrote an article "On the Rev. S. Haughton's Paper on the Bee's Cell and Origin of Species." Reverend Haughton had again taken issue with the theory of the origin of species. It is interesting to speculate whether Wallace had ever read Haughton's denunciation of the Linnean meeting, his accusation that Darwin was too unoriginal and that Wallace was too original.

With his outpouring of scientific papers, Wallace transformed the geometry of Darwin's "cabinet" of Hooker, Lyell, and Huxley from a quadrangle to a pentagon.

Wallace's major contribution in this period was a paper in the *Anthropological Review* in May 1864, which tentatively suggested that in man "the action of natural selection is checked." As Wallace explained, "[Man] is social and sympathetic, in the rudest tribes the sick are assisted, at least with food; less robust health and vigour than the average does not entail death. Neither does the want of perfect limbs, or other organs, produce the same effects as among animals. Some division of labour takes place; the swiftest hunt, the less active fish, or gather fruits; food is, to some extent, exchanged or divided."

In a letter to Wallace, Darwin described the paper as admirable and took the opportunity to chide Wallace for attributing the theory of the origin of species to Darwin alone. "You ought not in the Man paper to speak of the theory as mine; it is just as much yours as mine," Darwin protested. "One correspondent has already noted to me your 'high-minded' conduct on this head."

Darwin may have had cause to come about. The more high-minded was Wallace, the more guilt-ridden was Darwin.

Darwin added that he had passed Wallace's paper around, doubtlessly among Hooker, Lyell, and Huxley, and that "they have been equally struck by it," but that he, Darwin, felt the subject of Man required additional inquiry. "I have collected a few notes on Man," Darwin told Wallace, "but I do not suppose I shall ever use them." Darwin offered the notes to Wallace.

Once again Wallace appeared to be a length ahead of Darwin and Darwin ruefully admitted that the theory that man was in a position to put a brake on natural selection was a "great leading idea [and] is quite new to me."

In reply, Wallace disagreed with Darwin's assessment about the origin of *Origin*. "As to theory of Natural Selection itself, I shall always maintain it to be actually yours and yours only," Wallace wrote. ". . . My paper would never have convinced anybody or been noticed as more than ingenious speculation. . . . All the merit I claim is having been the means of inducing *you* to write and publish at once."

As for the subject of man, Wallace wrote that "I may possibly some day go a little more into this subject and, if I do, will accept the kind offer of your notes."

Man's descent, within the framework of natural selection, was obviously now haunting both men as the species question had before, but neither was ready to put on armor and enter the lists. Darwin and his closest associates still dragged their feet on this issue because of their ties to the Establishment and their deference to their families' religious beliefs. *Origin* was already creating enough furor, as observed earlier, among devout Protestants, Catholics, and Jews, and even among nonconformists. As for Wallace, he must have been struggling with a way to rationalize his Utopian socialist convictions in light of the brutal facts of natural selection as the principal mechanism of evolution—a struggle he would resolve later in an original way.

In that letter to Darwin, Wallace remarked that if it were true that Africa is the oldest existing continent, "here, then, is evidently the place to find *early man*"—a conclusion borne out in our time in the graveyard of ancient primates, Tanzania's Olduvai Gorge.

For Wallace, things were looking up. His relations with Darwin had evolved into a mutual admiration society; his scientific papers were being published and widely read; he had begun work on *The Malay Archipelago*; Stevens was still selling duplicate specimens; and, above all, perhaps, Wallace was still welcomed at Mr. L.'s house. In Miss L. he "saw signs of a change in her feelings towards me."

In the summer of 1864, Wallace renewed his proposal to Miss L. This time he did not write her directly but asked Mr. L. to explore his daughter's wishes "and, if she was now favorable, to grant me a private interview." The interview was granted, and Wallace cavorted on clouds.

He and Miss L. met regularly, two or three times a week, to discuss their future and "everything went on smoothly for some months." Wallace introduced her to his mother and Fanny, and a wedding date was fixed for Christmas week.

That December Wallace was perplexed to learn that Miss L. had abruptly gone off on a trip. The next day Wallace received a note from Mr. L. requesting that the engagement be broken off. "The blow was very severe," a depressed Wallace said, "and I have never in my life experienced such intensely painful emotion."

When Miss L. wrote, Wallace was more perplexed than ever. She complained that he rarely talked about himself or his family and therefore concluded that he must "have something to conceal." She also said she had heard gossip that Wallace was friendly with the widow of an Indian Army officer and friend of his mother's. Wallace was shaken; he had no more thought of the widow in terms of marriage than he would an aunt or grandmother. Wallace dashed off a reply and reassured Miss L. of his devotion. "But I received no reply," he said, "and from that day I never saw, or heard of, any of the family."

The incident not only is a measure of Wallace's difficulty in dealing with his own people as compared with the ease with which he dealt with people in the middle of the Amazon or the East Indies, but also of his intimacy with Darwin. Wallace confided in Darwin about the affair, and in a letter to Wallace dated January 29, 1865, in which Darwin said he was stunned by the originality of Wallace's recent papers in the *Geographical Journal*, Darwin added, "Do try what hard work will do to banish painful thoughts."

The advice, Wallace later openly conceded, referred "to my broken engagement."   ·

In a postscript, Darwin asked Wallace a question about the wild pigs of Aru. "Am I not right in inferring that these must have been introduced and run wild?" Darwin asked. "If you have a clear opinion on this head, may I quote you?"

Obviously, if scarlet fever was treated evenly with the species question, then wild pigs took precedence over an *affaire de coeur*.

Two days later Wallace replied. As for the broken engagement, he wrote, "Many thanks for your kind letter." Then he, too, plunged into the origin of Aru's wild pigs and expressed the firm belief that Darwin was wrong and that the Aru species was a distant form peculiar to those found in adjacent New Guinea.

But Wallace's thought of wild pigs did not put an end to his burning desire to find an "affectionate" wife.

Chapter 30

WHEN WALLACE RETURNED to England in 1862, the year Victoria's prince consort, Albert, died, the queen was in the twenty-fifth year of her sixty-four-year reign. Britain was in a golden age. In almost every field of human endeavor, her era stood second to none; it was radiant, and England was bursting with energy and enthusiasm, confident of present and future.

The long shadow cast by the Linnean conclave of July 1, 1858, was already influencing the future course of not only the sciences, but the very history of the world. Like much of the British aristocracy, Victoria was oblivious to the revolution set in motion by Wallace and Darwin; in the Queen's voluminous correspondence, there is not a single reference to the controversy which swirled beyond the moats and crenellated walls of her palaces. Little matter. Wallace was right in deciding to return home when he did. London was the epicenter of the world.

During those first days at Westbourne Grove, sitting by the fire and rebuilding his strength, his mother and Fanny fluttering around him, Wallace took a crash course in current events. He had been out of touch with the West for so long that the gap in his background would never really be filled.

Like Darwin, Wallace enjoyed a daily newspaper—the London *Times*—but also several others. The big news, of course, was the American civil war and the papers were filled that week with an account of what one journal called "the great naval fight . . . the contest between the *Merrimack* and the *Monitor*." Britannia ruled the waves and, as reflected in the press, had every intention of continuing to do so. The newspapers were filled with letters calling upon the empire to refit the Royal Navy and build "iron-cased" or "iron-clad" ships.

Some of the news was stale. The Irish Question was still being debated in Parliament, just as it was when Wallace left eight years earlier. But there were new "questions," such as the unification of Italy. And Germany—Prussia, really—was beginning, under Bismarck, her quest for a place in the sun; later that same year the Iron Chancellor would provoke Europe with the declaration that "not by speeches and majorities will the great questions of the day be decided . . . but by iron and blood!"

As a financial and cultural center, London bustled as never before. Railroad stocks, Wallace was amused to read, had recovered from their previous beating and as the empire expanded overseas, so did trade. The theater was booming and *Our American Cousin*—the play at which Lincoln was to be assassinated three years later—was the current hit. At St. James Hall, Picadilly, Charles Dickens read passages from *David Copperfield*; tickets cost four shillings for a sofa, one shilling for a gallery seat.

The scientific-industrial-military revolution sweeping the country was detectable everywhere: for example, weather dispatches to the newspapers, Wallace duly noted, were now transmitted "by submarine and magnetic telegraph." As for the papers themselves, they flourished and their columns bulged with advertisements. Two sets of ads especially attracted Wallace's attention.

For the first time Wallace appreciated fully his brother-in-law's success. Photography was the rage. Photo albums were in great demand, a "very handsome one, bound in embossed Morocco, and capable of holding twenty portraits," Wallace read, sold for six shillings, six pence. Adorning a visiting card with a photograph of the bearer was the vogue and the papers were filled with advertisements for *carte de visite* vignette portraits, as they were called.

Something else captivated the public—spiritualism. The medium and the séance were as popular, and often as dubious, as the analyst and the couch today.

Unlike Darwin, Wallace was not wholly satisfied with their conception of the descent of man. Wallace was groping toward a theory that natural selection alone could not account for man's unique characteristics among animals, his sense of spiritual need and being, his mental faculties, his ability to calculate, reason abstractly, conceive of infinity, and speculate about a tomorrow. Thus Wallace's curiosity was stirred —as it had been when he experimented with mesmerism at the Reverend Hill's school almost twenty years earlier—when he read, for example, in the London *Times* of April 2, 1862, such front-page advertisements as this:

SPIRIT RAPPING EXTRAORDINARY: Royal Colosseum [sic]. Mr. Taylor's Exposition of the Secret of Spirit Rapping and Spirit Mediums, Names on the Paper Pellets, the Mystic Writing on the Arm of the Medium etc. Everyday at 2 a.m. [sic] and 7 p.m.

But Wallace had little time to satisfy his curiosity about this latest fad, if fad it was. The demands on him, despite his indifferent health that first year, were heavy.

In this situation, Wallace learned firsthand about the impact of the theory of natural selection on man himself. The world would never be the same again. Then, and for the remainder of his life, Wallace was part of the storm, and he marveled at the nature of the tempest. The American Civil War and spiritualism paled in significance alongside the tumultuous reception the theory had received and was still receiving.*

Scientific, literary, and clerical circles were in perpetual turmoil. In the *Spectator*, the respected Cambridge geologist Adam Sedgwick raised the question of what caused new species. "I say *creation*. . . ," he thundered, "the operation of power quite beyond the powers of a pigeon-fancier." Louis Agassiz, one of the most powerful voices in the American scientific establishment, branded the theory a "scientific mistake, untrue in its facts, unscientific in its method, and mischievous in its

---

* And still does. In 1973 Tennessee adopted a new textbook law requiring that textbooks on evolutionary theory give equal emphasis to all accounts, including Genesis. Similar laws have been introduced in Ohio, Florida, and other states. Tennessee, of course, was the site of the Monkey Trial more than fifty years ago when John T. Scopes, a teacher, tested a law, later repealed, prohibiting the teaching of the theory of natural selection. In 1978, in a modern version of the Scopes Trial, a Federal judge ruled against three plaintiffs who sought to compel the Smithsonian Institution, which was opening a permanent exhibit on evolution, to include the Biblical story contained in the First Book of Moses. Dale Crowley, Jr., executive director of the National Foundation for Fairness in Education, a plaintiff, complained that people who believe in Genesis are offended that tax money is spent to promote "hostility toward religious faith." The heart of his argument is that "if we believe we descended from animals, we are going to act like animals," a point which may be unfair to animals. This debate is unchanged since Wallace's time. Robert C. Cowens, science editor of *The Christian Science Monitor*, expressed the belief last year in *Technology Review* that this long debate "has damaged the teaching of sound biological science."

tendency." He exploded, "There is no evidence of a direct descent of later from earlier species." A Bostonian, Dr. Peabody, charged that the theory denies supernatural revelation. "Christ is not risen," he declared, "and we are yet in our sins!" In Paris, M. Flourens, a prominent member of the Académie Française, roared, "Any theory which attempts to ignore design as manifested in God's creation is a theory, I say, which attempts to dethrone God!"

Scientists were particularly incensed by the lack of hard evidence to support the theory. Huxley and others defended Darwin and Wallace by citing the incompleteness of the geological record, giving rise to the continuing search for "missing links." Princeton's Charles Hodge, who described Wallace as "the companion and peer of Mr. Darwin," pointed up this aspect of the debate—the disappearance of the immediate predecessors of present-day species and the disappearance of *their* immediate predecessors—by recalling the story of the man who commissioned an artist to paint the "Passage of the Israelites over the Red Sea." In due time the artist produced a large canvas painted in red.

"What is that?" the gentleman asked.
"Why," said the artist, "the Red Sea."
"But where are the Israelites?"
"Oh, they have passed over."
"And where are the Egyptians?"
"They are under the sea."

On a later occasion, Wallace sought to turn back these assaults with the observation that "I for one cannot believe that the world would turn to chaos if left to law alone." This prompted botanist George Henslow, who prided himself as an evolutionist and had forecast that the theory would "lapse into oblivion [because] it is utter impossibility," to single out Wallace's statement for reply. "It is clear that design is what Mr. Darwin and Mr. Wallace repudiate," said Henslow gravely.

But perhaps the most celebrated incident, which did more to publicize the theory than any other until the Scopes Trial, occurred shortly before Wallace returned to England. In 1860, at Oxford, Bishop Wilberforce and Huxley engaged in what was, figuratively, the first monkey trial. Seven hundred persons packed the hall as the Bishop solemnly declared that "there is nothing in the idea of evolution: rock-pigeons are what rock-pigeons have always been." Then the Bishop snidely asked Huxley, "Was it through your grandfather or your grandmother that you claim descent from a monkey?" As the crowd howled, Huxley was heard to whisper, "The Lord hath delivered him unto mine hands."

There are many versions of the incident. But they come down to this: Huxley presented a lucid, brilliantly orchestrated rebuttal (no copy of it exists) and coolly concluded that "I should feel it no shame to have risen from the origin of a monkey but I should feel it a shame to have sprung from an ignorant Bishop!" The audience roared and, in the grand Victorian tradition, a woman in the crowd fainted.

Matthew Arnold, for one, was amused by the storm. "I cannot understand why you scientific people make such a fuss [about the theory]," he told a friend. "Why, it's all in Lucretius."* And, in a manner of speaking, it is.

Against this ongoing background, in that first year in England, Wallace plunged into the fray. He attended numerous meetings of the Zoological, Entomological, and Linnean societies, where "I . . . greatly enjoyed the society of people interested in the subjects that now had almost become the business of my life," he said with relish. Almost. In truth, Wallace wished science would become the business of his life, but he still had no prospects for regular employment in the field. Writing monographs and delivering occasional lectures at learned societies did not pay, any more than his forays into publishing—the book on palm trees, which was too technical for the lay public, and the book on travels in the Amazon, which sold indifferently.

A Wallace would have been a plus on a campus or as a researcher for a learned society, the think-tanks of the age. But he lacked the scholarly credentials; worse, he lacked social grace and his family origins were undistinguished. In Victorian England these barriers were virtually insurmountable in obtaining the sort of post for which he was ideally fitted. Yet he was in demand.

Wallace's birds of paradise at the Zoological Gardens, for example, stirred excitement in scientific circles as well as among strollers and nannies. Six weeks after his return from Southeast Asia, at the invitation of the Zoological Society, he gave his first talk in London. Nature, he observed, had taken every precaution that these birds, "her choicest treasures" [not man?], would not be easily observed or obtained. They dwelt in the interior of New Guinea, whose harborless, inhospitable coast was exposed to the full swell of the Pacific. The interior, rugged

---

* See pp. 28 and 77.

and mountainous, was covered with jungles, swamps, escarpments, and serrated ridges, posing an "almost impassable barrier [to man]." Yet in these trackless wilds, Wallace continued, the birds of paradise displayed the exquisite beauty and marvelous development of plumage calculated to excite the admiration and astonishment of man. It was, of course, Wallace's old theme, expressed in private letters, that the productions of nature were not made solely for man, the implication being that man was not at the center of creation.

Given the tidal wave of evangelism sweeping the Victorian age, Wallace may have unintentionally ruffled some feathers and, perhaps from amusement, he sought to smooth them out. "A feather in itself is a wonderful and beautiful thing," he told his audience. "A bird clothed with feathers is almost necessarily a beautiful creature."

For the next several years Wallace was thrust into the vortex of London's fast-paced, sophisticated society. But he fared badly. He felt uncomfortable, as uneasy as during that first year after his return from the Amazon before setting out for the Malay archipelago. "Talking without having anything to say," he later wrote in his memoirs, "and merely for politeness or to pass the time, was most difficult and disagreeable." Lady Lyell's impressions of him when she met him in 1863 for the first time, at a lunch given by Lyell, provide a devastating insight into Wallace's discomfort. She found him, "shy, awkward and quite unused to good society."

Yet among his scientific colleagues, in a small, intimate circle, when the talk turned to substantive matters, Wallace glowed. His originality astonished his contemporaries, especially since they recognized in him a self-educated, free-ranging, undisciplined, unstructured mind. Between 1862 and 1867—the first five years following his return from the Malay archipelago—he operated as a one-man research bureau. He wrote more than a dozen major papers on ornithology, several on physical and zoological geography, six on anthropology, and four on entomology. Two of the monographs alone filled two hundred pages of the Entomological Society's prestigious *Transactions*, and, of course, he contributed a half-dozen articles on his, and Darwin's, concept of evolution through natural selection, the hottest scientific subject of the day.

Yet entomology was by far Wallace's greatest interest and, he confessed, "if I had not had wider and more varied interests—evolution, [biological] distribution, physical geography, anthropology, the glacial period, geological time, sociology, and several others—I might have spent the rest of my life upon similar work."

In the autumn of 1864, while he courted Miss L., Richard Spruce, the English botanist whom Wallace and Bates had befriended in the Amazon, returned to London—like them—"in very weak health." He tarried briefly in the city and settled at Hurstpierpoint in Sussex, far from the bustling scene, a small village twice the distance of Down from London. Spruce selected Hurstpierpoint primarily to be near William and Elizabeth Mitten, his closest friends. Mitten was the village pharmacist and, as a member of the modern Wallace family has recalled, "quite well-known as an authority on mosses."

In the summer of 1865, after the disastrous affair with Miss L. had run its course—notwithstanding Darwin's admonition that hard work banished painful thoughts—Spruce invited Wallace to Sussex to meet the Mittens. Wallace's interest in mosses was quite genuine—the same may be said of him on almost any scientific subject—and, he observed before the year was out, this similarity of taste led to a close "intimacy" between Mitten and himself. Thereafter, although the journey was lengthy and uncomfortable, Wallace was a frequent visitor to Hurstpierpoint, where, it is often said, the setting resembles the sea, hills and dales rising and falling to the horizon like waves. Wallace did not visit Spruce as often as Mitten. But Wallace's interest ranged beyond mosses.

Annie Mitten was the youngest of Mitten's four daughters and was known in the family as "Annie the beautiful." She was born on February 12, 1846—two years before a twenty-five-year-old Wallace set off for the Amazon—and she had matured into an attractive young woman of nineteen, with soft brown eyes matching her soft brown tresses. As Wallace, then forty-two, gracefully phrased it, as a consequence of his increasing number of journeys to Sussex, he not only became intimate with Mitten but also "with his family."

Spring and autumn marriages were as much in vogue in the mid-Victorian period as photography and spiritualism. After the disastrous "Affair L.," a more experienced Wallace realized the necessity of making plain to Annie his honorable intentions. In 1866 the couple was married at Hurstpierpoint. This marked the beginning of a life together which fell only three years shy of a golden wedding anniversary.

The bride was accustomed to the life-style of the naturalist. She herself had been raised amid shelves of journals and specimen boxes. She was accustomed to scientific talk at the table and, like her father and the groom, Annie Wallace possessed not one but two green thumbs.

The couple honeymooned at Windsor and that autumn went on a holiday in northern Wales where "every day revealed some fresh object of interest as we climbed among the higher cwms." Even during their honeymoon, Wallace's thoughts focused on the natural world around him. He and Annie, he wrote, "thoroughly enjoyed" the ice-groovings, striations, smoothed rock-surfaces, *roches moutonnées*, moraines, perched locks, and rock-basins which made up the Welsh valleys. Wallace did not let the opportunity slip by to take notes, and in the January 1867 issue of the *Quarterly Journal of Science*, his first article on geology, written during their "holiday," appeared, entitled, "Ice-marks in North Wales." Once again his originality sprang to the fore. Wallace was the first scientist to put forth a detailed explanation of how glaciers were formed, demolishing the accepted theory that the Welsh *cwms* had been formed by the action of the sea. He demonstrated that glaciers formed lake basins by a grinding process and as a result of pressure, not, as widely supposed at the time, by a "scooping out" process. Wallace's concept was novel; today it is taken for granted.

In the summer of that year Wallace's newfound interest in glaciers took the couple to Switzerland on a second holiday. Botany overtook him there (Annie's influence is apparent), and Wallace later recalled that "we greatly enjoyed beautiful subalpine flowers then in perfection."

Wallace was fond of calling his wife "my dear Annie," and, in correspondence between the two which has survived, botany and horticulture ranked high in their domestic priorities. In 1895, for example, in the course of a journey he made alone to the Ruhr Valley, Wallace wrote, "The violets and anemones were lovely, I have got two species of glorious gentians." As a gift, he sent her a choice box of specimens for her garden.

Judging from their letters, the only objects which took priority in their household over entomology and botany were their three children, the first of whom was born a year after their marriage and christened Herbert Spencer, after the English philosopher and champion of individualism, whom Wallace admired strongly.

There would appear to be difficulty in reconciling the admiration of Wallace—a Utopian socialist and Owenite—for a rugged individualist, so rugged that he coined the phrase "survival of the fittest" to popularize the Wallace–Darwin theory of the origin of species. Yet, although they doubtlessly disagreed on many socioeconomic matters, Spencer and Wallace respected each other's originality and vibrancy. As editor of numerous political and economic journals, Spencer frequently asked Wallace, as the devil's advocate, to contribute articles. He also had Wallace read over the proofs of *Principles of Sociology* which appeared as a series of ten volumes, starting in 1860, and which, together with *The Man Versus the State*, which was published in 1884, is among Spencer's most important works. In his articles for Spencer, Wallace blended his radical views with the Baconian conviction that science was the key to universal peace and happiness.

Wallace, accompanied by Bates, met Spencer shortly after his return from the Malayan archipelago. They called on him in the expectation that Spencer could provide an answer to "the great unsolved problem of the origin of life—a problem which Darwin's *The Origin of Species* left in as much obscurity as ever," Wallace said.

"Our hopes were dashed at once," he added, when Spencer observed that the question was "too fundamental a problem to even think of solving at present."*

Darwin was not happy with the Wallaces' selection of their first child's name. "I heartily congratulate you on the birth of 'Herbert Spencer,'" Darwin wrote them, "and may he deserve his name, but I hope he will copy his father's style and not his namesake's." Darwin entertained misgivings about Spencer, and although he borrowed Spencer's phrase "survival of the fittest," Darwin's attitude toward Spencer was akin to his view of Robert Chambers. In a phrase, Darwin thought that Spencer often shot from the hip and asked questions later. As Huxley jestingly described him, "Spencer's idea of a tragedy is a deduction killed by a fact."

Whatever the case, Herbert Spencer Wallace's life was short-lived. He died in 1874, at the age of seven, from pneumonia.

The child died during a visit to his maternal grandmother's home at Hurstpierpoint. "On coming home this evening I received the news of poor little Bertie's death—this morning at eight o'clock," Wallace wrote on April 24, 1874. "I left him only yesterday forenoon, and had then considerable hopes for we had just commenced a new treatment which a fortnight earlier I am pretty sure might have saved him."

Wallace took the child's death so deeply to heart that, according to a friend, "during the remainder of his life he never mentioned him except when obliged, and then with tears in his eyes." In Wallace's two-

---

* Forty years later Wallace confessed that the origin of life was "as great a mystery as ever." Since then scientists have classified nearly two million different kinds of existing plants and animals on earth and, according to Herbert H. Ross, the entomologist, "[we] expect that the total inventory will be at least double this number." It is doubtful if man is any closer to answering Wallace's question today than in Wallace's time.

volume autobiography, there is no reference to Herbert Spencer Wallace's existence.

The couple had two other children, Violet Isabel, born in 1869 (she died, unmarried, in 1945), and William Gore, who was born in 1871 and passed away in 1951.

In Annie Mitten, Wallace had found more than "an affectionate wife." He had found the intellectual partner that he and Silk had talked about in their boyhood. As an ardent gardener, Annie tried fruitlessly to steer her husband from fauna to flora, but to the end of their life together, on walks across the heath, the couple shared the excitement of discovery whenever they came across a new species of plant or beetle. Wallace's home life, like that of Darwin, was happy and stable, and it was in these pleasant circumstances that both Wallace and Darwin did their major work. "He was very domestic," Violet and William, Wallace's two surviving children, later recalled in a joint memoir, "and loved his home."

This domestic tranquillity spilled over into Wallace's relations with his in-laws, the Mittens. The senior Mitten wrote him frequently and a typical letter, dated December 8, 1879, opens thusly: "I have looked over *Schrimper's Synopsis of European Mosses. . . .*" It then goes on into a lengthy critical commentary of the volume. Only in the last paragraph does Mitten refer to family matters, as if his personal life were an afterthought. "We are all pretty well, have had much snow, all covered now, frost severe," he said. "Ma has been well so far. . . . With love to Annie and Violet and Willie."

Within four years of his return to England from the jungles of Asia, Wallace had accomplished, breathtakingly, three of his four priorities: he had found a wife; he had met Darwin; and he had sorted out his great collection of specimens and started work on the first wave of a flood of scientific papers.

But the fourth objective, regular employment—a steady income—eluded him, and now that he was married and raising a family, the need for a job was greater than ever.

Chapter 31

IN HIS MEMOIRS, published when he was eighty-two, Wallace reminisced, "Up to the age of 21 I do not think I ever had a sovereign of my own." He should have added that after acquiring his first sovereign, he could not hold on to it, nor to those that followed.

Wallace's travels in the Malay archipelago were as much a financial as a scientific success. The monies he received from his species collections alone were, he confessed, "beyond my expectations." Almost all of his specimens were from *terrae incognitae* and of inestimable scientific curiosity; the bidding for them was brisk. Furthermore, Stevens, Wallace's shrewd agent, wisely invested Wallace's earnings while he was abroad in a manner of which Darwin would have heartily approved: Stevens invested them in railroad stocks—not the speculative kind which had brought about the collapse of the market on the eve of Wallace's journey to the Amazon, but the gilt-edged variety. When Wallace returned to England he found himself, much to his surprise and delight, in possession of real money for the first time. His portfolio was earning a handsome return of ·£300 annually. This was a respectable middle-class income (although by comparison, Darwin's meat and poultry bill alone at Down House equalled that princely amount to almost the last farthing!).

In addition to his portfolio, Wallace also possessed private collections of rare species which, after cataloging and describing, he disposed of serially through Stevens at handsome profits. Properly invested, these monies would bring an additional £200 a year. With an income of £500 annually, Wallace would not only be comfortably fixed but, more importantly, in a position to fulfill his wildest dream—the life of an English countryside squire, pursuing research to his heart's content in the grand style of a Darwin.

"But I never reached that comfortable position," Wallace said. ". . . I was wholly ignorant of the numerous snares and pitfalls that beset the ignorant investor."

In plain talk, Wallace was a dreadful businessman and a miserable administrator.

At the urging of newly acquired friends, upon his return home Wallace cashed in his blue chips for speculative stocks, "whose fluctuations in value I was quite unable to comprehend." This venture resulted in the loss of his portfolio, he said brokenheartedly, and "the loss was so great as to be almost ruin."

Wallace then invested in a slate quarry—"quite a safe thing," he was told—and promptly lost another £1,000. He also invested in a lead mine, only to be wiped out when the price of lead collapsed in 1870 with the discovery of lead (and silver) in Nevada. "The result of all this was that by 1880 a large part of the money I had earned at the risk of health and life was irrecoverably lost," he lamented.

That was not all. When he decided to build a house at Grays for Annie and their growing family, it turned out that he had selected a notoriously dishonest contractor, and not only lost another bundle of money but literally wound up building the house himself.

Yet worse lay ahead. "The most regrettable incident in my life," Wallace called it.

In the January 12, 1870, issue of *Scientific Opinion*, John Hampden, the relative of a prominent bishop, challenged the scientific community to prove that the world was round (350 years after Magellan). Hampden, the editor of flat-earth journals, put up a stake of £500. Wallace could not resist a challenge; his feats in the Amazon and Malay archipelago attest to that. He leaped at Hampden's challenge like a trout for an artificial fly. And Lyell encouraged him. "Should I take on Hampden?" Wallace asked. "Certainly," Lyell replied. "It may stop these foolish people."

To make a long story short—and it was long, the ensuing litigation lasting almost twenty years—Wallace selected the Old Bedford canal in Norfolk, which had a stretch of six straight miles between two bridges—to prove that the earth was round. In the manner of a duel, each man selected a second and J. H. Walsh, the respected editor of

Field, was jointly selected as referee. Wallace, of course, had been a surveyor and quickly demonstrated the truth of the earth's curvature by setting up a series of stakes and markers. He brought along a six-inch telescope for Hampden's benefit.

"Mr. Walsh decided without any hesitation that I had proved what I undertook to prove," Wallace said triumphantly. The world was not flat.

But Hampden refused to accept the evidence and his second, a William Carpenter, who had written a book to uphold the "flat-earth theory," supported his sponsor. Hampden now launched a one-man campaign against Wallace, proclaiming him a "liar," "thief," and "swindler," and publicized his views in letters, postal-cards, leaflets, and pamphlets. Wallace was astounded. So were Walsh and, for that matter, Lyell, Darwin, Hooker, and Huxley. They thought it was a joke, but Hampden was deadly serious. Wallace realized the gravity of the situation when Hampden sent Annie the following letter:

> Mrs. Wallace,
> Madam—If your infernal thief of a husband is brought home some day on a hurdle, with every bone in his head smashed to pulp, you will know the reason. . . . You must be a miserable wretch to be obliged to live with a convicted felon [sic].

The mild-mannered Wallace, whose faith in man's goodwill was so naive as to border on the limits of credulity, was angered one of the few times in his life. Wallace hauled Hampden before a police magistrate and Hampden was bound over to keep the peace for three months. But that was only the beginning. When the period expired, Hampden was back at his grist mill, attacking Wallace; he sent letters to the presidents of the Linnean, Geographical, Entomological, and other learned societies, denouncing Wallace as a "cheat, swindler, and imposter." None of Wallace's colleagues took the matter seriously. "I was grieved to see in the [London] *Daily News*," Darwin wrote him, "that the madman about the flat earth has been threatening your life."

Wallace sued for libel and in 1871 Hampden was convicted at Old Bailey, and bound over to keep the peace for one year. But in 1872 Hampden again renewed his offensive. An infuriated Wallace again sued for libel and won a £600 judgment, but Hampden had slyly transferred his property to a son-in-law, a solicitor, and Wallace was unable to collect a penny, winding up paying heavy legal costs. In 1873 Wallace won a second libel suit against Hampden and the court compelled Hampden to print a retraction. London's newspapers carried this recantation as a paid advertisement:

PUBLIC APOLOGY.—I, the undersigned John Hampden, do hereby absolutely *withdraw* all libellous statements published by me, which have reflected on the character of Mr. Alfred Russel Wallace, and apologize for having published them; and I promise that I will not repeat the offence.—JOHN HAMPDEN.

Several months later, however, the flat-earth theorist waged a new campaign of calumny against Wallace and this time he was remanded to Newgate Prison. Within a year of his release, Hampden was back at it. In 1875 he was again indicted for libel, and further costly litigation ensued. Wallace ran up astronomical legal bills.

As late as 1885 Hampden, still undeterred, wrote Huxley, "I have thoroughly exposed that degraded black leg, Alfred Russel Wallace, as I would every one who publicly identifies himself with such grossly false science." For the only time in his life, the articulate Huxley was speechless.

In his assaults, Hampden also circulated tracts proclaiming that Wallace engaged in "scientific villainy and roguery," and one of these pamphlets suggests that Hampden's incessant campaign against Wallace was motivated, beyond his flat-earth theory, by an effort to destroy Wallace's theory of the origin of species. In an 1885 broadside, Hampden describes himself as "the well-known champion of the Mosaic cosmogony . . . against . . . the pagan mystic, who is, at the end of fifteen years' conflict, still holding his ground. . . ."

Curiously, like the Reverend Haughton some years earlier, when he ignored Darwin's contribution to the July 1 Linnean Society as unoriginal, Hampden concentrated on Wallace and ignored Darwin's broader role in the development of the theory.

To this day, an outgrowth of the Hampden affair is the public's confusion over Wallace's role in the flat-earth controversy; while I was engaged in research at the Royal Geographical Society, for example, one reference librarian showed me a folder of clippings about the Hampden-Wallace battle and remarked, "Did Wallace really believe the earth was flat?"*

---

* The International Flat Earth Society, founded by Hampden and associates in 1888, still functions today. The current president is an American, Charles K. Johnson (from California, of course). The Society claims that space travel, eclipses, photographs of the earth taken by satellites, and other scientific findings demonstrating that the earth and moon are spherical, are a hoax.

But besides losing his investments and paying massive legal fees to defend himself against Hampden, Wallace also fared badly in job-hunting.

The first job to open up came in 1864, two years after his return to England. It was custom-crafted—the position of assistant secretary of the Royal Geographical Society. But the fates were unkind to Wallace —and to Bates. Unknown to one another, both applied for the same job. The Society was in a quandary.

Bates was now married and raising a family, and, like Wallace, was in desperate financial straits. The month that Wallace returned to England, Bates had applied for a post in the zoological department of the British Museum but was rejected on grounds both of being too old (he was thirty-seven) and of failing to pass an examination. In Bates' place, the Museum trustees nominated a younger man who had written credible poetry. Darwin heard about this gaffe and wrote Bates a consoling letter.

Bates replied that after eleven years in the Amazon he had barely saved £800 and was at a loss to know where next to turn. Darwin encouraged him to write *A Naturalist on the Amazons* and provided him with a letter to John Murray, who had published *Origin*.

In a private memoir, Francis Galton, Darwin's cousin, who played an active role in the Royal Geological Society, described the competition between Bates and Wallace for the secretaryship of the Society as "difficult." He also disclosed that Murray's intervention in the affair resolved the dilemma. Whether Galton, or Murray, or both, had consulted Darwin about the "difficult" choice is speculative. Whatever the case, Bates won the appointment. There is little doubt that both men shared superb scientific credentials, but that Bates had a distinct advantage over Wallace in one major respect. As Galton put it, Bates was "orderly and efficient." Wallace was no administrator.

Shortly after Bates' appointment, Darwin wrote him a note of congratulation. "You are very kind to inquire after my personal affairs," Bates replied on January 28, 1865; ". . . I like my present position very much."

In short order, Bates rose to the position of permanent secretary of the Society and held this post until his death in 1892 at the age of sixty-seven.

In an obituary notice published by the Society, W. L. Distant, an entomologist and intimate friend of Bates and his family, linked Bates with Wallace and Darwin as a member of the "early band" of evolutionists who preached the origin of species through natural selection. In the biological sciences, Distant wrote, there are usually three kinds of researchers: field workers, theorists, and systematizers. "Bates almost uniquely proved himself a master in each," Distant wrote, "and with the exception of his old travelling companion, Wallace, is approached in that respect by scarcely another living entomologist."

Wallace himself privately considered Bates better fitted for the Society's post because of his business experience as a hosiery apprentice and clerk in a brewery during the time of their first meeting at Leicester. "Besides," Wallace said, "the confinement and the London life would, I am sure, have soon become uncongenial to me. . . . I am therefore glad I did not get it, and I do not think I felt any a disappointment at the time."

In 1869, with Annie carrying her second child, Wallace was presented with a second opportunity to secure a regular job. The government announced plans to open a branch of the South Kensington (now Victoria and Albert) Museum at Bethnal Green in London's east end. Darwin, Lyell, and Hooker, who felt uneasy about their mugging of Wallace at the Linnean in 1858, conspired to support Wallace's application for the job (Huxley joined the trio). Wallace was so confident that he would land the position that he moved to Barking to be close to the site of the new museum.

Wallace was as ideally suited for the job as the poet who wound up in the British Museum's Zoology department. The branch, which was completed in 1872, was filled with the Mainwaring collection of French and German furniture, the Duke of Saxe-Coburg's collection of gold caskets, and the Dixon collection of paintings. But when the branch opened, the government, for reasons of economy, decided that it would require no special director and Wallace's hope for regular employment dissolved. Wallace must have been badly shaken. From Down, on September 2, 1872, Darwin, who observed Wallace's deepening financial troubles with mounting alarm, wrote, "I am extremely grieved to hear about the Museum; it is a great misfortune."

Another opportunity for acquiring regular pay materialized seven years later, in 1878, when the government proclaimed Epping Forest an "open space," and Wallace, who was now desperate, hurriedly applied for the post of superintendent. Epping comprised 5,560 acres, all that was left of the great forest of Waltham, a royal hunting ground which, until the Napoleonic Wars, stretched almost to London.

"This position would have suited me exactly," Wallace admitted, and his hopes were high. Everyone pitched in with recommendations—Darwin, Hooker, Lyell, Huxley, members of Parliament, presidents of learned societies, seventy letters of recommendation in all. But Wallace blew it.

He was so enthralled about the prospect of preserving what was left of a great forest as a national treasure—not unlike the American Yosemite, Yellowstone, Great Smoky Mountains, and other national parks—that he rushed into print in *Fortnightly Review* with an imaginative article entitled, "Epping Forest, and How Best to Deal with It." In essence, Wallace suggested, the forest should be left alone. London's commercial interests exploded in rage. Real estate brokers, merchants, and other businessmen formed a bloc and demanded that a "practical man" be appointed the head of the forest. They wanted Epping thrown open to development: skating rinks, golf courses, hotels, and, as Wallace remarked in a moment of bitterness, "other such amusements more suited to a beer garden."

Wallace lost the job. "My failure to obtain the post at Epping Forest was certainly a disappointment," he acknowledged. It was more than a disappointment; it was a personal and national disaster. But with his article, and the uproar it generated, Wallace indirectly influenced the future development of the forest as a "wild natural woodland for the enjoyment and instruction of successive generations of nature lovers."

Wallace's failure to obtain a job turned not only on his lack of administrative ability and business acumen, but also upon his radical political and scientific views. He was, after all, a Utopian socialist, an advocate of the nationalization of land, among other things. In search of something beyond natural selection to account for the descent of man, he also began to experiment with spiritualism, a subject which the scientific establishment summarily dismissed as a field fit for investigation by quacks, an area of inquiry infested with cranks, crooks, and charlatans.

Wallace did not know it, of course, but after his return to England he would never secure a regular job. In point of fact, the last regular position he ever held was at the age of twenty-one, when he taught at the Reverend Hill's school for boys.

Chapter 32

LOOKING BACK on summer during the winter of his life, Wallace concluded that his failure to settle into a regular job was "really for the best, since it left me free to do literary work." The phrase "literary work" is quaint, and as unassuming as Wallace was during his lifetime. His scientific output—books, monographs, essays, reviews—put him in the first rank of the scientists of his day. Two eminent biologists, Sir Patrick Geddes and J. Arthur Thomson, surveyed the tumultuous mid- and late-Victorian periods shortly after the turn of the century and concluded that "in our own science of biology, we may recall the Grand Old Men, second to none in history —Darwin, Wallace, and Hooker."

Wallace would have been amused at the thought of being placed between Darwin and Hooker, to whom he had dedicated two of his important works.

In all, Wallace published twenty-four books, including works destined to hold their place in science (and literature) as among the greatest contributions of the nineteenth century. Only one, however, was a financial success: *The Malay Archipelago*, which appeared in Wallace's time in a dozen editions. It stands with Darwin's *Voyage of the Beagle* as an imperishable work of scientific inquiry and adventure.

In 1869, the year Violet Isabell, the Wallaces' second child, was born, the *Archipelago* was published, and he dedicated it to Darwin "not only as a token of [my] personal esteem and friendship but also to express my deep admiration for his genius and his works." Darwin was moved by Wallace's words. "Let me congratulate you heartily," Darwin wrote him. ". . . Let me thank you for the very great honour which you have done me by your dedication."

Darwin was not simply being courteous. The *Archipelago* received rave reviews. *The Saturday Review* concluded, "We may safely say that we have never read a more agreeable book of its kind." Lyell greeted it enthusiastically with the observation, "Nothing equal to it has come out since Darwin's *Voyage of the Beagle*." Independently, Charles Kingsley, Canon at Cambridge University, drew the same conclusion. The *Archipelago*, he wrote Wallace, "has not its equal (as far as I can recollect) since our friend Darwin's *Voyage of the Beagle*."

In the *Archipelago*, Wallace gave the world the Wallace Line and, more important scientifically, the concept of such a line. He astonished lay and scholarly readers by dividing the East Asian insular chain into two clear-cut parts. "The [Bali] strait is here fifteen miles wide so that we may pass in two hours from one great division of the earth to another," Wallace wrote, "differing as essentially in their animal life as Europe does from America."

In 1876 Wallace brought out his two-volume *The Geographical Distribution of Animals*, and stunned the scientific aristocracy. The work was a study of the relationship between living and extinct animals as elucidating the last change of the earth's surface. His study became a building block for contemporary paleontology and zoology. "It is a memorable book," Darwin commented, "the basis of all future work on the subject." A London *Times* reviewer added, "It is a wonderful and fascinating story, whatever objections may be taken to theories founded upon it [natural selection]." A century later, Wilma George, the Oxford zoogeographer, wrote, "By synthesizing several branches of natural history, geology, paleontology, zoology and the theory of evolution by natural selection, Wallace succeeded in classifying the world, as he had originally classified the islands of the Malay Archipelago." She added: "It was revolutionary . . . [and] *The Geographical Distribution of Animals* has not been surpassed."

In it Wallace demonstrated the need for scientists to avoid pigeon-holes and to move from discipline to discipline in plumbing the complexities of nature. Wallace divided the earth into six biospheres and in doing so was the first scientist to recognize the Ice Age as a factor in the distribution of animals and in the descent of man. He also expanded on Bates' discovery of mimicry—with full credit to Bates—

and established laws governing this phenomenon. He excited the imagination of young students by declaring that mimicry offers "an almost unworked and inexhaustible field of discovery for the zoologist," and he egged on his peers to widen the search into the "incalculable combinations of laws which we term chance or . . . [the] volition of the Creator."

In 1871, two years after publication of *The Geographical Distribution*, in *Tropical Nature*, Wallace expanded on the theme of mimicry and divided an animal's coloring into classifications of protective (to conceal), warning (to disabuse an enemy), sexual (to distinguish sexes from afar), and so forth. He had touched briefly on the subject of mimicry in papers in 1864 and 1867, but as a contemporary scientist noted recently, "brief as they were, they represented the only theoretical statement on color in general with the exception of those in [Darwin's] *The Descent of Man*, which was published in 1871."

Wallace's treatment was more thorough than Darwin's and in 1964 Oxford's Wilma George wrote, "had Wallace expanded and stated his views in a book devoted entirely to colour, probably he would have lent his name on this branch of biology as indelibly as he has on natural selection and geographical distribution."

In 1880 Wallace published one of his greatest works, *Island Life*, and it was immediately acclaimed by botanists and entomologists. Wallace dedicated it to Hooker, "who more than any other writer, has advanced our knowledge of the geographical distribution of plants . . . as a token of admiration and regard."

Darwin was amazed by Wallace's eclecticism, leaping from fauna to flora as easily as the long-armed Siamang of Sumatra, allied to the genus *Hylobates*, swings effortlessly from tree to tree. "It is quite excellent," Darwin wrote Wallace, "and seems to me the best book which you ever published." And in a characteristic Darwinian aside, he confided, "I had a note the other day from Hooker and I can see that he is much pleased with the dedication."

In *Island Life* Wallace propounded a host of original theories; for example, the theory of the "aerial dispersal" of plant life which, he felt, accounted in part for the geographical distribution of the Earth's plant life. Aerial distribution is a commonplace concept today and studies have demonstrated that spores and pollens are airborne around the globe—like the radioactive fallout of atmospheric nuclear tests— as far as the Arctic Circle and at heights as great as five thousand feet.

Hooker was the greatest living botanist of the epoch, with the possible exception of his American colleague, Asa Gray—to whom Darwin had inexplicably revealed his theory of natural selection and who was unknowingly drawn into the drama of the Linnean "arrangement" many years earlier. "I am only two-thirds through Wallace and it is splendid," Hooker wrote Darwin. "What a number of cobwebs he has swept away."

Books, however, were only the literary and scientific peaks of Wallace's great range of works. He also contributed a veritable avalanche of articles to the *Annals and Magazine of Natural History; Proceedings of the Zoological Society; Transactions of the Linnean Society, Proceedings of The Royal Geographical Society* (edited, of course, by Bates); *The Journal of Botany; The Zoologist;* and many more. These were among the periodicals Darwin subscribed to, and filed. Clearly, Wallace was never far from Darwin's mind, nor from Lyell's or Hooker's, and, for that matter, we can speculate that the "delicate arrangement" surrounding the Linnean meeting of 1858 was also never lost in their thoughts. As *l'éminence gris* behind the affair, Darwin's sense of misgiving was perhaps the deepest.

Science aside, Wallace was compelled to write constantly, as if manning the bilge pump of a sinking vessel, to earn money to keep his family afloat financially. He loved his children and, of course, in their first days, weeks, and months of life he could not help but study and compare their behavior with that of his first baby, the "ugly red-haired . . . little duck of a darling" orang-utan he had nursed in Borneo in 1855, although, surprisingly, he never published a comparative paper on the subject.

In her own quiet way, meanwhile, Annie Wallace was another Emma Darwin, hovering over Wallace when she was not hovering over the children, running the household, and, in Annie's case, with her background in botany, tending to her vegetable and flower beds.

Wallace rose at six each morning, sipped a cup of tea, and promptly returned to bed for two hours. He rarely slept soundly; too many ideas floated about in his head like the swallow-tailed *Papilio* of the Amazon and the Malay archipelago. "Frequently he lay awake during the night," his children recounted in a memoir, "and then it was that he thought out and planned his work."

Wallace's workday lasted an intensive four hours, not unlike Darwin's most productive period of concentration. The work period began with a hot cup of cocoa, in both winter and summer, and Wallace worked steadily at his writing board until 1 P.M., sometimes jumping up to get a book from a shelf to verify a fact. His heaviest meal was at lunch, which he ate with Annie and the children. The luncheon highlight, aside from the gravy boat, was "a little Canary sack" mixed with a dash of soda water. Sherry and soda water? That was not all; he also added a spoonful of plum jam to the concoction. After lunch he napped and later in the day joined Annie in the garden. They took tea at 4 P.M. and, after supper, which was usually served at seven, spent the evening reading until eleven before they retired for the night.

The routine was broken only when there were visitors.

Wallace's house was a scene of domestic peace; for that matter, so were the households of Darwin, Hooker, Lyell, and Huxley.

During that first decade after returning to England—1862 to 1872— Wallace was briefly drawn into the vortex of the carriage set. "After my marriage," he recalled, "we occasionally dined with [Lyell] or went to his evening receptions." Through Sir Charles and Lady Lyell, Wallace was introduced to the glittering names of the scientific establishment, the Duke of Argyll, Sir Charles Wheatstone, Sir John Lubbock, "and a great many others." The abnormally tall, abnormally shy Wallace felt out of place. Arabella Buckley, Lyell's personal secretary, often had to "point out to me the various celebrities who happened to be present," Wallace said.

In London his most intimate friends were Huxley, Hooker, Sir John Lubbock (Darwin's neighbor), and Francis Galton (Darwin's cousin). "All these I met very frequently at scientific meetings," Wallace said, "or at some of their houses."

Although he saw Lyell more often than the others, he became the most intimate with Huxley and often visited Huxley's London residence at Marlborough Place or his country home at St. John's Wood. Huxley was everything Wallace was not—sophisticated, hot-tempered, extroverted, articulate, witty, at ease with small or big talk, and a veritable walking encyclopedia. Yet Wallace felt comfortable only at Huxley's house as compared to the homes of other members of the scientific aristocracy. "Mrs. Huxley was exceedingly kind and pleasant," he said, "and the whole domestic tone of the house was such as to make me quite at my ease which," he added, "is what happens to me with only a few persons."

It was at Huxley's that Wallace met the great Russian anthropologist Muklucho Maklay, who was en route to New Guinea. Since Wallace had been the first European to live alone in that *terra incognita*,

Huxley brought them together at his table. Maklay felt that you could learn nothing of another people unless you lived among them and "above all, won their confidence."

Maklay planned to be deposited on the island by a Russian warship accompanied by two servants, one Swedish and the other Polynesian. He did so and no sooner had the vessel disappeared than Maklay and his party were surrounded by Papuans brandishing bows and spears. But, although arrows were shot close to his head and body, Maklay never flinched. He sat still and smiled, knowing, the experienced Wallace said, "that if they really meant to kill him that was hardly the way they would do it, and that in any case he could not possibly escape." Maklay lived contentedly among the Stone Age people of the island for fifteen months, learning their language and customs. "I know of no more daring feat by any traveller," said Wallace.

Apparently Wallace made a good impression on the Russians because thereafter he was frequently visited by Russian specialists on their travels to the West. Conversely, his contacts with the Russians sparked interest in Russia in Wallace's work, and three of his major publications, including *Darwinism*, were translated into Russian and issued between 1878 and 1898 at St. Petersburg and Moscow. However, when one Russian scientist visited his home and mixed a spoonful of marmalade in his tea, Wallace was shaken. "I love delicacies myself, and little eccentricities interest me," he wrote, "but I draw the line at marmalade and tea."*

Darwin often invited the Wallaces to Down—"his quiet home" is the way Wallace characterized Down House—and occasionally he and Annie spent a weekend there. But Wallace's most frequent encounters with Darwin occurred in London. Each year, whenever the chronically ill Darwin felt up to it, he journeyed to his brother Erasmus' home on Queen Anne Street to catch up on friends and the latest scientific gossip. "On these occasions I usually lunched with him and his brother," Wallace said. Occasionally, Darwin called on the Wallaces at their home "for a quiet talk and to study some of Wallace's collections."

Between visits, Darwin and Wallace engaged in heavy correspondence. Like Lyell and Hooker, Darwin often turned to Wallace for advice. For example, in 1867 Darwin asked Bates, who was then secretary of the Royal Geographical Society, "why are caterpillars sometimes so beautifully and artistically coloured?" Darwin could not

---

* Personally, I draw the line at sherry and a spoonful of plum jam!

fathom why, through natural selection, they would acquire bright colors and thereby place themselves at a disadvantage against predatory birds. Bates confirmed Darwin's observation and recalled that "the most gaudy caterpillar [I] ever saw in the Amazon was conspicuous at a distance of yards."

As for the explanation, Bates threw his hands up. "You had better ask Wallace," he said. And Darwin did.

"On reading [Darwin's] letter," Wallace said, "I almost at once saw what seemed to be a very easy and probable explanation of the facts."

Wallace knew that showy and slow-flying butterflies often had a peculiar odor or taste which protected them from attack and this "led me at once to suppose that the gaudily-colored caterpillars must have similar protection."

On February 26 of that year, three days after receiving Darwin's letter, Wallace dashed off a hurried note of explanation. Darwin was flabbergasted by Wallace's powers of inductive reasoning. "Bates was quite right," Darwin replied in admiration. "You are the man to apply to in a difficulty. I never heard anything more ingenious than your suggestion, and I hope you may be able to prove it true."

As it developed, Jenner Weir, the entomologist, reported at the time that birds in his aviary avoided one of Britain's common moths, *Spilosoma menthrastri*. Weir was puzzled because the moth's color was white, making it conspicuous and therefore an easy prey at night. Wallace added one and one, and came up with two. "As a *white* moth is as conspicuous in the *dusk* as a *colored* caterpillar in the *daylight*, this case seemed to me so much on par with the other that I felt almost sure my explanation would turn out correct," Wallace said.

It did, and Darwin wrote him, "That is a splendid fact about white moths; it warms one's very blood to see a theory thus almost proved to be true."

London's glitter, however, was gradually wearing down Wallace. The Darwins, Hookers, Lyells, and Huxleys were delightful. But the city's gadflies—the rent-a-celebrity type—appalled him. He found it "impossible . . . to make conversation with them," Wallace said. He considered their remarks vapid and trivial and in their presence he gave the false impression that he was gloomy, whereas, he explained, "I was merely bored."

Like Darwin, despite the outward signs of a placid, graceful existence, Wallace was a coil of nervous energy who felt there was too much to do and too little time in which to do it. He could not afford to waste his time on small talk; he would rather moon about his garden in his "free time."

Thus, Wallace began a slow retreat from London, moving from one house to another (Dorking, Croydon, Godalming, Parkstone, and so on) until he ended up over a period of twenty years in Dorset, Thomas Hardy country, and in the spirit of Hardy's great novel of the period, *Far From the Madding Crowd*. Wallace's last move was to remote Broadstone, more than one hundred miles west of London. If Darwin and his contemporaries thought the sixteen-mile journey from London Bridge to Down was awesome, a trip to Broadstone was tantamount to a visit to a distant planet.

Wallace's retreat from society was hardly surprising. The London set was too articulate, too glib, and too affluent. As for the last, the Wallaces simply could not keep up with them, since Wallace was continually courting financial disaster.

"I had now to depend almost entirely on the little my books brought me in," he said, "together with a few lectures, reviews, and other articles."

The situation was so bad that if it had not been for the kindly intervention of a cousin of his mother's, "I should have been in absolute want," he admitted. She had intended to leave him £1,000 in her will, but realizing his financial plight, she transferred the money to him while she lived. "It was most welcome," a relieved and gratified Wallace acknowledged.

Wallace apparently was unaware of or ignored the Victorian admonition that three household moves were equal to an uninsured fire. With each move, his financial situation worsened and he was compelled to write faster and faster to maintain his family.

Chapter 33

WALLACE'S FAILURE to land a regular job cannot be attributed simply to his lack of formal education or social status. Darwin, Lyell, Hooker, and Huxley lowered the drawbridge for him, but Wallace never crossed the moat. He felt uncomfortable in affluent society. He could not afford to keep up with it and, more importantly, had no desire to do so; worse still, he deprecated his own achievement and value. And there were other problems. His Utopian socialist views tuned out the political establishment. His experiments in spiritualism turned off the scientific community.

Wallace's political naivete matched his innocence in financial matters. Scientists have a sorry record in politics, as witness in our own era the Bertrand Russells, Linus Paulings, and J. B. S. Haldanes. This list is intolerably long. Russell, for example, once advocated that the United States use the atomic bomb against the Soviet Union to save Western civilization; later he denounced American involvement in Vietnam as "criminal." Wallace's political record was not as grotesque.

Like many scientists before and after him, Wallace believed that harnessing science to society would bring about the Utopia described by Bacon in his *New Atlantis*, where science was the linchpin of universal happiness. Unlike many utopians, however, Wallace did not ignore defects in human nature. While his optimism was as hardy as a garden perennial, he admitted that he was "amazed" at the amount of goodness and humanity in man despite the degrading influences at work on the species.

Wallace was a prolific writer on political affairs, and carried aloft the banner of socialism in books such as *Bad Times*, *Moral Progress*, *The Revolt of Democracy*, and *Land Nationalization* (which went into three editions and appeared in both "limp cloth" and "paper cover"). Some of Wallace's "radical" opinions are so commonplace today that it is hard to believe that they were once considered novel, if not revolutionary. Yet a close friend of Wallace's confessed that he considered Wallace's political outlook "rank heresy and almost blasphemy."

Wallace defined socialism as "the organization of the labour of all for the equal benefit of all." To this end, he was an advocate of the nationalization of land and, as president of the Land Nationalization Society for ten years, was at the eye of a perpetual storm. He wrote powerful tracts against the "inhumanity, cruelty and immorality" of child and woman labor in the raw capitalist system of his era, particularly in the Welsh coal mines. He fought against "red-tapism" in government; railed against sweatshops, industrial blight, and urban decay; he championed the breakup of monopolies and trusts; and warned against pollution of air and water by "poisonous vapors." He favored free bread for the needy through the novelty of food stamps; greenbelts around towns and cities to provide recreation for urban dwellers; creation of food and drug administrations and laws against manufacture of "junk" foods; the redistribution of wealth through income and estate taxes; and the establishment of minimum wage and hour laws. He also favored conservation of natural resources. Unlike many other socialists, however, Wallace recognized the middle class as the "very backbone of the country" and sought to strengthen and broaden it through reforms. He advocated strong labor unions, the use of the strike as a weapon in the struggle for improved working conditions, and higher wages tied to increased productivity to offset inflation.

As for colonialism and the ever-expanding British empire, Wallace wrote, "It is evident that we have here a state of things which cannot go on indefinitely."

The most pernicious element in colonialism, Wallace felt, was racism, and he often cited as an example the white man's treatment of the "natives" who inhabited the Pacific. "These people are declared by numerous independent and unprejudiced observers to be both [sic] physically, morally and intellectually our equals, if not superiors," he said. "It has always seemed to me one of the disgraces of our

civilization that these fine *people* have not in a single case been protected from contamination by the vices and follies of our more degraded classes." (Italics added.)

In Victoria's time, such positions were shocking.

Some of his other views, while still unacceptable, appear today to be
gaining support. Wallace, for example, opposed gambling on the
ground that "whenever one wins, someone else loses," and he felt that
the acquisition of wealth through state lotteries contributed nothing
useful to the social order of which the gambler was a part. He would
have been appalled at off-track betting, state lotteries, and similar
revenue-raising gimmicks based on gambling. He also opposed foreign
aid as enabling "despotic rulers to gratify their passions, their follies, or
even their vices at the expense of their subjects." As the ultimate
idealist, Wallace argued *against* the welfare state. "The worker does
not want charity," Wallace asserted. "The worker wants dignity. He
feels that he is entitled to a man's share of the wealth he has produced,
and he wants it assured to him, not as a charity," Wallace declared,
"but as a citizen's right."

Wallace was among the foremost exponents of women's liberation
in Victorian-Edwardian England, and on grounds so ingenious, so
revolutionary, that the current feminist movement has not yet caught
up with him.

As an evolutionist whose theorizing often went far beyond Darwin's,
Wallace foresaw that the future moral progress of mankind would be
governed by the acceleration of women's rights. "The position of
women in the not distant future will be far higher and more important
than any which has been claimed for or by her in the past," he forecast. "While she will be conceded full political and social rights and
equality with man, she will be placed in a position of responsibility and
power which will render her his superior, since future moral progress
of the race will so largely depend upon her free choice in marriage."

Wallace's thesis was as much biological as sociopolitical and socioeconomic. As women acquire greater economic independence, he held,
they will also acquire a more effective power in selecting or rejecting
a suitor. Through this process of "natural selection," the human species
would make its most spectacular advance. "In a state or society in
which all women are economically independent, are all fully occupied
with public duties and social or intellectual pleasure, and had nothing
to gain by marriage as regards material well-being or social position,"

Wallace wrote, "it is highly probable that the numbers of the un-married from choice would increase." The powerful biological agency of reproduction would be exercised increasingly by the female of the species and the custom of a woman marrying for economic or social reasons would fade. In Wallace's utopian view, women would exploit this new independence by rejecting idle or utterly selfish males, the chronically diseased or intellectually weak. Thus, through a combina-tion of women's liberation and natural selection, Wallace foresaw the moral progress of mankind.

While some of Wallace's radical ideas are presently accepted and others are in the process of acceptance, some of them are so utopian as to be outlandish to this day. An illustration makes the point: Wallace advocated that one day a week or one week a month each person engage in gardening to "add much to the interest and enjoy-ment of their lives." The proposal, in an era before the introduction of mechanized agriculture, had a practical aspect—the creation of a large agricultural labor force to assist farmers at critical harvests. But the enrichment and quality of life was his basic concern. It never occurred to Wallace that some people hate gardening!

Karl Marx, living in obscurity in mid-Victorian London, was aware of the Linnean Society's extraordinary 1858 meeting and its explosive aftermath. For example, Marx attended Huxley's lectures on the Wallace–Darwin theory of evolution and, a friend of Marx later re-called, "spoke of nothing else for months." For that matter, Marx wrote Friedrich Engels, his collaborator, that the new theory provided a "basis in natural history for class struggle."

During the 1860s and 1870s, Marx, Darwin, and Wallace lived, in a manner of speaking, within hailing distance of each other. Yet Marx never met either Darwin or Wallace. In Wallace's case, this is especially surprising because of Wallace's unending denunciation of the capitalist system and his espousal of socialism. Yet there is no evidence that Wallace and Marx ever crossed paths even at the socialist clubs springing up in London in that period, forerunners of the founding in 1901 of the present-day British Labor Party. Nor is there any evidence that they ever exchanged a letter.

Marx probably viewed Wallace with disgust as a utopian whose focus, however radical among the ruling elite, was on reform, not revolution. Equally surprising is that in Wallace's books and political tracts, peppered with references to Adam Smith, Owen, Bellamy,

Spencer, Henry George, Swedenborg, John Stuart Mill, and Walter Bagehot, there is not a solitary reference to Marx. This must have been deliberate on Wallace's part. Wallace probably considered *Das Kapital*, which was published in 1867 as Wallace completed *The Malay Archipelago*, as a misapplication of economic to biological theory, pitting class (species) against class (species) in a struggle for survival and, through dialectics, the emergence of a new class (species).

For his part, Marx's enthusiasm for natural selection was short-lived. By the 1870s, he concluded, as had Wallace before him, that the link between biological evolution and economics is suspect. "Human history," Marx observed, "differs from natural history." Marx did not amplify this remark. Obviously, human history is man-made. But natural history? Moreover, biology is a science; human affairs, anything but a science.

Marx's newfound misgivings notwithstanding, he sent Darwin a copy of *Das Kapital* in 1873, inscribed, "on the part of his sincere admirer." Darwin was astonished by its receipt and, pursuing a policy of thanking those who troubled to send him a book or letter, wrote Marx a polite note in which he commented that his knowledge "of the deep and important subject of political economy" was scanty. And scanty it remained. Darwin never read beyond the first 105 pages of Marx's 927-page work. The remaining pages, presently at Down House, are uncut. The pages Darwin scanned are not even annotated in Darwin's almost indecipherable hand. Darwin did not consider either politics or economics a science, and therefore worth his time.

Six years later, in 1879, from out of nowhere as far as Darwin was concerned, Marx wrote Darwin a second (and last) letter. Darwin was now seventy—Marx was nine years his junior and five years Wallace's senior—and in this letter Marx requested permission to dedicate his next volume to Darwin. This was surely hypocritical since Marx had concluded that there was no relationship between the biological sciences and socioeconomic theory. As Ralph Colp, Jr., a Darwinian, aptly expressed it, Marx was not ashamed to "perform hypocritical actions in order to advance his ideas." Darwin flatly turned down Marx, and did so with the biting observation that such a dedication would imply "to a certain extent my approval of the general publication, about which I know nothing."

In his letter to Marx, Darwin added a line which is intriguing in the light of the "Marxist" regimes which have since sprung up and have rigidly, without exception, barred civil liberties, including such essential liberties, especially for the scientist, as freedom of thought. "I am a strong advocate of free thought," Darwin reminded Marx, "on all subjects." Although the reference was made within the context of atheism and evolutionary theory, it may well have reflected Darwin's premonition that his and Wallace's theory of the origin of species had killed God and that the consequences for the future of mankind were incalculable. Darwin, as observed earlier, was pessimistic; indeed, Wallace recalled that "during my last conversation with Darwin [shortly before Darwin's death] he expressed a very gloomy view on the future of mankind. . . ."

Darwin's pessimism has been, thus far, borne out; Wallace's naive vision of a brave new world, shattered. In a letter to a German naturalist that Christmas, a few weeks after turning down Marx, Darwin wrote, "What a foolish idea seems to prevail in Germany on the connection between socialism and evolution through natural selection."

In brushing off Marx and his mislabeling of his theory of socialism as "scientific"—curiously, although a scientist, Wallace never considered socialism "scientific"—Darwin hit the mark. It is fun to speculate that in doing so he applied an old saw that Hooker, his confidant, never tired of retelling. "There is a story somewhere of an Englishman, Frenchman, and German being each called on to describe a camel," Hooker often said. "The Englishman immediately embarked for Egypt, the Frenchman went to the zoo, and the German shut himself up in his study and thought it out!"

Nevertheless, since the days of Wallace and Darwin, Germany has provided a seedbed for materialist philosophies which have had a baleful influence on the course of human history within, and beyond, her frontiers. She has been the potting shed of communism and nazism, the twin holocausts of this century.

For Germans who shut themselves up in their studies, the theory of the origin of species by natural selection has had irresistible philosophical appeal. When *Origin* was translated into German for the first time, the translator, Professor H. G. Bronn, said he did so from a sense of duty but also with qualms. "Creation," he felt, "is supernatural and cannot be explained by a law of nature." Rudolf Virchow, a forceful figure in Bismarck's "*Kulturkampf*" and the confidant of Heinrich Schliemann, the pauper-to-riches discoverer of Homer's Troy, was frightened by the future. The theory, Virchow warned, would give birth to "dogmatism and fanaticism." It would lead to "revolution, socialism and disaster."* Indeed, at German universities, as Wallace returned from Malaya, it was said that the choice was heathenism or Christianity. *"Heidentum oder Christentum,"* the students shouted, *"die Fragen der Zeit!"*

Manifestly, in the mentality of the political dogmatist and fanatic—whether from the "right" or the "left"—natural selection, in Galton's words, can be replaced by "other processes" in the interminable, dialectic struggle for absolute power. For the dogmatist and fanatic, politics, economics, and sociology are "sciences." Indeed, despite Marx's own refutation of a link between natural and human history, Engels, at Marx's gravesite, did link the two. "Just as Darwin discovered the law of evolution in organic nature," Engels claimed, "so Marx discovered the law of evolution in human history."**

Wallace was as annoyed as Darwin over this confusion between natural and human history as "sciences." Wallace was stunned when Professor Joseph Le Coute, an American, wrote that "if you are to have any race improvement at all, the dreadful law of destruction of the weak and helpless must, with Spartan firmness, be carried out voluntarily and deliberately." And when another so-called Social Darwinian of the capitalist school railed against workman's compensation and old-age insurance as propping up the sick, the weak and helpless, Wallace was aghast.

A typical exponent of this misapplication of the theory of natural selection to political economy was William Matthew Flinders-Petrie, a founder of modern Egyptology and the mentor of Howard Carter, who discovered the tomb of Tutankhamen in 1922. "Nature," Professor Flinders-Petrie intoned, "knows no right of maintenance but only the necessity of getting rid of those who need it. . . ." Wallace con-

---

* When disaster struck in the form of "national" socialism, Emanuel Radl, professor of natural history, University of Prague, wrote in 1930, "Darwinism . . . [has] found a spiritual home in Germany." It had found it earlier in "Marx" and Engels, and in the robber barons of the Industrial Revolution.

** To his credit, Engels disagreed with Marx's conclusion and clung to the theory of natural selection as a clue to man's sociopolitical development, airing his views in 1876 in "The Part Played by Labor in the Transition from Ape to Man." By labor, Engels meant the ability of man's progenitors to employ tools. Interestingly, one of the hottest conflicts surrounding present-day biology is waged between Marxists and sociobiologists. There is a strange tie-back between them to Wallace. For example, in *Sociobiology: The New Synthesis* by Edward O. Wilson (Cambridge, Mass.: Harvard University Press, 1975)—the "bible" among sociobiologists—Wilson credits Wallace with "the first published record of tool-using in animals below primates." This refers to Wallace's observations about the black cockatoo *Probosciger arterrimus* in the "horrible" Aru Islands which uses a leaf to get hold of a nut for cracking it open.

sidered the statement cruel and he damned Petrie. "The whole book is full of such statements," Wallace fumed.

Unlike Wallace, who entered the lists to battle for his political convictions, Darwin kept his political opinions hidden from the public. In private, however, as Darwin's son William observed, "[My father] had an enthusiasm for liberty of the individual and for liberal principles." Wisely, Darwin felt that the theory of evolution had encountered enough opposition among scientists and clergymen without taking on the political and economic establishments. Darwin carried his self-discipline to the point that he "never answered criticism excepting those made by scientific men." Darwin was content to advance science (and his own place in history), and in a letter to Wallace in 1873 advised him to do likewise. "I hope to Heaven," Darwin wrote, "that politics will not replace Natural Selection."

But Wallace was impatient with the human condition, outspoken and independent-minded. J. W. Sharpe, a near neighbor of his in Dorset, felt that Wallace was stimulated by novelty and opposition. "An uphill fight in an unpopular cause, for preference a thoroughly unpopular one, or any argument in favor of a generally despised thesis, had charms for him that he could not resist," Sharpe said. The prospect of writing a new book or article with the purpose of disrupting doctrinaire scientific or political thinking, of rattling the academic community, Sharpe continued, always acted upon Wallace like a tonic.

This posture handicapped Wallace in landing a job. But probably the straw that broke the back of Hooker's camel was Wallace's experiments in spiritualism.

Chapter 34

EVER SINCE his introduction to mesmerism at Leicester, Wallace retained a residual curiosity in what is today called parapsychology. What makes this astonishing is that from the age of fourteen, when he lived with his brother William and was forced to quit school and go to work, Wallace was raised in an atmosphere, as he expressed it, of "advanced liberal philosophical opinions." In sum, William was a skeptic, an agnostic (before the word was invented).

It was not until after his return from the Malay world, however, that Wallace plunged into spiritualism. During his travels in the Amazon and Southeast Asia, where animism is still alive and well, he dismissed the many examples of black magic he encountered as "superstitions."* The Amazonian Indians, Wallace observed, "scarcely seem to think that death can occur naturally." Wallace was so turned off by what he saw, despite his early interest in mesmerism, that he later admitted, "I could not at that time find a place in my mind for the conception of spiritual existence, or for any other agencies in the universe than matter and force."

But, above all, Wallace was a scientist, a Baconian. "Facts are stubborn things," he later said in defense of his tilt toward spiritualism. "Facts beat me." But was the spiritualism that swept Victorian England based on facts?

---

* Darwin did likewise. He also witnessed many forms of the occult during the journey of the *Beagle*. In the Indian Ocean, among the Cocos Islands, he attended a black magic ritual and contemptuously described it as a "foolish spectacle."

The modern history of parapsychology barely goes back to Wallace's days at Leicester. No other branch of science, the London *Economist* recently observed, has encountered such contempt and hatred as research into psychic phenomena. And Brian Inglis, in his recent *Natural and Supernatural*, made the point that "any scientist who became identified with physical research ran the risk of being ridiculed, or worse." Yet the subject attracted a number of intelligent, outstanding Victorians, among them William Gladstone, John Ruskin, Lord Tennyson—and Alfred Wallace. Nor was Wallace the first scientist attracted to the occult. Johannes Kepler, the seventeenth-century founder of modern astronomy, the author of laws of dynamics and gravitation, launched his career casting horoscopes and ended it as court astrologer to the Duke of Wallenstein.

Wallace's views on spiritual existence underwent a slow, perceptible modification while he was abroad. On at least three occasions he had confronted death personally and, he said, each occasion made him feel, "in a way nothing else can do, the mystery of the universe." Wallace had a lust for life, a lust as intense as it was different from that of van Gogh. It defied Wallace's powers of reasoning that death should reduce living matter to nothingness. "It seems . . . ," Wallace said, groping for a word, "unnatural."

By the late 1860s Wallace had shifted his point of view so strongly that he became convinced that there "*must* be a hereafter for us all." But he admitted that he was, to the end of his life, beset by qualms of doubt despite the strength of his conviction, doubt which he attributed to the skepticism ingrained in him during his youth.

Wallace's first major declaration on this subject was contained in his first complete work on evolution, published in 1870, *Contributions to the Theory of Natural Selection*. The volume—which was critically acclaimed and went into a second edition within a year—included an essay on man, which concluded that man's evolution was distinct from that of other creatures. In it, Wallace argued that while natural selection accounted for man's bodily frame, it could *not* account for man's emergence as a spiritual being. The brainpan of the "uncivilized" peoples Wallace encountered in his travels, such as the Papuans, he observed, was virtually on a par with that of the most "civilized" people he met in London. Yet both were immensely superior to that of their simian relations, the anthropoid apes.

Natural selection, Wallace concluded from the "facts," could not provide primitive man with a brain disproportionate to his requirements. Natural selection was a mechanism of evolution. How could something evolve before it was needed? That was putting the cart before the horse. Wallace felt it "utterly inconceivable" that man's development as a spiritual being resulted from natural selection.

With trepidation—"these speculations are widely held to be far beyond the bounds of science," Wallace conceded—he suggested that "a superior intelligence has guided the development of man . . . and for a special purpose, just as man guides the development of many animal and vegetable forms."

In essence, as one goldfish remarked to another. "There *must* be a God, or who changes the water?"

Wallace's treatment of man marked the first major theoretical divergence of thought between Wallace and Darwin. Wallace insisted that there is a "difference of kind, intellectually and morally, between man and other animals" which natural selection could not account for. Darwin rejected Wallace's thesis outright. Darwin reasoned that man's whole nature, physical, intellectual, and moral, developed from lower animals by laws of natural selection.

"I hope you have not murdered too completely your own and my child," Darwin wrote Wallace. And in another letter to Wallace he added, "I groan over Man . . . and you the author of the best paper that ever appeared in the *Anthropological Review!*" Darwin signed the letter, "Your miserable friend."

Darwin also wrote Lyell about Wallace's conclusion and confessed, "I was dreadfully disappointed about Man, . . . had I not known to the contrary, [I] would have sworn it had been inserted by some other hand." But Darwin suspected that the devout Lyell would find the theory of outside agency in man's development appealing, and Lyell did. In 1873, in a revised edition of his *Antiquity of Man*, Lyell subscribed to Wallace's position, observing that "the perpetual adaptation of the organic world to new conditions leaves the argument in favour of design, and therefore of a designer, as valid as ever." And in a letter to Darwin, Lyell admitted that "as I feel that progressive development or evolution cannot be entirely explained by natural selection, I rather hail Wallace's suggestion that there may be a Supreme Will and Power which may not abdicate functions of interference, but may abide by the forces of laws of nature."

Darwin's neighbor, Sir John Lubbock, also thought Wallace on the proper track in separating man's intellectual and spiritual development from his physical origin. And Robert Chambers, whose *Vestiges* was the most influential book on evolution before the publication of *Origin* and whom Darwin held in contempt, wrote Wallace, "My idea is that the term 'supernatural' is a gross mistake [and] we have only to enlarge our conceptions of the natural and all will be bright."

In *Descent of Man*, published a year after Wallace's *Natural Selection*, with its heretical essay on man, Darwin sought to refute Wallace's thesis and check the defection of the Lyells and the Lubbocks. Unlike the first edition of *Origin*, in whose preface he ignored his forerunners, Darwin—now that his priority was assured—behaved generously toward his precursors. He mentioned Wallace fifty-five times as compared to only twice in the first edition of *Origin*. One reference dealt with their profound differences about man.

Darwin attributed man's development as the most dominant animal on earth to the development, through natural selection, of the human powers of observation, memory, curiosity, imagination, and reason, each developed through natural selection. "I cannot, therefore, understand how it is that Mr. Wallace maintains that 'natural selection' could only have endowed the savage with a brain a little superior to that of an ape," he said.

After reading *Descent*, Wallace hurriedly wrote Darwin. "I have to thank you for the great tenderness with which you have treated me and my heresies," he said, adding, "of course, I fully agree with every word and every argument which goes to prove the evolution or development of man out of a lower form." Darwin replied that he was relieved to learn that Wallace had not abandoned the core of "our theory."

Although Darwin categorically rejected the idea that an outside agency had contributed to the development of man, in his *Autobiography*, at several points, he referred to his father's "almost supernatural powers" in reading the thoughts of others. Moreover, one of Darwin's principal physicians, James M. Gully, believed in clairvoyance and frequently attended séances at which, he swore, apparitions floated around the room. Yet, although he characterized Gully's naivete as a "sad flaw," Darwin retained full confidence in Gully's hydropathy or water cure treatments for his chronic ailments.

On one occasion Gully induced Darwin to accompany him to a clairvoyant, but Darwin came away from the experience unconvinced. Although he remained a skeptic, however, Darwin remained intrigued by the subject. Francis Galton, his nephew, who founded eugenics, also delved into spiritualism, attending three séances, and in 1872 wrote

Darwin that perhaps there was something to it because he, Galton, was "utterly confounded by the results, and very disinclined to discredit them." And six years later Darwin confessed that while biologists appeared to have accepted the idea of evolution through natural selection, there was still room for inquiry into "how far natural selection has acted, and . . . whether there exists [in man] some mysterious innate tendency to perfectability." Wallace had forced Darwin to turn the idea over in his mind.

But the overwhelming evidence suggests that Darwin took a dim view of spiritualism and of the charlatans of the period who practiced it. In his library at Down House, to this day, are copies of such works as *The Supernatural and Natural* and *An Inquiry into the Reality of Divine Revelation*. As in the case of Marx's *Das Kapital*, many of the pages in these volumes are uncut. But until his death, Darwin toyed with Wallace's heresy. In the May 13, 1897 issue of *The British Weekly*, Professor Michael Foster cited Darwin's interest in the supernatural, and concluded, "We shall never know the countless hypotheses which passed through Darwin's mind and which, however wild and improbable, were tested by an appeal to nature and were finally dismissed."

Had Wallace simply stated his views, he would have probably emerged, like Lyell, Galton, Gully, and others, unscathed by heresy. But Wallace was ever the activist and he exposed himself to considerable ridicule when he joined the Society for Physical Research and became involved in experiments in spiritualism. Wallace's naive acceptance of floating figures and rapping tables dismayed his scientific colleagues. Inglis put the situation well: "By his magnanimous gesture in leaving to Darwin the full credit for the theory of evolution (over which Wallace, if he had published his own version first, as he could have done, could have claimed at least squatter's rights), Wallace had established a reputation for integrity as well as for scientific acumen."

Wallace's credentials were impeccable. Therefore, his interest in spiritualism had to be considered purely objective, scientific; he was neither a charlatan nor the kind to ride a fashionable bandwagon in quest of cheap notoriety or celebrity. He confounded the scientific establishment.

Many of the leading scientists of the day were moved to view Wallace charitably. Lord Kelvin, the brilliant physicist who developed the second law of thermodynamics, considered researchers like Wallace "innocent, trusting minds, who are victims of imposture." The description certainly fitted Wallace.* "I am well aware that my scientific friends are somewhat puzzled for what they consider to be my delusion," Wallace admitted. But his friends were more than "somewhat puzzled."

The irrepressible Huxley dismissed spiritualism as "twaddle" and wrote Wallace jocularly, "I am neither shocked nor disposed to issue a Commission of Lunacy against you." Hooker was astounded by Wallace's behavior. "That such a man should be a spiritualist," Hooker wrote Darwin, "is more wonderful than all the movements of all the planets!" As for Wallace's family, they were bemused by his acceptance of spiritualism and humored him. "If you are once convinced of the facts and teachings of spiritualism," Wallace wrote his son Will, "you will think more as I do." But Will never did.

Wallace's connection with the spiritualist movement accomplished what Darwin dreaded: it provided ammunition to critics of the Darwin–Wallace theory of evolution. Professor G. J. Rommanes, a powerful opponent of Darwin and Wallace, publicly denounced Wallace's experiments in parapsychology as "absurd."

Although Wallace was badly taken in by fakes and charlatans, not unlike some people deceived today by some psychologists, psychiatrists, mystics, and evangelists, he was not a complete fool. He read widely on the subject of reincarnation and concluded that it "does not seem to me rational." And to a correspondent who discussed astrology, Wallace replied, "I am quite astonished at your wasting your money on an advertising astrologer. . . . [They] calculate to lead you to send more money, and you get in reply more words and nothing else."

Wallace admitted, however, that his interest in the supernatural had impaired his reputation. By the turn of the century, he wrote, "I never go, willingly, to London now . . . I am so widely known as a 'crank.' " A close friend of Wallace's put it more diplomatically: "Wallace held himself very much aloof from the London whirlpool."

As observed earlier, unlike Wallace, Darwin hewed rigidly to science and kept publicly distant from politics. He adhered to the admonition of de Buffon—the great French naturalist of his grandfather Erasmus' day—to never ask *why*, but only *how*. But Wallace's overweening curiosity about *why* was insatiable. And he plunged into spiritualism,

* But the weight of Kelvin's arguments against the occult was seized upon later by spiritualists who pointed out that Kelvin considered X-rays a "hoax" and heavier-than-air machines a physical impossibility.

just as he had into politics, while Darwin contended, rightly, that their theory was controversial enough without such red herrings as parapsychology and politics.

And so Wallace lived perpetually in the midst of a maelstrom, simultaneously advancing the heretical theory of evolution through natural selection, founding such disciplines as biogeography and social anthropology, writing books which have since become classics of science and travel, waging endless court battles against proponents of a flat earth, publicly espousing socialism and spiritualism, waging compaigns against vaccination and vivisection, fighting off creditors, and steadily retreating farther and farther from London, the seat of the world.

Through these convulsions, Wallace remained, with Annie and the children at his side, imperturbable, outwardly placid, characteristically shy and retiring; inwardly, he remained the unreconstructed optimist, who, had he been aboard the *Titanic*, would probably have thought that it had stopped to pick up ice.

As Wallace's financial situation worsened, however, Darwin, Hooker, and Lyell grew increasingly uncomfortable.

Chapter 35

IN 1880 Wallace's *Island Life* appeared and, despite the book's critical success, he found himself in a state of "ever-increasing anxiety." The situation was desperate.

"I saw no way of increasing my income," he said grimly, "which was then barely sufficient to support my family and educate my two children in the most economical way."

Darwin's disquiet over Wallace's plight deepened. "I wish you could obtain some quiet post and have leisure for moderate scientific work," Darwin wrote him that year. The suggestion, on the surface, appeared to be a contradiction in terms—Wallace should get a job so that he could have the leisure to pursue his scientific interests. But Wallace knew exactly what Darwin meant. Science would not pay the greengrocer and leisure meant the opportunity for creative work. It was during moments of "leisure" that Darwin and Wallace worked hardest.

Bates, now entrenched as secretary of the Royal Geographical Society, came to Wallace's financial aid by getting him a part-time job as assistant examiner in geography for the Society, and a similar position for the Indian Civil Service. Wallace earned roughly £30 a week over a three-week period annually in these roles and, he boasted, "occasionally even more."

The work was "drudgery," and Wallace's children recalled that the job gave him "a very strenuous time." He read an average of fifty papers a day; read until his eyes were bleary, his mind blurred. But the jobs provided a steady income of £90 a year and he kept them for twenty years, until the age of seventy-four.

Wallace also corrected scientific papers for Darwin's cousin, Galton, who taught at University College, London. Most of the papers were good, he wrote Galton on one occasion, but Wallace complained, "There is also a small batch of wretchedly bad papers, showing such an utter ignorance of [biology] that it is difficult to understand how these boys were permitted to compete."

Lyell also came to Wallace's financial rescue. Wallace edited the last four editions of Lyell's masterwork, *Principles of Geology*, and Lyell paid him at a rate of five shillings ($1.20) per hour. In a rare criticism of his benefactor, Wallace wrote to Darwin, "This is confidential [but] I do not think this quite enough for the class of work." When Darwin himself proposed that Wallace consider editing the second edition of Darwin's *Descent of Man*, Wallace, in desperation, indicated he would do so for seven shillings an hour ($1.40). But both Darwin and Wallace appeared to entertain misgivings about the collaboration and the matter was dropped. During this period of financial distress, Wallace canvassed jobs alternately as a librarian, registrar, and curator at the Birmingham College of Science—without success.

At this time Wallace's "most intimate and confidential friend," he wrote disarmingly in his autobiography, was Arabella Buckley, Lyell's personal secretary until Lyell's death in 1875 at the age of seventy-eight. Wallace mentioned his financial problems "to her alone"—that is, outside of Annie and the family circle—and on a subsequent visit to Down House, she made a passing reference to Wallace's desperate situation.

For a troubled Darwin, the "Wallace–Darwin episode," as his son put it, or the "delicate arrangement," as Huxley's son put it, loomed ever larger. As a man of integrity whose great human weakness was that momentary infatuation with priority (and, in this instance, therefore immortality), Darwin felt the Linnean affair grow in his mind as a great stain darkening his personal code of honor. Wallace's dire financial straits compounded this. To complicate matters, the naive, innocent Wallace had evolved into a true friend and the bonds of affection between them had grown stronger with the years. The guilt-ridden Darwin felt Wallace his moral superior and in a letter as early as April 14, 1869, as if under a compulsion to tell Wallace the truth about the conspiracy and cover-up leading to the Linnean meeting, Darwin wrote in admiration, "You are the only man I ever heard of who persistently does himself an injustice and never demands justice."

The following year, in the preface to his *Natural Selection*, Wallace hailed Darwin as having been "best fitted for the great work" of producing *Origin*. Darwin read those words with a sense of shame.

"There never has been passed on me or indeed on anyone, a higher eulogism than yours," he wrote Wallace. "*I wish that I fully deserved it.*" (Italics added.) Then, with the Linnean affair haunting him, Darwin added: "Very few things in my life have been more satisfactory to me [than] that we have never ever felt any jealousy towards each other, though in one sense rivals. I believe that I can say this of myself with truth, and I am absolutely sure that it is true of you."

The last line of that letter tells more than Wallace perceived. Darwin "believed" he himself harbored no envy toward Wallace, but was "absolutely sure" that this was true of his rival. In other, similar letters to Wallace, Darwin sought to purge himself of the shroud of dishonor which enveloped the 1858 Linnean meeting like a London fog.

Arabella's news profoundly agitated Darwin. For days and nights he turned Wallace's problem over and over in his mind, and suddenly hit upon a grandiose solution—"scheme," is the word Darwin used to characterize it. He would write Hooker, Huxley, and others to petition the Crown to give Wallace a government pension in recognition of his scientific accomplishments. In a letter to their daughter, Henrietta, Emma Darwin wrote that December that "he [Darwin] is so full of Wallace's affair he has not time for his own, and has concocted provisional letters to Gladstone [then Prime Minister] and the Duke of Argyll."

The Duke was close to Victoria and once caused the unsmiling queen to burst into a rare display of public laughter when he dropped the crown and brought it into the Robing Room—as Herbert Tingsten, the Swedish journalist described the scene—"looking like a collapsed pudding." The Duke was also a friend of Darwin's and had met Wallace several times at the late Lyell's evening soirées.

Darwin tried his hand at writing "memorials" to Victoria but quite literally threw up his hands and turned the task over to Huxley, who, by far, was the best writer of Down's inner circle. On December 11, 1880, Huxley completed the memorial to the throne, describing Wallace as a magnificent naturalist whose work for science had brought him but little material return. By Christmas Eve, working rapidly, as if against time, Darwin had circulated the memorial widely and obtained a dozen prominent signatures to the document, including, of course, his own and those of Hooker and Huxley. Were Lyell alive, he most assuredly would have hurriedly signed it.

The stage was now set and Huxley undertook to direct the production. He instructed Darwin to write Gladstone. "Mr. Gladstone," Huxley explained, "can do a thing gracefully when he is so minded, and unless I greatly mistake, he will be so intended if you write him."

Darwin promptly followed through, and the "scheme" was launched.

In the first week of January, Darwin dispatched the memorial to No. 10 Downing Street. In the normal course of events, a letter to the Prime Minister, especially during the first week of the New Year, would have been promptly lost in the bureaucratic shuffle. But the envelope bore the return address of Charles Darwin; the name turned the trick, and the memorial was brought to William Gladstone's immediate attention. That Wallace's future lay in the hands of Gladstone and Victoria was a prank of history. Gladstone, like Wallace, was widely considered a "crank." He was among the last persons Darwin or Wallace would have thought to communicate with. He was a flame-throwing evangelist who, as an Homeric scholar, sought to blend Greek mythology with Christianity (he read his wife and daughter the Greek classics at breakfast and was a patron of Heinrich Schliemann, the discoverer and excavator of Troy). Gladstone took a dim view of "curious, infidelic, so-called scientists who trace their ancestry to troglodytes," as he phrased it.

But Gladstone sought to tread a thin line between his private beliefs and what he believed was in the general public interest. He was also intensely human and empathized with the plight of the poor. Although he had second thoughts about evolutionists who defied the Mosaic cosmogony, he immediately passed the memorial on to Victoria.

For her part, Victoria was oblivious to the Darwins and Wallaces; worse, she despised Gladstone, whom she considered a "socialist." But the signatures on it—those of the Duke of Argyll, Lord Avebury, Sir Joseph Dalton Hooker, and other eminent men—rendered to the memorial an air of stability and authority, and, above all, loyalty to the crown. Victoria, who was thirty-nine years old when the Wallace–Darwin communications were read at the Linnean Society, and was now in her sixty-second year, promptly approved the memorial.

On January 7, 1881, the postrider deposited at Down House the day's usual sack of mail—journals, newspapers, and letters. Parslow, the family butler, who had first handled Wallace's envelope from Ternate twenty-two years earlier, was now seventy-one and might, on an off-chance, have again handled the day's mail. A small white envelope, bearing No. 10 Downing Street as the returnee's address, was clearly the most important communication of the day.

In the living room, Darwin tore it open. "Hurrah!" he cried out to an astonished Emma. "Hurrah!" The letter bore the news that the pension had been granted to Wallace. Darwin bounded to his study and enclosed Gladstone's letter with a note of his own to Huxley.

"Good heavens! how pleased I am," Darwin wrote. He also rushed off a letter to Wallace. "I have just received a note in Mr. Gladstone's own handwriting, in which he says 'I lose no time in apprising you that although the [pension] Fund is moderate and at present poor, I shall recommend Mr. Wallace for a pension of £200 a year."

Wallace, who had been kept abreast of Darwin's "scheme" by Arabella Buckley, was elated. "The amount you say Mr. Gladstone proposes to recommend is considerably more than I expected would be given," Wallace wrote Darwin, "and it will relieve me from a great deal of the anxieties under which I have laboured for several years."

"Today," he reminded Darwin, "is my fifty-eighth birthday, and it is a happy omen that your letter should have arrived this morning."

The matter of the £200 should be placed in perspective: that self-same year, the Darwin household spent £223 for meat at Down House.

For Darwin, his success in securing Wallace a measure of security for the remainder of his natural life was an act of expiation. Darwin had atoned for his behavior in the sordid conspiracy and cover-up surrounding his obsession with priority. Darwin was now in his seventy-second year, tired, weary. His face was heavily creased, his brow furrowed and his somber mood and outlook darkened by the black coat and black clerical hat that he wore on his daily round of the Sandwalk. But his white beard highlighted his face like the light entering through the window of a Vermeer painting. "My scientific work tires me," Darwin had written only the year before. He felt that his life was drawing to a close—"a year or two," he forecast with in-difference.

In July 1881, in the last letter Darwin wrote Wallace, he said, "Life has become very wearisome to me." He rambled on about whether or not there existed a God; Darwin felt that he had yet to atone for what he believed was the murder of God. The great naturalist was completely exhausted, and he complained to Wallace, "everything tires me, even seeing scenery."

An explanation for Darwin's deep depression is perhaps best found in the eloquence of Charlotte Brontë, who died three years before the Linnean meeting's proclamation of the theory and who, in 1851, upon reading her first exposition of avowed atheism and materialism, from the pens of Harriet Martineau and her collaborator Henry George Atkinson, in *Letters of the Nature & Development of Man*, wrote, "[This is] the first unequivocal declaration of disbelief in the existence of a God or a future life I have ever seen. . . . Sincerely, for my own part, do I wish to find & know the Truth; but if this be Truth, well may she guard herself with mysteries, & cover herself with a veil. If this be Truth, man or woman who beholds her can but curse the day he or she was born."

On April 18, 1882, barely a year after he had made peace with his conscience by securing Wallace a pension for life, Darwin died. He had always wanted to be buried at his beloved Down, but, against his wishes, he was laid to rest a week later at Westminster Abbey amid the pomp and circumstance that he had avoided all his life. There were ten pallbearers. Hooker and Huxley were among them. And, of course, Alfred Russel Wallace.

Chapter 36

W ITH A PENSION IN HAND, an annual income from cor-
recting student papers, and hit-and-miss royalties from his books, Alfred
Russel Wallace found himself in 1883, at the age of sixty, free of
financial burdens for the first time since the age of fourteen.

Among the pallbearers at Darwin's funeral was the American
ambassador to the Court of St. James, James Russell Lowell, better
known among his countrymen as abolitionist, editor, poet, a doyen of
New England's intellectual aristocracy, and a member of the family
that produced poets Amy and Robert Lowell.

Lowell and Wallace struck up an agreeable acquaintanceship and
three years later the Lowell Institute at Boston invited Wallace to give
a series of lectures in the United States. For Wallace this was an opportunity to revisit the Western Hemisphere and, for the first time,
to observe the flora and fauna of North America. It also provided him
with the opportunity to promote the theory of evolution through
natural selection across the Atlantic.

During a ten-month, whirlwind tour of the United States and
Canada, at colleges and universities, at meetings of scientific bodies, and
at literary teas, Wallace preached the theory of evolution and delivered
a series of brilliant variations on the theme during the question-and-
answer period that followed each talk. In the United States, which he
described as a land of "novelty and excitement," large crowds turned
out to hear his controversial views and after his first lecture on November 2, 1886, the Boston *Transcript* reported, "The first Darwinian,

Wallace, did not leave a leg for anti-Darwinism to stand on when he had got through his first Lowell lecture last evening."

Wallace, the incorrigibly shy, inarticulate, retiring speaker, who was as paralyzed by large gatherings as by small talk at receptions, was perhaps the most surprised person in Boston that night. "Mr. Wallace," the *Transcript* continued, "though not an orator, is likely to become a favourite [sic] as a lecturer, his manner is so genuinely modest and straight-forward." And to his utter astonishment, Wallace discovered that he did not require the orator's polish, the well-turned phrase, the cultivated voice to win audiences; his knowledge of the subject and his unbridled enthusiasm did the trick.

Among those on hand to greet him at Boston was Asa Gray, excerpts of whose letter from Darwin were read together with Wallace's Ternate Paper at the Linnean Society that memorable July 1, 1858. "The first American botanist," Wallace called him. "America's Hooker" would have been more descriptive. At dinners and luncheons, arranged through Gray and others, Wallace met a gallery of great Americans— Oliver Wendell Holmes, Henry George, William James. He also met the President, Grover Cleveland. Wallace's visit to the White House made a strange impression on him. "There was no ceremony whatever," the startled Wallace said.

During his American odyssey, he sometimes had to shake hands with as many as sixty guests at a reception, some of whom seemed as puzzled as he was bemused. "I've never heard of him," Wallace over-heard one person remark. "Nor I," a companion said. "He's an Englishman, lecturing on Darwin and such things." "Well," said the first one, "he hasn't much of an English accent."

Wallace kept a detailed diary of his North American tour, styled along the lines of the notebooks he had written during his ventures in the Amazon and the Malay archipelago. He calculated, for example, that the cost of his 310-day visit, including ten days in Canada, worked out to $3.25 per day, including travel, lodging, food, and tips, and excluding seventy days during which he was entertained by hosts. The principal notebook, which is in excellent condition, is owned by the Linnean Society and during the past couple of years there has been talk of publishing it as a commentary on the America of the late 1880s.

Occasionally Wallace talked politics—Utopian socialism, that is— and, he admitted, "my ideas seemed very wild." Spiritualism was much in vogue in the United States, particularly in New England, and he joined a circle of Harvard professors at séances. He attended his first Fourth of July celebration in the Midwest, complete with fireworks, and described the country's observance of its independence day as a "carnival." He found the Americans ingenious and among the most marvelous objects he discovered was a wooden, two-foot ruler which could be folded up and put in a vest pocket. "I had never seen one like it in any English tool-shop," the former apprentice carpenter and surveyor said. He also found Americans wasteful, and he was horrified at the way they squandered their natural resources for quick profits. "It is the misfortune of the Americans," he observed sagely, "that they have such a vast continent to occupy."

Race relations troubled him in both the postbellum North and South. "We gave them slavery both white and black," Wallace wrote, "a curse from the effects of which they still suffer and out of which a wholly satisfactory escape seems as remote as ever."

In California he met his brother John, whom he had not seen since he had left for the Amazon in 1848. John had acquired an American wife, children, and grandchildren, and like many immigrants before him, prospered on American soil.

Wallace spent much of his time making copious notes on North America's flora and fauna; his biggest disappointment was that he never encountered a rattlesnake although, he said boyishly, "I was always on the look out."

Many of Wallace's observations about American society were Tocquevillean in character. Immigration he viewed as a form of natural selection. "A nation formed by emigrants from several of the most energetic and intellectual nations of the old world, for the most part driven from their homes by religious persecution or political oppression, including from the very first all ranks and conditions of life—farmers and mechanics, traders and manufacturers, students and teachers, rich and poor—the very circumstances which drove them to emigrate led to a natural selection of the *most* energetic, the *most* independent, and in many respects the *best* of their several nations," he concluded. ". . . It is not surprising that these conditions with such a people should have resulted in that mad race for wealth in which they have beaten the record, and have produced a greater number of multi-millionaires than all the rest of the world combined, with . . . disastrous results." Wallace, the socialist, considered the inheritance of wealth socially immoral. "To allow one child to be born a millionaire and another a pauper is a crime against humanity," he declared, "and for those who believe in a deity, a crime against God."

But, he conceded, this was only one side of American character. As for the other side, he observed, "everywhere there are indications of a deep love of nature, a devotion to science and to literature fully proportionate to that of the older countries, while in inventiveness and in the application of science to human needs they have long been in the first rank."

Wallace's vaulting optimism put the whitest lining on the darkest clouds he observed in the American sky. "It is to America that the world looks to lead the way towards a just and peaceful modification of the social organism, based upon a recognition of the principle of equality of opportunity, and by means of the organization of the labour of all for the equal good of all."

The historical significance of Wallace's tour was his popularization of evolutionary theory in the United States. Wherever he went he spread his own—and Darwin's—gospel. He called his lectures "The Darwinian Theory." He played down his own role in the discovery and development of the theory; indeed, few of his listeners were aware of his Sarawak Law, Ternate Paper, and other works. But for Wallace, transcending all other considerations was the discovery during his journey of people repeatedly telling him that they had not grasped the theory of natural selection until they listened to his explanation of it.* Wallace's exposure to the general public opened his eyes to the failure of *Origin* to spell out the theory of natural selection cogently, lucidly. But, after all, had not Huxley, Hooker, and Lyell complained that Darwin's presentation made it one of the most difficult books to read?

Wallace was not only the greatest living authority on the theory— its co-discoverer, if not discoverer—but he also possessed the ability to put forth his ideas in plain, jargon-free language. In America an idea began to take shape in his mind to write a popular book on evolution and it was with this idea in his head that he returned to England on August 11, 1887.

The impetus to write such a book was given a push from an unexpected source—the late Darwin's son, Francis.

---

* This situation had its counterpart last year, during the observation of the Einstein Centenary. The general public admitted that it had no clear conception of the meaning of $E=mc^2$.

In November John Murray, the publisher, brought out Francis' *Life and Letters of Charles Darwin*, containing its unsatisfactory explanation of the disappearance of Darwin's most critical correspondence during 1855 to 1858, the period between Wallace's publication of the Sarawak Law and the events leading up to the July 1 Linnean meeting. The preface contains an unusual statement for a book of collected letters. "Of letters addressed to my father," Francis wrote, "I have not made much use." Thus, he neatly avoided the issue of "missing letters." Francis Darwin sent advance copies of the book to each of his father's pallbearers. Wallace was stunned to learn that his Ternate Paper had shaken Down House to its foundations. On November 10, 1887, in a note to Francis, Wallace acknowledged receipt of *Life and Letters* and added, with an air of incredulousness, "I was not aware before that your father had been so distressed—or rather disturbed—by my sending him my essay from Ternate."

For the first time Wallace had an inkling of the Darwinian conspiracy and cover-up—twenty-nine years after the event. Among the principals in the affair, Darwin and Lyell were dead. Hooker was the sole survivor. Momentarily, Wallace was confronted by a dilemma. Should he confront Hooker and probe the events leading up to the 1858 Linnean meeting? Or should he, as his Malay friends were wont to say, leave ancient pools undisturbed?

For almost thirty years Wallace had deferred to Darwin. Close and true ties had developed between them. It was Darwin who had secured him a pension for life. Reviewing his correspondence with Darwin, Wallace reinterpreted the hints Darwin had continually thrown out about the injustice done to Wallace. Darwin was trying to bring himself directly to tell Wallace the truth of the "Wallace–Darwin episode" but was unable to do so. Darwin treasured his relationship with Wallace, whom he viewed as a rare human being, trusting and totally honest; he could not bring himself to hurt this unsuspecting, innocent man. It was not in Darwin's character—the Linnean affair notwithstanding—the Darwin who wept when he was forced to kill a pigeon to advance science.

For that matter, Wallace himself opted to remain in character. After his first note to Francis, Wallace entertained misgivings and, in a bid to reassure Francis of fidelity to his father, he hurriedly penned another note in which he declared for the first time that too many people were apt "to give me too much credit" for the natural selection theory but that he always felt, "and [I] feel still," that his own role in the discovery of the mechanism and the principle of divergence was "very small an affair."

Yet more skim ice formed not long after, in 1893, when Jane Loring Gray's collection of her husband Asa's correspondence appeared, containing her perplexing discovery, when she wrote the Darwins, that her husband's correspondence to Darwin for the critical period of 1855 to 1858 was largely missing.

Wallace was no more a saint than Darwin or any other mortal. He would not have been human had he not occasionally slipped from his self-imposed historical role as spear-carrier in the drama of evolutionary biology.

The first slip occurred in 1891 in a reprint of his 1870 edition of *Contribution to Natural Selection*, retitled *Natural Selection and Tropical Nature*. The volume contained in its entirety the Ternate Paper, exactly as written by Wallace in the Moluccas during the malarial attack, dispatched to Darwin, and read before the Linnean Society. But the new edition contained a footnote that did not appear in the first edition. "It must be remembered," Wallace wrote, "that the writer had no opportunity of correcting the proofs of this paper."

The footnote was meaningless to anyone—other than a Hooker or Francis Darwin—reading the paper for the first time without some hint of what had happened during the eventful days leading up to the paper's original publication. Furthermore, in an introductory note which Wallace failed to list in the preface as an addition to the book, and which was not listed in the book's table of contents and has apparently been overlooked by historians, Wallace observed that the immediate result of his Ternate paper was to force Darwin at once to prepare *Origin* for publication "instead of waiting an indefinite number of years to complete a work on a much larger scale which he had partly written."

And then Wallace slipped. "I feel much satisfaction in having thus aided in bringing about the publication of this celebrated book," he said, "and with the ample recognition by Darwin himself of my independent discovery of 'natural selection.'"

As evidence of "the ample recognition" Darwin accorded him, Wallace wryly offered two citations: the *sixth* edition of *Origin* and Francis Darwin's *Life and Letters*, published, of course, *after* Darwin's death. Wallace's backhanded commentary is devastating.

In 1901, in *The Wonderful Century*, Wallace slipped again. He confessed that on the basis of his initial exchange of letters with Darwin he had expected the Ternate Essay to come as a surprise to the latter. After all, had not Darwin written that he was at work on a theory of evolution but that "my work will not fix or settle anything." Within that time frame, Wallace's Ternate Paper fixed and settled everything. "I was therefore surprised," Wallace admitted for the first time, "to find that he had really arrived at the very same theory as mine."

Five years later, from a new and unexpected source, Wallace learned more of the intrigue encapsulating the Linnean affair. John Murray published *The Life of Sir Charles J. F. Bunbury*, edited, no less, by Bunbury's sister-in-law, Lyell's wife, Mary, and containing an introduction by Hooker. The book was essentially Bunbury's diary and an entry marked July 14, 1858, provided Wallace with another, still fresher, clue about the confusion and uproar he had created at Down with his Ternate Paper. "Darwin has been engaged for nearly twenty years in a work on the general question of species, which is not yet nearly ready for publication," Bunbury confided to his diary, "but at last, as there was some danger of his being forestalled—for Mr. Wallace, who is employed as a natural history collector in the Eastern islands, had independently taken up some of the same theories, and sent home a Paper containing his own views—therefore Lyell and J. Hooker persuaded Darwin to allow one chapter of his work to be published."

Wallace may have been naive, but the true picture was gradually coming into sharper focus. Wallace would, however, go to his death without seeing the picture completely in focus; for example, until Leonard Wilson came along only ten years ago, nobody realized the traumatic impact of the Sarawak Law upon Lyell, who had probably discussed it with his wife Mary, since she took most of his notes and wrote his letters because of his poor eyesight.

Darwin had once described Wallace as a "good Christian," and in *Moral Progress*, Wallace's last book, published in 1913, when he was ninety, Wallace turned the other cheek and forgave Darwin his irrepressible passion for exclusivity. "Everyone's experience of life, and especially the example of his friends and associates, leads him to repress his passion, regulate his emotions, and in general to see his judgment before acting, so as to secure the esteem of his fellows and greater happiness for himself," wrote Wallace, "and these restraints, becoming habitual, may often give the appearance of an actual change of character till some great temptation or violent passion overcomes the usual restraint and exhibits the real nature, which is usually dormant."

Did Darwin's great temptation and violent passion for priority overcome the usual restraint and reveal his real, dormant nature? Wallace
does not say, but within the context of the Linnean episode, the inference is indisputable.

On one occasion, Oxford University invited Wallace to unveil a
statue of Darwin and Wallace declined. Professor Poulton, Wallace's
good friend at Oxford, later recalled, "I well remember the sly
humour with which he hinted that Sir Joseph Hooker would be a far
more appropriate central figure at the ceremony."

Wallace did, however, take part in the July 1, 1908, Linnean Society
observance of the fiftieth anniversary of the Darwin–Wallace communications and in this instance Poulton believed that Wallace "was
moved by a sense of duty to disregard his own preferences." On that
occasion, Wallace resumed his self-styled role as a footnote in history.
He referred to a "more daring few who have decided that I was the
first to discover it [the theory of natural selection] and that I gave way
to Darwin!" He chided such interpreters of history as under a "complete misapprehension." But on that same occasion he also observed
that "without any apparent warning my letter, with the enclosed
[Ternate] Essay, came upon him [Darwin], like a thunderbolt from
a cloudless sky!" This, Wallace explained, forced Darwin into "pre-
mature publicity" while Hooker and Lyell, "his two friends, undertook
to have our two papers read before this Society." Wallace himself,
eighty-five years old at the time of the anniversary meeting, contributed to the myth that "two papers" were read on that occasion.
Of course, there was only one paper, Wallace's.

But the most important result of Wallace's gradual realization of
the true role he played in the history of evolution was his decision to
turn out one last work on the subject. As observed earlier, Wallace
had no sooner returned from the United States with thoughts of
writing a popular account of natural selection than he received Francis'
Life and Letters. Wallace promptly dropped everything to write his
own version of the theory of natural selection. He spent a year on the
project and with a touch of irony entitled the book, *Darwinism*. The
book was his answer to the revelations contained in *Life and Letters*
and for all practical purposes it was the book that Wallace told Bates
he had begun to write in 1858 when he was preempted by Darwin.*

In a sense, *Darwinism* is a rewrite of *Origin*. It is also a defense of

* See page 221 and page 42.

the theory of natural selection and the principle of divergence. It cut off Darwin's slow retreat from natural selection in later editions of *Origin*, particularly Darwin's backsliding into Lamarckism, the theory of the inheritance of acquired characteristics, a concept which Darwinians to this day consider the great heresy of evolutionary theory. Thus, it was left to Wallace to restore faith in Darwinism and to answer critics of Darwin and himself who sought "to minimize the agency of natural selection."

At the outset of *Darwinism*, Wallace cited a subtle but significant difference between himself and Darwin. "A weakness in Darwin's work has been that he based his theory, primarily, on the evidence of variation in domesticated animals and cultivated plants," Wallace wrote. "I have endeavoured to secure a firm foundation for the theory in the variation of organisms in a state of nature."

In this memorable work, Wallace provided the most precise definition of the theory of natural selection up to that date, "the continuous adjustment of the organic to the inorganic world." By inventing the word *Darwinism*, Wallace subtly forced scientists to focus on the subject of natural selection to the exclusion of heresies such as Lamarckism. The book also provided a hint of things to come in biological evolutionary theory, touching on the modern concept of genetic drift. As Gerald Henderson observed in an unpublished analysis of *Darwinism*, Wallace's "basic work and theoretical formulation in many respects seem as solidly grounded and in some instances much more in advance of his time than were those of his great colleague."

Darwinism, however, was not a put-down of Darwin's seminal *Origin*. "The present work," Wallace wrote in the preface of the first edition, dated March 1889, "treats the problem of the *Origin of Species* on the same general lines as were adopted by Darwin; but from the standpoint reached after nearly thirty years of discussion, with an abundance of new facts and the advocacy of many new or old theories." Among the new theories Wallace put forth was a refined, reinforced concept of natural selection. No longer did he view evolution simplistically as a field of perpetual battle. Wallace downplayed Huxley's notion of natural selection as "the law of the jungle," or as Spencer put it, "survival of the fittest." Wallace now viewed nature as a compromise between life and death, an arena of mutual aid—a theory popularly and wrongly attributed to the Russian geographer and socialist, anarchist, and nihilist, Peter Kropotkin, who may have first read Wallace in Russian translation. In our time, the theory of natural selection has been revived and has become increasingly fashionable, one of its most articulate proponents being the anthropologist Ashley Montagu. The "incessant warfare" of nature, Wallace observed, is the very means by which beauty, harmony, and enjoyment in nature are produced, and it is the process which affords "one of the most important elements in bringing about the origin of species."

Wallace opposed the poet's vision of "nature red in tooth and claw." He himself was a staunch believer in the concept of mutual aid, and in *Darwinism* wrote, "On the whole . . . the popular idea of the struggle for existence entailing misery and pain on the animal world is the very reverse of the truth. What it really brings about, is, the maximum of life and of the enjoyment of life with the minimum of suffering and pain. . . . It is difficult even to imagine a system by which a greater balance of happiness could have been secured."

In *Darwinism*, Wallace also fortified Darwin's *Descent of Man* and restated his own Sarawak Law that "in his bodily structure, [man] has been derived from the lower animals, of which he is the culminating development." Thus, Wallace argued, man is compelled to reject the idea of "special creation" as unsupported by facts, as well as in the highest degree improbable. But he qualified man's development in a manner which Darwin in his day, and Darwinists today, continue to reject. "Because man's physical structure has been developed from an animal form by natural selection," Wallace averred, "it does not necessarily follow that his mental nature, even though developed *pari passu* with it, has been developed by the same causes only."

Wallace returned to the theme he outlined in 1869, specifically, that man's moral and intellectual nature suggest that "some other influence, law or agency is required to account for them." Wallace was convinced more than ever that man's mathematical, musical, and artistic faculties were not developed by laws of natural selection.

In *Darwinism* there emerged a determined effort by Wallace to counter the mechanistic, materialistic philosophies to which *Origin* had given rise, notably, that "we, in common with the rest of nature, are but products of blind eternal forces" and that all the agony of martyrs, all the groans of victims, all evil and misery, all struggles for freedom, all efforts toward justice, all aspirations for the virtue and wellbeing of humanity, are hopeless, baseless, useless—that there is neither rhyme nor reason in man's existence. The origin of man's spirit, his love of truth, delight in beauty, passion for justice, thrill of exultation in acts of courage and self-sacrifice, cannot be found in natural selection, Wallace argued, adding that this in no way lessens the fundamental scientific truth of natural selection as a mechanism of evolution.

"I therefore claim for my book," Wallace said with finality, "the position of being the advocate of pure Darwinism."

Wallace's *Darwinism* ran 494 pages. It was his *Origin*, and it was an immediate success. The first edition appeared in May 1889; a second edition followed in August of that year, new printings in October and in March, 1890.

Among the critics of *Darwinism* was Herbert Spencer. "I regret that you have used the title *Darwinism*," Spencer complained, ". . . [because] you will, by using it, tend greater to confirm the erroneous concept almost universally current." Spencer felt there was no need to spell out the "erroneous concept" to Wallace: among other things, an apparent worldwide belief that Darwin was the sole discoverer of evolutionary theory, that he came up with his theory in a vacuum, and that none came before him.

Ironically, critics accused Wallace of being "more Darwinian than Darwin," a charge that stuck fast to Wallace for the remainder of his life. "Some of my critics declare that I am more Darwinian than Darwin himself," he said with a wry smile, "and in this, I admit, they are not far wrong." But, by being more Darwinian than Darwin, Wallace was simply being himself.*

---

* In *Ever Since Darwin* (New York: Norton, 1977), Stephen Jay Gould, an engaging writer, perpetuated this view, describing Wallace as having "far out-Darwined Darwin." Interestingly, in the August 16, 1979, *New York Review of Books*, Gould, an enthusiastic Darwinian, observed that ". . . in part, and more dubiously, Darwin did treasure the notion of priority, and did pursue it with perhaps too much zeal."

Chapter 37

Wallace's waning years followed a double track, the two parts running in opposite directions. For as he drifted into obscurity, he was showered with honors.

The drift was understandable. In the biological sciences after the turn of the century, "Darwinism" was in decline as genetics moved into stage center.

In 1865 Gregor Mendel, an Austrian monk and scientist, delivered a paper to the Brünn Society for the Study of Natural Science in which he revealed the principles of heredity based on experiments with peas. This historic paper founded the science of genetics, although the reaction to it was even less deafening than the reaction to Wallace's Sarawak Law some ten years earlier. In point of fact, Mendel and his paper were completely ignored.

Hugo de Vries, a botanist at the University of Amsterdam, working on the problems of heredity in evolution—which had eluded both Wallace and Darwin—resurrected Mendel's work at the turn of the century. *Time-Life* publications are generally considered poor source material and the presentation of the roles of Mendel, de Vries, Darwin, and Wallace in the *Evolution* volume of the Life Nature Series is a classic of distortion. The volume describes de Vries' discovery of Mendel's work thus: "Like Darwin confronted with Wallace's work, de Vries did not hesitate. In a paper read before the German Botanical Society on March 21, 1900, the Dutch botanist gave full credit for one of the most momentous discoveries in scientific history to the man to whom it belonged."

De Vries' action, of course, was precisely the opposite of Darwin's. Darwin did not hesitate, either. But instead of proclaiming Wallace's Ternate Essay to the world, he entered into a delicate arrangement to head off Wallace at the pass, the Linnean Society meeting of July 1, 1858.

Mendel was familiar with the work of Wallace and Darwin; a well-marked copy of *Origin*, with its two references to Wallace in the preface, was found in the Austrian monk's library. The failure of Mendel to get in touch with his contemporaries in England and the failure of Darwin, Wallace, Lyell, Huxley, and, above all, Hooker— the botanist of the quintet—to read the Brünn paper, as Hans Stubbe, the German biologist and historian observed, "is one of the incomprehensible facts about the history of our science."

But Stubbe provided himself an answer: "There is hardly any doubt," he concluded, "that a number of lines of biological research were neglected or even completely forgotten amid this ferment." By ferment, of course, Stubbe meant the Wallace–Darwin episode at the Linnean Society and its aftermath. May the same be said for genetics in our time?

As genetics pushed the role of natural selection into the wings, Darwin's surviving colleagues, including Wallace himself, who was seventy-seven when de Vries made his discovery, and Hooker, who was eighty-three, went on the defensive. Both were grieved to learn from a Cambridge correspondent, for example, that the Mendelians had "gained the upper hand. . . . Even Francis Darwin is more or less within their domain."

Wallace was uncharacteristically bitter. Mendelian theory, he conceded, is "new, and within its very limited range, important, as leading to conceptions as to causes and laws of heredity but only misleading when adduced as the true origin of species in nature."

One of Wallace's mental blocks in grasping Mendelian genetics was, despite his training as a surveyor and a delight in statistics, his apparent inability to work in higher mathematics. "I find it quite impossible for me to follow their detailed studies and argument," he wrote a colleague about genetics. "It wants a mathematical mind, which I have not."

Thus, Wallace clung ever more desperately to nature, to the real, visible world around him, and was annoyed that the Mendelians claimed "all wisdom, before which we poor Darwinians must hide our diminished heads." When genetics swept the United States, Hooker consoled Wallace. "The Americans" a saddened Hooker wrote Wallace in 1906, "are prone to believe any new things."

But Wallace's chief complaint with Mendelian theory had nothing to do with "higher mathematics." He accused the geneticists of failing to make the distinction that he himself drew between evolution and life. Natural selection, he said, is capable of explaining the facts of the continuous development of species from species, "from amoeba to man." But, he added, both he and Darwin recognized that this has nothing whatever to do with the basic mysteries of life. "Yet I am at once howled at, or sneered at, for pointing out the facts that such problems exist, that they are not in any way touched by evolution but are far before it," he said.

In 1908, as the genetic revolution swept biology, the Linnean Society observed the fiftieth anniversary of the "joint communication" in spectacular fashion, casting a gold Darwin–Wallace medal,* and inviting many of the most important scientists of the day to participate in the ceremonies, in the manner of a Nobel Prize in our time. Attention was refocused on the theory of natural selection and on Wallace as its living cofounder. Wallace was the recipient of a veritable flood of honorary degrees, medals, and citations.

As usual, Wallace took the adulation calmly. "The fact is," he confessed, "I have at all times a profound distaste for all *public* ceremonies."

The wavecrest of Wallace's return to the limelight was his receipt of the Order of Merit from King Edward in December 1908. The Order of Merit is the highest decoration for achievement given by the Crown to those who have distinguished themselves in science, literature, and the arts. It is given in their old age. Edward had founded the Order on the occasion of his coronation in 1901, perhaps partly to display independence of his mother and also to bestow royal recognition on those whom Victoria had ignored. (In 1907, Edward had awarded the Order to Florence Nightingale). During Victoria's reign, Darwin received no recognition from the Crown; ironically, the best he could do was the Prussian order of *Pour le Mérite* in Bismarck's day.

Wallace had attended the Linnean Society's celebration the previous July but, on the ground of infirmity, he avoided an audience at

---

* Wallace, ironically, was the first recipient of his own medal.

Buckingham Palace. "To my great relief," he sighed, "the king dispensed with my personal attendance at the investiture." Edward sent an aide to Broadstone, Dorset, to enact the ceremony. Wallace probably blushed when he was handed the badge of the Order, a cross of red and blue enamel overlaid by an imperial crown and bearing in gold the inscription, "For Merit." An elated Wallace wrote his son Will, "Ma gave him [the aide] some tea." The aide, a colonel, showed Wallace how to wear the Order's ribbon—garter blue and crimson—around the neck and, Wallace said, "We were all pleased." He never wore it.

This sudden ascent to celebrity must be viewed for what it really was. It was symbolic—and irrelevant to the true issue of priority surrounding the Linnean affair of 1858. Wallace had become a grand-old-man-of-science; he was destined to be the last surviving member of the cast in what was perhaps the greatest drama in the history of science. Thus, he was honored, as one of Darwin's inner circle, as "codiscoverer," as it was euphemistically now called, of the theory.

Wallace was aware of the new situation. He was amused by his celebrity and joshed about it. He believed in socialism and spiritualism, experimented in phrenology, waged campaigns against vaccination and vivisection, and was frequently characterized as a "crank." Still, one reviewer compared him to Newton and critics hailed him as the greatest tropical naturalist of the nineteenth century. "Of course, [they] praise my biology up to the skies—there I am wise—everywhere else I am a kind of weak, babyish idiot!" Wallace laughed. "It is really delightful."

In contrast to the atmosphere of gloom that shrouded Darwin during his last years at Down, Wallace eschewed black cloaks and remained youthful and cheerful to the end. Like Darwin, however, he became increasingly stoop-shouldered and the pace of his daily walk through the garden slowed appreciably with each advancing year. After 1900 and their move to Broadstone—Old Orchard, Wallace christened their last home—he and Annie, who was now fifty-two and suffered from arthritis, rarely left their house. Daughter Violet, who tutored private students for a living, moved in with them.

At first Violet feared that the chatter and laughter of her four or five wards would upset her father's routine, his tranquillity. But childlike himself, Wallace reveled in the company of the youngsters. When a visitor once remarked to Violet, "What a wonderful old man your father is," she was taken aback. "This was quite a shock," she recalled, "for to us he was not old." One of her wards, an eight-year-old boy, later recalled that Wallace's favorite drink was Canary sack and that "he always treated me with great kindness, patience and indulgence, which is somewhat remarkable considering my age, and how exasperating I must have been sometimes." The former student had disregarded de Buffon's admonition and kept asking "why" about everything; one suspects that this constant interrogation by children served as a stimulus for Wallace's own creative thought processes. Another child also persisted in asking him why. For example, the child asked why he sometimes removed his spectacles when reading and Wallace replied solemnly, with a Lewis Carroll-like twinkle, "Because I can see better." The child persisted, "Then why do you wear glasses?" Wallace replied solemnly, "Because I can see better."

Like Darwin, as Wallace aged, he also grew more and more fond of solitude. "Really, the greatest kindness my friends can do me is to leave me in peaceful obscurity," he wrote a colleague, "for I have lived so secluded a life that I am more and more disinclined to crowds of any kind." Yet scientists and others persisted in writing him, and Wallace left no letter unanswered. As late as October 29, 1913, Ellsworth Huntington of Yale University's Peabody Museum wrote Wallace for assistance in preparing a map on animal distribution. Wallace was approaching ninety-one years of age, and in a postscript Huntington, a distinguished zoologist, wrote from New Haven, Connecticut, "May I add a word to express a high appreciation . . . for the originality of thought which you continue to display."

In the British Museum's collection of Wallace letters, there is a sweeping assortment of scientific correspondence, ranging from biology to entomology to paleontology. Among his private papers is a note from an A. J. Bidwell of Singapore.

"My wife," explained Bidwell, "is a daughter of the late Charles Allen." Allen! That bumbling youngster who accompanied Wallace on his voyage from England to the Malay archipelago more than half a century earlier. "Her father was never tired of telling his children of the happy times he spent with you," Bidwell wrote. "There is a feeling in the Straits [Singapore and Malaya] that you do to a certain extent belong to us."

Wallace also had to bear up to a stream of visitors, including some whom he—of all people, considering how most people viewed him—described as "cranks." These were individuals who were largely interested in spiritualism. Although they wasted his time, he was reluctant to turn away anyone who journeyed the hundred miles from London to seek him out. "He was loath to hurt their feelings," Violet recalled.

But distinguished scientists, old friends, and "cranks" were not the only visitors. All his life Wallace had sallied forth to meet nature in her own setting, and as he aged and his movements became limited to his house and garden, uncannily, as if to repay him for his interest, nature came to him.

At the age of eighty-five, a correspondent in Argentina—like the young Darwin's, Wallace's correspondence was now global in character —shipped him several bagged and burlapped orchids. While examining one clump, three beetles droped out "and I managed to catch two of them," Wallace said joyously. To his surprise, however, the intrepid coleopterist did not recognize them. Embarrassed, he dispatched them to the British Museum (Natural History) for identification. The Museum's entomologists were agitated. The beetles were rare species of the large South American genus *Ibidion*, and the Museum did not have a single specimen in its vast holdings. Then, on the Sunday before Christmas Day that same year, 1908, in a manner reminiscent of the detective Nero Wolfe, Wallace made the evening round of his orchid rooms. Suddenly a large insect flew by him and settled on a workbench. Its lower wings were brilliant orange, the upper, brownish-orange. Wallace wrote his son Will, "At first I thought it was a butterfly that mimicked a moth, but I had never seen anything like it before."

In great excitement, he and Annie captured the insect the following morning. Wallace sent it to Lord Rothschild, a close friend and enthusiastic coleopterist who served as an unofficial, unpaid curator of entomology at the British Museum. Rothschild identified the specimen as a *Castnia*, a strange South American moth which resembles a butterfly. He and other Museum officials checked their collection of *Castnia* and although the Museum boasted a large collection of these moths, there was no sample to match Wallace's find, only a drawing of it with the notation that it was extremely rare.

The mystery of how this rare insect turned up in Wallace's house was quickly solved. The *Castnia* had been hidden in a chrysalis on an orchid; Wallace found the empty covering on the floor of his plant room. As James Marchant, his friend and admirer, later wrote, "It was certainly a strange . . . coincidence that these creatures should find themselves in Dr. [sic] Wallace's greenhouse, where alone they would be noticed and appreciated." The mountain had come to Mohammed.

As the guns of August were wheeled into position in 1913, Wallace wrote a series of powerful tracts in which he warned that the Great Powers were on the slippery slide leading to a catastrophic global conflict. For Wallace, ever on the barricades, there appeared to be no journey's end. But Wallace sensed that his life was drawing to a close. His children, Violet and William, in their joint memoir, recalled that although he was still able to mount barricades, he had abandoned thoughts of embarking on "a major work because," he confided, "he felt he had but a few more years to live."

Hooker, the last member of the Linnean conspiracy, had died two years earlier, in 1911, at the age of ninety-four. The Hooker family had been invited to bury him at Westminster Abbey alongside Darwin, but Hooker had expressed a strong desire before his death to be buried at Kew Gardens among the plants he had nurtured through a lifetime, as his father had done before him. By now, Huxley was long gone, having died in 1895 at the age of seventy. It therefore fell to Alfred Russel Wallace to be the sole survivor of the greatest scientific revolution since Copernicus in the annals of the species *Homo sapiens*.

Suddenly, on November 2, 1913, after a short tour of his "Sandwalk," Wallace felt faint and was overcome by an onslaught of violent chills. He shivered uncontrollably, as he had on that stifling hot day in the Moluccas when the theory of the origin of species, with all its nuances, had flashed in his mind.

Annie summoned the family physician, and there was talk that perhaps he had suffered a recurrent attack of malaria. Annie (now sixty-four), Violet (forty-four), and Will (forty-two) overheard Wallace and the physician laughing merrily in the study.

"Wonderful man! he knows so much," the doctor said as he departed. "I can do nothing for him."

The next day Wallace sank into semiconsciousness and at 9:25 A.M., Friday, November 7, 1913, as the sun rose high in the sky and dried off the bedewed leaves of his garden, as new species, through natural selection, struggled into existence, Wallace died in his sleep, at peace with the real world of nature. His children put it poignantly: "[He] quietly passed on to that other life in which he was such a firm believer."

There were immediate demands in London that he should be buried alongside Darwin at Westminster Abbey. But Annie and the family objected. Earlier, Wallace—like Darwin and Hooker before him—had expressed adamant opposition to such a procedure. He wanted to be buried in the soft loam of his treasured English countryside, and his last wish was fulfilled.

Three days later he was laid to rest with touching simplicity, as his good friend Marchant recalled, in the little cemetery at Broadstone, on a pine-clad hill, surrounded by fields of heather, swept by sea breezes, and abounding with life—butterflies by day and moths by night.

Within a fortnight of his burial, a committee of scientists, including the president of the Linnean Society, petitioned the Dean and Chapter of Westminster Abbey for permission to erect "a suitable national memorial to [him] . . . believing that no position would be so appropriate as Westminster Abbey, the burial-place of his illustrious coworker, Charles Darwin."

Dean Herbert T. Ryle and the Chapter unanimously approved the petition. A memorial plaque was unveiled on November 1, 1915, by coincidence All Souls' Day, together with a medallion in honor of Hooker.

Thus, in a poetic sense, the spirits of Darwin, Lyell, Hooker, and Wallace, the principals in the adventure surrounding the theory of the origin of species and the descent of man, are linked forever in the north nave of the Abbey. Lyell's last resting place is situated forty-one paces from Darwin's; Darwin's six paces from Wallace's plaque, and Wallace's plaque four paces from Hooker's. Huxley's eulogy, delivered on the occasion of Darwin's death, befits all four:

For each of them there was no fear in facing the unknown. Their lives had been one long experience with the laws of nature that govern the universe and they would calmly entrust themselves to those laws through eternity.*

---

* With Wallace's death, his Civil List Pension ended abruptly. An ill Annie could not afford to retain Old Orchard and the family was forced to sell it in early 1914. As it turned out, Annie, "the beauty of the Mitten family," died December 13, 1914, almost within a year of Wallace, and was buried at his side.

In 1964 Old Orchard was bulldozed to make way for a housing development. An effort was made to save the site for posterity—the developer had paid £16,000 for the house and three acres—but as an official of the Linnean Society said in a letter to the Wallace family, "I cannot see that much can be done about this unfortunate matter."

At this writing, rubble still litters the spot, bricks and bits of glass from Wallace's plant rooms, an odd beam from his study. The road running through the development is named Wallace Court. More likely than not, none of the residents have ever heard of him.

On the Law which has Regulated the Introduction of New Species*

BY ALFRED RUSSEL WALLACE

Geographical Distribution dependent on Geologic Changes.

EVERY naturalist who has directed his attention to the subject of the geographical distribution of animals and plants, must have been interested in the singular facts which it presents. Many of these facts are quite different from what would have been anticipated, and have hitherto been considered as highly curious, but quite inexplicable. None of the explanations attempted from the time of Linnæus are now considered at all satisfactory; none of them have given a cause sufficient to account for the facts known at the time, or comprehensive enough to include all the new facts which have since been, and are daily being added. Of late years, however, a great light has been thrown upon the subject by geological investigations, which have shown that the present state of the earth and of the organisms now inhabiting it, is but the last stage of a long and uninterrupted series of changes which it has undergone, and consequently, that to endeavour to explain and account for

---

* The Sarawak Law shook Darwin, who had yet to publish a line on evolutionary theory, and stunned his close friend Sir Charles Lyell, forcing Lyell into opening his own species notebook.

its present condition without any reference to those changes (as has frequently been done) must lead to very imperfect and erroneous conclusions.

The facts proved by geology are briefly these:—That during an immense, but unknown period, the surface of the earth has undergone successive changes; land has sunk beneath the ocean, while fresh land has risen up from it; mountain chains have been elevated; islands have been formed into continents, and continents submerged till they have become islands; and these changes have taken place, not once merely, but perhaps hundreds, perhaps thousands of times:—That all these operations have been more or less continuous, but unequal in their progress, and during the whole series the organic life of the earth has undergone a corresponding alteration. This alteration also has been gradual, but complete; after a certain interval not a single species existing which had lived at the commencement of the period. This complete renewal of the forms of life also appears to have occurred several times:—That from the last of the geological epochs to the present or historical epoch, the change of organic life has been gradual: the first appearance of animals now existing can in many cases be traced, their numbers gradually increasing in the more recent formations, while other species continually die out and disappear, so that the present condition of the organic world is clearly derived by a natural process of gradual extinction and creation of species from that of the latest geological periods. We may therefore safely infer a like gradation and natural sequence from one geological epoch to another.

Now, taking this as a fair statement of the results of geological inquiry, we see that the present geographical distribution of life upon the earth must be the result of all the previous changes, both of the surface of the earth itself and of its inhabitants. Many causes, no doubt, have operated of which we must ever remain in ignorance, and we may, therefore, expect to find many details very difficult of explanation, and in attempting to give one, must allow ourselves to call into our service geological changes which it is highly probable may have occurred, though we have no direct evidence of their individual operation.

The great increase of our knowledge within the last twenty years, both of the present and past history of the organic world, has accumulated a body of facts which should afford a sufficient foundation for a comprehensive law embracing and explaining them all, and giving a direction to new researches. It is about ten years since the idea of such a law suggested itself to the writer of this essay, and he has since taken every opportunity of testing it by all the newly-ascertained facts with which he has become acquainted, or has been able to observe himself. These have all served to convince him of the correctness of his hypothesis. Fully to enter into such a subject would occupy much space, and it is only in consequence of some views having been lately promulgated, he believes, in a wrong direction, that he now ventures to present his ideas to the public, with only such obvious illustrations of the arguments and results as occur to him in a place far removed from all means of reference and exact information.

A Law deduced from well-known Geographical and Geological Facts.

The following propositions in Organic Geography and Geology give the main facts on which the hypothesis is founded.

GEOGRAPHY

1.   Large groups, such as classes and orders, are generally spread over the whole earth, while smaller ones, such as families and genera, are frequently confined to one portion, often to a very limited district.

2.   In widely distributed families the genera are often limited in range; in widely distributed genera, well marked groups of species are peculiar to each geographical district.

3.   When a group is confined to one district, and is rich in species, it is almost invariably the case that the most closely allied species are found in the same locality or in closely adjoining localities, and that therefore the natural sequence of the species by affinity is also geographical.

4.   In countries of a similar climate, but separated by a wide sea or lofty mountains, the families, genera and species of the one are often represented by closely allied families, genera and species peculiar to the other.

GEOLOGY

5.   The distribution of the organic world in time is very similar to its present distribution in space.

6.   Most of the larger and some small groups extend through several geological periods.

7.   In each period, however, there are peculiar groups, found nowhere else, and extending through one or several formations.

8. Species of one genus, or genera of one family occurring in the same geological time, are more closely allied than those separated in time.

9. As generally in geography no species or genus occurs in two very distant localities without being also found in intermediate places, so in geology the life of a species or genus has not been interrupted. In other words, no group or species has come into existence twice.

10. The following law may be deduced from these facts:—*Every species has come into existence coincident both in space and time with a pre-existing closely allied species.*

This law agrees with, explains and illustrates all the facts connected with the following branches of the subject:—1st. The system of natural affinities. 2nd. The distribution of animals and plants in space. 3rd. The same in time, including all the phænomena of representative groups, and those which Professor Forbes supposed to manifest polarity. 4th. The phænomena of rudimentary organs. We will briefly endeavour to show its bearing upon each of these.

The Form of a true system of Classification determined by this Law.

If the law above enunciated be true, it follows that the natural series of affinities will also represent the order in which the several species came into existence, each one having had for its immediate antitype a closely allied species existing at the time of its origin. It is evidently possible that two or three distinct species may have had a common antitype, and that each of these may again have become the antitypes from which other closely allied species were created. The effect of this would be, that so long as each species has had but one new species formed on its model, the line of affinities will be simple, and may be represented by placing the several species in direct succession in a straight line. But if two or more species have been independently formed on the plan of a common antitype, then the series of affinities will be compound, and can only be represented by a forked or many branched line. Now, all attempts at a Natural classification and arrangement of organic beings show, that both these plans have obtained in creation. Sometimes the series of affinities can be well represented for a space by a direct progression from species to species or from group to group, but it is generally found impossible so to continue. There constantly occur two or more modifications of an organ or modifications of two distinct organs, leading us on to two distinct series of species, which at length differ so much from each other as to form distinct genera or families. These are the parallel series or representative groups of naturalists, and they often occur in different countries, or are found fossil in different formations. They are said to have an analogy to each other when they are so far removed from their common antitype as to differ in many important points of structure, while they still preserve a family resemblance. We thus see how difficult it is to determine in every case whether a given relation is an analogy or an affinity, for it is evident that as we go back along the parallel or divergent series, towards the common antitype, the analogy which existed between the two groups becomes an affinity. We are also made aware of the difficulty of arriving at a true classification, even in a small and perfect group;—in the actual state of nature it is almost impossible, the species being so numerous and the modifications of form and structure so varied, arising probably from the immense number of species which have served as antitype for the existing species, and thus produced a complicated branching of the lines of affinity, as intricate as the twigs of a gnarled oak or the vascular system of the human body. Again, if we consider that we have only fragments of this vast system, the stem and main branches being represented by extinct species of which we have no knowledge, while a vast mass of limbs and boughs and minute twigs and scattered leaves is what we have to place in order, and determine the true position each originally occupied with regard to the others, the whole difficulty of the true Natural System of classification becomes apparent to us.

We shall thus find ourselves obliged to reject all those systems of classification which arrange species or groups in circles, as well as those which fix a definite number for the divisions of each group. The latter class have been very generally rejected by naturalists, as contrary to nature, notwithstanding the ability with which they have been advocated; but the circular system of affinities seems to have obtained a deeper hold, many eminent naturalists having to some extent adopted it. We have, however, never been able to find a case in which the circle has been closed by a direct and close affinity. In most cases a palpable analogy has been substituted, in others the affinity is very obscure or altogether doubtful. The complicated branching of the lines of affinities in extensive groups must also afford great facilities for giving a show of probability to any such purely artificial arrangements. Their death-blow was given by the admirable paper of the lamented Mr. Strickland, published in the "Annals of Natural History," in which he so cleverly showed the true synthetical method of discovering the Natural System.

Geographical Distribution of Organisms.

If we now consider the geographical distribution of animals and plants upon the earth, we shall find all the facts beautifully in accordance with, and readily explained by, the present hypothesis. A country having species, genera, and whole families peculiar to it, will be the necessary result of its having been isolated for a long period, sufficient for many series of species to have been created on the type of pre-existing ones, which, as well as many of the earlier-formed species, have become extinct, and thus made the groups appear isolated. If in any case the anti-type had an extensive range, two or more groups of species might have been formed, each varying from it in a different manner, and thus producing several representative or analogous groups. The Sylviadæ of Europe and the Sylvicolidæ of North America, the Heliconidæ of South America and the Euplœas of the East, the group of Trogons inhabiting Asia, and that peculiar to South America, are examples that may be accounted for in this manner.

Such phænomena as are exhibited by the Galapagos Islands, which contain little groups of plants and animals peculiar to themselves, but most nearly allied to those of South America, have not hitherto received any, even a conjectural explanation. The Galapagos are a volcanic group of high antiquity, and have probably never been more closely connected with the continent than they are at present. They must have been first peopled, like other newly-formed islands, by the action of winds and currents, and at a period sufficiently remote to have had the original species die out, and the modified prototypes only remain. In the same way we can account for the separate islands having each their peculiar species, either on the supposition that the same original emigration peopled the whole of the islands with the same species from which differently modified prototypes were created, or that the islands were successively peopled from each other, but that new species have been created in each on the plan of the pre-existing ones. St. Helena is a similar case of a very ancient island having obtained an entirely peculiar, though limited, flora. On the other hand, no example is known of an island which can be proved geologically to be of very recent origin (late in the Tertiary, for instance), and yet possess generic or family groups, or even many species peculiar to itself.

When a range of mountains has attained a great elevation, and has so remained during a long geological period, the species of the two sides at and near their bases will be often very different, representative species of some genera occurring, and even whole genera being peculiar to one side, as is remarkably seen in the case of the Andes and Rocky Mountains. A similar phænomenon occurs when an island has been separated from a continent at a very early period. The shallow sea between the Peninsula of Malacca, Java, Sumatra and Borneo was probably a continent or large island at an early epoch, and may have become submerged as the volcanic ranges of Java and Sumatra were elevated. The organic results we see in the very considerable number of species of animals common to some or all of these countries, while at the same time a number of closely allied representative species exist peculiar to each, showing that a considerable period has elapsed since their separation. The facts of geographical distribution and of geology may thus mutually explain each other in doubtful cases, should the principles here advocated be clearly established.

In all those cases in which an island has been separated from a continent, or raised by volcanic or coralline action from the sea, or in which a mountain-chain has been elevated in a recent geological epoch, the phænomena of peculiar groups or even of single representative species will not exist. Our own island is an example of this, its separation from the continent being geologically very recent, and we have consequently scarcely a species which is peculiar to it; while the Alpine range, one of the most recent mountain elevations, separates faunas and floras which scarcely differ more than may be due to climate and latitude alone.

The series of facts alluded to in Proposition (3), of closely allied species in rich groups being found geographically near each other, is most striking and important. Mr. Lovell Reeve has well exemplified it in his able and interesting paper on the Distribution of the Bulimi. It is also seen in the Hummingbirds and Toucans, little groups of two or three closely allied species being often found in the same or closely ad-

joining districts, as we have had the good fortune of personally veri-
fying. Fishes give evidence of a similar kind: each great river has its
peculiar genera, and in more extensive genera its groups of closely allied
species. But it is the same throughout Nature; every class and order of
animals will contribute similar facts. Hitherto no attempt has been made
to explain these singular phænomena, or to show how they have arisen.
Why are the genera of Palms and of Orchids in almost every case confined to one hemisphere? Why are the closely allied species of brown-
backed Trogons all found in the East, and the green-backed in the
West? Why are the Macaws and the Cockatoos similarly restricted?
Insects furnish a countless number of analogous examples;—the Goliathi
of Africa, the Ornithopteræ of the Indian Islands, the Heliconidæ of
South America, the Danaidæ of the East, and in all, the most closely
allied species found in geographical proximity. The question forces itself
upon every thinking mind,—why are these things so? They could not
be as they are had no law regulated their creation and dispersion. The
law here enunciated not merely explains, but necessitates the facts we
see to exist, while the vast and long-continued geological changes of the
earth readily account for the exceptions and apparent discrepancies
that here and there occur. The writer's object in putting forward his
views in the present imperfect manner is to submit them to the test of
other minds, and to be made aware of all the facts supposed to be
inconsistent with them. As his hypothesis is one which claims acceptance
solely as explaining and connecting facts which exist in nature, he ex-
pects facts alone to be brought to disprove it, not *à priori* arguments
against its probability.

Geological Distribution of the Forms of Life.

The phænomena of geological distribution are exactly analogous to
those of geography. Closely allied species are found associated in the
same beds, and the change from species to species appears to have been
as gradual in time as in space. Geology, however, furnishes us with
positive proof of the extinction and production of species, though it
does not inform us how either has taken place. The extinction of species,

however, offers but little difficulty, and the *modus operandi* has been well illustrated by Sir C. Lyell in his admirable "principles." Geological changes, however gradual, must occasionally have modified external conditions to such an extent as to have rendered the existence of certain species impossible. The extinction would in most cases be effected by a gradual dying-out, but in some instances there might have been a sudden destruction of a species of limited range. To discover how the extinct species have from time to time been replaced by new ones down to the very latest geological period, is the most difficult, and at the same time the most interesting problem in the natural history of the earth. The present inquiry, which seeks to eliminate from known facts a law which has determined, to a certain degree, what species could and did appear at a given epoch, may, it is hoped, be considered as one step in the right direction towards a complete solution of it.

High Organization of very ancient Animals consistent with this Law.

Much discussion has of late years taken place on the question, whether the succession of life upon the globe has been from a lower to a higher degree of organization. The admitted facts seem to show that there has been a general, but not a detailed progression. Mollusca and Radiata existed before Vertebrata, and the progression from Fishes to Reptiles and Mammalia, and also from the lower mammals to the higher, is indisputable. On the other hand, it is said that the Mollusca and Radiata of the very earliest periods were more highly organized than the great mass of those now existing, and that the very first fishes that have been discovered are by no means the lowest organised of the class. Now it is believed the present hypothesis will harmonize with all these facts, and in a great measure serve to explain them; for though it may appear to some readers essentially a theory of progression, it is in reality only one of gradual change. It is, however, by no means difficult to show that a real progression in the scale of organization is perfectly consistent with all the appearances, and even with apparent retrogression, should such occur.

Returning to the analogy of a branching tree, as the best mode of representing the natural arrangement of species and their successive creation, let us suppose that at an early geological epoch any group (say a class of the Mollusca) has attained to a great richness of species and a high organization. Now let this great branch of allied species, by geological mutations, be completely or partially destroyed. Subsequently a new branch springs from the same trunk, that is to say, new species are successively created, having for their antitypes the same lower organized species which had served as the antitypes for the former group, but which have survived the modified conditions which destroyed it. This new group being subject to these altered conditions, has modifications of structure and organization given to it, and becomes the representative group of the former one in another geological formation. It may, however, happen, that though later in time, the new series of species may never attain to so high a degree of organization as those preceding it, but in its turn become extinct, and give place to yet another modification from the same root, which may be of higher or lower organization, more or less numerous in species, and more or less varied in form and structure than either of those which preceded it. Again, each of these groups may not have become totally extinct, but may have left a few species, the modified prototypes of which have existed in each succeeding period, a faint memorial of their former grandeur and luxuriance. Thus every case of apparent retrogression may be in reality a progress, though an interrupted one: when some monarch of the forest loses a limb, it may be replaced by a feeble and sickly substitute. The foregoing remarks appear to apply to the case of the Mollusca, which, at a very early period, had reached a high organization and a great development of forms and species in the testaceous Cephalopoda. In each succeeding age modified species and genera replaced the former ones which had become extinct, and as we approach the present æra, but few and small representatives of the group remain, while the Gasteropods and Bivalves have acquired an immense preponderance. In the long series of changes the earth has undergone, the process of peopling it with organic beings has been continually going on, and whenever any of the higher groups have become nearly or quite extinct, the lower forms which have better resisted the modified physical conditions have served as the antitypes on which to found the new races. In this manner alone, it is believed, can the representative groups at successive periods, and the rising and fallings in the scale of organization, be in every case explained.

Objections to Forbes' Theory of Polarity.

The hypothesis of polarity, recently put forward by Professor Edward Forbes to account for the abundance of generic forms at a very early period and at present, while in the intermediate epochs there is a gradual diminution and impoverishment, till the minimum occurred at the confines of the Palæozoic and Secondary epochs, appears to us quite unnecessary, as the facts may be readily accounted for on the principles already laid down. Between the Palæozoic and Neozoic periods of Professor Forbes, there is scarcely a species in common, and the greater part of the genera and families also disappear to be replaced by new ones. It is almost universally admitted that such a change in the organic world must have occupied a vast period of time. Of this interval we have no record; probably because the whole area of the early formations now exposed to our researches was elevated at the end of the Palæozoic period, and remained so through the interval required for the organic changes which resulted in the fauna and flora of the Secondary period. The records of this interval are buried beneath the ocean which covers three-fourths of the globe. Now it appears highly probable that a long period of quiescence or stability in the physical conditions of a district would be most favourable to the existence of organic life in the greatest abundance, both as regards individuals and also as to variety of species and generic group, just as we now find that the places best adapted to the rapid growth and increase of individuals also contain the greatest profusion of species and the greatest variety of forms,—the tropics in comparison with the temperate and arctic regions. On the other hand, it seems no less probable that a change in the physical conditions of a district, even small in amount if rapid, or even gradual if to a great amount, would be highly unfavourable to the existence of individuals, might cause the extinction of many species, and would probably be equally unfavourable to the creation of new ones. In this too we may find an analogy with the present state of our earth, for it has been shown to be the violent extremes and rapid changes of physical conditions, rather than the actual mean state in the temperate and frigid zones, which renders them less prolific than the tropical regions, as exemplified by the great distance beyond the tropics to which tropical forms penetrate when the climate is equable, and also by the richness in species and forms of tropical mountain regions which principally differ from the temperate zone in the uniformity of their climate. However this may be, it seems a fair assumption that during a period of geological repose the new species which we know to have been created would have appeared, that the creations would then exceed in number the extinctions, and therefore the number of species would increase. In a period of geological activity, on the other hand, it seems probable that the extinctions might exceed the creations, and the number of species consequently diminish. That such effects did take place in connexion with the causes to which we have imputed them, is shown in the case of the Coal formation, the faults and contortions of which show a period of great activity and violent convulsions, and it is in the formation immediately succeeding this that the poverty of forms of life is most apparent. We have then only to suppose a long period of somewhat similar action during the vast unknown interval at the termination of the Palæozoic period, and then a decreasing violence or rapidity through the Secondary period, to allow for the gradual repopulation of the earth with varied forms, and the whole of the facts are explained. We thus have a clue to the increase of the forms of life during certain periods, and their decrease during others, without recourse to any causes but these we know to have existed, and to effects fairly deducible from them. The precise manner in which the geological changes of the early formations were effected is so extremely obscure, that when we can explain important facts by a retardation at one time and an acceleration at another of a process which we know from its nature and from observation to have been unequal,—a cause so simple may surely be preferred to one so obscure and hypothetical as polarity.

I would also venture to suggest some reasons against the very nature of the theory of Professor Forbes. Our knowledge of the organic world during any geological epoch is necessarily very imperfect. Looking at the vast numbers of species and groups that have been discovered by geologists, this may be doubted; but we should compare their numbers not merely with those that now exist upon the earth, but with a far larger amount. We have no reason for believing that the number of species on the earth at any former period was much less than at present; at all events the aquatic portion, with which geologists have most acquaintance, was probably often as great or greater. Now we know that there have been many complete changes of species; new sets of organisms have many times been introduced in place of old ones which have become extinct, so that the total amount which have existed on the earth from the earliest geological period must have borne about the same proportion to those now living, as the whole human race who have lived and died upon the earth, to the population at the present time. Again, at each epoch, the whole earth was no doubt, as now, more or less the theatre of life, and as the successive generations of each species died, their exuviæ and preservable parts would be deposited over every portion of the then existing seas and oceans, which we have reason for supposing to have been more, rather than less, extensive than at present. In order then to understand our possible knowledge of the early world and its inhabitants, we must compare, not the area of the whole field of our geological researches with the earth's surface, but the area of the examined portion of each formation separately with the whole earth. For example, during the Silurian period all the earth was Silurian, and animals were living and dying, and depositing their remains more or less over the whole area of the globe, and they were probably (the species at least) nearly as varied in different latitudes and longitudes as at present. What proportion do the Silurian districts bear to the whole surface of the globe, land and sea (for far more extensive Silurian districts probably exist beneath the ocean than above it), and what portion of the known Silurian districts has been actually examined for fossils? Would the area of rock actually laid open to the eye be the thousandth or the ten-thousandth part of the earth's surface? Ask the same question with regard to the Oolite or the Chalk, or even to particular beds of these when they differ considerably in their fossils, and you may then get some notion of how small a portion of the whole we know.

But yet more important is the probability, nay almost the certainty, that whole formations containing the records of vast geological periods are entirely buried beneath the ocean, and for ever beyond our reach. Most of the gaps in the geological series may thus be filled up, and vast numbers of unknown and unimaginable animals, which might help to elucidate the affinities of the numerous isolated groups which are a perpetual puzzle to the zoologist, may there be buried, until future revolutions may raise them in their turn above the waters, to afford materials for the study of whatever race of intelligent beings may then have succeeded us. These considerations must lead us to the conclusion, that our knowledge of the whole series of the former inhabitants of the earth is necessarily most imperfect and fragmentary,—as much so as our knowledge of the present organic world would be, were we forced to make our collections and observations only in spots equally limited in area and in number with those actually laid open for the collection of fossils.

Now, the hypothesis of Professor Forbes is essentially one that assumes to a great extent the completeness of our knowledge of the whole series of organic beings which have existed on the earth. This appears to be a fatal objection to it, independently of all other considerations. It may be said that the same objections exist against every theory on such a subject, but this is not necessarily the case. The hypothesis put forward in this paper depends in no degree upon the completeness of our knowledge of the former condition of the organic world, but takes what facts we have as fragments of a vast whole, and deduces from them something of the nature and proportions of that whole which we can never know in detail. It is founded upon isolated groups of facts, recognizes their isolation, and endeavours to deduce from them the nature of the intervening portions.

Rudimentary Organs.

Another important series of facts, quite in accordance with, and even necessary deductions from, the law now developed, are those of rudimentary organs. That these really do exist, and in most cases have no special function in the animal œconomy, is admitted by the first authorities in comparative anatomy. The minute limbs hidden beneath the skin in many of the snake-like lizards, the anal hooks of the boa constrictor, the complete series of jointed finger-bones in the paddle of the Manatus and whale, are a few of the most familiar instances. In botany a similar class of facts has long been recognised. Abortive stamens, rudimentary floral envelopes and undeveloped carpels, are of the most frequent occurrence. To every thoughtful naturalist the question must arise, What are these for? What have they to do with the great laws of creation? Do they not teach us something of the system of Nature? If each species has been created independently, and without any necessary relations with pre-existing species, what do these rudiments, these apparent imperfections mean? There must be a cause for them; they must be the necessary results of some great natural law. Now, if, as it has been endeavoured to be shown, the great law which has regulated the peopling of the earth with animal and vegetable life is, that every change shall be gradual; that no new creature shall be formed widely differing from anything before existing; that in this, as in everything else in Nature, there shall be gradation and harmony,—then these rudimentary organs are necessary, and are an essential part of the system of Nature. Ere the higher Vertebrata were formed, for instance, many steps were required, and many organs had to undergo modifications from the rudimental condition in which only they had as yet existed. We still see remaining an antitypal sketch of a wing adapted for flight in the scaly flapper of the penguin, and limbs first concealed beneath the skin, and then weakly protruding from it, were the necessary gradations before others should be formed fully adapted for locomotion. Many more of these modifications should we behold, and more complete series of them, had we a view of all the forms which have ceased to live. The great gaps that exist between fishes, reptiles, birds, and mammals would then, no doubt, be softened down by intermediate groups, and the whole organic world would be seen to be an unbroken and harmonious system.

Conclusion.

It has now been shown, though most briefly and imperfectly, how the law that "*Every species has come into existence coincident both in time and space with a pre-existing closely allied species,*" connects together and renders intelligible a vast number of independent and hitherto unexplained facts. The natural system of arrangement of organic beings, their geographical distribution, their geological sequence, the phænomena of representative and substituted groups in all their modifications, and the most singular peculiarites of anatomical structure, are all explained and illustrated by it, in perfect accordance with the vast mass of facts which the researches of modern naturalists have brought together, and, it is believed, not materially opposed to any of them. It also claims a superiority over previous hypotheses, on the ground that it not merely explains, but necessitates what exists. Granted the law, and many of the most important facts in Nature could not have been otherwise, but are almost as necessary deductions from it, as are the elliptic orbits of the planets from the law of gravitation.

On the Tendency of Varieties to Depart Indefinitely from the Original Type*

BY ALFRED RUSSEL WALLACE

Instability of Varieties supposed to prove the permanent distinctness of Species.

ONE of the strongest arguments which have been adduced to prove the original and permanent distinctness of species is, that *varieties* produced in a state of domesticity are more or less unstable, and often have a tendency, if left to themselves, to return to the normal form of the parent species; and this instability is considered to be a distinctive peculiarity of all varieties, even of those occurring among wild animals in a state of nature, and to constitute a provision for preserving unchanged the originally created distinct species.

In the absence of scarcity of facts and observations as to *varieties* occurring among wild animals, this argument has had great weight with naturalists, and has led to a very general and somewhat prejudiced belief in the stability of species. Equally general, however, is the belief in

---

*The Ternate Paper Wallace mailed to Darwin March 9, 1858, from the Moluccas (present-day Indonesia), setting in motion the conspiracy and cover up surrounding the Linnean Society meeting of July 1 that year and the publication of *The Origin of Species* the following year.

what are called "permanent or true varieties,"—races of animals which continually propagate their like, but which differ so slightly (although constantly) from some other race, that the one is considered to be a *variety* of the other. Which is the *variety* and which the original *species*, there is generally no means of determining, except in those rare cases in which the one race has been known to produce an offspring unlike itself and resembling the other. This, however, would seem quite incompatible with the "permanent invariability of species," but the difficulty is overcome by assuming that such varieties have strict limits, and can never again vary further from the original type, although they may return to it, which, from the analogy of the domesticated animals, is considered to be highly probable, if not certainly proved.

It will be observed that this argument rests entirely on the assumption, that *varieties* occurring in a state of nature are in all respects analogous to or even identical with those of domestic animals, and are governed by the same laws as regards their permanence or further variation. But it is the object of the present paper to show that this assumption is altogether false, that there is a general principle in nature which will cause many *varieties* to survive the parent species, and to give rise to successive variations departing further and further from the original type, and which also produces, in domesticated animals, the tendency of varieties to return to the parent form.

The Struggle for Existence.

The life of wild animals is a struggle for existence. The full exertion of all their faculties and all their energies is required to preserve their own existence and provide for that of their infant offspring. The possibility of procuring food during the least favourable seasons, and of escaping the attacks of their most dangerous enemies, are the primary conditions which determine the existence both of individuals and of entire species. These conditions will also determine the population of a species; and by a careful consideration of all the circumstances we may be enabled to comprehend, and in some degree to explain, what at first sight appears so inexplicable—the excessive abundance of some species, while others closely allied to them are very rare.

The Law of Population of Species.

The general proportion that must obtain between certain groups of animals is readily seen. Large animals cannot be so abundant as small ones; the carnivora must be less numerous than the herbivora; eagles and lions can never be so plentiful as pigeons and antelopes; the wild asses of the Tartarian deserts cannot equal in numbers the horses of the more luxuriant prairies and pampas of America. The greater or less fecundity of an animal is often considered to be one of the chief causes of its abundance or scarcity; but a consideration of the facts will show us that it really has little or nothing to do with the matter. Even the least prolific of animals would increase rapidly if unchecked, whereas it is evident that the animal population of the globe must be stationary, or perhaps, through the influence of man, decreasing. Fluctuations there may be; but permanent increase, except in restricted localities, is almost impossible. For example, our own observation must convince us that birds do not go on increasing every year in a geometrical ratio, as they would do, were there not some powerful check to their natural increase. Very few birds produce less than two young ones each year, while many have six, eight, or ten; four will certainly be below the average; and if we suppose that each pair produce young only four times in their life, that will also be below the average, supposing them not to die either by violence or want of food. Yet at this rate how tremendous would be the increase in a few years from a single pair! A simple calculation will show that in fifteen years each pair of birds would have increased to nearly ten millions! whereas we have no reason to believe that the number of the birds of any country increases at all in fifteen or in one hundred and fifty years. With such powers of increase the population must have reached its limits, and have become stationary, in a very few years after the origin of each species. It is evident, therefore, that each year an immense number of birds must perish—as many in fact as are born; and as on the lowest calculation the progeny are each year twice as numerous as their parents, it follows that, whatever be the average number of individuals existing in any given country, *twice that number must perish annually*,—a striking result, but one which seems at least highly probable, and is perhaps under rather than over the truth. It would therefore appear that, as far as the continuance of the species and the keeping up the average number of individuals are concerned,

large broods are superfluous. On the average all above *one* become food
for hawks and kites, wild cats and weasels, or perish of cold and hunger
as winter comes on. This is strikingly proved by the case of particular
species; for we find that their abundance in individuals bears no relation
whatever to their fertility in producing offspring. Perhaps the most
remarkable instance of an immense bird population is that of the passenger pigeon of the United States, which lays only one, or at most
two eggs, and is said to rear generally but one young one. Why is this
bird so extraordinarily abundant, while others producing two or three
times as many young are much less plentiful? The explanation is not
difficult. The food most congenial to this species, and on which it thrives
best, is abundantly distributed over a very extensive region, offering
such difference of soil and climate, that in one part or another of the
area the supply never fails. The bird is capable of a very rapid and long-
continued flight, so that it can pass without fatigue over the whole of
the district it inhabits, and as soon as the supply of food begins to fail
in one place is able to discover a fresh feeding-ground. This example
strikingly shows us that the procuring a constant supply of wholesome
food is almost the sole condition requisite for ensuring the rapid increase
of a given species, since neither the limited fecundity, nor the unrestrained attacks of birds of prey and of man are here sufficient to check
it. In no other birds are these peculiar circumstances so strikingly combined. Either their food is more liable to failure, or they have not sufficient power of wing to search for it over an extensive area, or during
some season of the year it becomes very scarce, and less wholesome sub-
stitutes have to be found; and thus, though more fertile in offspring,
they can never increase beyond the supply of food in the least favourable seasons. Many birds can only exist by migrating, when their food
becomes scarce, to regions possessing a milder, or at least a different
climate, though, as these migrating birds are seldom excessively abundant, it is evident that the countries they visit are still deficient in a
constant and abundant supply of wholesome food. Those whose organization does not permit them to migrate when their food becomes
periodically scarce, can never attain a large population. This is probably the reason why woodpeckers are scarce with us, while in the
tropics they are among the most abundant of solitary birds. Thus the
house sparrow is more abundant than the redbreast, because its food is
more constant and plentiful,—seeds of grasses being preserved during
the winter, and our farm-yards and stubble-fields furnishing an almost
inexhaustible supply. Why, as a general rule, are aquatic, and especially

sea birds, very numerous in individuals? Not because they are more prolific than others, generally the contrary; but because their food never fails, the sea-shores and river-banks daily swarming with a fresh supply of small mollusca and crustacea. Exactly the same laws will apply to mammals. Wild cats are prolific and have few enemies; why then are they never as abundant as rabbits? The only intelligible answer is, that their supply of food is more precarious. It appears evident, therefore, that so long as a country remains physically unchanged, the numbers of its animal population cannot materially increase. If one species does so, some others requiring the same kind of food much diminish in proportion. The numbers that die annually must be immense; and as the individual existence of each animal depends upon itself, those that die must be the weakest—the very young, the aged, and the diseased,—while those that prolong their existence can only be the most perfect in health and vigour—those who are best able to obtain food regularly, and avoid their numerous enemies. It is, as we commenced by remarking, "a struggle for existence," in which the weakest and least perfectly organized must always succumb.

The Abundance or Rarity of a Species dependent upon its more or less perfect Adaptation to the Conditions of Existence.

It seems evident that what takes place among the individuals of a species must also occur among the several allied species of a group,—viz., that those which are best adapted to obtain a regular supply of food, and to defend themselves against the attacks of their enemies and the vicissitudes of the seasons, must necessarily obtain and preserve a superiority in population; while those species which from some defect of power or organization are the least capable of counteracting the vicissitudes of food, supply, &c., must diminish in numbers, and, in extreme cases, become altogether extinct. Between these extremes the species will present various degrees of capacity for ensuring the means of preserving life; and it is thus we account for the abundance or rarity of species. Our ignorance will generally prevent us from accurately tracing the effects to their causes; but could we become perfectly acquainted with the organization and habits of the various species of animals, and could we measure the capacity of each for performing the different acts necessary to its safety and existence under all the varying circumstances by which it is surrounded, we might be able even to calculate the proportionate abundance of individuals which is the necessary result.

If now we have succeeded in establishing these two points—1st, *that the animal population of a country is generally stationary, being kept down by a periodical deficiency of food, and other checks*; and, 2nd, *that the comparative abundance or scarcity of the individuals of the several species is entirely due to their organization and resulting habits, which, rendering it more difficult to procure a regular supply of food and to provide for their personal safety in some cases than in others, can only be balanced by a difference in the population which have to exist in a given area*—we shall be in a condition to proceed to the consideration of *varieties*, to which the preceding remarks have a direct and very important application.

Useful Variations will tend to Increase; useless or hurtful Variations to Diminish.

Most or perhaps all the variations from the typical form of a species must have some definite effect, however slight, on the habits or capacities of the individuals. Even a change of colour might, by rendering them more or less distinguishable, affect their safety; a greater or less development of hair might modify their habits. More important changes, such as an increase in the power or dimensions of the limbs or any of the external organs, would more or less affect their mode of procuring food or the range of country which they inhabit. It is also evident that most changes would affect, either favourably or adversely, the powers of prolonging existence. An antelope with shorter or weaker legs must necessarily suffer more from the attacks of the feline carnivora; the passenger pigeon with less powerful wings would sooner or later be affected in its powers of procuring a regular supply of food; and in both cases the result must necessarily be a diminution of the population of the modified species. If, on the other hand, any species should produce a variety having slightly increased powers of preserving existence, that variety must inevitably in time acquire a superiority in numbers. These results must follow as surely as old age, intemperance, or scarcity of food produce an increased mortality. In both cases there may be many individual exceptions; but on the average the rule will invariably be found to hold good. All varieties will therefore fall into two classes—those which under the same conditions would never reach the population of the parent species, and those which would in time obtain and keep a numerical superiority. Now, let some alteration of physical conditions occur in the district—a long period of drought, a destruction of vegetation by locusts, the irruption of some new carnivorous animal seeking "pastures new"—any change in fact tending to render existence more difficult to the species in question, and tasking its utmost powers to avoid complete extermination; it is evident that, of all the individuals composing the species, those forming the least numerous and most feebly organized variety would suffer first, and, were the pressure severe, must soon become extinct. The same causes continuing in action, the parent species would next suffer, would gradually diminish in numbers, and with a recurrence of similar unfavourable conditions might also become extinct. The superior variety would then alone remain, and on a return to favourable circumstances would rapidly increase in numbers and occupy the place of the extinct species and variety.

Superior Varieties will ultimately Extirpate the original Species.

The *variety* would now have replaced the *species*, of which it would be a more perfectly developed and more highly organized form. It would be in all respects better adapted to secure its safety, and to prolong its individual existence and that of the race. Such a variety *could not* return to the original form; for that form is an inferior one, and could never compete with it for existence. Granted, therefore, a "tendency" to reproduce the original type of the species, still the variety must ever remain preponderant in numbers, and under adverse physical conditions *again alone survive*. But this new, improved, and populous race might itself, in course of time, give rise to new varieties, exhibiting several diverging modifications of form, any of which, tending to increase the facilities for preserving existence, must by the same general law, in their turn become predominant. Here, then, we have *progression and continued divergence* deduced from the general laws which regulate the existence of animals in a state of nature, and from the undisputed fact that varieties do frequently occur. It is not, however, contended that this result would be invariable; a change of physical conditions in the district might at times materially modify it, rendering the race which had been the most capable of supporting existence under the former conditions now the least so, and even causing the extinction of the newer and, for a time, superior race, while the old or parent species and its first inferior varieties continued to flourish. Variations in unimportant parts might also occur, having no perceptible effect on the life-preserving powers; and the varieties so furnished might run a course parallel with the parent species, either giving rise to further variations or returning to the former type. All we argue for is, that certain varieties have a tendency to maintain their existence longer than the original species, and this tendency must make itself felt; for though the doctrine of chances or averages can never be trusted to on a limited scale, yet, if applied to high numbers, the results come nearer to what theory demands, and, as we approach to an infinity of examples, become strictly accurate. Now the scale on which nature works is so vast—the numbers of individuals and periods of time with which she deals approach so near to infinity, that any cause, however slight, and however liable to be veiled and counteracted by accidental circumstances, must in the end produce its full legitimate results.

The Partial Reversion of Domesticated Varieties explained.

Let us now turn to domesticated animals, and inquire how varieties produced among them are affected by the principles here enunciated. The essential difference in the condition of wild and domestic animals is this,—that among the former, their well-being and very existence depend upon the full exercise and healthy condition of all their senses and physical powers, whereas, among the latter, these are only partially exercised, and in some cases are absolutely unused. A wild animal has to search, and often to labour, for every mouthful of food—to exercise sight, hearing, and smell in seeking it, and in avoiding dangers, in procuring shelter from the inclemency of the seasons, and in providing for the subsistence and safety of its offspring. There is no muscle of its body that is not called into daily and hourly activity; there is no sense or faculty that is not strengthened by continual exercise. The domestic animal, on the other hand, has food provided for it, is sheltered, and often confined, to guard it against the vicissitudes of the seasons, is carefully secured from the attacks of its natural enemies, and seldom even rears its young without human assistance. Half of its senses and faculties are quite useless; and the other half are but occasionally called into feeble exercise, while even its muscular system is only irregularly called into action.

Now when a variety of such an animal occurs, having increased power or capacity in any organ or sense, such increase is totally useless, is never called into action, and may even exist without the animal ever becoming aware of it. In the wild animal, on the contrary, all its faculties and powers being brought into full action for the necessities of existence, any increase becomes immediately available, is strengthened by exercise, and must even slightly modify the food, the habits, and the whole economy of the race. It creates as it were a new animal, one of superior powers, and which will necessarily increase in numbers and outlive those inferior to it.

Again, in the domesticated animal all variations have an equal chance of continuance; and those which would decidedly render a wild animal unable to compete with its fellows and continue its existence are no disadvantage whatever in a state of domesticity. Our quickly fattening pigs, short-legged sheep, pouter pigeons, and poodle dogs could never have come into existence in a state of nature, because the very first step towards such inferior forms would have led to the rapid extinction of the race; still less could they now exist in competition with their wild allies. The great speed but slight endurance of the race horse, the unwielding strength of the ploughman's team, would both be useless in a state of nature. If turned wild on the pampas, such animals would probably soon become extinct, or under favorable circumstances might each lose those extreme qualities which would never be called into action, and in a few generations would revert to a common type, which must be that in which the various powers and faculties are so proportioned to each other as to be best adapted to procure food and secure safety,— that in which by the full exercise of every part of his organization the animal can alone continue to live. Domestic varieties, when turned wild, *must* return to something near the type of the original wild stock, *or become altogether extinct.**

Lamarck's Hypothesis very different from that now advanced.

We see, then, that no inferences as to varieties in a state of nature can be deduced from the observation of those occurring among domestic animals. The two are so much opposed to each other in every circumstance of their existence, that what applies to the one is almost sure not to apply to the other. Domestic animals are abnormal, irregular, artificial; they are subject to varieties which never occur and never can occur in a state of nature; their very existence depends altogether on human care: so far are many of them removed from that just proportion of faculties, that true balance of organization, by means of which alone an animal left to its own resources can preserve its existence and continue its race.

The hypothesis of Lamarck—that progressive changes in species have been produced by the attempts of animals to increase the development of their own organs, and thus modify their structure and habits—has been repeatedly and easily refuted by all writers on the subject of varieties and species, and it seems to have been considered that when this was done the whole question has been finally settled; but the view here developed renders such an hypothesis quite unnecessary, by showing that similar results must be produced by the action of principles constantly at work in nature. The powerful retractile talons of the falcon-

---

* That is, they will vary, and the variations which tend to adapt them to the wild state, and therefore approximate them to wild animals, will be preserved. Those individuals which do not vary sufficiently will perish.

and the cat-tribes have not been produced or increased by the volition of those animals; but among the different varieties which occurred in the earlier and less highly organized forms of these groups, *those always survived longest which had the greatest facilities for seizing their prey.* Neither did the giraffe acquire its long neck by desiring to reach the foliage of the more lofty shrubs, and constantly stretching its neck for the purpose, but because any varieties which occurred among its anti-types with a longer neck than usual *at once secured a fresh range of pasture over the same ground as their shorter-necked companions, and on the first scarcity of food were thereby enabled to outlive them.* Even the peculiar colours of many animals, especially insects, so closely re-sembling the soil or the leaves or the trunks on which they habitually reside, are explained on the same principle; for though in the course of ages varieties of many tints may have occurred, *yet those races having colours best adapted to concealment from their enemies would inevi-tably survive the longest.* We have also here an acting cause to account for that balance so often observed in nature,—a deficiency in one set of organs always being compensated by an increased development of some others—powerful wings accompanying weak feet, or great velocity making up for the absence of defensive weapons; for it has been shown that all varieties in which an unbalanced deficiency oc-curred could not long continue their existence. The action of this prin-ciple is exactly like that of the centrifugal governor of the steam engine, which checks and corrects any irregularities almost before they become evident; and in like manner no unbalanced deficiency in the animal king-dom can ever reach any conspicuous magnitude, because it would make itself felt at the very first step, by rendering existence difficult and extinction almost sure to follow. An origin such as is here advocated will also agree with the peculiar character of the modifications of form and structure which obtain in organized beings—the many lines of diver-gence from a central type, the increasing efficiency and power of a par-ticular organ through a succession of allied species, and the remarkable persistence of unimportant parts such as colour, texture of plumage and hair, form of horns or crests, through a series of species differing con-siderably in more essential characters. It also furnishes us with a reason for that "more specialized structure" which Professor Owen states to be a characteristic of recent compared with extinct forms, and which would evidently be the result of the progressive modification of any organ applied to a special purpose in the animal economy.

Conclusion.

We believe we have now shown that there is a tendency in nature to the continued progression of certain classes of *varieties* further and further from the original type—a progression to which there appears no reason to assign any definite limits—and that the same principle which produces this result in a state of nature will also explain why domestic varieties have a tendency to revert to the original type. This progression, by minute steps, in various directions, but always checked and balanced by the necessary conditions, subject to which alone existence can be preserved, may, it is believed, be followed out so as to agree with all the phenomena presented by organized beings, their extinction and succession in past ages, and all the extraordinary modifications of form, instinct, and habits which they exhibit.

Written at Ternate, February, 1858

Author's Note

IN 1947, as a war correspondent, I journeyed from Java to the Celebes (now Sulawesi) in a Catalina flying boat and, as we flew over the Straits of Macassar, I was told we were crossing the Wallace Line. Like many people, I had never heard of it. About a year later, Graham Jenkins, a Reuters correspondent, came down with jaundice and the handful of foreign correspondents in Batavia (Jakarta), covering the Indonesian–Dutch conflict, paid him a visit. Jenkins was a history buff and among his books was Wallace's *The Malay Archipelago*. "Wallace of the Wallace Line?" I inquired. Jenkins replied laconically, "The same Wallace." I borrowed the book, and was fascinated.

As matters were to turn out, my wife came from Dutch Guiana (Surinam), and in the course of time, I read *A Narrative of Travels on the Amazon and Rio Negro* by "the same Wallace." In neither of these works was there a hint of the high drama encapsulating the enunciation in 1858 of the theory of the origin and divergence of species by natural selection. I then discovered that although Wallace had exercised incalculable influence on the course of human events, he had written more books than were written about him. In point of fact, the shelving on Wallace was almost as bare as Mother Hubbard's cupboard.

A major source on Wallace is his published works, virtually all of them unfortunately out of print, but numbering twenty-four books, from *Palm Trees on the Amazon* (London: Van Voorst, n.d. [1853]) to *The Revolt of Democracy* (New York: Funk & Wagnalls, 1914), and 242 essays, monographs, and articles from "On the Umbrella Bird," published in 1850 in the *Proceedings of the Zoological Society of London*, to his last essay, "The Nature and Origin of Life," written in 1912 but misplaced and unpublished after his death the following year.

As a start, I opened Wallace's two-volume *My Life: A Record of Events and Opinions* (New York: Dodd, Mead, 1905), an autobiography in the grand Victorian tradition which carried reticence to exasperating lengths; for example, it contained a single reference to Wallace's Annie, describing her as "Mr. Mitten's eldest daughter, then about eighteen years old." Her Christian name was not given. Perhaps reticence is a misnomer, because Wallace discussed his unsuccessful pursuit of "Miss L." in detail in *My Life* and, as one of Wallace's descendants remarked, "We often wonder how grandmother felt about that!"

Another rich source of published Wallaceana is found in the two-volume biography *Alfred Russel Wallace: Letters and Reminiscences* by James Marchant (London: Cassell, 1916), which contains a complete list of Wallace's published works. Marchant's work has a curious history. Wallace suggested to his good friend and admirer that he write a comparative study, entitled *Darwin and Wallace*, and Marchant agreed. "Alas! soon after the agreement with the publishers was signed and in the very month the plan of the work was to have been shown to Wallace," Marchant wrote, "his [Wallace's] hand was suddenly stilled by death and the book remains unwritten."

Apparently Marchant started out with a comparative study in mind, but the structure soon collapsed. The only published attempt at such a study is *Biologist Philosopher* by Wilma George (London: Abelard-Schuman, 1964), the English zoogeographer, an outstanding work. She puts Wallace ahead of Darwin in many areas of biological inquiry and concludes that Wallace is responsible for his own relative obscurity, "for it was he who gave the word Darwinism to all areas of the theory of evolution by natural selection."

A splendid, unpublished dissertation by the late Gerald M. Henderson, entitled *Alfred Russel Wallace: his role and influence in nineteenth-century evolutionary thought* (Ann Arbor, Michigan: University Microfilms, 1958) also engages in a comparative study and suggests that Wallace's basic theories were much more in advance of his time than those of Darwin. "For too long," Henderson said, "Wallace has been ignored or ridiculed for his unorthodox ideas on human evolution."

The time of Wallace's death may have had something to do with his obscurity. He died shortly before the outbreak of World War I, and it is doubtful if many people had much time for Wallace then or for Marchant, whose biography appeared in the same year that saw Verdun, Jutland, and the Somme.

Works about Wallace are almost nonexistent. Aside from Marchant and George, the only other full-length treatment—besides a children's book—is *Darwin's Moon* by Anabel Williams-Ellis (London: Blackie, 1966), and the less said about it the better.

Whatever the case, these works—despite the existence of several thin lines of inquiry into the "delicate arrangement"—ignore the chain-reaction of events that led up to the July 1, 1858, Linnean meeting. Above all, there are the surviving correspondence and notebooks of Darwin and his cabinet, which are laced with hints about the affair; circumstantially, Darwin's "missing" correspondence of 1855 to 1858; Wallace's correspondence of the period; the publication of the Sarawak Law and Ternate Essay before *Origin*; and Wallace's confessed surprise when the cover-up surrounding the affair was partially cleared after Darwin's death. The sum total of this evidence did not reveal itself as the proverbial tip of an iceberg, but as skim ice.

This was the greatest moment in the history of science since Copernicus' revolutionary proclamation that the Earth was neither at rest nor at the center of the universe. What is unfathomable is that the drama surrounding the event was permitted to devolve into fable, that so few attempts have been made to research the affair. In almost every book about Darwin, Wallace is brushed aside simply as Darwin's "co-discoverer" of the theory of natural selection.

How the myth about the Linnean meeting developed is not difficult to follow. A typical example appeared in *The Coming of Evolution* by John Judd (Cambridge: Cambridge University Press, 1910), in which the author, a Fellow of the Royal Society, observed that "fortunately we are not called upon for anything like a judicial investigation" into the affair. This sort of smoke suggests a fire, but why not open an inquiry into the "delicate arrangement"? Judd explained: "Had these two men been of less noble and generous nature, the history of science might have been dishonoured by a painful discussion on a question of priority." But, as Judd makes patently clear, Wallace was ignorant of what happened in England in 1858. Accordingly, the "painful discussion" was avoided on the strength of the "noble and generous nature" of one man, not two. That man was Alfred Russel Wallace. One may ask, however: Has not the failure to cauterize the affair by sunlight dishonored the history of science?

My quest for Wallaceana took me on a crazy-quilt journey across England, from London to Down to Broadstone to Bournemouth, across the channel to Amsterdam, and beyond. Wherever I went, people were helpful, directly and indirectly, and I hereby acknowledge their assistance: In London, A. M. Rose, acting executive officer of The British Library, gave me access to the Student's Room where I have worked before, and Dr. C. J. Wright, research assistant, provided me with a list of material from the Library's printed catalogues and "rough register." The cornucopia included Wallace's correspondence from 1856 to 1912, twenty-nine folders or "volumes," including the 1889 draft of Wallace's *Darwinism* and—holy of holies—"Vol. XXI Correspondence with Charles Darwin, 1857–1881." The material was presented to the Library by Wallace's son William.

Th. O'Grady, executive secretary of the Linnean Society of London, kindly provided me not only with Wallace's Malay and American notebooks but also a folder of correspondence from Wallace's descendants (more about that later). To my regret, the meeting room in which the Wallace–Darwin "joint communication" was read is no longer in existence. Dr. Paul Whalley, secretary of the Royal Entomological Society, was likewise exceedingly helpful. I pulled him away from his microscope at the British Museum (Natural History) and he gave me a Cook's tour of the Society's building, leading me to the august conference room where Wallace's worn, ink-stained writing slate is still in use at the head of the table. Whalley remarked, "I have always thought Wallace lived in Darwin's shadow." Dr. Peter Whitehead, president of Ensoc, as entomologists fondly call their group, took the trouble to open the Society's walk-in vault in search of Wallaceana, but the pickings were meager. At the British Museum (Natural History), Mrs. A. Datta, reference librarian, provided me with additional Wallace notebooks, including four water-stained journals on the fishes of the Rio Negro, among the few items that survived Wallace's disaster at sea. In London, too, John Hemming, director and secretary of the Royal Geographical Society, permitted me to use the Society's archives which are normally "open only to Fellows of the Society," and Mrs. C. Kelly, archivist, made copies for me of several Wallace documents. I am also truly grateful for the assistance provided by other reference librarians, including J. Percival, archivist, University College, London, where the Wallace–Galton papers are stored; J. Pingree, college archivist, Imperial College of Science and Technology, London, which holds several Huxley–Wallace letters; Peter Gautrey, assistant under-librarian, Charles

Darwin Collection, Cambridge University Library, who provided my emissary, Professor Bruce Bassett of Columbia University, with assistance in obtaining a copy of Darwin's notes on Wallace's Sarawak Law; and D. Outram, research assistant, The Royal Commission on Historical Manuscripts, whose aid was invaluable.

At Down, Mrs. Philip Titheradge greeted me at the same door where Parslow received the Ternate Essay and later met Wallace on his first visit to Darwin, and her husband, the curator of Down House, went out of his way to provide me with an intimate glimpse of Darwin's home, opening Darwin's library cases and permitting me to take notes in Darwin's study—at Darwin's own table, no less. The highlight of my visit to Down was a solitary journey through the Sandwalk, the same path over which Darwin and Wallace trod on many occasions.

Wallace's Malay archipelago, today embracing Indonesia, Malaysia, and Singapore, required no introduction since it was my habitat—as it was Wallace's—for eight years, and my wife was literally at home in the Amazon (she lived there longer than Wallace).

In The Netherlands, I am grateful to F. Deeleman, secretary general of the Koninklijk Instituut voor de Tropen or Royal Institute for the Tropics, who put me in touch with the lively Duth zoologist, Dr. D. Hellenius, author of *De Vreemde Eilandbewoner (The Strange Inhabitant of the Island)* (Amsterdam: Arbeiderspers, 1967), and a member of the University of Amsterdam's Instituut van Toxanomische Zoologie or Institute for Zoological Taxonomy, who has an ongoing interest in the Wallace–Darwin relationship.

Here at home, I am deeply indebted, as I have been frequently in the past, to Mary Kohn, chief reference librarian of the Ruth A. Haas Library, Western Connecticut State College, where I am a member of the faculty, and to her able assistant, Marion Pfender. Both retained their aplomb however outrageous my requests for help. I should also like to acknowledge the suggestions of my editor, Roger Jellinek, who, after reading the manuscript, described the Linnean affair, in a memorable phrase, as "intellectual murder."

Indeed, except for my publisher and Gerri K. Lewis, a journalism major who typed the manuscript, none of the individuals named above knew what I was about, and it is likely that several of them would be either startled or appalled by the result. I should hastily add in this era of "factional fiction" and "docudramas" that all the quotations in this book are authentic; the only changes are in spelling or verb tense.

Ms. Lewis' comment when she finished the job was poignant. "By

the middle of the book I was so engrossed with this guy that I was getting quite angry with him," she said of Wallace. ". . . It seems that if
a man like Wallace could devote such time and energy to not only
living but understanding life and still be relatively unknown, well, I
don't see how I'll ever leave my mark. . . . I kept hoping he would get
the recognition he apparently deserved and yet I knew through history that he wouldn't."

The utopian Wallace would be distressed to learn that not everyone
was cooperative, testifying to the generalization that the exception
makes the rule. The exception here was H. Lewis McKinney. In his
Wallace and Natural Selection (New Haven: Yale University Press,
1972), and elsewhere, McKinney referred to Wallace's grandsons,
A. J. R. and R. R. Wallace. In October 1977, preparatory to revisiting
England, I wrote McKinney, acknowledging his work on Wallace and
requesting the addresses of the grandsons. I received no reply. I wrote
again in November, and again I received no reply. In December, I tele-
phoned the University of Kansas, where McKinney is a member of
the faculty, and left a message asking him to call me collect. He never
did. In American parlance, three strikes and you're out. (Later I learned
that he treated others similarly; for example, a British zoologist from
Birmingham, England, wrote to McKinney three times and his letters
were ignored.) The dismaying aspect of this episode is that I, and other
taxpayers, partly helped finance McKinney's research on Wallace.
McKinney took handouts from two foundations and the Federal government's National Institutes of Health. The records of the Statistics
and Analysis Branch, Division of Research Grants, NIH, show that
he received at least $16,850 in support of his Wallace research and that
the figure may be as high as $22,000, but the files for the first year of his
application, 1962, have since been destroyed and there is "no way of
tracing back," according to M. Oakleaf, Acting Chief of the Office of
Grants Inquiries. In any case—simple courtesy and the spirit of Western
scholarship aside—an individual who accepts public money has an obli-
gation to the public. I did not investigate how much money McKinney
got from the two foundations since these sources were not financed by
my money.

I knew the Wallaces lived in Britain, but, as I soon found out, there
are a lot of Wallaces there, 151 in the London telephone directory alone.
Accordingly, I contacted the Society of Genealogists, which had proven
helpful in the past. But they retreated in horror, overwhelmed in that
period by commissions following the showing of *Roots* in America.

In desperation I turned to my former colleagues in journalism, and a senior editor of a major news organization in New York cabled his London bureau. The reply highlights Alfred Russel Wallace's obscurity not only here but in England. The cable read:

> Re Alfred Russel Wallace's descendants. With the limited info you've given me on his grandsons I haven't been able to find them for you after contacting several entomology societies, museum and science libraries. It might interest you to know that some of the entomolgy [sic] societies had never heard of Wallace, let alone his progeny. Sorry.

My capricious goddess, Chance, entered. In London, while working through a folder of correspondence from Wallace's descendants, I noticed that over a period of years, A. J. R. Wallace gave the same home address: 61 East Avenue, Bournemouth (I later learned that Wallace's son Will built the house). I had found A. J. R. (John) Wallace and his wife, Daphne; the other grandson, R. R. (Dick) Wallace, owned and operated a small dairy farm at Hazelhurst Farm, Sway, Lymington, Hampshire. John turned out to be a cloning of his father, as Will is described in Hubbard (see below), and bore a striking resemblance to his grandfather.

Journalists and academicians note: The Wallace descendants possess fifty-five letters of their grandfather's, several from the Amazon and several from the Malay archipelago. Among them is the sensational letter and envelope which Wallace sent from Ternate to Bates' brother at the same time he mailed the Ternate Essay to Darwin, establishing a time frame for Darwin's receipt of it—a time period that does not coincide with Darwin's claim that the essay arrived June 18. Two weeks earlier is more likely. The Wallaces also possess Wallace memorabilia, including in this case their grandfather's grandfather clock and many of his books.

The Wallaces tread gingerly on the Wallace–Darwin relationship. "Grandfather was Darwin's Boswell," John said. As for the missing Wallace wrapper on his Darwin correspondence (see frontispiece), he observed, "My father lent Marchant a number of letters and they were not all returned, and when my father wrote Sir James about them we got a very offhanded reply." Thus, many Wallace letters are lost or mislaid. "They were valuable," John added. Asked what he and the Wallace descendants thought had happened to the missing Darwin letters of 1855 to 1858, Wallace's grandson replied wryly, "You'd better ask Charles Darwin about his missing letters."

Like Alfred Russel himself, it appears the Wallace descendants prefer to leave ancient pools undisturbed.

Fortuitously, several scholars, whose work has escaped public notice, are not prepared to do so. In Amsterdam, Dr. Hillenius observed, "In reading Wallace I detect a tone of faint complaint," adding, "I admire and like Darwin, but he is, after all, only human, and he was ambitious. If Darwin was sincere in his protestations about preferring the solitude of Down, of desiring to remain in the background, he and his friends would have published Wallace's Linnean paper alone." And Charles Coulston Gillispie conceded in *Forerunners of Darwin* (Baltimore: Johns Hopkins, 1959) that Wallace has been treated "unjustly" by history, but he did not elaborate.

In 1979 I asked Professor Gillispie, who is a member of Princeton's program in the history and philosophy of science, to elaborate; he generously turned the matter over in his mind for three weeks and then wrote:

> What I shall say in conjecture. I believe that it now seems to me less of an injustice that the theory of natural selection should be associated primarily with Darwin than it did when I wrote the sentence that you quote to me.* . . . I have come to have what may be a more mature appreciation of the intrinsic importance of institutional factors, and contextual factors, in making a scientific theory viable. Darwin was in an enormously better position than Wallace, personally, socially, financially, as to influence. . . . He was in a position to get a hearing. . . . I would doubt, for example, that Wallace would have received anything like the hearing that Darwin did. . . . Whether this is an injustice or simply a contrast in circumstance, I would not altogether wish to say. But I think that I would be more inclined to emphasize the contrast now than the injustice.

Yet several scholars have cited history's treatment (and Darwin's) of Wallace as "unjust," among them, the late C. F. A. Pantin, former president of the Linnean Society, a man with the courage of a lion, who observed in "Alfred Russel Wallace: His Pre-Darwinian Essay of 1855" (*Proceedings of The Linnean Society of London*, Vol. 171, Part 2, 1958–1959) that "it is perhaps less generally realized . . . how great [Wallace's] contribution to the whole question of evolution was." And in another paper, "Alfred Russel Wallace, F. R. S. and His Essays of 1858 and 1855" (*Notes of the Royal Society of London*, Vol. 14, 1959,

* See pp. 84-85.

pp. 67–85), Pantin concluded that if there had been no *Origin*, Wallace's Ternate Essay would have been given pride of place in the history of evolution. "He dealt with the theory more thoroughly and logically than Darwin did." The result, however, he averred, would be a "somewhat different book by a *very* different author."

On November 23, 1975, in the television series *The Ascent of Man*, Bruce Mazlish, director of humanities at the Massachusetts Institute of Technology, drew an identical conclusion. He made the point that a discoverer leaves his imprint on his discovery. Asked what the impact on history would have been if the Wallace–Darwin roles were reversed, Mazlish concluded, "*very* different." Said Mazlish: "The place where we could see this difference is in their attitude to the savages, the lower order of the human race. Wallace saw them as friendly beings, as equals. The Western world was not their bullies. Darwin came out [with] a *very* different view of the savage. . . . The fact of the matter is, through his attitude, wittingly or otherwise, he provided a footing for racism of the sort Wallace would not."

Mazlish felt that Darwin's view of the theory gave rise to Social Darwinism. "It would have been a difficult matter to get Social Wallaceism," he said. However, as in the case of Gillispie, cited above, Mazlish concluded, "Intriguing as the possibility of Wallaceism is, it was not in the cards. Wallace came from a different stratum of society and he would not have gotten the attention [of a] Darwin. . . . Wallace was from a lower class and did not have the same kind of connections in the British scientific establishment as Darwin."

The Ascent, produced by the BBC in London, appeared on public broadcasting stations in the United States and probably marked the first time in the history of the medium that Wallace's name was mentioned.

I am grateful to James Paradis, a member of the Department of Humanities at M.I.T. and a colleague of Mazlish, for providing me in private correspondence with a deep insight into the Wallace–Darwin relationship. Paradis wrote, "The key to both men's studies, I believe, was partially the survey they conducted of archipelagos; their awareness of land masses and the apparent relationship between physical environment and animal distribution provided them an ingress to thinking about chronology and species development. Both men were familiar with the work of Lyell; both men had a knowledge of surveying techniques; both men, thus, took a precise view of species geography with regard to possible shifts in large land masses. The archipelago arrangements enabled them to observe gradations in related species in a laboratory fashion. In effect, they could observe the results of evolution under certain fixed boundary conditions, including the condition of a limited food supply which is normally most pronounced in an island environment. These conditions prepared them, in my opinion, for their respective readings of Malthus."

Paradis is a warm admirer of Darwin. Yet he added, "I find Wallace, personally, a more sympathetic and interesting intellect, in certain respects. He was a speculator whose sojourn into land tenure, spirit-rapping, and religion took some fascinating directions. He was an independent traveller whose empathy for the *native peoples* he met in his travels was intelligent and well-informed. . . . Wallace, almost alone among the great naturalists of the Victorian era, was a social critic whose criticisms extended to his own society, as well." (Italics added.) Paradis displays refreshing vigor and independence in not automatically putting down Wallace for his adventures into parapsychology, an area of inquiry which is, rightly or wrongly, more often than not, summarily dismissed as unworthy of scientific investigation.

The tie-back between Darwinism and racism also appears in *Social Darwinism in American Thought* by Richard Hofstadter (Philadelphia: University of Pennsylvania Press, 1944), who observed that colonialists and racists in the last century partly rationalized their policies by citing Darwin and the *Origin*'s subtitle, *The Preservation of Favored Races In the Struggle for Life*.

Another scholar, the Oxford botanist and geneticist, C. D. Darlington, made a shambles of Darwin's priority in *Darwin's Place in History* (Oxford: Blackwell, 1959). Darlington convincingly achieved his objective, which he described in these terms: "We can, and no doubt we shall . . . change Darwin's place in history."

Among Americans, Barbara Beddall stands above all others for her dogged inquest into the "delicate arrangement." Her conclusions appeared in two brilliant essays in the *Journal of the History of Biology*, "Wallace, Darwin, and the Theory of Natural Selection" (No. 1, 1968) and "Wallace, Darwin and Edward Blyth: Further Notes on the Development of Evolution Theory" (Vol. 5, No. 1, Fall, 1972). She also commented on the affair in the epilogue of her *Wallace and Bates in the Tropics: An Introduction to the Theory of Natural Selection* (London: Collier-Macmillan, 1969). An adventurous scholar who was among the first to accept and advance the theory of continental drift to explain the dispersal of organic life on the planet, Beddall considered Darwin's receipt of the Ternate Essay "a calamity" for Darwin.

In an interview last year, Mrs. Beddall explained her interest in the Linnean affair. "It came as a surprise to me," she said. "I was working on Wallace when I came on the Linnean meeting, and I was surprised by the episode and the paucity of material on it." She said she found it "very odd" that the most critical correspondence in Darwin's files was missing. "I think Darwin was much more aware about Wallace than he let on," Beddall said. "Somebody cleaned up the file." In her opinion, Francis Darwin destroyed the "missing" letters. Mrs. Beddall also believes that in writing to Asa Gray in 1857, Darwin deliberately selected someone outside of England and sought to "protect himself and get something on the record" after publication of Wallace's Sarawak Law in 1855. She considers it convenient that the only critical surviving correspondence in Darwin's 1855 to 1858 file was a copy of his letter to Gray.

John L. Brooks, the biologist who formerly taught at Yale University and is currently a senior official in the National Science Foundation at Washington, D.C., stands right behind, if not alongside, Beddall. Brooks has been at work on the biological antecedents of Wallace's works and the relationship between Wallace and Darwin since the 1960s. "This is the hardest story in science, and one day it is going to blow up," Brooks said in an interview. "It is a very complicated story and there's going to be a lot of flack from Darwinphiles. It is a great cover-up and seems to make Watergate pale." Brooks has made, in addition to a continuing analysis of Wallace's contributions to the biological sciences, an inquiry into Dutch mail schedules for the 1850s and has concluded that the average length of time involved in the shipment of mail from the Indies to Holland and England was about ten weeks. "The heart of my hypothesis on the Wallace–Darwin relationship," Brooks said, "is that when Wallace mailed his manuscript to Darwin, Darwin received it May 18, 1858." Brooks feels that the fascinating aspect of this untold story is that it has been covered up for more than a century.

Brooks has told part of the story in "Extinction and the Origin of Organic Diversity," (*Connecticut Academy of Arts and Sciences, Transactions*, Vol. 44, December, 1972), where he charges that Darwin appropriated Wallace's divergence theory and other parts of Wallace's species hypothesis without acknowledgement, and documents it as a scientist and scholar by analysis of the excerpts Hooker and Lyell selected from the unpublished Darwin Essay of 1844 for the Linnean meeting. Among other observations, Brooks pointed out that the excerpts clearly demonstrated that "Darwin had no idea of the manner in which race formation leads to species formation."

A comprehensive review of contemporary Darwin literature is found in John C. Greene's "Reflections on the Progress of Darwin Studies," (*Journal of the History of Biology*, Vol. 8, No. 2, Fall, 1975). Greene, however, avoids airing the theories of Beddall, Brooks, George, Henderson and others who have explored the "delicate arrangement."

Yet the skim ice surfaced almost ninety years ago. Francis Darwin's astonishing explanation for the disappearance of his father's most important correspondence for 1855–58—especilly for June, 1858—is first revealed in *The Life and Letters of Charles Darwin* (New York: Appleton, 1898). These two volumes include Francis' cut version of his father's *Autobiography*. The mystery surrounding the missing letters deepens in *More Letters of Charles Darwin*, edited by Sir Francis and A. C. Seward (New York: Appleton, 1903). And the affair is compounded by Sir Francis' *The Foundations of the Origin of Species* (Cambridge: University Press, 1909), in which he reported how he found his father's unpublished 1842 essay hidden in a cupboard "which was not used for papers of any value, but rather . . . for matter which he did not wish to destroy." *Emma Darwin: A Century of Family Letters* by Henrietta Litchfield (New York: Appleton, 1915) consists of two volumes of correspondence edited by her daughter, among them letters about Darwin's role in obtaining Wallace's pension. *Erasmus Darwin* by Ernst Krause (New York: Appleton, 1880) contains the lengthy introduction by Charles Darwin which ignited the bitter Darwin–Butler controversy. In this connection, see *The Note-Books of Samuel Butler*, edited by Henry Festing Jones (London: Fifield, 1913), in which Butler rejoices over the "exposure and discomfiture of Charles Darwin and Wallace and their followers" as the result of Butler's *Evolution Old and New, Luck or Cunning?* and other works. In *The Autobiography of Charles Darwin* edited by Nora Barlow (New York: Harcourt, Brace, 1958), Francis' original cuts are restored and Darwin's granddaughter makes a valiant attempt to bring about a reconciliation between Darwin and Butler, to which both would accord their spectral approval.

Other pieces of the 1858 puzzle are found in Darwin's *Journal*, edited by Sir Gavin de Beer (London: *Bulletin of The British Museum* [*Natural History*], Historical Series 2, 1959). This is Darwin's damaging "pocket diary" which contains no reference to the arrival of the Ternate Paper nor to the Linnean meeting. The texts of Darwin's 1842 and 1844 unpublished sketches, with an excellent introduction, appear in de Beer's *Evolution by Natural Selection* (Cambridge: Cambridge University Press, 1958). Darwin's "M" and "N" notebooks can be found in *Darwin on Man* by Howard E. Gruber (New York: Dutton, 1974). Gruber's discussion of Darwin's problem with the principle of divergence is noteworthy. *Charles Darwin's Natural Selection* by R. C. Stauffer (London: Cambridge University Press, 1972) contains the second part of Darwin's unpublished "big book." Stauffer observes that "in the spring of 1858 he [Darwin] returned to Chapter VI to *revise* and expand it, particularly by interpolating a *new* discussion on divergence some forty folios long." (Italics added.) This was completed June 12, 1858, four days after Darwin told Hooker that he had solved the problem of the principle of diversity in natural selection and nine days after Darwin's apparent receipt of the Ternate Essay which spelt out the principle. What sparked this revision? Stauffer does not say.

Darwin's failure to uncover the principle of divergence until 1858 is discussed in a stimulating paper on the influence of Malthus, Bentham, Adam Smith, and other economists on Darwin in "Darwin and the Political Economists: Divergence of Character," to be published this year in the *Journal of the History of Biology*. I am indebted to the author, Silvan S. Schweber of Brandeis University, for sending me an advance proof of his work, and to Charles Gillispie at Princeton for putting me on Schweber's trail. Schweber observed that Darwin wrote out the principle between April 14 and June 12, 1858, as confirmed by Stauffer; and, citing McKinney, Schweber concluded that Darwin did not receive the Ternate Essay from Wallace before June 3, 1858, and that "there can be no doubt that Darwin had the concept of divergence of character before May or June of 1858." But if Darwin received the Ternate Essay on June 3, Darwin would have had more than a week to rework a problem that had baffled him for almost two decades.

A spirited defense of Darwin's failure to develop the principle of divergence before 1858 appears in Huxley's obituary of Darwin (London: *Proceedings of the Royal Society of London*, 1882), in which Huxley ingeniously explained that there was no need for Darwin to enunciate the principle because it was always implicitly there!

As for Darwin's relations with his inner circle, *vis-a-vis* Wallace, see *Life, Letters and Journals* of Sir Charles Lyell, edited by Katherine Murray Lyell, his sister-in-law (London: Murray, 1881), particularly for Lyell's slide into Wallace's camp in 1869 when Wallace suggested design may have played a part in man's descent. Lyell's views on evolution appear in *Antiquity of Man* (London: Murray, 1869 and 1873). Alongside Lyell's *Life and Letters* stands Leonard G. Wilson's spectacular find of 1961, *Sir Charles Lyell's Scientific Journals on the Species Question* (New Haven: Yale, 1970), in which Lyell reveals the crushing impact of Wallace's Sarawak Law on himself and Darwin. As for Lyell's "missing" letters to Darwin of 1855 to 1858, Wilson confessed in a private communication that "I do not know why Lyell's letters to Darwin have for the most part not survived," and added that "I hesitate to attribute any particular significance to the fact that most of Lyell's letters to Darwin appear not to have survived."

Wilson also reported that "in talking to the scholars who are currently editing a collected edition of Charles Darwin's correspondence, I have learned that certain portions of Darwin's incoming correspondence were lost in storage as a result of dampness, and the portions of the correspondence thus lost may have included a group of Lyell letters." This is an interesting development since even Francis Darwin did not ascribe the loss of the missing letters of 1855 to 1858 to rot. The project Wilson referred to has been in progress now for five years.

Dr. Frederick Burkhardt, former president of the American Council of Learned Societies, which is sponsoring the collected edition of Darwin's letters, in response to a query, wrote from Cambridge, where he spends part of the year, "As for Wallace, the famous letter from Ternate has been the object of a search for many years. I even went to Taylor's papers at the Printing Institute (he was printer and secretary of the Linnean Society at the time) but no luck. It was probably returned to Hooker or Lyell when the paper was sent to them for proof-reading and *may* have been kept—but Hooker and Wallace knew one another well in later years and neither seems to have a memory of seeing it."

As for the "missing" Darwin correspondence of 1856–58, Burkhardt suggested that there is "no evidence that more than one Wallace letter is missing from that year. . . . I have no explanation of the missing Wallace to Darwin letters (if there are more than one missing). There would seem to be no motive for destroying it."

Eight scholars and research assistants, working out of Cambridge, are engaged on the project. They expect to complete Darwin's letters for 1821–46, with a calendar, by October of this year.

Life and Letters of Sir Joseph Dalton Hooker by Leonard Huxley

(London: Murray, 1918), "collected and arranged by Lady Hooker," provide insight into Hooker's relations with Darwin and his ultimate rejection of the doctrine of the fixity of species. In Hooker's *The Botany of the Antarctic Voyage* (London: Reeve, 1844) and *Introductory Notes on the Flora of Tasmania* (London: Reeve, 1859), Darwin's closest associate does an about-face and, in the words of an 1860 reviewer, "frankly adopts . . . the Darwin–Wallace theory." See also Hooker's obituary by Sir Ray Lankester, "A Great Naturalist: Sir Joseph Hooker" (*Quarterly Review*, October, 1918) for further insight into the life and times of a remarkable botanist. Another valuable source of material is *The Life of Sir Charles J. F. Bunbury* edited by Mrs. Henry Lyell (London: Murray, 1906), which contains an introductory note by Hooker.

Asa Gray's role in the Wallace–Darwin episode appears in the *Letters of Asa Gray*, edited by Jane Loring Gray (Boston: Houghton Mifflin, 1893). The issue is skirted in *Asa Gray* by A. Hunter Dupree (Cambridge, Massachusetts: Harvard University Press, 1959). The part played in the post-Linnean period by Huxley is portrayed in *Life and Letters of Thomas Henry Huxley* by Leonard Huxley (New York, Appleton, 1901), a two-volume work from which the title of this book is extracted. See also *Darwiniana* by Thomas H. Huxley (New York: Appleton, 1896), a collection of Huxley's superb essays, including those attended by Karl Marx, on the Wallace–Darwin joint theory of the origin and divergence of species by natural selection. Finally, for this early period, see the Wallace letter in which he first proposed his theory of zoogeography, "A Letter from A. R. Wallace to F. P. Pascoe, Written from Ternate, 20 December 1860" (London: *Proceedings of the Royal Entomological Society*, Vol. 14, 1939), with a note by Professor Hale Carpenter. The opposition to the startlingly new theory, particularly the concept later dubbed The Wallace Line, is covered in the *Encylopedie van Nederlandsche-Indië*, Vol. 5 (Den Haag–Leiden: Ze Druk, 1921).

The relationship between Bates and Wallace is detailed in *The Naturalist on the River Amazons* by Henry Walter Bates (London: Murray, 1892), which contains a memoir by Edward Clodd and is a reprint of the original 1863 Murray edition. Wallace's obituary of Bates appeared in *Nature*, February 25, 1892. Sir Francis Galton's obituary of Bates, in which Galton revealed that Murray influenced Bates' appointment over Wallace as the Royal Geographical Society's secretary, is found in *Proceedings of the Royal Geographical Society*, April, 1892.

For firsthand glimpses of Wallace see *Impressions of Great Naturalists* by Henry Fairfield Osborn (New York: Scribner's, 1924), *The Life of Sir James Brooke by Spenser St. John* (Edinburgh: Blackwood, 1879), and *Notes of a Botanist on the Amazon & Andes* by Richard Spruce (London: Macmillan, 1908, 2 volumes), which was edited by Wallace. Finally, for a view of Wallace's son William in America, see *Little Journeys to the Homes of Great Scientists* by Elbert Hubbard (East Aurora, New York: Roycroft, 1905).

Many books contain sketches or references to Wallace (indeed, it is quite impossible to write about Darwin without some, albeit vague, reference to Wallace). Among the more notable of these are "Alfred Russel Wallace" by Edward D. Cope in *Evolution in Science, Philosophy and Art* (New York: Appleton, 1891), and *The History of Biological Theories* by Emanuel Radl (London: Oxford University Press, 1930)—who commits the common *non sequitur* of many writers dealing with Darwin and Wallace, observing that although Wallace entertained "peculiar" views, his Ternate Essay caused Darwin "considerable embarrassment, for he [Darwin] saw himself robbed of the fruits of his own labor." Invariably, in these sketches and references, Darwin's failure to resolve the principle of divergence until Wallace appeared on the scene is omitted. In *English Worthies* by Grant Allen (New York: Appleton, 1885), the author observed that "if Charles Darwin had never existed at all," the Ternate Essay would have taken its place at the forefront of evolutionary theory (the conclusion also drawn by Pantin). In "War Darwin ein originelles Genie?" by J. H. F. Kohlbrugge (*Biologisches Zentralblatt*, Vol. 35, 1915), the Utrecht historian destroys Darwin's contention that he conceived of the theory in a vacuum and cites Wallace among his precursors. (I am grateful to Frater Orantus, Paramaribo, Surinam, for translating this lengthy document for me into English.) In *Alfred Russel Wallace: The Story of a Great Discoverer* by Lancelot T. Hogben (London: Society for Promoting Christian Knowledge, 1918), the author puts forth the thesis that Wallace's discovery, independent of Darwin's, "focusing as it did the attention of scientific minds upon one idea approached from such diverse standpoints, may have lent more weight to their joint discovery." *An Exposition of Fallacies in the Hypothesis of Mr. Darwin* by C. R. Bree (London: Longmans, Green, 1872) attacks the theory of mimicry and, dismissing Darwin, attributes it to "the sole production of the fertile brain of Mr. Wallace." In point of fact, it was Bates who first developed the idea and Wallace who refined and expanded upon it, making the study of mimicry a centerpiece of natural selection. *What is Darwinism?* by Charles Hodge (New York: Scribner, Armstrong, 1874), is an excellent summary of the pros and cons of debate which swirled around the theory; Hodge makes frequent reference to Wallace as "companion and peer of Mr. Darwin."

Excellent source material may also be found in the following: *The Darwin–Wallace Celebration* (London: The Linnean Society of London, 1908), a special edition to commemorate the fiftieth anniversay of the "joint communication," and which includes a treasure trove of commentaries, including those of Hooker and Wallace; *Down: The Home of the Darwins by Sir Hedley Atkins* (London: Royal College of Surgeons of England, 1974), an engaging, informative account; *Historical and Descriptive Catalogue of the Darwin Memorial at Down House, Downe, Kent* (n.d., n.p., 31 pp.); *Charles Darwin and Down House* by Jessie Dobson (Edinburgh: Churchill Livingstone, 1959); *To Be An Invalid* by Ralph Colp, Jr. (Chicago: University of Chicago Press, 1977) —by far the best analysis of Darwin's illnesses, real and perceived; and *Charles Darwin: A Portrait*, by Geoffrey West (New Haven: Yale University Press, 1938).

The feeling of the Wallace–Darwin era is captured in William H. Edwards' *A Voyage Up the River Amazon* (London: Murray, 1847), the book which sent Wallace off to the Amazon; *Vestiges of the Natural History of Creation with a Sequel* by Robert Chambers (New York: Harper, 1875), first published anonymously in 1844, denounced by Darwin and praised by Wallace; *A Manual of British Coleoptera* by James Francis Stephen (London: Longman, Orme, Brown, Green, and Longmans, 1839), a favorite of both Wallace and Darwin; and the *Journal of the Geological Society of Dublin* (Dublin: Gill, 1860), a rare find which contains Haughton's devastating commentary on the Linnean's "joint communication."

The Making of Species by Douglas Dewar and Frank Finn (London: John Lane The Bodley Head [sic], 1909) is off the well-travelled track. The authors treat Wallace and the "Wallaceian school of biologists" as separate and distinct from Darwin and the Darwinian school and, although they are strongly critical of Wallaceians, as they call his supporters, the authors concede that England gained "scientific supremacy . . . in the middle of [the] last century by the labours of Charles Darwin and Alfred Russel Wallace." The authors develop a familiar theme, that Wallace "out-Darwined Darwin"—without explaining that

Wallace was merely being Wallace, the discoverer of a theory which Darwin worked out independently of him.

The "party line" of the history of the theory of natural selection is hewed to in a constant stream of books about Darwin, each serving to reinforce the myth of the generation before it. Two examples—old and new—will suffice here: *Pioneers of Evolution from Thales to Huxley* by Edward Clodd (New York: Appleton, 1897), in which the author blatantly contended that Darwin, Hooker, and Lyell never considered "claims of priority" in arranging the Linnean meeting, and *Darwin, Wallace and the Theory of Natural Selection* by Bert James Loewenberg (Cambridge: Arlington, 1959), who observed that "Wallace's paper on the introduction of new species published in 1855 impressed Darwin but aroused no feeling of intellectual competition," adding, "on the contrary, he [Darwin] welcomed it with his customary warmth and generosity." To his credit, however, Loewenberg, chairman of the 1959 Darwin Anniversary Committee, empathized with Wallace. "Alfred Russel Wallace still remains a relatively unknown figure," he wrote. "He is hardly more than a character in the *legend* of which Charles Darwin is the hero. No theory attaches to his name [Loewenberg omitted the Wallace Line]. . . . He created his own historical image by his conduct." (Italics added.)

The theory of natural selection absorbed the shocks of Mendelian genetics and rebounded in the late 1920s. For an authoritative analysis see *The Genetical Theory of Natural Selection* by R. A. Fisher (Oxford: Clarendon, 1930), who helped replace the Wallace–Darwin concept in the mainstream of evolutionary theory. Fisher states that the theory of mimicry, for example, is "the greatest post-Darwinian [sic] application of natural selection." This is borne out in modern genetic studies, where genes found in man, with a composition closely similar to the genetic composition of monkeys—a species "closely-allied to man," as Wallace would put it—are the focal points of experiments into the origin of species and of life. For example, Simian virus 40 (SV40) are virogenes, and resemble certain genetic strands in *both* monkeys *and* man.

In one respect, this has been a painful book to write: Darwin is a warm and agreeable character who possessed many admirable qualities. Like everyone else, he had weaknesses; his great weakness was a Ninevite vanity. In books written for students and laymen—for example, *Darwin's Century* (New York: Doubleday, 1959)—the late Loren

Eiseley waxed poetic about Darwin and his accomplishments. In an arcane essay, however, entitled "Charles Darwin, Edward Blyth, and the Theory of Natural Selection" (*American Philosophical Society Proceedings*, Vol. 3, No. 1, 1959), Eiseley confessed that in his hero there was a "hunger to possess the theory os totally his own." Eiseley cannot have it two ways. This was the hunger that overpowered Darwin at a moment of truth, and led him into the "delicate arrangement."

Posthumously, Eiseley expanded on this theme in *Darwin and the Mysterious Mr. X* (New York: Dutton, 1979). He considered Wallace, for example, "in some respects a more able anthropologist than Darwin," an unusual admission since Eiseley, who died in 1977, was Benjamin Franklin Professor of Anthropology and the History of Science at the University of Pennsylvania. Eiseley's Mr. X was not Wallace; it was Edward Blyth. As for Wallace, Eiseley indicated that he had shied away from writing full treatment of him because "it is comparatively easy to give a fair account of a man who dies within his own generation. He is encapsulated in his own time, and his follies and achievements can be comprehended accordingly. It is not so simple to evaluate the career of [a Wallace]. . . . His was a full life—that much can be said. A lengthy biographical study would have to incorporate much. . . . Many of his ideas . . . outran with a flashing brilliance even his friend and colleague, Darwin."

As for Wallace, Darwin's hunger resulted in Wallace's failure to win the priority, acclaim, and recognition that were justly his. Wallace never completed his own "big book" on the theory, *Darwinism* notwithstanding. Wallace was forced to set off in a myriad of directions, flitting from project to project, subject to subject, in a desperate effort to keep his family afloat financially. This wide-ranging activity dissipated his time, energy and, above all, originality. Wallace lost his place in history; worse, history lost whatever further contributions Wallace would have made had he stuck to evolutionary theory and continued to advance his theory of the origin of species. Wallace wound up, as he himself cheerfully admitted and Julian Sorell Huxley aptly noted in *The Dictionary of National Biography, 1912–21*, as a "crank." But Huxley hurriedly qualified that designation, observing that when Wallace "was handling the facts of nature and the ample speculations of evolutionary theory, this could not show itself."

Thus fate, in the guise of Darwin, intervened in Alfred Russel Wallace's life and played an unfair trick on him. So perhaps there is a moral in the Wallace story: that however gifted an individual, whatever his or her opportunities and accomplishments, each is governed by chance. Wallace lucked out, although it is only fair to observe that luck is also partly the residue of design. The Armenians have a toast which befits this tale: To the inexplicable, in us, and above us. Wallace would have liked that; Darwin, probably not.

In a letter to Asa Gray, Darwin remarked, "False facts are highly injurious to the progress of science, for they often endure long; but false views, if supported by some evidence, do little harm, for everyone takes a salutary pleasure in proving their falseness: and when this is done, one path towards error is closed and the road to truth is often at the same time opened."

The same may be said of writing history and biography. This is the "Darwinian" spirit in which this book was written.

Index